SWEATSHOP USA

SWEATSHOP USA
The American Sweatshop in Historical and Global Perspective

Daniel E. Bender
and Richard A. Greenwald,
Editors

ROUTLEDGE
NEW YORK AND LONDON

Published in 2003 by
Routledge
29 West 35th Street
New York, NY 10001
www.routledge-ny.com

Published in Great Britain by
Routledge
11 New Fetter Lane
London EC4P 4EE
www.routledge.co.uk

10 9 8 7 6 5 4 3 2 1

Library of Congress Cataloging-in-Publication Data

Sweatshop USA : the American sweatshop in historical and global
perspective / Daniel E. Bender and Richard A. Greenwald, editors.
        p. cm.
  ISBN 0-415-93560-1 (alk. paper) — ISBN 0-415-93561-X (pbk. : alk.
paper)
1. Sweatshops—United States—History.   I. Bender, Daniel E.   II.
Greenwald, Richard A.
  HD2339.U6S9 2003
  332.25—dc21

                                                                    2003009696

For Mimi and Debbie

Contents

Acknowledgments ix

Foreword xi
DANIEL J. WALKOWITZ

Introduction: Sweatshop USA: The American Sweatshop
in Global and Historical Perspective 1
DANIEL E. BENDER AND RICHARD A. GREENWALD

Producing the Sweatshop

1 "A Foreign Method of Working": Racial Degeneration, Gender
Disorder, and the Sweatshop Danger in America 19
DANIEL E. BENDER

2 Fashion, Flexible Specialization, and the Sweatshop:
A Historical Problem 37
NANCY L. GREEN

3 Bringing Sweatshops into the Museum 57
PETER LIEBHOLD AND HARRY R. RUBENSTEIN

Sweatshop Migrations

4 Labor, Liberals, and Sweatshops 77
RICHARD A. GREENWALD

5 "An Industry on Wheels": The Migration of Pennsylvania's
Garment Factories 91
KENNETH C. WOLENSKY

6 Sweatshops in Sunset Park: A Variation of the Late-Twentieth-
Century Chinese Garment Shops in New York City 117
XIAOLAN BAO

7 Offshore Production 141
EDNA BONACICH AND RICHARD P. APPELBAUM et al.

8 Globalization and Worker Organization in New York City's
Garment Industry 169
IMMANUEL NESS

Sweatshop Resistance

9 Sweatshop Feminism: Italian Women's Political Culture
in New York City's Needle Trades, 1890–1919   185
JENNIFER GUGLIELMO

10 Consumers of the World Unite!: Campaigns Against
Sweating, Past and Present   203
EILEEN BORIS

11 The Rise of the Second Antisweatshop Movement   225
ANDREW ROSS

12 Students Against Sweatshops: A History   247
LIZA FEATHERSTONE

13 The Ideal Sweatshop?: Gender and Transnational Protest   265
ETHEL BROOKS

Contributor Biographies   287

Index   291

Acknowledgments

Scholarly projects are inherently collective, and this one is no exception. We must thank Danny Walkowitz, who shaped us as much as this project, Kitty Krupat, Mary Nolan, Michael Hanagan and the folks at *International Labor and Working Class History.* Karen Wolny and her staff at Routledge were wonderful to work with and deserve much thanks.

Daniel Bender would like to thank Ardis Cameron, David Offenhall, and Rosanne Currarino for their close and sympathetic reads.

Richard Greenwald would like to thank Dick Oestreicher, Stanely Aronowitz and Danny Walkowitz for comments on this as well as my larger project. I must also thank my Dean, Warren Mazek and my Chair, Jane Brickman for providing institutional support for this project, and George Billy and Don Gill of the USMMA library.

Foreword

The modern sweatshop era may be said to have begun in the spring of 1996, when America rediscovered the sweatshop. "Capitalist or Child-slaver?" screamed one headline that spring of Kathie Lee Gifford, America's apple-cheeked talk-show host. Gifford, reports announced, profited and endorsed a clothing line made in Honduras in "monstrous sweatshops of the New World Order" by workers paid "slave wages." But the news also hit closer to home when it was revealed that Gifford's clothing was also produced in a Manhattan "sweatshop" by children who were being paid 31 cents an hour for laboring under horrific conditions. And worse—their paltry wage had not been paid in weeks!

Gifford tried to minimize the damage, first claiming there were only "a handful of unethical manufacturers," and then issuing a tearful apology. But Gifford's apology notwithstanding, news of the exploitative conditions under which Wal-Mart—and the parent corporation, the Disney Company—contracted for these goods unleashed a storm of protest and galvanized a new national social protest movement with global reach. Honduras, Haiti, Taiwan, Thailand, and other poor countries were havens for U.S. corporations seeking cheap labor markets, but one did not have to look abroad to find the problem. Labor Secretary Robert Reich pointed out in response to Gifford, the "handful" of companies were in reality probably half the 22,000 cutting and sewing shops in the United States at the time!

In this timely collection, editors Daniel Bender and Richard Greenwald make clear the vastness of this struggle. The essays also suggest some salutary lessons to activists about analyses of the sources of abuses and strategies for ending them. To begin, sweatshops are neither new, nor are they confined to the garment industry. The term originated in the nineteenth century, and horrific working conditions—meager wages and long hours in dangerous and cramped workplaces—was associated with much labor in finishing goods and assembly work as well as garment labor. Yet one of the extraordinary and underappreciated secrets of labor history was the success of the labor movement in establishing the term as prima facie evidence of managerial abuse. The charge that a workplace was a sweatshop, if it stuck, transformed debates about inequality and dependence to virtually universally accepted claims for justice.

To be sure, the gains did not easily translate into fundamental restructuring of the wage system or of an industry; sweatshops were usually consigned to the realm of bad capitalists needing reform. Moreover, reformers—and male trade unionists—seeing exploited women and children as most poignant victims of sweatshop labor, mounted a paternal (and sometimes maternal) focus on protective legislation as a palliative. But lest we be consigned to forget the past once again, these wonderful essays both remind us there is a history to the sweatshop and struggles against it, and there are lessons for present and future struggles to be learned from that history.

Daniel J. Walkowitz
New York University

Introduction
Sweatshop USA
The American Sweatshop in Global and Historical Perspective

DANIEL E. BENDER
University of Waterloo

RICHARD A. GREENWALD
United States Merchant Marine Academy

The United States has rediscovered its sweatshops. Newspapers and magazines, often otherwise reluctant to give column space to workplace issues, regularly publish dramatic exposés of shocking working conditions in garment sweatshops as nearby as New York and as far afield as El Salvador. In fact, as Smithsonian curators Peter Liebhold and Harry Rubenstein note, the 1995 raid on a sweatshop in El Monte, California, where seventy-two Thai workers labored in shocking conditions and in captivity produced an extraordinary 842 newspaper and magazine stories.[1] This newfound concern about the sweatshop and sweated work has made its way into everyday conversation and popular culture—perhaps more so than any other kind of labor or workplace. As the journalist Liza Featherstone suggests, shoppers standing outside the Gap in the local mall might very well be discussing the company's use of sweatshop labor.[2]

Journalistic coverage and public concern about substandard, shocking conditions, often in shops producing goods for "celebrity" clothing lines or for high-profile clothing stores, has nurtured a loose alliance of antisweatshop activists, from college students to reinvigorated trade unionists. This coalition is centered around the Union of Needle, Industrial, and Technical Employees (UNITE!)—the leading American garment workers' union—the National Labor Committee, United Students Against Sweatshops (USAS), and numerous grassroots and religious groups. With all its potential political power and moral authority, the contemporary antisweatshop movement has advanced an understanding of production in the "global village" opposed to that celebrated by mainstream politicians and transnational corporations. Rather than lauding the growth of global networks of trade and information, antisweatshop activists are highlighting the bleak aspects of globalization. Their voices can be clearly heard in protests at meetings of the World Bank and the International Monetary Fund. The tactics, rhetoric, and language of these antisweatshop activists, while responding powerfully to today's reality of "free trade" and "globalization," often mirror the efforts of their predecessors of the late nineteenth and early twentieth centuries.

The sweatshop remains a powerful concept. Images of its horrific conditions and its debilitating social and cultural effects have been the backbone of some of the most powerful organized activism in the United States since the 1960s. The antisweatshop movement has begun to challenge what once seemed like a corporate juggernaut. Why does the sweatshop carry such enormous moral weight?

Moral repulsion toward the sweatshop has endured, despite the passage of time. The sweatshop has a long history. The use of the word "sweat" to describe dangerous, arduous labor stretches back centuries. Garment work, preformed by immigrant women, was condemned as "sweated" as early as the 1830s and the "sweatshop" itself was first defined in the 1890s.[3] While understandings of the roots, meaning, and problems of the sweatshop have changed since the 1890s, the word is still used to mobilize efforts to reform working conditions.

These essays, a cross-section of the expanding field of sweatshop studies, unite the historical, cultural studies, sociological, anthropological, and political-science literature on sweatshops. Together, they trace the changing meanings of the sweatshop. In what ways has the definition of the sweatshop changed? Do older conceptions of the sweatshop still influence contemporary understandings? Why does the label "sweatshop" still ellicit repugnance, even as definitions of the sweatshop have shifted? At the same time, these essays examine the emotional, moral, political, literary, and economic responses to the sweatshop. Together, they highlight the connection between debates about the roots and meanings of the sweatshop—what might be called the politics of definition—and efforts to eradicate sweatshops. Activists, workers, and policymakers have often called upon the moral weight of the sweatshop in broader efforts at social resistance and reform.

These essays also explore the tension between the local and the transnational that remains omnipresent in attempts to define, regulate, and, ultimately, eliminate sweatshops. From its first usage in the United States, the definition of the sweatshop has reflected social anxiety about global flows and exchanges of people, goods, culture, and capital. Thus, where the sweatshop is cast in the beginning of the twenty-first century as the worst expression of the new unregulated, global economy, it was understood at the beginning of the twentieth century as the dangerous outgrowth of unrestricted immigration and urbanization. As the economics of the sweatshop is distinctly transnational, so, too, is its politics. For example, those American, Canadian, and European policy makers in the 1890s who first defined the sweatshop exchanged concerns, methods of industrial investigation, and theories of social reform—they even shared the very word *sweatshop*. Yet antisweatshop campaigns remain profoundly national—even as they target the inequalities of the global economy. Regulations and antisweatshop organizations exist almost exclusively within a national context, despite international treaties about trade and tentative efforts at cross-border organizing.

The Morality and Economics of the Sweatshop

In 1901, the U.S. Industrial Commission attempted to define the "sweating system." In the heightened tension of an age rife with urban congestion and industrial strife, the Commission pledged to find the ties between industrial disorder and the peculiar character of the nation's new immigrants. For the Commission's members and for many of its witnesses, the growing urban dangers of disease and crime reflected the debased racial character of the residents of new Southern and Eastern European and Asian immigrant neighborhoods. According to the members of the Commission and its expert witnesses, these immigrants were distinct races, vastly inferior physically and morally to American "stock." The arrival of immigrants threatened the racial purity of the nation, not only because of their higher birthrate, but also because they carried with them and bred the germs of contagious disease in their cramped neighborhoods and filthy tenements. Most important, immigrants imported degraded ways of working that seemed antithetical to an American factory imagined as clean, scientific, and orderly. For the Commission's members, the sweatshop was the worst example of that immigrant way of working and they associated the sweatshop, at least at first, with Eastern-European Jews and, to a lesser extent, with Italians.[4]

For the Commission, the sweatshop was more than simply a specific type of factory or manner of production. It was a disorderly, immoral, dangerous workplace that reflected the racial inferiority of its immigrant workers and owners. Eastern-European Jews, the immigrant group the Commission largely blamed for the sweatshop, were too "individualistic" for the discipline of the modern, American factory. Instead, they seemed willing to accept the uncivilized conditions of the sweatshop because of its lax discipline. Indeed, the Commission even blamed Jews' supposed racial inclination to filth, rather than the effects of unbridled competition, for the conditions of garment shops. For the Commission, race could explain the economics of the sweatshop.[5]

Thus, when the economist John R. Commons testified to the Commission that the "sweating system" was "a system of subcontract, wherein work is let out to contractors to be done in small shops or homes," his definition remained inflected with conceptions of racial difference and moral judgments in several crucial ways. First, he saw the "sweating system," not simply as a peculiar form of industrial organization, but as a direct contrast to the "factory system" that he—and so many other social reformers and policy makers—associated with American efficiency and "civilization." Second, Commons regarded the sweatshop as at the center of a rising immigrant economy that threatened to undermine not only the health and racial position of immigrants, but also the wages and well-being of "American" workers. Thus, the Commission set out to measure the social and cultural dangers caused by the "foreign-born labor in the clothing trade."[6]

The Industrial Commission and Commons were not alone in their condemnation of the sweated garment work as the degraded labor of immigrants. They joined a range of reformers, politicians, public health advocates, and journalists in branding the sweatshop the archetype of a dangerous trend in immigrant work. Indeed, the sweatshop emerged as the preeminent focus of reformist and government concern about immigrant labor. It was the target of House of Representatives hearings in 1892 and was the primary impetus behind and target of factory inspection laws in New York, Illinois, and Massachusetts, among other industrialized states. In addition, the sweatshop was the focus of numerous journalistic investigations of immigrant labor. Thus, the Commission in investigating the sweatshop was drawing from and contributing to a broad conversation about immigration, race, and labor that was, at times, shrill and accusatory and, always, anxious.[7]

For these policy makers, social reformers, public health officials, factory inspectors, and journalists who sought to define the sweatshop in the years after 1890, the sweatshop was both an economic and cultural term. It was, at once, a form of production, the industrial embodiment of immigrant's racial inferiority, and the epitome of an exploitative workplace. To label the garment workplaces in New York, Chicago, Rochester, Cincinnati, and Boston—the cities investigated by the House of Representatives—"sweatshops" was a sad acknowledgment of a massive transformation in American garment manufacture, from large-scale, mechanized production to small, poorly capitalized workplaces. It was also a moral judgment about the garment industry, immigrant workers, and bosses.[8]

And, yet, the sweatshop could also serve as the basis for cross-class organizing. While immigrant workers and their trade union leaders eschewed the harsh racialized language of social reformers, they did seize upon the word "sweatshop" as a way of expressing outrage. Indeed, on the rare occasions when workers were called to testify to government hearings about the garment industry, they condemned an economic and class system that preyed on the desperation of recent immigrants. If the sweatshop, for a range of Progressive-Era American critics from workers to reformers, was a tragic result of unrestricted immigration and unregulated industry, the advent of factory legislation and inspection beginning in the 1890s was a move toward "civilization" and the assimilation of immigrants.[9]

As historian Nancy Green suggests, the understandings of the sweatshop forged in the 1890s serve as "classic descriptions" that politicians, reformers, and workers continue to refer to, even as the economics of the garment industry have changed and as fears about the sweatshop have shifted from concerns about racial degradation and the spread of disease to anxiety about the loss of jobs, growing inequality, and the disruption of working-class families.[10] By the 1920s and early 1930s, unionists, factory inspectors, and reformers considered "jobbers"—a kind of contractor operating within larger manufacturing establishments—rather than subcontractors as the principal urban sweatshop employer. Meanwhile, critics worried about the spread of small shops that were located outside of the major, urban garment manufacturing centers and that employed only women. To capture the severity of working conditions, critics labeled these small factories "sweatshops." Thus, at the height of the Great Depression, the Secretary of Labor Frances Perkins saw the "sweatshop" lurking behind the $4.95 red silk dress. For Perkins, an eyewitness to the 1911 Triangle Shirtwaist Factory Fire, an event perhaps more than any other that captures popular fears about sweatshop exploitation, the "return of the sweatshop" during the Great Depression was a step away from "civilized industrial order." While she was concerned about the fate of a female—not necessarily immigrant—workforce, she still recalled older images of the sweatshop. She worried about the return of shops where "shop conditions are usually far below standards and the picture of such a plant is a look back to the sweatshops . . . at the turn of the century."[11]

The persistence of the sweatshop—both on the economic landscape and in the discourse about labor—represents an ongoing anxiety about immigration, race, gender, and work. Nonetheless, contemporary politicians have sought to find an objective definition, perhaps to divorce the sweatshop from its historical moral gravity. In 1994, the United States General Accounting Office (GAO) defined a sweatshop as a workplace "that violates more than one federal or state labor law governing minimum wage and overtime, child labor, industrial homework, occupational safety and health, workers compensation, or industry regulation." Nonetheless, the focus on child labor, homework, health, wages, and the lengths of the workday clearly evoked earlier, more emotionally charged understandings.[12]

And, the contemporary discourse about sweatshops remains profoundly subjective, especially in its ongoing dependence on "classic descriptions." Thus, when the New York *Daily News* published a four-day exposé on the city's sweatshops, they self-consciously recalled sweatshops of the 1890s in their depiction of immigrant workers, laboring to exhaustion in cramped, dangerous workplaces. One factory in the garment district, for example, the newspaper compared to the Triangle Shirtwaist Factory. (Interesting, when the Triangle Factory was built, it was considered a factory, the opposite of the sweatshop.

Today, it often serves as the archetypical historical sweatshop.) At the same time, in a post-Communist era when the market economy has sometimes appeared beyond reproach and leading corporate executives like General Electric's Jack Welch are hailed as national heroes (at least before recent disclosures of high-profile corporate corruption and subsequent dramatic bankruptcies), the moral repugnance evoked by the sweatshop has provided a language to criticize conditions in a range of industries far removed from garment manufacture. Thus, Bruce Raynor, now the president of UNITE!, declared that "supermarket and restaurant delivery workers, servers at catered parties, cabdrivers, child-care providers, home healthcare workers and apartment cleaners" are "workers in service-sector sweatshops."[13]

Raynor's proclamation suggests a paradox in the "politics of definition" of the sweatshop. Labeling a workplace a sweatshop condemns its conditions, its owners, and, often still, its workers. The "classic description" of the sweatshop could open the doors to alliances between workers and those concerned with the broader social effects of their labor. Most notably, it gave the garment labor organizing of the 1890s a singularity of purpose as workers' sought to rise "out of the sweatshop."[14] At a time when politicians were wary of unions, the close alliances forged between workers, reformers, and policy makers were unprecedented. Indeed, as historian Steve Fraser has argued, they served as a "dress rehearsal" for the New Deal. At the same time, such alliances depended on the concept of the sweatshop as an unnatural and foreign workplace and the sweatshop itself as primitive capitalism easily fixed by economic progress, efficiency, and government regulation. Such understandings helped set sweatshop laborers apart as foreign, potentially contagious, even immoral.[15]

The Global American Sweatshop

The sweatshop, as both a form of production and as a label for an immoral workplace, emerged from the turn-of-the-last-century exchanges of people, goods, capital, and ideas in what historian Daniel Rodgers calls "Atlantic Crossings." Rodgers argues that, in an era of unprecedented immigration, industrial trade, and imperial expansion, American and European social reformers and politicians kept their eyes carefully focused across the Atlantic. Efforts to understand and regulate industry were formulated in a transatlantic, rather than a solely national, context. Leading American economists and reformers, often educated in Europe, imported Western and Northern European notions of social insurance and factory legislation. They applied these notions to the regulation of the labor of Southern and Eastern Europeans, in particular.[16]

Nowhere was this more true than in the case of the sweatshop. The sweatshop was defined simultaneously in the United States, Canada, and Britain. The U.S. House of Representatives, for example, began their groundbreaking hearings at almost the same moment that the British House of Lords was holding high-profile investigations into the "sweating system." They defined the sweatshop and the threats that it posed in similar ways. In both places, the sweatshop was cast as a primitive form of production, and an immigrant workplace. British and French investigators visited American sweatshops and American inspectors even testified to the House of Representatives about European conditions. So, too, did Americans and Europeans exchange ideas about the regulation of sweatshops. Americans carefully studied the English Factory Act that emerged from the House of Lord's investigations of the "sweating system." After all, as *Nation* editor E. L. Godkin declared: "We have in this city, probably in all our large cities . . . exactly the kind of abuse which the English Factory Act was intended to correct."[17]

Transatlantic conversations about the sweatshop that began in the 1890s were so intense in large measure because American and European observers were convinced that the sweatshop was the direct result of immigration. They carefully noted the similar conditions of sweatshop, in particular in New York and London. In each city, inspectors were quick to point out that sweatshops were located in tenement apartments in the heart of immigrant and, largely, Jewish neighborhoods, like New York's Lower East Side and London's East End. American inspectors also noted that London was often a stopping point for Eastern European migrants on their way to New York.

The sweatshop was never a stagnant or stationary form of production. With little capital, even less technology and available cheap labor, the sweatshop was a movable system in the new world system. Regional migration of labor and capital were seamlessly connected to globalism—that is, global migration of capital, production, and fashion trends. "Out of town" shops sprang up in Philadelphia and other cities as early as the Progressive Era. By the 1930s, production found its way to Western Pennsylvania. By the 1950s, production moved to Asia, and by the 1960s, the Caribbean and Latin America. The mobility of capital, coupled with the growth of international trade in the mid- to late-twentieth century and the abundance of cheap labor saw sweatshops expand dramatically.[18]

Contemporary observers also understand the sweatshop as transnational. The contracting and subcontracting system that was once limited to a single nation or, more likely, a single city, is now global. The American athletic shoe and clothing company Nike has become, for antisweatshop activists, the archetypical sweatshop employer. Yet Nike has no factories of its own. All its production is contracted out; it owns few nonretail facilities beyond its sprawling Oregon corporate campus. In fact, Nike does not even contract with American employers. Its entire production is abroad and overseas, where it is difficult to trace and almost impossible to regulate. It is in this context that contemporary critics argue that the roots of the resurgence of the sweatshop can be found in the multilateral trade negotiations that began in the early 1970s and accelerated in the 1990s. These negotiations ended tariffs that once maintained national systems of garment production. As contracting has "gone global," so, too, has consumption. As journalist Naomi Klein points out, universally recognized logos have helped transform regional and local markets into national and transnational demands.[19] The Nike swoosh stands for Nike no matter where the garment or shoe is produced. But, global consumption depends on high demand in the United States, Canada, and Europe, and low wages in the Global South. Where American sweatshops once produced for a national or local market—New York retailers in the 1890s generally contracted with sweatshops only as far away as Boston or Baltimore—the contemporary sweatshop often produces goods for distant markets. A London Fog raincoat destined for northern U.S. and Canadian marketplaces might be manufactured in Malaysia, where a raincoat is an alien garment. Clothing manufactured in Global South sweatshops might return—if ever—from the United States only as part of a global "rag" trade.[20]

The inequalities of global consumption help maintain perceptions of the sweatshop as "foreign." For policy makers and activists alike, the reemergence of mass immigration to the United States since the 1960s is intimately linked to return of the sweatshop. Sweatshop labor is constructed as foreign because it is associated with the labor of "foreigners" and because it is still perceived as an alien form of labor, contrary to powerful ideals of male breadwinning and of the mechanized industrial workplace. This enduring sense of sweatshop labor as a "foreign method of working" continues to shape the popular imagination of the typical sweatshop laborer as nonwhite, non-European or non-American, young, unskilled, and female.

The moral weight of the sweatshop—few would truly endorse a sweatshop—makes it an obvious focus for critics of globalization and for workers seeking to publicize their plight. Thus, when contemporary activists point out the dangers of the global economy, they point to the sweatshop. As Klein argues, activists have used the visibility of the logos of companies like Nike or the Gap to focus attention on otherwise hidden contracting practices. Nonetheless, supporters of free trade can also rely on the alien nature of the sweatshop to issue "two cheers for sweatshops," as economists Nicholas Kristof and Sheryl WuDunn put it. While lamenting the poor conditions of the sweatshop, they suggest that, given cultural differences, Western consumers should be wary about rejecting the sweatshop. Asian workers might really want sweatshop labor. Thus, they cast the sweatshop as the first stage in a process of capitalist development that Third World nations must pass through in their integration into the global economy.[21]

Given that the sweatshop exists at the nexus of global exchanges of capital, people, ideas, and goods, is there an "American sweatshop"? Thomas Bender's notion of transnationalizing American history is helpful in understanding the tension between the transnational and national contexts of the sweatshop. As Bender suggests, the goal of a writing a transnational history is not to ignore the nation altogether, but to imagine the nation as "a partially bounded historical entity imbricated in structures and processes that connect to every part of the world."[22] National borders matter insofar as historically they have bounded efforts at regulation, reform, and resistance—even as production, capitalization, and the migration of workers have always remained global. When turn-of-the-last-century American and European social scientists and reformers exchanged ideas about the origins and dangers of the sweatshop—and arrived at almost identical conclusions—they still proposed national- and state-oriented reforms and regulations. Unlike French and British efforts, American reform was hampered by judicial constraints that until the Great Depression, outlawed prohibitions on tenement apartment labor. Thus, American reformers, handcuffed by the courts, were much more willing than their European counterparts to forge alliances with immigrant unionists to eradicate sweatshops and civilize capitalism—and its employees. In addition, many American reformers at the turn of the last century saw the sweatshop as the direct product of liberal immigration law. Closing America's ports, they argued, might help keep out the sweatshop. American critics effectively closed the door to European immigrant workers in 1924. New immigration quotas allowed only the smallest numbers of Jewish and Italian immigrants. The effort to protect a national garment industry and market also led reformers and unionists to seek restrictions on garment imports. In the post–World War II round of trade negotiations, garments and textiles were exempted from restrictions on tariffs, and the 1973 Multi Fiber Arrangement regulated import tariffs and the flow of trade. So, too, was unionism national. The "international" in the ILGWU's name was more irony than reality. The ILGWU organized mostly in the United States and in only a few cities in Canada. Historically, the union was reluctant to organize waves of new immigrants and migrants, first, Puerto Ricans and African Americans and, later, Asians. Only recently has UNITE!, the union formed in 1995 from the merger of the ILGWU and the other major garment union, the Amalgamated Clothing and Textile Workers' Union, focused energetically on the unionization of the so-called "new" immigrants.[23]

Immigration restrictions, protective tariffs, and unionization strategies together worked to carve out a solidly national sphere within the fundamentally transnational system that encouraged the rise of the sweatshop. The more national a market and workforce, the easier it would be to regulate. Thus, policymakers from the 1890s to the early 1920s and beginning again in the 1930s imposed stringent regulations on the site and conditions of garment work. These regulations were enforced not only by government inspectors, but also by alliances between government, labor, and business—the kinds of tripartite labor accords that were lauded until the 1970s as the bright future of liberal labor relations. Some manufacturers sought to avoid the regulatory gaze by escaping union strongholds like New York and Chicago. They formed the basis of a "runaway" industry. Other large employers applauded the restrictions on small manufacturers that could otherwise undercut prices and ratchet up competition.[24]

This effort to consolidate a national market through the restriction of transnational flows of people and goods—but not significantly of ideas about reform and manufacture or of capital—depended on the notion, indeed, the myth, that the sweatshop could be eradicated in one country. In 1910, after a lengthy strike in New York, the garment worker and unionist Abraham Rosenberg declared that the "many-headed hydra" of the sweatshop was finally defeated. His metaphor of the hydra is telling. After all, the hydra was never fully killed. One of its heads was immortal and could be kept from regenerating only by keeping it under the weight of a heavy rock. Rosenberg, a practical trade unionist, recognized that the sweatshop could never be fully banished, only regulated.[25]

The premature epitaph of the sweatshop has been composed and rewritten many times, often in the heady optimism that followed massive garment strikes. Rosenberg offered his epitaph after a 1910 clockmakers' strike that established the ILGWU as a permanent force in the New York garment industry. A landmark labor agreement, the "Protocol of Peace" ended the strike by instituting a system of regulation that encouraged the reemergence of a factory system of production. The "Protocol," though it lasted only six troubled years, helped solidify an alliance between Progressive reformers and the labor movement that lasted until the early 1920s. By the 1920s, union leaders were again lamenting the return of the sweatshop. The epitaph for the sweatshop was rewritten again in the 1930s. A massive strike in 1933 and New Deal labor policy helped restore the vigor of the ILGWU. In particular, the passage of the Fair Labor Standards Act in 1938—still the major antisweatshop legislation—set hour and wage standards in the garment industry. *Life* magazine declared the sweatshop banished this time. In 1938, it printed an article, complete with pictures of healthy, American garment workers on the cover, that looked back to "thirty years ago" when "the industry stank of the sweatshop." In 1938, though, "the sweatshop is virtually gone . . . "[26] By the 1950s, the arrival of Puerto Rican and African American migrants, and later Asian immigrants from China, Korea, and Southeast Asia, signaled a downtown in wages and the return of the sweatshop. At around the same time, the federal government was backing away from restrictive trade policies. Cold warriors encouraged garment manufacture in the Caribbean basin as a way of strengthening anti-Communist governments. After the end of the Cold War, the federal government, under both Republican and Democratic leadership, cast loosening restriction on the garment trade as central to free-market economic politics.

The suggestion of the New York *Daily News* that "enforcement, enforcement, enforcement" is a solution to the city's sweatshop problem highlights the persistence of the myth of ending sweatshops in one country, city, or region. Most unionists, activists, politicians, and workers, however, would recognize that the sweatshop is central to a truly global system of production and consumption. Still, even as they gaze globally, these actors organize nationally.

USAS, the leading student activist group, in focusing on transnational corporations has built a series of successful alliances, exchanging ideas and strategies with workers in Mexico and elsewhere. They remain, however, an American activist group, firmly grounded in American universities and solely focused on changing American political and economic culture. Similarly, the federal government, when concerned at all about sweatshops, has shrunk from assuming an international regulatory role—even as it encourages foreign production. Thus, the Clinton administration in 1996, in the aftermath of the raid on the El Monte sweatshop, assembled the White House Apparel Industry Partnership. The best it proposed was voluntary monitoring of working conditions. Even then, the focus of the Clinton administration was clearly national, not international. Secretary of Labor Alexis M. Herman in 1999 condemned sweatshops in the strongest terms in a generation. "Sweatshops," she declared, "are repugnant to our moral core." Yet, for Herman, the sweatshop was a *national* problem: "And it is such an 'underground' problem that there is no definitive source on how many sweatshops operate in this country. But we know this: One is one too many."[27]

The national myopia of Herman and the Clinton Administration represents a tacit admission that the global sweatshop is beyond national reform. But, the American sweatshop *is* global. The American sweatshop is not necessarily in the United States. It is equally in New York or in El Salvador. Examining the American sweatshop means looking at workplaces located in the United States *and* abroad, but tied to the United States through ongoing exchanges of people, goods, resources, capital, and ideas. There is a persistent tension between the global roots of the sweatshop and nationally based efforts at reform and regulation. It is in this context that the American sweatshop need not exist in the United States but remains intimately and in highly historically specific ways linked to American political and economic culture. Indeed, the American sweatshop might equally be a Chinese, Vietnamese, or Mexican sweatshop!

The American sweatshop might be located abroad, but it is surely producing clothing for an American manufacturer, or it might be producing clothing for an American consumer. Then again, it might exist because of a national economic policy that is encouraged by the United States or by American foreign aid or lending agencies. The American sweatshop might also be located within the borders of the nation, all the while depending on the labor of immigrants and avoiding the gaze of regulators. The sweatshop may exist in one country and still be perceived as foreign. It may be linked to economic, political, and cultural demands from another part of the world—or another part of the same city.

Studying the American sweatshop means examining its many paradoxes. The economic roots of the sweatshop are international, but efforts at its control are national. Historically, the sweatshop carries a moral weight that has helped spur vigorous reform and organizing and cross-class, cross-ethnic so-cial movements. However, labeling a workplace a sweatshop casts its workers as foreign, alien, and dangerous. Such paradoxes help explain why antisweat-shop movements carry the importance of moral, abolitionist movements and also why the sweatshop seems like an immortal hydra.

Sweatshop USA

These essays are investigations of the cultural, political, ethnic, racial, and gen-dered discourse around the sweatshop and of its historic globalization. The social history of the diverse and changing sweatshop workforce and of antisweatshop activists and reformers is embedded in each of these essays.[28] The very idea of the "return of the sweatshop," the notion that contemporary sweatshops re-flect those of a century ago, suggests that the history of the sweatshop must move beyond a straight-line chronology. Thus, the essays in this collection are organized thematically in order to emphasize the important role of history in today's discussions about the sweatshop. Paradoxically, contemporary notions about the sweatshop as the precursor to industrial revolution in the Third World can be traced to turn-of-the-century racist descriptions of the sweat-shop as a primitive, foreign form of production. It also highlights how, in the evolution of antisweatshop organizing, reformers, consumer activists, and unionists continue to confront the difficulties of perceived racial, gender, and class divisions and the reality of a garment industry constantly on the run. In presenting a long view of the garment production, this collection confronts the assumption that the globalization of the industry is simply a movement of work away from metropoles—industrial centers in the West, like New York, Chicago, or Los Angeles (or London and Paris)—to less industrialized regions in Western nations and, finally, to the postcolonial developing world. Instead, garment production has always been dependent on worldwide migrations, even when markets were largely local or domestic.

The collection is divided into three sections. The first, "Producing the Sweatshop," examines the cultural and economic dialogues that surrounded the original defining of the sweatshop and that continue to shape ideas about its persistence and return. Daniel Bender describes how reformers and factory inspectors in the 1890s, drawing on a transatlantic discourse about race and biology, considered the sweatshop a sign of a dangerous process of racial de-generation effecting recent immigrant arrivals. Workers, instead, saw the phys-ical decline they suffered in the sweatshop as the evidence of class exploitation. In the end, however, workers and inspectors came to agree on the gendered ef-fects of sweated labor, in particular the threats that sweatshops seemed to pose to the sexual division of labor within the family. Nancy Green extends the analysis of the cultural discourse around sweatshops by linking it to economic debates about whether flexible production—small workshops dependent on contracting and subcontracting—is the wave of the future or an archaic type of work. At the same time, she questions the idea of a "return of the sweatshop." She argues that, despite the best efforts of workers and outside critics of the sweating system, the organization of the garment industry and the shifting demands of fashion have led to persistent exploitation. Peter Liebhold and Harry Rubenstein share their own experiences of being at the center of a stormy debate over sweatshops. They were curators for the 1998 Smithsonian Exhibition *Between a Rock and a Hard Place: A History of Sweatshops, 1820–Present,* mounted partly in response to the raid on the El Monte sweatshop. They examine the furor over the exhibition and ask provocative questions about whether a nation that tries to deny its sweatshop history can effectively confront its sweatshop present.

The second section, "Sweatshop Migrations," connects the movement of sweatshop production in and out of industrial centers like New York and Los Angeles to migrations of people, capital, and ideas. The first section connected the initial debates over the sweatshop to the arrival of European immigrants in the 1890s; this section connects the flow of production out of American industrial centers beginning in the 1930s. Richard Greenwald's essay looks at the strategy adopted by the garment unions to combat sweatshops and runaway shops in the twentieth century. Using oral histories of former garment workers and unionists, Ken Wolensky contradicts the idea that the sweatshop is a necessary evil that comes before real industrial development. Instead, he points out that garment producers, escaping unionized New York City and no longer able to depend on arrivals of desperate immigrants, arrived in Pennsylvania in the aftermath of deindustrialization: the closure of coal mines. He explores how the International Ladies' Garment Workers' Union (ILGWU) chased this mobile industry. In creating a union community in Pennsylvania, union leaders did not imagine that the runaway industry would soon be leaving. Finally, Xiaolan Bao explores the ethnic and family networks among Chinese immigrants in Sunset Park, Brooklyn and their ties to the neighborhood's garment industry. Simple economic explanations alone cannot explain the rise of sweating. Complex family and ethnic ties link immigrants, often undocumented, to their employers and workers' anger over low wages and overtime is often directed at new immigrants. Edna Bonacich and Richard Appelbaum investigate the relationship between offshore garment production and the Los Angeles industry, one of the few American cities that has witnessed a growth in garment manufacture. They connect the expansion of the garment industry in Los Angeles to city's image as a center of fashion and popular culture and the effects of a "global race to the bottom" in wages. The city, with its large immigrant population, has become the center of a vast network of small shops and contractors, largely hidden from the gaze of government inspectors. Manny Ness presents a contrasting image in his exploration of the New York garment industry. Especially after the terrorist attacks of September 11, 2001, New York manufacture has declined dramatically—despite a large immigrant population. As part of a study of the place in the city's industry in an era of global production, he traces how the UNITE! and the Chinese Staff and Workers' Association (CSWA), an activist organization critical of the union, are seeking alternatives to traditional unionizing strategies in response to the ability of management to shift production quickly.

The final section, "Sweatshop Resistance," explores efforts to combat sweatshops by workers, consumers, unionists, activists, reformers, and policy makers. It examines how antisweatshop social movements have relied on the moral repugnance elicited by the sweatshop, but suggests that strategies might have distinct limitations. The essays in this section point to the difficulty of organizing against the sweatshop in the face of the movement of people and production. Ethnicity has always been central to understanding both sweatshops and the garment industry. Jennifer Guglielmo's essay explores the often overlooked role of Italian-American women's oppositional culture in the period leading up to the Great Depression. She rejects the notion that Italian women were docile unionists and workers constrained by patriarchy. Instead, she argues, they waged an important struggle "outside of and in opposition to" garment unions. In the next essay, Eileen Boris looks at the various campaigns against sweatshops from the Progressive Era up to the present. She studies three distinct periods, the Progressive Era, the New Deal and present, in the hope that history can inform current political and policy debates.

The final three essays present different interpretations of the contemporary antisweatshop movement. Andrew Ross presents the most optimistic view. He explores how activists in the First World have harnessed the moral power of the word "sweatshop" to present a critique of global production that stretches far beyond simply the garment industry. Through dramatic exposés of working conditions, activists have struck transnational corporations at their weakest spot: their public image. Antisweatshop activists are beginning to establish the basic ideas of labor rights in the new global economy. Liza Featherstone presents a case study of USAS, one of the most successful antisweatshop groups. In examining several of the group's major campaigns, for example, over the monitoring of conditions in factories making clothing with university logos, Featherstone suggests that the antisweatshop movement is trying to move beyond telling "horror stories" about sweatshop conditions while confronting images of collegiate activists as privileged elites. Ethel Brooks presents a counterpoint to Ross' arguments about activism in the First World focused on conditions in the Third. Brooks questions how much power transnational antisweatshop movements afford Third World women workers. She explores a new kind of migration: the arrival of Third World women workers in the United States for speaking tours arranged by activists to highlight working conditions. Efforts at offshore reform of offshore production transforms such women into victims, whose voices can only speak about local conditions. In a global economy characterized by pervasive inequality, can there truly be an equitable antisweatshop movement?

The thirteen essays in this collection offer the reader a current window into what we have called "sweatshop studies"—the interdisciplinary study of the sweatshop. By bringing these authors together, we hope, in some small way, to bring this diverse community of scholars and activists closer. We hope to spark a conversation in which history informs the present and becomes a tool for social and economic change.

Notes

1. Peter Liebhold and Harry R. Rubenstein, *Between a Rock and a Hard Place: A History of American Sweatshops, 1820–Present* (Los Angeles: UCLA Asian American Studies Center, Simon Wiesenthal Center Museum of Tolerance, 1999), 12.
2. Liza Featherstone and United Students Against Sweatshops, *Students Against Sweatshops* (London: Verson, 2002).
3. Christine Stansell, "The Origins of the Sweatshop: Women and Early Industrialization in New York City." In Michael H. Frisch and Daniel J. Walkowitz, eds. *Working-Class America: Essays on Labor, Community, and American Society* (Urbana: University of Illinois Press, 1983), 78–103; Daniel E. Bender, *Sweated Work; Weak Bodies: Anti-Sweatshop Campaigns and Languages of Labor* (New Brunswick: Rutgers University Press, 2003); N. N. Feltes, "Misery or the Production of Misery: Defining Sweated Labour in 1890." *Social History* 17 (October, 1992), 441–452.
4. "Reports of the Industrial Commission on Immigration," XV (Washington: Government Printing Office, 1901). See, in particular, the testimony of the economist John R. Commons reprinted in John R. Commons, ed., *Trade Unionism and Labor Problems* (Boston: Ginn & Company, 1905), 316–335.
5. The Commission wrote, for example, that "The Jewish immigrant . . . is not by nature a wage-earner, and he keeps before himself continually the goal of emancipation from hard work." "Reports of the Industrial Commission on Immigration," 323–347.
6. Commons, *Trade Unionism and Labor Problems*, 316–335.
7. For a discussion of this discourse, see Nancy L. Green, *Ready-to-Wear and Ready-to-Work: A Century of Industries and Immigrants* (Durham: Duke University Press, 1997), 137–160.
8. House of Representatives, Committee of Manufactures, 52nd Congress, 2nd Session, "Report on the Sweating System under House Resolution" (February 13, 1892).
9. This idea of moving from sweatshops to "civilization" not only shaped the response reformers and unionists, but also has influenced the historiography of the American garment industry and the sweatshop, see Leon Stein, ed., *Out of the Sweatshop* (New York: Quadrangle, 1977); Joel Isaac Seidman, *The Needle* Trades New York: Farrar & Rinehart, 1942); Landon Storrs, *Civilizing Capitalism: The National Consumers' League, Women's Activism, and Labor Standards in the New Deal Era* (Chapel Hill, University of North Carolina Press, 2000).
10. Green, *Ready-to-Wear and Ready-To Work*, 156–157. For a comparative study of turn-of-the-century and contemporary sweatshops, see Daniel Soyer, "Garment Sweatshops, Then and Now." *New Labor Forum* 4 (Spring–Summer, 1999), 35–46.
11. Green, *Ready-to-Wear and Ready-To Work*, 56–58; Frances Perkins, *Survey Graphic* (February 1933).
12. General Accounting Office (GAO), Report to the Chairman, Subcommittee on Commerce, Consumer, and Monetary Affairs, Committee on Government Affairs, Committee on Government Operations, House of Representatives, "Garment Industry Efforts to Address the Prevalence and Conditions of Sweatshops," GAO/HEHS-95–29 (November 2, 1994).
13. "Sweat & Tears Still in Fashion in City" *Daily News*, July 8, 2001; Bruce Raynor, "Serfs of the Service Economy." *New York Times*, November 16, 1999.

14. Stein, ed., *Out of the Sweatshop*.
15. Steve Fraser, "Dress Rehearsal for the New Deal: Shop-Floor Insurgents, Political Elites, and Industrial Democracy in the Amalgamated Clothing Workers" in Frisch and Walkowitz, eds., *Working-Class America: Essays on Labor, Community, and American Society*, 212–255; Christopher T. Martin, "New Unionism at the Grassroots: The Amalgamated Clothing Workers of America in Rochester, New York, 1914–1929," *Labor History* 42 (May, 2000): 237–253.
16. Daniel T. Rodgers, *Atlantic Crossings: Social Politics in a Progressive Age* (Cambridge: The Belknap Press of Harvard University Press, 1998). Also see Martin J. Sklar, *The Corporate Reconstruction of American Capitalism, 1890–1916: The Market, the Law and Politics* (New York: Cambridge University Press, 1988).
17. Sheila Blackburn, " 'Princesses and Sweated-Wage Slaves Go Well Together': Images of British Sweated Workers, 1843–1914," *International Labor and Working-Class History* 61 (Spring, 2002), 24–44; James Schmiechen, *Sweated Industries and Sweated Labour the London Clothing Trades, 1860–1914* (Urban: University of Illinois Press, 1984); E. L. Godkin, "Our 'Sweating System,'" *Nation* (June 19, 1890).
18. On this, see Ellen Israel Rosen, *Making Sweatshop: The Glogalization of the U.S. Apparel Industry* (Berkeley: University of California Press, 2002); Jefferson R. Cowie, *Capital Moves: RCA's Seventy-Year Quest for Cheap Labor* (Ithaca: Cornell University Press, 1999); and Ken Wolensky's essay in this volume.
19. Rosen, *Making Sweatshops*.
20. Tom Vanderbilt, *The Sneaker Book: Anatomy of an Industry and an Icon* (New York: The New Press, 1998).
21. Nicholas Kristoff and Sheryl WuDunn, "Two Cheers for Sweatshops," *New York Times Magazine* (September 24, 2000).
22. Thomas Bender, ed., *Rethinking American History in a Global Age* (Berkeley: University of California Press, 2002), 11.
23. Rosen, *Making Sweatshops*, 13–176.
24. Richard A Greenwald, *Law and Order in Industry: The Protocols of Peace, the Triangle Fire and Industrial Democracy in the Making of the New Industrial Relations in Progressive Era New York* (Philadelphia: Temple University Press, forthcoming).
25. *Justice*, July 28, 1922, 6; Abraham Rosenberg, *Memoirs of a Cloakmaker*, trans. Lynn Davison (New York: Unpublished, 1920), 310–311.
26. "International Ladies' Garment Workers' Union: A Great and Good Union Points the Way for America's Labor Movement," *Life* (August 1, 1938).
27. Leibhold and Rubenstein, *Between a Rock and a Hard Place*, 36.
28. Among the large number of social histories of workers laboring in sweatshops, at least within North America, see: Miriam Ching Yoon Louie, *Sweatshop Warriors: Immigrant Women Workers Take on the Global Factory* (Cambridge: South End Press, 2001); Jo Ann Argersinger, *Making the Amalgamated: Gender, Ethnicity, and Class in the Baltimore Clothing Industry, 1899–1939* (Baltimore: The Johns Hopkins University Press, 1999); Ruth Frager, *Sweatshop Strife: Class, Ethnicity, and Gender in the Jewish Labour Movement in Toronto, 1900–1939* (Toronto: University of Toronto Press, 1992); Susan Glenn, *Daughters of the Shtetl: Life and Labor in the Immigrant Generation* (Ithaca: Cornell University Press, 1990); Xiaolan Bao, *Holding Up More than Half the Sky: Chinese Women Garment Workers in New York City, 1948–92* (Urbana: University of Illinois Press, 2001).

1
Producing the Sweatshop

1

"A Foreign Method of Working"

Racial Degeneration, Gender Disorder, and the Sweatshop Danger in America

DANIEL E. BENDER
University of Waterloo

Beginning in the 1880s, a veritable army of journalists, politicians, and inspectors explored New York's Lower East Side, the crowded neighborhood where Eastern-European Jewish and Italian immigrants had found work and cramped housing. These outside observers brought back with them tales of a foreign quarter to share with a curious and frightened middle-class and elite American audience. They described the strange habits of the Lower East Side's residents and the filth and squalor of the area's tenement apartments. Most important to their audience, these critics described the neighborhood's garment contract shops. After all, it was through these shops—and the clothing produced in them—that American, middle- and upper-class New York was linked to working-class and immigrant New York.

The reports of these visitors filled the pages of the city's newspapers and the nation's magazines. Exposés of working and living conditions on the Lower East Side were highly personal reactions of outside observers who contrasted their shock, disgust, and revulsion with immigrants' seeming comfort in the filth and immorality of the garment workplace. Observers described exotic workplaces, rife with dangers, and redolent of the smells of dirty workers and strange food; they were hazy with dust and filled—probably—with invisible germs ready to land on newly produced garments. These were "un-American" shops, the products of urban crowding and unrestricted immigration.

Such personalized narratives of exploration and disgust helped provoke a city, national, and, indeed, international fervor about the dangers posed by these immigrant garment workshops. Local and national politicians, with the aid of factory inspectors, began widely publicized investigations into garment production, in particular into systems of contracting in which retailers contracted out "bundles" of precut cloth to be assembled into garments in small Lower East Side workshops. Two high profile government committees—in 1892, a House of Representatives committee and, in 1901, the Federal Industrial Commission on Immigration—sought to determine the social effects and perils of "foreign-born labor in the clothing trade," especially Eastern-European Jews. States, including New York, Massachusetts, and Illinois, with sizable garment industries and immigrant populations, also launched their own investigations of immigrants' garment work.[1] Citing the findings of these investigations, New York State, the epicenter of the American garment industry, passed the Factory Inspection Law in 1886 and substantially revised it in 1892. The law regulated some conditions of labor and required that all tenement garment manufacturers have a permit.[2]

Politicians sought to differentiate these contracting shops from the "American" factory by labeling them "sweatshops." The association of these shops with "sweated labor," a term long associated with immigrants' jobs, garment work, and arduous, physically draining toil, helped distinguish them as a "foreign method of working." Condemnations of the sweatshop, thus, merged with and often subsumed criticism of immigrants and fears about the larger social effects of unrestricted immigration. In particular, investigators and politicians came to see the sweatshop as reflective of supposed Jewish racial characteristics. Contemporary understandings of race and, specifically, the process of racial degeneration shaped understandings of the dangers of the sweatshop.

In their investigations, inspectors, journalists, and policymakers claimed to have found the frightening evidence of "racial degeneration." They argued that sweatshop labor had sent Jewish immigrants, who composed the majority of the sweatshop workforce, tumbling down the racial hierarchy that so many Progressive Era observers used to distinguish differences among immigrant groups. These critics of the sweatshop argued that immigrant groups were part of distinct races capable of ascending or descending a complex and unstable hierarchy. In this way, understandings of the economics of the sweatshop became intertwined with notions of race. This racialization of the economics of the garment industry was part of a larger convergence of biological science and economic theory. Industrialization, many economists and social scientists between 1880 and 1930 argued, was a step in a process of "social evolution." The workplace itself was now the primary site of evolutionary struggle and the urban marketplace was where the losers and winners of this struggle confronted each other. Thus, class and ethnicity represented more than simple social categories; they were markers of biological status, divisions between winners and losers, civilized and uncivilized.[3]

Drawing on a vibrant transnational biological and economic discourse that saw the working class itself as divided into a hierarchy with dependants and "defectives" incapable of labor on the bottom and respectable, skilled workers at the top, policymakers cast sweatshop workers as the detritus of "social" or "industrial evolution." As a class and as a race—these categories were often used interchangeably—Jewish sweatshop workers displayed symptoms of

racial degeneracy. As poor immigrants, they necessarily faced the perils of evolutionary, economic struggle. They were neither artisans nor "defectives"—
yet. However, they showed all the signs of falling from the ranks of the
"industrial" to the "parasitic" classes. In particular, policy makers pointed to
moral turpitude, family breakdown, and the rising prevalence of disease
among Jewish workers as outward, individual signs of a collective, racial
degradation.[4]

This degradation was all the more obvious and threatening because the
sweatshop was fundamentally an urban problem. The urban crucible accelerated
the process of racial degeneration. As the economist John Commons argued, the
city attracted the most defective and dependant of immigrants who sought the
plethora of resources and aid offered by social reformers and city governments.
Thus, the "least self-reliant or forehanded . . . races" migrated to the city. For
critics, like Commons, worried about the effect of unrestricted immigration, the
closing of the American frontier meant that immigrants were huddled in a few
urban, industrial centers. Public intoxication, crime, vagrancy, prostitution, family abandonment, and epidemic disease were evidence that "the dangerous effects of city life" were forcing immigrants and their children into the ranks of the
"truly parasitic."

Even worse, racial degeneration, in the heightened economic, evolutionary
struggle of the city, could be hereditary. The congestion and economic exchanges of the urban center also meant that racial degeneration was a problem
effecting the most "civilized." The "poverty and pauperism" of immigrant
races effected—and, indeed, infected—American classes. Vagrancy, crime, and
drunkenness tumbled into the streets and out of ethnic enclaves. Germs and
disease bred in the filthy environments of immigrant homes and workplaces,
like the tenement sweatshop, and in the bodies of racially less resilient immigrants might lead to urban plagues. And, most ominous, according to some
observers, science and urban social reform helped preserve those individuals
who would otherwise perish through natural selection. For others, the dynamics of economic competition favored those immigrant races willing to work in
abominable conditions. Biological, industrial competition seemed to favor the
least desirable immigrants. Such observers feared, as well, that the least resilient, the most immoral, and the least civilized immigrant races—the "low-
skilled and inefficient labour"—were reproducing faster than American stock.
Rising percentages of foreign-born in cities seemed to confirm this counter-
selection. As one worried observer put it immigration hinted at "race suicide"
as it was merely "the substitution of one kind of man for another."[5]

The process of defining the sweatshop in the 1880s and 1890s, as a symp-
tom, cause, and effect of racial degeneration, focused on immigrants. It included them initially only as subjects. Yet even though communication
between immigrants and outside observers was difficult—few factory inspectors

spoke Yiddish and few garment workers spoke fluent English—the idea of the sweatshop entered immigrants' own discourse about work. In turn, immigrants' ideas about the dangers of the sweatshop that generally eschewed notions of racial degradation came to influence reform strategies. In particular, immigrants, reformers, inspectors, and policy makers came to agree that one of the worst problems of the sweatshop was that it had become a source of family disruption and physical (if not, racial) decline.

Race, Biology, and the Sweatshop

In the 1890s, observers in different American states and on both sides of the Atlantic sought to isolate the multiple causes of the sweatshop. Their conclusions depended on a combination of biological, evolutionary, and economic thought.[6] They argued that sweatshops sprang up because of the system of contracting and subcontracting in which the onus of production was passed on from a manufacturer to a contractor to a subcontractor and, all too frequently, to a subsubcontractor. Shop owners' compensation was "sweated" from their employees.[7] The system of contracting and subcontracting degraded working conditions, because contractor shops located work in the home. Also, because of its location, sweatshop wages were so low that male as well as female workers had to work to support their families.[8] As economist Frank Tracy Carlton argued, "the distinguishing characteristics usually found in a sweated industry are low wages, a long working day, insanitary workshops, and speeded-up workers." For Carlton, the "adjectives" "low, long, insanitary, and speeded-up" suggested that the sweatshop was fundamentally an urban and immigrant problem. "The conditions favorable to the development of sweated industries," he wrote, "are found in large cities . . . where it is easy to obtain immigrant, women, and children laborers . . . " Because the immigrant sweatshop workforce was one that might, through the process of racial degeneration, become dependent on the benevolence of urban social insurance and reform, the sweatshop was "a 'parasitic industry.'" It sapped the vitality, strength, and health of its workers while undermining the "factory system."[9]

Factory inspectors and politicians were so diligent in reporting the immigrant composition of the sweatshop workforce because they considered "the wide development of the contract system . . . a phase of immigration" and an archaic form of production that had preceded the factory system in the larger process of social evolution. As the sweatshop might cause racial degeneration, its proliferation represented a counterevolutionary development.[10] It was, after all, a type of workplace favored by those from the "least civilized sections of Europe."[11] In defining the sweatshop as a "foreign" workplace, New York's factory inspectors directly contrasted it to the glorified "American factory" where "you find everything in keeping with the American idea." Thus, the sociologist and anthropologist Maurice Parmelee suggested that, in the process of social evolution, the "large shop, the factory, and the large capitalist should replace the home and small shop industries and the small capitalist."[12] But, the racial characteristics of Jews, arriving in large numbers, prevented that from happening.

Inspectors and observers blamed the "racial characteristics of the Jew" for the problems of the sweatshop. The Industrial Commission, for example, explained that racially Jews were unfit for factory production. As a race, they were too "individualistic" for the "discipline of the factory." Piecework proliferated and workdays lengthened "because the Jewish people are peculiarly eager to earn a big day's wages, no matter at what sacrifice."[13] The inferior, internal characteristics of Jews, inspectors seemed to suggest, were mirrored in the condition of their bodies; mind and body were intertwined. After all, as economist Commons insisted, a worker "can only exercise the gifts which nature has endowed him." Thus, according to Commons, the Jew "prefers the sweat-shop."[14] The individualism of Jews was reflected in the weakness of their bodies. As a "race subject to contempt," the economist Jesse Pope argued, Eastern-European Jews lacked the skills or strength for factory production. They "were the most helpless and inefficient immigrants that have ever entered this country." Jewish immigrants' body-type drew them naturally to "such light occupations as sewing."[15]

For inspectors, the racial character of Jews explained the economics of contracting. Economic competition was, as the University of Wisconsin economist Richard Ely reminded, a biological process. "Nothing could well be more unscientific in the present age of science," he wrote, "than to leave evolution out of account in our examination of anything so fundamental in society as competition." If the sweatshop was driving other garment factories out of business, that was a biological phenomenon. But, it was a process that favored the least desirable of races; the fittest were not necessarily the strongest. Even in his paean to competition, Ely worried that "a kind of society is possible, in which the beggar has this fitness . . . " As Commons wrote, immigrants could triumph because they would accept lower standards of living than the more advanced races they were replacing: " . . . competition has no respect for superior races. The race with lowest necessities displaces others."[16] As Robert Hunter agreed, "it is a competition of standards, and the lowest standard prevails. Among the common laborers in . . . the clothing and textile trades, this competition is too intense. It amounts, at times, almost to a race war . . ."[17]

Thus, for Commons, in the history of American industrial evolution, the Irish had displaced the "educated sons and daughters of American stock" in the textile mills of New England—but were, in turn, supplanted by French Canadians. But, when these French Canadians made the mistake of acquiring "a higher standard," they were replaced by Syrians, Poles, and Italians. Similarly, in the garment industry, the Irish and German took the jobs of more advanced English and Scotch tailors. In turn, "Russian Jews" were steadily taking their jobs—but their own positions seemed to be threatened by the arrival of

Italians. Industrial evolution, in short, was the "substitution of races" leading to a downward spiral in racial standards: "Each comes from a country lower in the scale than that of the preceding, until finally the ends of the earth have been ransacked in the search for low standards of living . . ." Commons suspected—and worried—that eventually even the most debased of European races would be supplanted by immigrants from "China, Japan, and India."[18] For some observers, like Hunter, this process of racial displacement threatened to lead to the degeneration of supplanted races. He argued that among "displaced classes" there were rising numbers of "defective" and "dependent" "hoodlums, tramps, and paupers."[19] For others, industrial competition might lead to race suicide. As sociologist Edward Ross, among many others, warned, the arrival of immigrants—the "hunger-bitten hordes from the man-stifled neighbor lands"—was lowering the birthrate of more desirable native "stocks." The arrival of the "foreign element" threatened the "annihilation of the native element."[20] Thus, as Cornell professor Frank Fetter mourned: "the ignorant, the improvident, the feeble-minded are contributing far more than their quota to the next generation."[21]

The biological competition that favored the least advanced races of immigrants hinted at larger social dangers of "race suicide." It could also explain the abominable conditions of sweated labor. Inspectors' reports—like the testimony of politicians and the exposés of journalists—seem to measure their racial, class, and moral distance from workers. In particular, inspectors contrasted their repulsion with the smells and filth of the garment workshop with immigrants' seeming comfort. In effect, inspectors were reaffirming hierarchies of race in the context of the reform relationship. The ability to countenance dirt and smells was a marker of one's place on the evolutionary ladder. The lower the race, the lower the expectation of sanitation. A "Hebrew" comfort in filth explained the smells of the sweatshop and provided evidence of Jews' place in the hierarchy of races.[22] Thus, George McKay, the principal factory inspector for the Lower East Side in the late 1880s and early 1890s, was typical when he declared that sweatshops "smell as powerfully and poisonously as the wretched toilers themselves." One sweatshop he described as "nauseating . . . and the stench abominable."[23] The stench of the sweatshop revealed the racial differences separating inspectors and workers.

If sweatshop conditions already reflected Jews' low racial status, inspectors worried that they might catalyze a process of degeneration. Critics like the journalist Eva McDonald Valesh pointed to the declining bodies of sweatshop workers as evidence of racial decline. Valesh insisted that Jewish workers' physical weakness was accented by their work in sweatshops: ". . . gaunt figures now and then emerge . . . All, even to the babies, have that pallid, haggard expression, characteristic of the quarter. Not one of the multitude exceeded the average height, and many fell below it."[24] The noted critic of tenements and urban squalor Jacob Riis, in a similar fashion, noted that Eastern-European Jewish workers labored until "mind and muscle give out together."[25] For Riis and Valesh, the Jewish proletarian body was increasingly frail and decrepit with poor muscle structure and twisted spines.[26] Jews, as Parmelee worried, seemed to be "physically unfit for the strain of sweated labor"—despite their natural attraction to sewing.[27]

Even worse, this physical decline might be inherited, either through a process of Lamarckian evolution in which negative acquired characteristics reappeared in workers' children or through a Darwinian evolution in which the conditions of work led to a breakdown in workers' morality leading to degeneration and overbreeding. Either way, as one inspector testified to the House committee, immigrant Jews were becoming "a race enfeebled by the strain of terribly long hours, lack of air, and bad sanitary conditions."[28] Eastern-European Jews' "ill-fed and poorly clad bodies," another inspector insisted, left them "unclean in person and degraded in mind."[29] The sweatshop sent Jewish immigrants tumbling down the hierarchy of races. "We may see the low level of civilization to which they have been forced," one inspector mourned. Hunter insisted that given the "squalor," "foul odors," and "promiscuous mixing of all ages and sexes" of the tenement sweatshop, Jewish immigrants had become a degenerate race. The Jews of "the Russian Pale are better off morally, physically," he wrote, "than those of the east side of New York."[30]

Valesh and Riis, among other observers of Jewish immigrant workers, claimed to have discovered a particularly brutalized race of workers. But, the plight of Jews was part of a larger problem. Fears about the racial degeneration of immigrants was part of broader transatlantic anxiety about the decline of the lower classes. At the outbreak of the Crimean War, the British "Committee on Physical Deterioration" was horrified at the numbers of working-class men rejected for military service because of physical unfitness. Similar surveys in the United States of military recruits and of working-class communities in the steel center of Pittsburgh and the garment center of New York also revealed degradation.[31] Thus, the influential writer on the causes of poverty, John Hobson noted that "modern life has no more tragical figure than the gaunt, hungry laborer . . . begging in vain for . . . the rough food and shelter for himself and his family, which would be practically secured to him in the rudest form of society."[32]

The role of inspector, thus, was that of defender of the race and protector of civilization. Only inspection and laws could prevent sweatshop workers from "being a menace to civilization."[33] Inspectors were "sweeping back new social evils which follow the ever-coming tides of lower and lower classes of labor every generation."[34] And, they were defending "civilization" from very real and immediate "evils," even beyond the looming dangers of race suicide. When inspectors described themselves as fighting the "evils of the sweatshop," they were referring specifically to the contagious diseases they claimed to have found in every sweatshop they visited.[35] In cities, like New York, where immigrants were linked to middle- and upper-class native-born Americans through geography and economic exchanges, disease could not be quarantined in immigrant neighborhoods or, as they were often called, "colonies." As Parmelee worried, the "evils" of the sweatshop for immigrant workers could lead to "the dissemination of disease throughout the community at large, because the germs of disease are carried by the products of sweated industries to the consumers." For McKay, "the danger from the . . . obnoxious smells that abound therein to those employed is only equaled to that which may be caused by the spread of infectious disease through clothing . . . made up under those conditions." In labeling the tenement factories of New York City, "lung sweatshops" because of the dangers of tuberculosis in the dust, Hunter worried that "a consumptive of the sweatshop, spraying the garments he sews by sneezing . . . may convey to some delicate lad or girl in a far-distant part of the country or in a wealthy part of the city the disease which the sweatshop has given him."[36]

Such fears of disease, coupled with concerns about the evolutionary challenges posed by the arrival of immigrants, shaped the first regulations of sweatshops, proposed on both sides of the Atlantic in the 1890s. These laws, especially in the United States where legal precedents restricted the possible scope of industrial regulation, linked antisweatshop campaigns to larger efforts for immigration restriction, public health legislation, and urban sanitary reform. Like these other urban-based movements, the initial drive for antisweatshop regulations aimed to protect middle-class consumers, not workers. Thus, reformers conceived of the first antisweatshop laws as bulwarks against the contagion nurtured in the filth of sweatshops and in the bodies of immigrants and passed on to middle-class consumers, especially women. As the Industrial Commission admitted: "the legislation . . . has been undertaken not on behalf of the workers, but on behalf of consumers. It is the protection of the public against contagious and infectious disease . . ."[37] At its best, such laws could be part of efforts to reverse a process of selection that favored the weak and undesirable. As Ely suggested, through sanitary regulation, "modern civilization increases the strength and vigor of those who do survive."[38] In effect, the laws passed in New York and elsewhere in the United States, and, similarly, in Europe during the 1890s that restricted the site and conditions of garment production were designed to regulate the biological interactions of race and class in the city.

Class and the Immigrant Sweatshop

For inspectors, reformers, and politicians, the sweatshop encapsulated the dangers of urban confrontations of race and class. For these observers, racial degeneration was a problem not simply for immigrants, but also of immigrants. This was especially true in an industrial city characterized by exchanges of goods and, thus, of germs. In this context, workers became, not necessarily allies to reform, but objects of—and, according to some inspectors, hindrances to—reform. With antisweatshop regulation defined as the protection of civi-

lization and consumers, many factory inspectors initially regarded "uncivilized" immigrant workers as an obstacle to effective investigation. Immigrants
were so obstinate in their habits and so comfortable in the filth of the sweatshop that they undermined efforts to confront the public health threats of the
sweatshop.[39]

However, the racial and class barriers of suspicion that divided workers and
inspectors were permeable. Immigrant voices could not be removed from the
discourse around sweatshops. Some Jewish immigrants testified at government hearings, including those held by the House of Representatives. When
they testified, workers shared at least part of inspectors' vocabulary. In particular, they focused on the health of immigrant sweatshop workers.[40] Also like
public critics of the sweatshop, Jewish workers noted connections between the
arrival of immigrants and the rise of contracting. Dr. Daniels reported that
immigrants she talked to explained the rise of a contracting system by pointing to "the increase in the numbers of those seeking employment, especially
greenhorns just come over." Jewish immigrants further echoed inspectors'
concerns about long hours of labor and the horrid conditions of sweatshops
located in workers' homes. Abraham Bisno, a cloakmaker who had lived and
labored in both New York and Chicago and, later, a union official, testified to
the House committee that immigrants "work in bedrooms and in shops where
there is nothing to breathe."[41] Dr. Daniels testified to the House hearings that
Jewish workers admitted to working "from fourteen to fifteen hours, and
sometimes as much as they could endure in two days."

Yet immigrants were, not surprisingly, unwilling to accept racialized, economic explanations for the sweatshop—even if they agreed on many of its
evils. Often, like the garment worker and labor leader Morris Feinstone, they
pointed to the logic of competition and the vulnerability of recent immigrant
arrivals. As Feinstone put it: "The products of this forced labor were offered in
the open market in competition with 'American' products which were higher
in price because native workers commanded higher wages for their labor."[42]
According to Feinstone, competition and exploitation, not race, explained the
difference between the "American" factory and the immigrant sweatshop. For
Jewish workers, their enfeebled bodies revealed the onerous conditions of
labor and the unfairness of the system. Immigrants saw the sweatshop as a
problem facing working-class Jews, not as a reflection of their biological and
racial status.[43]

For immigrant workers, the conditions of the sweatshop were the natural
result of arduous labor in cramped and degrading tenement apartments. They
were not the result of a Jewish racial trait. The worker and poet Morris Rosenfeld, for example, blamed his boss for the "damp and murky" sweatshop. In
one poem, he asked how if his "body is weak from the work's dreadful clutch,"
he can be expected to be clean.[44] Thus, immigrants pointed to the trauma of
labor, not to the process of racial degeneration, to explain their weak bodies.

Abraham Rosenberg, for example, called his fellow workers "pale, overworked shadows."[45] He argued that sweatshops turned hale immigrants into frail proletarians: "dark, dirty, overcrowded sweatshops . . . swallowed healthy immigrants . . ."[46] Disease and germs were intimately intertwined with the peril of labor, not with the danger of urban contact. For Rosenfeld, the immigrant in the sweatshop was a "pale operator . . . using up his strength." In his poem "The Tear on the Iron," Rosenfeld argued that his own weakness was caused by work in the "cold and dark" sweatshop: "My heart is weak, I groan and cough,—my sick breast scarcely heaves."[47]

Like inspectors, Jewish workers saw the sweatshop as linked to immigration. But the sweatshop preyed upon immigrants, it was not the reflection of their debased nature. Morris Feinstone, for example, stressed the class relationships that lay behind the sweatshop: "When these fugitives came to America seeking the promised land, they were taken off the boats by contractors . . . and set to work in subhuman surroundings, for a miserable wage, and under conditions which made protest utterly impossible."[48] The decline in workers' health belied class exploitation, not racial degeneration. Thus, the poet and sweatshop worker Yacob Adler traced the decline of one immigrant's health directly to the experience of sweated labor: "Weary and shaking,/ every bone breaking,/ home he comes aching,/ home from the shop . . ."[49]

For inspectors, the sweatshop rendered visible Jews' physical inferiority and revealed their low racial status. Physical decline further hinted at the presence of disease which might be passed on to middle-class consumers. For immigrants, physical weakness and disease revealed the evils of a system that preyed on recent immigrants. Given their divergent explanations for the ill health of workers, immigrants and inspectors could not build a cross-class antisweatshop movement solely on shared concerns about weakness and disease.

Gender, Racial Degeneration, and the Sick Immigrant

Gender proved a stronger common ground. Outside critics came to blame racial degeneration on the immoral mixing of men and women at work. Male and female Eastern-European Jewish immigrants lamented that their declining health was disrupting a sexual division of labor they saw as an American ideal. Both groups came to see the sweatshop as a family problem. For social reformers, factory inspectors, and public health officials, levels of women's wage work attested to the immorality of the sweatshop system and contributed to the debased condition of immigrants. Meanwhile, male Eastern-European Jewish immigrants, with the tacit and sometime vocal acceptance of women, declared the preservation of the ideal of the male breadwinner as the key to Jews' Americanization and social status. Together, especially after the turn of the century, workers and inspectors increasingly viewed the restriction of women's paid labor in their tenement homes as the goal of an antisweatshop movement.

Factory inspectors and journalists consistently protested the seemingly un-differentiated work of men and women. During their hearings, the House of Representatives committee, for example, asked witnesses to measure the effects of men and women working together.[50] For the witnesses to and members of the committee, high rates of women's wage work played a key role in workers' moral degradation and racial degeneration. John D. Warner, the chairman of the House committee, declared that the intermixing of male and female workers was a "promiscuous carrying out of the work." The factory inspector, George McKay, agreed that "so far as morals are concerned," the labor of men and women together in the cramped surrounding of the sweatshop was "prompting premature curiosity in young minds, and turning their attention to matters of sexual significance . . ."[51]

McKay worried especially that the degraded state of immigrants could become fixed by being passed down from sweatshop workers to the children produced by the promiscuity of the sweatshop. Echoing Lamarckian evolutionary theory, some inspectors were concerned that the physical and moral breakdown of immigrant workers would appear in the next generation.[52] As McKay put it, through immoral sexual relations, sweatshop workers would create "a race ignorant, miserable and immoral . . ."[53] Other inspectors eschewed such ideas of acquired characteristics, but still worried that the labor of women would lead to racial degeneration. Racial debasement would occur with the decline of male breadwinning. Women would be removed from their "natural" duties of child-rearing, setting in motion a process in which the most brutal children would survive. Women's labors could lead to the survival of the unfit. Thus, sweatshop work, one inspector argued, "will eventually bring forth ignorant, brutal, unhealthy men and women. This must be when a woman, in addition to the duties of wife and mother is forced to join with her husband as breadwinner." Similarly, Parmelee declared that "when the labor is so long and difficult as to interfere with the peculiar functions of the women and with the healthy development of the children, it is a great evil."[54] At the same time, Hunter suggested that the labor of women, along with the work of brutalized children, was the reason "so-called belated industries, like the sweating system" persist. Thus, through biological discourses, gendered concerns about the breakdown of the family were linked to racialized understandings of economics.[55]

Even as both male and female Eastern-European Jewish immigrants tended to downplay fears of racial decline, they still worried that the sweatshop would undermine what was increasingly a cherished social and cultural ideal: the notion of the male breadwinner. Immigrants recognized the ideal of the male breadwinner as an easily identifiable Victorian-American social standard. Male and female workers advanced models of women's labor that permitted, even encouraged, women's labor before marriage and allowed different forms of economic productivity, like shopkeeping, after marriage.[56] Nonetheless, both male and female Jewish immigrants discouraged married women's wage labor, especially in the garment industry.[57] Eastern-European Jewish immigrants generally came to regard married women's labor as a symbol of poverty and men's breadwinning as a sign of assimilation and success. In the years after their arrival, they sought to translate gendered cultural ideals into social reality. Thus, as the observer of the New York garment industry, Mabel Hurd Willet documented, for many Jewish women, marriage ideally meant the end of their garment wage work: "Among Jews the . . . period of industrial activity of a Jewish woman is normally a short one."[58]

The threat of married women's sweatshop labor became central to the way male and female factory inspectors, social reformers, and Jewish workers together came to define the dangers of sweated work. As part of a broad program of urban sanitary reform focused on immigrant housing, fears about the effects of work on the body and on gendered order came together around concern about the location of garment work in tenement apartments. Work in cramped, unsafe, and unsanitary tenement apartment sweatshops not only represented a significant threat to workers' and public health, but also encouraged the immoral labor of married women. Thus, when the Consumers' League of New York declared the sweatshop a "menace to the home," it referred not only to the homes of middle-class consumers who might purchase infected clothing, but also to the homes and families of working-class immigrants. The New York State Office of the Factory Inspector similarly declared: "The combination living-room and workshop is a positive menace to the health of the community."[59]

Especially after 1900, Eastern-European Jewish immigrants came to join factory inspectors in their crusade against garment work in tenement apartments as they sought Americanization and assimilation. More than other immigrant groups in New York, Jewish immigrants came to demand a differentiation between home and work. As historian Andrew Heinze suggests, especially after the turn the century, Jewish immigrants often decorated their apartments with material goods, like pianos, that declared the home as distinct from the workplace and symbolized their rising social status and assimilation.[60] Such emblems of leisure marked immigrants' rise from the time when they struggled to find an economic foothold, when their homes were, at best, purely functional. For newly arrived or for especially impoverished immigrants, a few scraps of wood might even suffice as furniture. Poor or new immigrants, especially men, might even sleep in the shop itself to save money.[61]

In addition, workers, especially men, would often carry work home after the day in the shop was completed. The whole family might work long into the night to supplement their miserable wages.[62] The cloakmaker Abraham Bisno described to the House committee how the most impoverished male workers took work home where they could rely on the help of their wives and children:

"The manufacturer runs his shop at ten hours a day only, but I, who have a desire to work longer than ten hours, take work home every night. The manufacturer says you can take the work home and produce it at home. He takes it home and he has the use of his wife and children and neighbors." For Bisno, with the pressures of subcontracting, the home became, not a site of leisure, but a dangerous workplace. "Sweat shops," he argued, "are shops at home."[63]

If the sweatshop was in the home, workers could never escape its dangers. Thus, social reformers, policy makers, inspectors, and male workers—and, on occasion, female workers—labeled the homework shop, a sweatshop located in workers' tenement apartments, the worst kind of sweatshop. In the homework shop, the boundaries between the industrial and the domestic disintegrated, conditions deteriorated, and gendered disorder increased. For inspectors, the homework shop accelerated the process of racial decline: "No pretense is made of separating the work from the household affairs, if such a term can be used to describe the existence of these people."[64] For "these people," the homework shop threatened their chance at Americanization. For both groups, the homework shop magnified the health dangers of sweated labor. Warner traced a hierarchy—much like the evolutionary hierarchy of races—within the sweated system with homework at the very bottom: ". . . through the contractor to the 'sweater' and on to the 'home worker,' the steps are steadily downward—of decreasing responsibility, comfort, and compensation."[65] In the homework shop, male workers turned the ideal of the male breadwinner on its head by converting family members into wage earners.

For Warner and other factory inspectors, the public health and moral dangers of the sweatshop were intensified by the destruction of a familial division of labor. "By introducing outsiders in his home and controverting it into a workroom," the reformer Joseph Lee told the House of Representatives hearings on sweated labor, "the occupier has already surrendered the privacy which makes the home sacred; and the results, both sanitary and moral, of the combination of home and factory are worse in degree than in any other class of cases we have been considering." Specifically, the United States Industrial Commission on Immigration argued, "the effect on the intelligence and personal initiative of the tailors is also depressing."[66] For the Industrial Commission, the racial decline caused by sweated labor was intimately intertwined with the corruption of male breadwinning.

In this context, inspectors came to see homeworkers either as the most degenerate of immigrants or as their wives: "The home-worker is generally a foreigner just arrived and frequently a woman whose husband is dead, sick, or worthless and whose children keep her at home."[67] Women homeworkers were, at once, the principal victims of the sweatshop and a symbol of the moral, physical, and racial perils of sweated work. Female homeworkers were, at worst, "defective in habits or physical or in mental capacity." At best, they were married, foreign women for "whom the death or worthlessness of her husband leaves to support a family, which prevents her leaving her home."[68]

Like middle-class observers, workers—men, in particular—identified homework as a threat to male breadwinning and as a moral danger. They worried about the "physical, psychological, and moral deterioration" caused by sweated homework.[69] Morris Feinstone, for example, blamed "the vicious 'homework' system" for "the steady degradation of whole families." He insisted that when they turned to homework, female immigrants and their families surrendered their "health, moral courage, and at the last even hope of deliverance."[70]

Thus, immigrants, led by male workers like Feinstone, came to advance their own ideas about degeneration, degradation, and deterioration. Their understandings of the dangers of sweated labor were stripped of racialized and class meanings, but were dependent on ideals of a sexual division of labor. In the process, immigrants identified a common ground about the dangers of the sweatshop with factory inspectors, social reformers, and public health advocates. Together, these male workers and outside critics would seek an anti-sweatshop movement grounded in gendered fears about the sweatshop. Accordingly, their primary goal was the "the restriction . . . of tenement-house work."[71] However, this "movement for stamping out of the disease-breeding infamous and un-American 'sweating system' " offered a limited alternative to the sweatshop. Instead of the sweatshop, they proposed only the "modern" factory. Instead, of family labor, they suggested only male breadwinning. [72]

Notes

1. House of Representatives, Committee of Manufactures, 52nd Congress, 2nd Session, "Report on the Sweating System under House Resolution" (Feb. 13, 1892), iii–xxix; "Reports of the Industrial Commission on Immigration," 316–344. On regulation in Pennsylvania and Massachusetts, see *Thirteenth Annual Report of the Factory Inspectors of the State of New York, 1898* (Albany: Wynkoop Hallenbeck Crawford Co., State Printers, 1899), 779–784.

2. *Seventh Annual Report of the Factory Inspectors of the State of New York, 1892* (Albany: James B. Lyon, State Printer, 1893), 113–211, 1–23.

3. For examples of this view of industrialization as a step in a larger process of evolution and the related idea that class is a marker of biological status, see Richard Theodore Ely, *Studies in the Evolution of Industrial Society* (New York: The Macmillan Company, 1903); Frank Tracy Carlton, *Education and Industrial Evolution* (New York: The Macmillan Company, 1913), 45–72; Carroll D. Wright, *The Industrial Evolution of the United States* (New York: Flood and Vincent, 1895); Thomas Nixon Carver, *Essays in Social Justice* (Freeport: Books for Libraries Press, 1970 [reprint from 1915]), 349–375; William Graham Sumner, *What Social Classes Owe to Each Other* (New York: Harper & Brothers, 1883). Like so many ideas about economics and class, this biological interpretation was influenced by European intellectual currents. See, for example, Herbert Spencer, *The Principles of Sociology* (London: Williams and Norgate, 1876); Benjamin Kidd, *Social Evolution* (New York: Macmillan, 1895); Carl Bücher, *Industrial Evolution* (New York: Henry Holt & Company, 1901). See also Daniel Pick, *Faces of Degeneration: A European Disorder, c.1848–c. 1918* (Cambridge: Cambridge University Press, 1989).

4. The arguments about working-class racial degeneration in many ways represented the intellectual precursor to the related ideas of immigration restriction and eugenics. On racial degeneration and immigration, see Robert Hunter, *Poverty* (New York: Grosset & Dunlop, 1904); Brooks Adams, *The Law of Civilization and Decay; An Essay on History* (New York: Macmillan, 1916); G. Frank Lydston, *The Diseases of Society (The Vice and Crime Problem)*

(Philadelphia: J. B. Lippincott Company, 1904); E. Ray Lankester, *Degeneration: A Chapter in Darwinism* (London: Macmillan and Co., 1880); Samuel Royce, *Deterioration and Race Education with Practical Application to the Condition of the People and Industry* (New York, Arno Press, 1972 [reprint from 1877]).

5. Maurice Parmelee, *Poverty and Social Progress* (New York: The Macmillan Company, 1916), 128; Hunter, *Poverty*, 305. Those economists, sociologists, and anthropologists who claimed that urban immigrants were undergoing a process of racial degeneration included those opposed to all immigration and those who favored restrictions; see John R. Commons, *Races and Immigrants in America* (New York: The Macmillan Company, 1907); William S. Sadler, *Race Decadence: An Examination of the Causes of Racial Degeneracy in the United States* (Chicago: A. C. McClurg & Co., 1922); Madison Grant, *The Passing of the Great Race; or, The Racial Basis of European History* (New York: C. Scribner, 1916); Hunter, *Poverty*, 261–317.

6. N. N. Feltes, "Misery or the Production of Misery: Defining Sweated Labour in 1890" *Social History* 17 (October 1992), 441–452; Sheila Blackburn, " 'Princesses and Sweated-Wage Slaves Go Well Together': Images of British Sweated Workers, 1843–1914," *International Labor and Working-Class History* 61 (Spring, 2002), 24–44.

7. "Report on the Sweating System," v–vi. For similar British definitions of the sweatshop, see Charles Booth, *Life and Labours of the People of London* (London: The Macmillan Company, 1892), 328; Beatrice Webb, "How to Do Away with the Sweating System" in Sidney and Beatrice Webb, *Problems of Modern Industry* (New York: Longmans, Green, and Co., 1902), 139–155.

8. The first use of the word 'sweatshop' in the United States that I have found is in the *Fifth Annual Report of the Factory Inspectors of the State of New York* (Albany: James B. Lyon, State Printer, 1891), 27–28. The earliest and most complete definition of the "sweat-shop" is in the "Report on the Sweating System," v–vi. For an example of a similar definition of the sweatshop, see: "Reports of the Industrial Commission on Immigration" Volume XV (Washington: Government Printing Office, 1901), 319–324. For details on the first use of the word "sweatshop" and "sweated," see Pope, *The Clothing Industry in New York*, 256–287; John R. Commons, "The Sweating System in the Clothing Trade" in John R. Commons, ed., *Trade Unionism and Labor Problems* (Boston: Ginn and Company, 1905), 316–335; Leon Stein, "Introduction" in Leon Stein, ed., *Out of the Sweatshop: The Struggle for Industry Democracy* (New York: Quadrangle, 1977), xv–xvi.

9. Frank Tracy Carlton, *The History and Problems of Organized Labor* (Boston: D. C. Heath & Company, 1911), 359; "Report on the Sweating System," 95.

10. Carlton, *The History and Problems of Organized Labor*, 359; "Reports of the Industrial Commission on Immigration," 324.

11. *Twelfth Annual Report of the Factory Inspectors of the State of New York, 1897* (Albany: Wynkoop Hallenbeck Crawford Co., State Printers, 1898), 47.

12. Parmelee, *Poverty and Social Progress*, 130; *Twelfth Annual Report of the Factory Inspectors of the State of New York*, 47.

13. "Reports of the Industrial Commission on Immigration," 323–347.

14. Commons, *Races and Immigrants*, 133. This notion of the body as the external image of the internal mental character as part of the biological, racial views at the turn of the century became part of the contemporary enthusiasm for the "strenuous life," as a way of combating race suicide, and for gymnasiums, as a way of encouraging racial progress among working-class immigrants. See, Gail Bederman, *Manliness and Civilization: A Cultural History of Gender and Race in the United States, 1880–1917* (Chicago: University of Chicago Press, 1995); T. Jackson Lears, *No Place of Grace: Antimodernism and the Transformation of American Culture, 1880–1920* (The University of Chicago Press, 1981); E. Anthony Rotundo, *American Manhood: Transformations in Masculinity from the Revolution to the Modern Era* (New York: Basic Books, 1993).

15. *Twentieth Annual Report of the Bureau of Labor Statistics for the Year Ended September 30, 1902* (Albany: The Argus Company, Printers, 1903), 79; "Reports of the Industrial Commission on Immigration," 325.

16. Richard T. Ely, "Competition: Its Nature, Its Permency, and Its Beneficence," *Publications of the American Economic Association* 2 (February, 1901), 55–70; Commons, *Races and Immigrants*, 151.

17. Hunter, *Poverty*, 295.

18. Commons, *Races and Immigrants*, 151–152;

19. Hunter, *Poverty*, 295.

20. For a discussion of the question of "race suicide" and its relation to class and immigration, see Edward A. Ross and respondents, "Western Civilization and the Birth-Rate," *American Journal of Sociology* 12 (March, 1907), 607–632; Hunter, *Poverty*, 303.

21. Ross and respondents, "Western Civilization and the Birth-Rate," 618.

22. *Ninth Annual Report of the Factory Inspectors of the State of New York, 1894* (Albany: James B. Lyon, State Printer, 1895), 876; "Report on the Sweating System," 187–193, 199.

23. George McKay, "The Effect Upon the Health, Moral and Mentality of Working People Employed in Overcrowded Work-rooms" in *Fifth Annual Report of the Factory Inspectors of the State of New York*, 77–80; George McKay, "The Sweating System" in *Eighth Annual Report of the Factory Inspector of the State of New York, 1893* (Albany: James B. Lyon, State Printer, 1894), 787–797.

24. Eva McDonald Valesh, "The Tenement House Problem in New York" *The Arena* 7 (April 1893), 582.

25. Jacob Riis, *How the Other Half Lives: Studies among the Tenements of New York* (New York: Telegraph Books, 1985), 80. Such descriptions of the typical "Hebrew" worker reflect the United States Immigration Commission's own "racial" profiles of the "Hebrew, Jewish, or Israelite." United States Immigration Commission, "Dictionary of Races or Peoples," *Reports of the Immigration Commission*, Vol. 5, 61st Congress, 3rd Session, Senate Doc. 748.

26. On the racialization of Jews and the relationship to older versions of anti-Semitism, see Matthew Frye Jacobson, *Whiteness of a Different Color: European Immigrants and the Alchemy of Race* (Cambridge: Harvard University Press, 1998), 174–182; Robert Singerman, "The Jew as Racial Alien: The Genetic Component of American Anti-Semitism," in David A. Gerber, ed., *Anti-Semitism in American History* (Urbana: University of Illinois Press, 1986), 103–128; Sander Gilman, *Franz Kafka: The Jewish Patient* (New York: Routledge, 1995), 41–100; Karen Brodkin, *How Jews Became White Folks and What That Says about Race in America* (New Brunswick: Rutgers University Press, 1998).

27. Parmelee, *Poverty and Social Progress*, 126.

28. *Ninth Annual Report of the Factory Inspectors of the State of New York*, 876; "Report on the Sweating System," xxviii–xxix.

29. *Ninth Annual Report of the Factory Inspectors of the State of New York, 1894*, 876.

30. *Ninth Annual Report of the Factory Inspectors of the State of New York, 1894*, 876; Hunter, *Poverty*, 154, 280–281.

31. Arthur Shadwell, *Industrial Efficiency* (New York: Longmans, Green & Co., 1906); Arnold White, *Efficiency and Empire* (London: Methuen & Co., 1901); Dr. Robert Rentoul, *Race Culture or Race Suicide* (London: The Walter Scott Publishing Co., 1906); Paul Underwood Kellogg, ed., *The Pittsburgh Survey* (New York: Charities Publication Committee, 1909–1914); E. E. Pratt, *The Industrial Causes of Congestion in New York City* (New York: Longmans, Green & Co., 1911)

32. John Atkinson Hobson, *Problems of Poverty: An Inquiry into the Industrial Condition of the Poor* (London, Methuen, 1891), 17.

33. "Reports of the Industrial Commission on Immigration," 321.

34. *Twelfth Annual Report of the Factory Inspectors of the State of New York*, 759.

35. *Twelfth Annual Report of the Factory Inspectors of the State of New York*, 759 ; "Report on the Sweating System," 199. On social reform and factory inspection, see Kathryn Kish Sklar, *Florence Kelley and the Nation's Work: The Rise of Women's Political Culture, 1830–1900* (New Haven: Yale University Press, 1995).

36. Parmelee, *Poverty and Social Progress*, 130–131; McKay, "The Sweating System," 794; Hunter, *Poverty*, 169–170.

37. "Reports of the Industrial Commission on Immigration," xxx.

38. Ely, "Competition," 64.

39. *Fifth Annual Report of the Factory Inspectors of the State of New York*, 27; George M. Price, *The Russian Jews in America*, trans. Leo Shpall, Reprinted from the *Publication of the American Jewish Historical Society* XLVIII (September–December 1958 [Original, St. Petersburg, Russia, 1893]), 54.

40. Morris Rosenfeld in his poems described the "*svetshop*" in Morris Rosenfeld, *Songs from the Ghetto*, trans. Leo Wiener (Boston: Small, Maynard and Co., 1900. Quoted in Melach Epstein, *Jewish Labor in the U.S.A.: An Industrial, Political and Cultural History of the Jewish*

Labor Movement, 2 Vols. in 1 (New York: Ktav Publishing House, Inc., 1969), 93. See, also, Bernard Weinstein, *Di Yidishe Iunions in Amerike* (New York: Fareinigte Idishe Gewerk-shaftn, 1929), 49–50 and Elias Tcherikower, *The Early Jewish Labor Movement in the United States*, translated and revised Aaron Antonovsky (New York: YIVO, 1961), 168. Epstein suggests that the three characteristics were "Unsanitary conditions, Long or unlimited work hours, Very low wages." Epstein, *Jewish Labor in U.S.A.*, 87.

41. "Report on the Sweating System," xiii, 93–94.
42. Morris C. Feinstone, "A Brief History of the United Hebrew Trades," in *Gewerkshaften: Issued by the United Hebrew Trades on the Occasion of Its 50th Anniversary as a Trade Union Central Body in Greater New York* (New York, 1938), 12.
43. Daniel Bender, "'A hero . . . for the weak': Work, Consumption, and the Enfeebled Jewish Worker, 1881–1924" *International Labor and Working-Class History* 56 (Fall, 1999), 1–22. Alan Kraut argues that at the same time that Jewish immigrants recognized their physical weakness, Eastern-European Jewish immigrants sought to dispel racialist notions that they were biologically inferior or had a propensity to filth. Alan Kraut, *Silent Travelers: Germs, Genes, and the "Immigrant Menace"* (New York: BasicBooks, 1994), 136–165.
44. Morris Rosenfeld, "Despair," YIVO; Morris Rosenfeld papers RG #431, Box 12, Folder 116.
45. Abraham Rosenberg, *Memoirs of a Cloakmaker*, trans. Lynn Davison (New York: Unpublished, 1920), Martin P. Catherwood Library; Cornell University, 25.
46. Rosenberg, *Memoirs of a Cloakmaker*, 25.
47. Rosenfeld, *Songs from the Ghetto*, 7–11.
48. Feinstone, "A Brief History of the United Hebrew Trades," 12.
49. Yacob Adler, "The Machine Worker" in Aaron Kramer, ed. and trans., *A Century of Yiddish Poetry* (New York: Cornwall Books, 1989), 91–92.
50. "The Slaves of the 'Sweaters,'" *Harper's Weekly* 34 (April 26, 1890), 335; J. D. Warner, "Sweating System in New York City," *Harper's Weekly* 39 (February 9, 1895), 135. Eileen Boris, *Home to Work: Motherhood and the Politics of Industrial Homework in the United States* (Cambridge: Cambridge University Press, 1994), 21–124; Eileen Boris, "Regulating Industrial Homework: The Triumph of 'Sacred Motherhood,'" *Journal of American History* 71 (March 1985), 745–763; David Rosner and Gerald Markowitz, "The Early Movement for Occupational Safety and Health, 1900–1917," in Judith Walzer Leavitt and Ronald L. Numbers, eds., *Sickness and Health in America: Readings in the History of Medicine and Public Health* (Madison: The University of Wisconsin Press, 1985), 507–52. For details on progressive-era debates about women's wage work, see Alice Kessler-Harris, *Out to Work: A History of Wage-Earning Women in the United States* (Oxford: Oxford University Press, 1982), 75–216; Alice Kessler-Harris, *A Women's Wage: Historical Meanings and Social Consequences* (Lexington: University Press of Kentucky, 1990). On working-class women's intervention into these debates, see Ardis Cameron, *Radicals of the Worst Sort: Laboring Women in Lawrence, Massachusetts, 1860–1912* (Urbana: University of Illinois Press, 1993), 47–72.
51. "Report on the Sweating System," 221; George McKay, "The Effect Upon the Health, Moral and Mentality of Working People Employed in Overcrowded Work-Rooms," in *Fifth Annual Report of the Factory Inspectors of the State of New York*, 88–89.
52. On the persistence of Lamarckian evolutionary theory and its importance for the study of class relations, see Mark Pittenger, "A World of Difference: Constucting the Underclass in Progressive America," *American Quarterly* 49 (March 1997), 26–65.
53. McKay, "The Effect Upon the Health, Moral and Mentality of Working People Employed in Overcrowded Work-Rooms," 84–85.
54. "Report on the Sweating System," 198; Parmelee, *Poverty and Social Progress*, 130. The idea of counter-selection or the "survival of the unfit" was a common theme in the Progressive Era study of class and immigration. It reached its most full development with the rise of eugenics. For some important examples that especially trace the role of women labors in counterselection, see Hunter, *Poverty*, esp. 293–294; Theresa Schmid McMahon, "Women and Economic Evolution or the Effect of Industrial Changes Upon the Status of Women," *Bulletin of the University of Wisconsin* 496 (1912), 5–124; Albert Keller, *Societal Evolution: A Study of the Evolutionary Basis of the Science of Society* (New York: The Macmillan Company, 1916), 169–207.
55. Hunter, *Poverty*, 244.
56. Women's economic roles as boarders and shopkeepers has been an important subject for historians of Eastern-European Jewish immigrant women, see Susan Glenn, *Daughters of*

the Shtetl: Life and Labor in the Immigrant Generation (Ithaca: Cornell University Press, 1990), 74–76; Sydney Stahl Weinberg, *The World of Our Mothers: The Lives of Jewish Immigrant Women* (Chapel Hill: The University of North Carolina Press, 1988), 135–136.

57. Glenn, *Daughters of the Shtetl*, 239–240; Kathie Friedman-Kasaba, *Memories of Migration: Gender, Ethnicity, and Work in the Lives of Jewish and Italian Women, 1870–1924* (Albany: State University of New York Press, 1996), 91–134; Weinberg, *The World of Our Mothers*, 185–224.

58. Mabel Hurd Willet, *The Employment of Women in the Clothing Trade* (New York: Columbia University Press, 1902), 86–89; Weinberg, *The World of Our Mothers*, 105.

59. Consumers' League of New York, "The Menace to the Home from Sweatshop and Tenement-Made Clothing" (New York, 1901); *Eleventh Annual Report of the Factory Inspectors of the State of New York, 1896* (Albany: Wynkoop Hallenbeck Crawford Co., State Printers, 1897), 28.

60. Andrew Heinze, *Adapting to Abundance: Jewish Immigrants, Mass Consumption, and the Search for American Identity* (New York: Columbia University Press, 1990), 105–146.

61. Corinne L. Gilb, *Oral History of Jennie Matyas*, April–October 1955, Martin P. Catherwood Library, Cornell University, 18; Rose Cohen, *Out of the Shadow: A Russian Jewish Girlhood on the Lower East Side* (Ithaca: Cornell University Press, 1995 [original, 1918]), 89; Interview with Isidore Wisotsky, YIVO; Irving Howe Papers RG #570, Box 1, 2; Yitzchak Yankel Doroshkin, *From Zhitkovitch Throughout the World (Episodes of My Life)*, 1974, YIVO; American Jewish Autobiographies (AJA) RG #102, #305, 59.

62. *Third Annual Report of the Bureau of Statistics of Labor* (Albany: The Argus Company, Printers, 1886), 289–290.

63. "Report on the Sweating System," 93.

64. "Report on the Sweating System," viii.

65. Warner, "The Sweating System in New York," 135. On turn-of-the-century antihomework campaigns, see Boris, *Home to Work*, 21–124; Cynthia Daniels, "Between Home and Factory: Homeworkers and the State" in Eileen Boris and Cynthia Daniels, eds., *Homework: Historical and Contemporary Perspectives on Paid Labor at Home* (Urbana: University of Illinois Press, 1989), 13–32.

66. "Report on the Sweating System," xxiii; "Reports of the Industrial Commission on Immigration," 373.

67. Warner, "The Sweating System in New York," 135.

68. "Report on the Sweating System," viii.

69. Tcherikower, *The Early Jewish Labor Movement*, 118.

70. Feinstone, "A Brief History of the United Hebrew Trades," 13.

71. "Reports of the Industrial Commission on Immigration," 350.

72. ILGWU, *3rd Annual Convention, Report of Proceedings* (1903), 6.

2

Fashion, Flexible Specialization, and the Sweatshop
A Historical Problem

NANCY L. GREEN
Ecole des Hautes Etudes en Sciences Sociales

When a foreman is in back of you, watching what you are doing—and God forbid you do just a little bit, he start screaming, he start yelling. . . . That's a sweatshop.[1]

Is the sweatshop merely a recurrent fin-de-siècle occurrence, "invented" at one turn of the century, rediscovered at another? From the first use of the term in the 1890s to its resurgence in the 1980s, has there been nothing in between? Debates over the sweatshop go to the heart of questions about historical knowledge. Does the reemergence of a category herald a direct reproduction of its historic past, or is the term simply a metaphor, used increasingly widely as a synonym for abysmal working conditions? Some authors, such as economist Michael Piore and social scientist Charles F. Sabel have argued that you cannot compare as similar the sweatshops of yore with conditions of the late twentieth century. Labor laws and generally better surroundings have intervened; the old sweatshop is necessarily dead. Others, from labor leaders to a state senator, have argued, on the contrary, that the sweatshop has returned, due to circumstances specific to late twentieth century garment capitalism.[2] Is the sweatshop dead, has it returned or does it live on as part of a continuing phenomenon?

It is no secret that one of the most persistent historical sites of the sweatshop has been the garment industry. Descriptions of urban garment shops today echo those of the past, and it is that resonance that needs to be reexamined as historical knowledge. A reading of over a century of ready-made history allows us to analyze core aspects of the industry's structure. With variations over time and space, a pattern clearly emerges. I want to examine here the social consequences of what may simply be one of the most transparent cases of the difficulties of tailoring supply to (highly fluctuating) demand. From pleats to shoulder pads, the extreme variability inherent in the fashion business has to this day meant high levels of labor turnover, seasonal unemployment, and poor working conditions. These conditions seem to be a common corollary to the highly competitive contracting-out system. The sweatshop as workplace and metaphor poses a challenge to theories of flexible specialization.

Flexibility as Seen from Below

Over the last fifteen years, a discourse on flexibility has radically challenged earlier histories of industrialization. It has done so by contrasting the fixed with the fluid, Ford with Benneton, that is, Ford's early twentieth-century centralized assembly line and Benneton's late twentieth-century reliance on outside subcontractors and by heralding alternative models of capital and labor organization. This interpretation has allowed an important corrective to smokestack-filled narratives of industrial development. In particular, in their important challenge to the Fordist model of production, Sabel and Piore, along with historical sociologist Jonathan Zeitlin, have postulated a theory of "flexible specialization" to provide a new explanation for past economic history as well as a prescription for the future. They have argued provocatively that the outcome of mass production was not as inevitable as once thought in the light of its successes from the 1920s to the 1970s, and that a craft model of production based on a community of producers, as developed in northern Italy textile mills, for example, in the late twentieth century, could rectify the rigidities of the assembly-line mode of production.[3] The argument is both historic and historiographic, and is itself a product of the 1980s recession that challenged previous models of economic success.

In this view, the women's garment industry has shifted dramatically from archaic to avant-garde. Reinterpreted as a proud rebel from the mass production model, the manufacture of fashion has been hailed as one of the harbingers of the new second industrial revolution.[4] The apparel trade's light industrial structure is another example of an artful balancing act between rigid forms of production and volatile demand; its form of flexibility is one that will save the industry from extinction in the West.[5]

Nonetheless, the sweatshop image remains. For social reformers and labor activists, it has come to symbolize recurrent abuses in the garment industry. At the turn of the twentieth century, a French social investigator climbed the dark, dank hallway of a New York tenement in order to examine a garment workshop first hand.

> *Visit to the "Sveating [sic] system."* . . . They were situated in the South-East portion of the city, in dilapidated-looking buildings; the wooden steps shook, narrow and nauseating toilets were in the stairway, medium-sized rooms where some twenty workers worked like demons, cutting, placing buttons, ironing, each according to his specialty. The windows were open and, although it was very hot, the temperature was not stifling; but the spectacle of such feverish ac-

tivity, of all of those hands following the movement of the machines made me think of one of the circles of hell in Dante.[6]

Minus the hyperbole, the image is similar today: "[V]entilation is poor; piles of fabric sit near boilers and gas burners; there are no fire exits."[7]

Two fundamentally different perspectives of the industry thus exist: one optimistic, one pessimistic, one heralding capital flexibility and entrepreneurial talent, the other focusing on grim unstable labor conditions. The two images have understandably collided in recent years as a political issue. Yet they also mask a question of historical understanding. Sociologists Alejandro Portes and Manuel Castells have argued that contemporary contracting is a *new* phenomenon, implying that it is thus immune to the ills of its predecessors: "An old form in a new setting is, in fact, new."[8] Others have argued that the sweatshop has *returned*, and that it has reproduced the ills of yesteryear.[9]

I will argue that, beyond a certain resurgence, there is a historic *continuity* in the forms of labor organization within the industry that are linked to the underlying extreme volatility of demand. Flexibility of production time and space have characterized one hundred years of garment work, and they have repeatedly led to excesses and abuses of the subcontracting system. A notion of continuity is neither to deny the heroic struggles engaged in by shop workers, union leaders, reformers, and government legislators to counter the sweatshop evils nor to ignore the historical variations over time—periods of relative amelioration of conditions when more stringent labor standards have been more or less enforced. But it is the repetitive necessity of these struggles, which speak to certain elements of the organization of garment work, that seem to lead continually to exploitative forms of labor. Much of that labor has moved further and further away from Manhattan, expanding the notion of "offshore" to ever-distant locations. This has only, in many cases, simply (and until very recently) moved the problem out of sight. But, as recent scandals have shown, deep pockets of dismal conditions persist within an industry dedicated to fashion and fads even in the "First World."[10]

Time and Space

The economics and politics of flexibility—from the viewpoint of capital—can be summarized by three basic elements, the avoidance of: fixed costs, a fixed labor force, and fixed rules. Flexibility permits the adjustment of supply to demand by cutting the risk of long-term investment, adjusting the labor force to production needs, and limiting rigidities due to union and legal restrictions that regulate wages, benefits, social welfare payments, and working conditions. At a systemic level of analysis, the flexible model has an inherent beauty. However, managing variability does not mean that it disappears. Responsibility and costs are shifted elsewhere.

One hundred years of industrial sewing can be summarized by three S's: skill, "seasonality," and subcontracting: relatively low skill needs; high seasonal fluctuations; and pervasive subcontracting. From men's shirts to women's blouses, the industry is comprised of different production units and numerous specialties. The important women's wear sector alone, which serves as the basis for the analysis below, is in itself a microcosm of the tensions between flexible production and standardization of products and labor processes. Seasonality and subcontracting—flexibility with regard to time and space—emerge as leitmotivs in over a century of archival documents and industrial reports. While labor legislation and generally better sanitary conditions have eliminated a certain amount of the dirt and dust, poor conditions have remained in garment discourse and reality. They provide a cautionary tale about the understanding of flexibility past and present.

The Time Factor: Seasonal Production and Seasonal Unemployment

The slack season is an ever-recurring complaint, although most garment professionals usually decry *their* era as a contemporary calamity, worse than ever before. Seasonality is a result of both the functional and the fashionable. Changes in climate (literal seasons) cause us to don swimsuits in summer and turtlenecks in winter. Beyond that, however, fashion intervenes, adding a powerful figurative dimension to the notion of seasons. Turtlenecks are not always "in."

Depending on the specialty, the slow season can last up to four or five months a year. Some garments are more (literally) seasonal than others: rainwear, swimwear, furs. But even in ordinary outerwear, dressier items worn in public tend to be more (figuratively) seasonal than garments worn around the house. Women's wear is more seasonal than men's. General economic conditions—appropriately called the economic "climate"—can exacerbate seasonality, especially when retailers wait until the last minute to order. In 1964, the International Labour Office (ILO) defined four different types of fluctuations as having an impact on this industry: long-term structural economic change; cyclical economic fluctuations; seasonal swings; and sectoral variations. Sociologist Carol Smith has suggested that we simply speak of regular and irregular seasonality.[11] The climatic season for swimwear is a known factor, but the latest fashion cut, a rainy summer, or a weak economy is not.

Dips in employment follow accordingly. The "slack," "slow," or "dull" season was endemic to the garment trade even before the advent of ready-made goods.[12] Women's-wear tailors complained of the cyclical nature of balls and weddings. Early clothing capitalists criticized seasonal ups-and-downs as one of the worst evils of the trade. In the spring of 1916, American clothiers complained that an increased tendency toward style changes meant "complete disorganization of whatever regularity there has been in an already irregular business."[13] Half a century later, at a (first) Technical Tripartite Meeting on the garment industry organized by the ILO (in 1964), even though general prosperity meant that seasonal perturbations were relatively better than before World War II, they were still considered enough of a constituent curse to be one of the three major themes of the ILO meeting. As ILGWU delegate to the meeting, Lazare Teper pointed out that, even in relatively good times, women's outerwear suffers from greater seasonal instability than most other goods. When a second tripartite meeting was held sixteen years later, seasonal fluctuations were still considered "a serious problem" and growing. Nothing much had changed by the 1995 meeting.[14] Today's ever-changing styles give even more urgent meaning to seasonal turbulence. And like their predecessors, current practitioners pronounce the hectic pace of change as unprecedented.

Yet ready-made goods were initially conceptualized as a remedy for seasonal oscillations. They were made up during the tailors' slack period. As ready-to-wear became a separate industry, it was conceived of as more orderly and less dependent on seasonal orders precisely because of its prefabricated nature. And to the extent that seasonal fluctuations were blamed on (female) capriciousness, the advance production of garments was seen as giving (male) manufacturers more control over such fashions and passions. (Marx predicted that steam power would lead to factory production that would eliminate the "murderous, meaningless caprices of fashion."[15])

However, as a method of regulating the rhythm of production, the ready-made industry failed. It soon developed the same bad habits as the tailoring trades, waiting until the last minute to create new styles. Ready-made methods shifted from being a "regulatory agent" to accentuating the "fits and starts and the periodic overwork."[16] Customers kept their bad habits, and ready-made manufacturers acquired them. Contemporary retailers and computer-tracking inventory programs have only exacerbated the problem of "just-in-time" ordering.

The problem of oscillating production schedules has thus plagued the industry for over a century. Manufacturers and labor unions have sought relief in different ways. Firms have sometimes tried dovetailing winter goods with summer ones. The ILGWU suggested at one point that if you cannot beat the seasons then join them: export to the southern hemisphere, where the seasons are the reverse of ours.[17] More frequently, producers have tried switching from expensive to cheap dresses or preparing more standard items during the slack season. However, switchable skills or sewing-machine attachments do not always match. Versatility can be checked by specialization. Unions have also tried to combat the oscillation of production by pressing for the elimination of overtime, insisting on extra money for it, and urging contractual limits on seasonal unemployment.

The historic agreements signed after the 1909–1910 garment strikes in New York addressed the problem of seasonal manufacture. The Protocol included a provision for employers to divide the work equitably among workers during slack periods. The ILGWU was indeed a pioneer in work-sharing, constantly lamenting the on-and-off work schedules and continually needling employers to even out workloads. The Committee on Resolutions stressed in 1922 that:

> We will insist on a shorter workday until such time when even the ladies' garment industry will recognize our rights to work normally and regularly throughout the year as human beings ought to work.[18]

A 1924 resolution was even more forceful:

> The present disgraceful system of uncertainty, of frequent job changing, of daily job hunting, of repeated privations, misery, and despondency in the homes of the families of our great membership must be abolished.[19]

However, the Committee also admitted that the enforcement of guaranteed employment was a pious wish. Shortly after the 1933–34 National Recovery Act codes were overturned, the ILGWU again complained about the "chiselers" who tried to continue their "old, nefarious ways and methods."[20] The industrial reports and labor press repeatedly emit a resigned sense of inevitability. Excessive overtime, alternating with periods of unemployment seemed to be constitutive of the "sweatshop system."

Only a minority of, mostly entrepreneurial, voices have admitted the virtues of seasonal fluctuations. Rush orders may be the bane of the industry's organization, but they are also the boon to its existence, the essential motor of ever-changing demand behind clothing and capital renewal. Even the effects on labor may not be so drastic in this view: the lag time gives women time to catch up on their responsibilities at home, its proponents have argued. Indeed, in spite of laws or rules, workers have been known to sneak into union shops after hours when needed, to work overtime and be paid double time.[21]

Yet when workers in one turn-of-the-twentieth-century New York shop went on strike to install a clock, they did so to protest against erratic hours.[22] Half a century later, the 1964 ILO meeting on seasonal fluctuations suggested several measures to reduce seasonal unemployment: increase consumption and thus clothing purchases; implement better production planning; build up inventories; manufacture complementary goods; simplify, standardize, and specialize production. However, recognizing the perhaps utopian nature of a call to eliminate variability in production, the ILO meeting report concluded with a series of suggestions designed to attenuate their effects: contractor registration; work-sharing; homework regulation; labor laws; unemployment insurance, etc.[23]

Over the last century, this dependence on variability, in fashion and labor conditions, has not gone unchallenged. Labor laws and union rules have sought to regulate excessive hours. Unemployment insurance has come to cover the gap between seasons.[24] Yet fashion fluctuation and the extremes of overtime and slack time have remained a constant of the industry, leading in many cases to sweatshop conditions. Highly fluctuating demand has repeatedly served as a disincentive to heavy investment in fixed capital and labor costs. And it has been a major factor in the organization of an industry dependent on contract immigrant labor at home, low wage work abroad. Long hours to fill an order are the modern equivalent of getting the gown to the ball on time.

Space: The Multiple Places of Production

If seasonality is the temporal expression of flexibility, subcontracting is its spatial manifestation. While seasonal unemployment shifts the burden of the slow season onto the worker, contracting shifts risk as well as costs, of equipment and upkeep, onto the contractor or homeworker.

Garments can be made just about anywhere. The division of sewing labor, the separation of the stages of production, the light weight and low cost of garment technology, and the relatively little space needed to set up a garment shop have allowed a division of sewing space. Industrial garment making has thus sprouted and survived in the interstices of the modern urban environment, proving, in contrast to other forms of industrialization, that a division of labor does not necessarily imply a concentration of same. Garments have been made in tenements, lofts, high rises, and suburban homes. Sewing machines have been set up in living rooms, bedrooms, dining rooms, attics, and garages in a creatively flexible use of space.[25] In what can be called the dispersed assembly line, home, workshop, and factory have all coexisted. While each has had its period of historical prominence, all three have persisted over the century and are interrelated. Manufacturing space, like the latest trend in sizing, can be classified as small, medium, and large.

Factory

Space usage has not remained uniform throughout the century. Prior to World War I, the factory seemed to be gaining ground in women's-wear production, as Marx had predicted.[26] Early ready-made enthusiasts envisioned garment-making along the classic lines of the Industrial Revolution and began concentrating capital and workers under one roof in order to save time in transportation and to ensure better supervision. At times, this had tragic consequences. The infamous Triangle Shirtwaist Factory in New York employed some 500 young immigrant women prior to the fire of 1911, which killed 146 of them. But it was not the urban tragedy that had manufacturers rethink their spatial organization.

Even the most successful large production units had their limits. Too great a fixed investment was risky in the face of regular and irregular seasonality.

Labor unrest—by "class-conscious flappers"—also encouraged New York manufacturers to redefine the economics of concentration. The early clothing capitalists kept the core of production inside the plant and relegated seasonal fluctuations to outside contractors and homeworkers. Ultimately, however, this gave way to another type of spatial division that was not simply seasonal. The different stages of making and marketing clothes themselves became disaggregated. Sewing became increasingly separated from design, cutting, and sales. And it became located in the contractors' shops.

Contracting and Subcontracting

The New York State Governor's Commission of 1925 was explicit: The small shop "permits greater elasticity and flexibility of employment."[27] Contracting had its heyday in the interwar period. "With $2,500, a few customers, and a colossal amount of nerve, almost anyone can go into the dress business," commented a 1930s' magazine article.[28] While large production sites continued to exist (although increasingly moving away from Manhattan), the women's wear firms of the urban center shrunk in size as sewing shifted to the contractors' shops.[29] Contracting became and has remained the most emblematic symbol of variable production, where supply must meet ever-changing demand. Here is where current controversy over the "return of the sweatshop" lies. And here is where most immigrants work.

The advantages of contracting are many. As a system, it provides overall flexibility. For manufacturers, it shifts certain risks, costs, and responsibilities onto the contractor. It has historically been a means of avoiding the constraints inherent in labor legislation and unionization. And contracting has always been more prevalent in women's wear than in more standardized production. In 1958, for example, jobbers and subcontractors employed 67 percent of all workers in the women's outerwear sector across the United States, while accounting for "only" 45 percent of employment in men's and boys' apparel and 38 percent in women's and children's underwear.[30]

Contracting also provides opportunities for newcomers. The low startup costs make entry into business easy, and contractors are most often immigrants who hire other immigrants, first their own co-ethnics but then the next "wave."[31] A readily available community labor pool has helped foster ethnic shops from the Lower East Side, the Jewish immigrant neighborhood in New York, at the beginning of the twentieth century to Chinatown, nearby in Lower Manhattan, at its end. In their most positive light, these shops have also been called "social shops," emphasizing their familial, ethnic, or simply more congenial character as compared to factories.[32]

Contractors come by various names and in various forms. New York contractors in the 1940s often had between thirty-five and forty workers, similar to the Chinatown shops forty years later.[33] However, contractors may or may not have a physical shop of their own; they may simply distribute work to subcontractors and/or a scattered (home) work force. Some contractors cut, most do not. They usually work for more than one jobber or manufacturer. One 1990 study found up to six levels of subcontracting.[34]

Regardless of their size or setup, contractors are generally characterized by their low-margin operations. It takes little capital to set up a sewing shop and could be done for as little as $50 in 1900, $2–3,000 in 1924, $10,000 in 1942, or $15–25,000 in 1959 in New York City. In the early 1980s, a 25- to 30-person shop could be started with $25,000 in New York's Chinatown.[35] The low amount of capital needed to begin with is generally correlated to a continued temptation to keep costs (of labor in particular) as low as possible. He or she who underbids the next contractor then gets the work. But the process can easily lead to a spiral of cost compression often abetted by sweatshop conditions.

And business closings are rampant. Low capital correlates with high turnover. The dress manufacturer, engaged in a "razor-edged" struggle of survival and "known to doctors for his 'dress stomach' and his frequent nervous breakdowns," has been estimated to have an average business life of five to seven years. High "firm mortality" and "entrepreneurial turbulence" affect manufacturers, contractors, and workers alike.[36] A study of 927 New York contract shops in 1926 showed that 68.2 percent of them had closed within the next three years. In the early 1980s, the Chinese Garment Makers' Association estimated that one-third of all firms folded each year.[37]

There have been basically two contrasting images of the contracting system and the contractor. Contractors have been compared to the ubiquitous cockroaches of New York City and have been criticized for buying labor on the "pig market" (*khazer markt* in Yiddish), a day-labor market.[38] A 1913 *Forverts* (Jewish socialist daily newspaper) article argued that workers felt more dignified, "somewhat higher *spiritually*" in a big factory than at the mercy of the "one-cent" soul of the hated small-time boss.[39] An ILGWU report described the interwar contractors as "irresponsible beggar employers," adventurers, and parasites. Jesse Carpenter, in his 1972 book on collective bargaining, preferred "industrial termites" as his insect metaphor.[40] The contractor has been blamed for everything from maintaining a backward ("primitive") mode of production to preventing assimilation by maintaining and encouraging ethnic ghettos to sustaining sweatshops.

However, contracting has also had its advocates. Contractors refute the image of oppressors: "We work harder than you. We earn sometimes less than you, in any case never more than you. We suffer from the hands of the manufacturers, what kind of exploiters are we?"[41] Jobbers and contractors alike have stressed the latters' independence. And workers too have been described as freer in the neighborhood shop context. In yet another *Forverts* article of 1913, the contractor's shop was described favorably: discipline is less rigorous than in the factory; workers can go home for lunch; they don't have to squeeze onto public transportation to get to work; and "the workman feels more at liberty."[42] Today the ethnic entrepreneur has become a new urban hero, while the immigrant contractor's shop can be, in short, a "cultural cushion" for employment.[43]

Yet key to its functioning is its place within the industrial sewing structure. The United States Industrial Commission that looked into twentieth-century labor conditions, wrote: "The contract system possesses as one of its advantages, not merely the cheaper cost of manufacture, but also the shifting of legal responsibility from the manufacturer to the middleman."[44] The contractor's labor costs may represent up to 75 percent of the price received for the made-up goods.[45] By managing the labor supply, contractors manage economic as well as social flexibility. Yet garment contracting relationships well illustrate what historian William Reddy has called assymetric exchange relationships: they displace costs and risks onto weaker bargainers, and are never engaged among equals.[46]

Homework

There is one more, ultimate, locus of even more flexible production: homework. As the contractor is to the manufacturer or jobber, so the homeworker is to the contractor: an elastic labor force, expandable and contractible according to the weather or the latest fad. Homework and subcontracting have been subsumed to the same function. The 1980 ILO report included homework as a category of subcontracting.[47]

Homework has persisted and thrived in the transition from one "socio-technological nexus" (in which certain social conditions and certain techno-logical forms of production co-exist) to another: from nineteenth-century tailors enrolling the help of their families to the more elaborate putting-out system that developed with the growth of ready-made clothes to the rise of large firms which often kept a fluctuating population of homeworkers (in what Marx called the "external department of the manufactories").[48]

Homework is a good example of the problems of historical analysis of recurrent phenomena. It is periodically proclaimed eradicated and just as frequently (re)discovered. The use of homeworkers has not been constant throughout the last century, although by their nature, homeworkers are difficult to count. New York State licensing laws (of 1892 and 1899) helped the N.Y. Commissioner of Labor keep track, although he kept complaining that he did not have enough inspectors to do so properly. In accordance with these laws, approximately 50,000 homeworkers were registered with the Department of Labor in New York City at the turn of the twentieth century, most of whom worked in the garment trade (cigar-making being the other most frequent occupation). But the number kept falling, down to approximately 20,000 in 1913. By the late 1920s, the N.Y. Commissioner of Labor patted himself on the back for the declining numbers while admitting other explanations for the steady decrease: the immigration restriction laws; labor troubles; poor business.[49]

Yet, not all homeworkers were registered. The 1912 New York State Factory Investigating Commission estimated that there were 125,000 homeworkers in Greater New York City in 1913. In the 1920s, approximately 20 percent of the women's garment firms sent their work out of state, beyond the control of the city labor inspectors. With the Depression, homework increased until the National Recovery Act codes of 1933–34 prohibited it in certain specialties altogether. These laws severely curtailed but did not eliminate it entirely, even when the New York state regulatory system took over after the Codes were deemed unconstitutional.[50]

In New York there was a recrudescence of homework after World War II as a quick way of getting back to work. In 1962, however, the New York State Department of Labor abolished its special homework unit due to its "apparent success" in policing homework and enforcing sanctions.[51] But the phenomenon finally decreased less because of legislation than due to the long postwar boom. Nonetheless, like contracting and the sweatshop, homework has made a marked comeback over the last twenty years, from making garments to processing insurance claims. By the early 1990s, union officials estimated that homeworkers constituted 20 percent of the New York City garment workforce, or approximately 30,000 people.[52]

The social science discussion of homework has often focused on gender roles, but it is also fundamentally a debate about the advantages and disadvantages of a flexible—perhaps the least visible, the most flexible, in terms of time as well as space—organization of work.[53] The boundaries between categories are themselves flexible. Shopworkers can turn into homeworkers at night, when they take extra work home to finish. Homeworkers may be employed or self-employed. While some work alone, others employ family members or boarders. Homework often means child labor as well.

At the same time, homework importantly provides work for some people who would otherwise be excluded from the labor market. Women with children, an unemployed husband, sick parent, or cultural traditions that make it difficult to work outside the home, have often turned to homework to contribute to the family budget. Women's seasonal employment can offset male seasonal unemployment. Immigrants have used homework as an entrée into the labor market and often continue to work at home for ethnic or religious reasons or simply to speak their own language. For all of these workers, informal recruitment networks and apprenticeships can be flexibility at its best.

Ultimately, however, from the turn-of-the-century Italian homeworker in New York balancing twenty pairs of pants on her head to the Chinese worker taking a duffle bag full of work home today, homework represents an extreme form of flexibility. In contrast to a discourse on choice and freedom emphasized by its proponents, jobbers' demands, unreasonable deadlines, and the imperatives of piecework (the more you do the more you earn) have often been the invisible supervisors regulating the homeworker's day. Even among homeworkers, there is a more and less stable group, those who get work regularly and those who work less frequently. The discourse on homework has been multivocal over the last century, ranging from idylls of the happy housewife or industrious immigrant combining home and work to denunciations of the horrors of the industrial revolution brought home.

The "Return" of the Sweatshop?

The sweatshop has often summarized the worst of the these conditions of overtime/slack time and dispersion of the places of production. From the late nineteenth century to now, the term "sweating system" has been an emotional one, implying cramped space, long hours, low wages, child, female, and immigrant labor, exploitative middlemen, and germs. The classic description of the sweatshop is almost formulaic, leading up a dingy narrow stairway to a dirty apartment where living and working space are intermixed. The workshop, too, has filthy walls, poor lighting, and bad ventilation, and it becomes "home" to newly arrived immigrants who stretch out at night on unsewn bundles or cutting tables.

As Judith Coffin and Eileen Boris have both shown, late nineteenth- and early twentieth-century "miserabilist" descriptions of sweatshops that emphasized the dirt, dust, and disease were part of the reformers' rhetoric of pathology, a repulsive, morbid vision designed to combat the sentimentalist vision of the fairy fingers of the imagined seamstress. Behind their critique, the social scientists were arguing for order versus chaos, productive rather than unproductive, and male rather than female work.[54]

However, beyond the exaggerated form that the moral critique took lay a multiform criticism of laboring conditions. "Sweating" as a metaphor for toiling and severe exertion dates back to the fifteenth century, but the term took on its modern meaning in the nineteenth century to describe conditions in the tailoring and ready-made shoe trades. At first sweating referred to those working outside of corporate norms and exploiting themselves. By the late nineteenth century, however, London social investigators Charles Booth and Sidney and Beatrice Webb combined two essential elements in their descriptions: hard or excessive work and contracting, that is, the sweating of others.[55]

The term "sweatshop" became as widespread as both the conditions themselves and the growth of reformers' literature in the late nineteenth century, but no country wants to take credit for its origins. The Oxford dictionary attributes it (as distinct from "sweating") to the United States (in 1892). New York State factory inspectors, however, defined the sweatshop as a "foreign method of working" in contrast to the clean, neat "American idea of doing business."[56]

If the classic descriptions of the sweatshop date to the period before World War I, the persistence of the phenomenon and its metaphorical use to denounce poor labor conditions have continued throughout the century. As one critical observer commented in 1935, in spite of turn of the twentieth-century labor legislation and the New Deal codes, "During the course of twenty years the needle trades have completed a cycle—from sweatshop back to sweatshop."[57] The Depression only gave it more scope.

While union pressures and government protective legislation have repeatedly worked to stem the worst of abuses, numerous indicators of historical continuity within change persist. Cloth particles and dust, poisonous gases from irons, and steam from the pressing machines chronically led to tuberculosis (the "tailor's disease") in the late nineteenth century. Today's workers suffer from bronchitis and asthma. Health and labor officials have tried to regulate dust and air, and the Triangle Fire was a powerful stimulus to reinforce fire safety controls and better factory conditions. However, air standards have only been as successful as garment industry regulations in general. New chemicals used to treat some fabrics have added new environmental and fire hazards. Even today, some garment workers call their factories and workshops a "death trap."[58] In times of relative regulation, pockets of miserable conditions have remained, a function of flexible needs of rush orders and the multiple loci of sew-by-night production.

Newspaper reports speak today of squalid conditions in deteriorating factory buildings where illegal immigrants work ten to eleven hours without overtime and for less than the minimum wage. In his widely reported 1979–82 investigation into the New York garment industry, then New York State Senator Franz S. Leichter (Democrat/Liberal, Manhattan/Bronx) described the contemporary contractors' shops as sweatshops. Drawing on an ILGWU evaluation, he estimated that there were approximately 3,000 sweatshops in Chinatown, the South Bronx, North Manhattan and other boroughs of New York, employing some 50,000 people, up from less than two hundred garment sweatshops, mostly in Chinatown, a decade earlier. Subsequent newspaper and magazine articles repeated these numbers.[59]

The evidence seems in some ways contradictory. The union itself has a double language. The International Ladies' Garment Workers' Union, now merged into UNITE! (the Union of Needletrades, Industrial and Textile Employees), has continually stressed its past successes in a linear interpretation of betterment. Yet it has also been at the front lines of criticism of contemporary sweatshops. On the one hand, the labor history of the industry, as seen through the union records, contrasts the sweatshops of the 1900s to the subsequent amelioration of conditions, thanks to union efforts and especially the legendary 1909–1910 strikes. Louis Levine's early triumphal history of the union, published in 1924, set the tone for succeeding accounts: thanks to the ILGWU, the garment industry had evolved "from the early sweatshop to the present status of industrial citizenship."[60] Subsequently, as union leader Pauline Newman stressed in 1965, from the perspective of over half a century of union struggles:

> I would like to tell the younger generation here . . . that my generation had the privilege, the great honor to fight and bleed in order to improve the conditions under which you work today. We worked 80 hours a week—I did anyway—in the Triangle Waist Company. You work 35. It took my generation to change conditions to those under which we work today. (Applause)[61]

Yet while hailing its past successes, the union has another discourse, recognizing and castigating current conditions in the workshops as anathema to everything for which the union stands. The two discourses are not contradictory. They are linked by the notion of return, which bridges the gap between memory and history. The theme of return does not conflict with the ILGWU's own representation of having brought about important, indeed heroic, improvements.[62]

Sociologists Roger Waldinger and Michael Lapp have questioned the view of return as overstated. As they have rightly pointed out, Leichter's figure was repeated over and again without apparent verification. However, the difference of interpretation is in part a difference of definition. Waldinger and Lapp defined sweatshops according to the OECD (Organisation for Economic Co-operation and Development) definition as illegal or concealed employment, which they argued is much less widespread than commonly believed, while Leichter englobed hazardous and unsanitary working conditions, illegal practices, and health or safety violations in his use of the term.[63]

Beyond differing definitions, an important historiographic issue lies between different views of the sweatshop, that of continuity versus rupture and the relationship of the sweatshop image to flexible specialization. The notion of return implies a break. There have been periods in which conditions have indeed been better than others, periods of greater or lesser regulatory compliance, and periods of more or less public interest in exploring and exposing workshop or homework conditions. Notions of hygiene and workers' rights have themselves changed over the century. Is the twentieth-century use of a late nineteenth-century term then simply a reformer's ploy, witness to the poverty/obstinacy of the reformers' vision? Or does it not also imply a continuity of form and content, the very repetition of the imagery revelatory of certain conditions linked to flexible specialization?

Piore and Sabel have explicitly rejected the idea that flexible specialization leads to sweating:

> Sweating, to underscore the point, is the generic response of embattled firms—whether mass or small producers—that cannot innovate. It is not a strategy peculiar to endangered flexible specialists.[64]

Obviously all flexible specialists are not sweaters. However, the concepts have too many characteristics in common for the parallel to be entirely dismissed. Flexibility in the garment industry has most often meant contracting within a context of cutthroat competition at all levels—between New York and Paris or Taiwan, among contractors, and also among workers for scarce jobs during the off-season—which lower wages and working standards. Flexibility, competition, and speed all seem to favor poor working conditions.

If dirt, dust, fire hazards, and excessive hours have thus permeated the definition of garment industry conditions to this day, I would argue that they have done so for two reasons: due to their very evocative power and their recurrence over time. The use of nineteenth-century terminology in the twentieth century serves to criticize twentieth-century practices *relative to* twentieth-century expectations. Despite or because of its multiple definitions and romanticized imagery, the "sweatshop" has become a metaphor for bad working conditions in general. Recent uses of the term have even moved the sweatshop outdoors, to include flower farms, asbestos removal, and taxi driving.[65] To dismiss the language as outdated misses the point. The power of its imagery is intended. The historic connotation is reused both because it has more generally passed into the language but also because it can be consciously harnessed as a mode of denunciation of current conditions in relation to contemporary standards.

Furthermore, the sweatshop has never really gone away. Even Michael Piore has recently recognized that sweatshops have in fact "never entirely disappeared."[66] True, the modes of production which emerged with the development of ready-made goods at the end of the nineteenth century have improved over time. However, interpretations often depend upon the time period highlighted: memories of the great strikes of 1909–1910, reflecting the heroism of labor insurgency and worker agency or the NRA period, stressing state regulation. A long-term history can yield the contradictory conclusion that although labor conditions have improved generally over time, contracting and many of its evils have also remained stubbornly present. Cloth particles in the air, long hours, and low pay were decried repeatedly in each period.

The rhetoric of return (of the sweatshop) has paralleled that of decline (of the industry). Sweatshops, like immigrant labor have been posited as last-ditch efforts to stem competition from low-cost imports or explained as a result of the Reagan years and loosening regulations. All are (partial) historical explanations for industrial decline, union regression and decreasing labor standards at the end of the twentieth century. Yet explaining the *return* of the sweatshop on industrial *decline* in the "First World" fails to see how similar conditions have prevailed ever since the late nineteenth-century period of *growth*. The history of the women's wear industry over the last century is a mirror image of the fashion dialectic: industrial conditions show a constantly renewed struggle between forces of order and of disorder, between efforts at standardization and the siren call of fashion change. Unions have fought the bosses in order to try to stabilize working conditions, while unions, manufacturers and their employees have at times all worked together to try to maintain the industry against runaway shops and foreign competition. At the same time, similarities in sewing have persisted, characterized by low skill needs, high seasonality, and widespread subcontracting. Flexibility, as it were, has been a constant. What strikes the historian of the *longue durée* is the *persistence* over time and space of complaints relating to the pitfalls of unbridled flexible response to volatile demand.

Notes

1. Virginia Yans-McLaughlin, "Metaphors of Self in History: Subjectivity, Oral Narrative, and Immigration Studies," in *Immigration Reconsidered*, ed. idem (New York: Oxford University Press, 1990), 276.
2. Michael Piore and Charles F. Sabel, *The Second Industrial Divide* (New York: Basic Books, 1984); New York State Senator Franz Leichter's report and labor's response to contemporary sweatshops are discussed further below. My article here draws heavily from my book *Ready-to-Wear and Ready-to-Work: A Century of Industry and Immigrants in Paris and New York* (Durham: Duke University Press, 1997), especially chapter 5, but it has been "tailored" for this volume; notably, although the book compares both cities, I draw particularly on the New York evidence here.
3. Piore and Sabel, *The Second Industrial Divide*; Charles F. Sabel and Jonathan Zeitlin, "Historical Alternatives to Mass Production: Politics, Market, and Technology in Nineteenth-Century Industrialization," *Past and Present*, 108 (August 1985), 133–76. The term "flexible specialization" is attributed to Sabel.
4. This interpretation, deeply rooted in nineteenth-century economic liberalism, is paralleled by the individualist interpretation of fashion. See, e.g., Gilles Lipovetsky, *L'empire de l'éphémère* (Paris: Gallimard, 1991; English edition: *The Empire of Fashion*, Princeton: Princeton University Press, 1994).
5. E.g., Jonathan Zeitlin and Peter Totterdill, "Markets, Technology and Local Intervention: The Case of Clothing," in *Reversing Industrial Decline? Industrial Structure and Policy in Britain and Her Competitors*, ed. Paul Hirst and Jonathan Zeitlin (Oxford: Berg, 1989). See also Roger Waldinger, *Through the Eye of the Needle: Immigrants and Enterprise in New York's Garment Trades* (New York: New York University Press, 1986).
6. Emile Levasseur, *L'ouvrier américain*, 2 vols. (Paris: L. Larose, 1898), 1:431. He adds, however, that these immigrants were probably better off in New York than they had been in their home countries.
7. Jo-Ann Mort, "Return of the Sweatshop," *Dissent* 35 (Summer 1988), 364; idem, "Immigrant Dreams: Sweatshop Workers Speak," *Dissent* 43 (Fall 1996), 85–87.
8. Alejandro Portes and Manuel Castells, "World Underneath: The Origins, Dynamics, and Effects of the Informal Economy," in *The Informal Economy*, Alejandro Portes, Manuel Castells, and Lauren Benton, eds. (Baltimore: The Johns Hopkins University Press, 1989), 13.
9. Senator Franz S. Leichter, "The Return of the Sweatshop," unpublished report, 3 vols. (1979–1982); Barbara Koeppel, "The New Sweatshops," *The Progressive* 5 (Nov. 1978), 22–26; *New York Times*, Oct. 12–13, 1983, and Sept. 6, 1987; Mort, "Return of the Sweatshop."
10. The El Monte scandal of 1995 shifted the focus from overseas sweatshops to American ones. A town-house complex in Los Angeles was raided, where some seventy Thais were working in sweatshop conditions and being held against their will. The employers (the owner was called "Auntie") had confiscated their passports and let no one out of the compound; money was deducted from wages to pay back the passage money and false documents. *Washington Post*, September 10, 1995. "A Stain on Fashion," *Washington Post*, September 12, 1995. Under a subtitle "Sweatshops Are Part of the Bargain," the article blamed the industry's "multiple layers, myriad players, fickle consumers and inherent pressures." See also the 1998 Smithsonian exhibit curated by Peter Liebhold and Harry Rubenstein: *Between a Rock and a Hard Place*: www.americanhistory.si.edu/sweatshops.
11. Organisation internationale du travail (OIT), *Réunion technique tripartite pour l'industrie du vêtement* (Geneva: Bureau International du Travail, 1964), report 3, *Les problèmes résultant des fluctuations de l'emploi dans l'industrie du vêtement*; Carol Joan Smith, "Women, Work, and Use of Government Benefits: A Case Study of Hispanic Women Workers in New York's Garment Industry" (Ph.D. diss., Adelphi University, 1980), 71ff.

12. Gertrud Greig, *Seasonal Fluctuations in Employment in the Women's Clothing Industry in New York* (New York: Columbia University Press, 1949). Cf. Christine Stansell, *City of Women: Sex and Class in New York, 1789–1860* (Urbana: University of Illinois Press, 1987); and Richard Stott, *Workers in the Metropolis: Class, Ethnicity, and Youth in Antebellum New York City* (Ithaca: Cornell University Press, 1990), 24–25, 118–19, and passim.

13. New York State Governor's Advisory Commission, *Cloak, Suit and Skirt Industry of New York City* (New York: The Evening Post job printing office, 1925), 22.

14. OIT, *Réunion tripartite* (1964), *Compte rendu sommaire*, p.36; ibid., report 3: *Fluctuations de l'emploi*; OIT, *2ème réunion tripartite* (1980), *Note sur les travaux*, 65; idem, *4ème réunion* (1995), 2:41.

15. Karl Marx, *Capital*, 3 vols. (London: Lawrence and Wishart, 1974), 1:450.

16. Pierre Du Maroussem, *La Petite industrie (salaires et durée du travail)*, Vol. 2, *Le Vêtement à Paris* (Paris: Imprimerie Nationale, 1896), 306.

17. *Justice*, May 15, 1946, cited by Robert Laurentz, "Racial/Ethnic Conflict in the New York City Garment Industry, 1933–1980," diss., SUNY-Binghamton, 1980, 192.

18. International Ladies' Garment Workers' Union (ILGWU), *Record of the 16th Convention* (1922), 93, 124. Jesse T. Carpenter, *Competition and Collective Bargaining in the Needle Trades, 1910–1967* (Ithaca: New York State School of Industrial and Labor Relations, 1972), 125–37, on the union's attempts to limit contracting; Benjamin K. Hunnicutt, *Abandoning Shorter Hours for the Right to Work* (Philadelphia: Temple University Press, 1988), 71–75, on work-sharing.

19. ILGWU, *Record of the 17th Convention* (1924), 229.

20. ILGWU, *Report of the General Executive Board* (23d Convention, 1937), 10–11.

21. City College Oral History Research Project, "Immigrant Labor Oral History Collection," Tamiment Library (New York City, n.d.), I-105. For late twentieth-century evidence, see, e.g., Smith, "Women, Work."

22. Hadassa Kosak, "The Rise of the Jewish Working Class, New York, 1881–1905," City University of New York, diss., 1987, p. 206; see also p. 120; and idem, *Cultures of Opposition: Jewish Immigrant Workers, New York City, 1881–1905* (Albany: SUNY, 2000).

23. OIT, *Réunion tripartite* (1964), 3: chaps. 4 and 5; and ibid, *Compte rendu sommaire*, 40–45.

24. See, for example, New York State Department of Labor, *The Women's Clothing Worker and Unemployment Insurance* (New York: Division of Employment, 1953). On unemployment insurance as a means of regulating the effect of fluctuating demand, see also Steven Fraser, *Labor Will Rule: Sidney Hillman and the Rise of American Labor* (New York: The Free Press, 1991), 215–18.

25. Contractors' shops have also been called "kitchen and bedroom" shops. Kosak, "Jewish Working Class," 205. See also Waldinger, *Eye of the Needle*.

26. Marx, *Capital*, 1:445–46.

27. New York State Governor's Advisory Commission, *Cloak, Suit*, 14.

28. *Fortune* magazine, cited in Roger Waldinger, "Another Look at the International Ladies' Garment Workers' Union: Women, Industry Structure and Collective Action," in *Women, Work, and Protest*, ed. Ruth Milkman (Boston: Routledge, Kegan Paul, 1985), 103.

29. In New York City, for example, the average number of workers per establishment in women's wear fell from 27.8 in 1899 to 17.9 in 1921. Louis Levine, *The Women's Garment Workers: A History of the International Ladies' Garment Workers' Union* (New York: B. W. Huebsch Inc., 1924), 521.

30. Cited in OIT, *Réunion tripartite* (1964), 1: table XII, 42.

31. For a discussion and critique of the co-ethnic network theory, see Green, *Ready-to-Wear and Ready-to-Work*, 285–290; Ivan Light, Richard B. Bernard, Rebecca Kim, "Immigrant Incorporation in the Garment Industry of Los Angeles," *International Migration Review* 33:1 (Spring 1999), 5–25.

32. New York State Governor's Advisory Commission, *Cloak, Suit*, p.43; ILGWU, *The Story of the ILGWU* (New York: ILGWU Educational Department, 1935), 25.

33. ILGWU, *Report of the General Executive Board* (26th Convention, 1947), 93; Abeles, et al., *The Chinatown Garment Industry Study* (New York: ILGWU Local 23–25 and New York Skirt and Sportswear Assn., 1983), 4.

34. Maurizio Lazzarato, Antonio Negri and Giancarlo Santilli, "La Confection dans le Quartier du Sentier," report, Ministère du travail, de l'emploi et de la formation professionnelle: MIRE, 1990, 186; Abeles et al., *Chinatown Study*, 4, 69, found that contractors work for an average of 4.6 jobbers, and manufacturers give out work to some 27 different contractors.

35. Levine, *Women's Garment Workers*, viii, 15; Roy Helfgott, "Women's and Children's Apparel," in *Made in New York: Case Studies in Metropolitan Manufacturing*, ed. Max Hall (Cambridge, Mass.: Harvard University Press, 1959), 30; Waldinger, *Eye of the Needle*, 137–38, and chap. 6; José R. De La Torre et. al., *Corporate Responses to Import Competition in the U.S. Apparel Industry* (Atlanta: Georgia State University College of Business Administration, 1978), 37, calculated that the average plant and equipment in the garment industry was $2,335 per production worker, compared to $24,245 for all manufacturing.

36. ILGWU, *Report of the General Executive Board* (27th Convention, 1950), 93; Helfgott, "Women's and Children's Apparel," 31; Joel Seidman, *The Needle Trades* (New York: Farrar and Rinehart, 1942), 42. See also Elaine Wrong, *The Negro in the Apparel Industry* (Reprint) (Philadelphia: University of Pennsylvania, 1974), table 7, 18, showing employment turnover in the apparel industry to be higher than that of all manufacturing sectors as a whole.

37. Meiklejohn, "Dresses," 329, 334, 324, 343; Leichter, "The Return of the Sweatshop," 2:28; cf. Peter Kwong, *The New Chinatown* (New York: Noonday Press, 1987), 68. See also, e.g., ILGWU, Report, Dress Industry Data, February 8, 1949, Dress Joint Series, Box 3, File 11, ILGWU Archives. Often firms close for legal and tax reasons, only to reopen under another name, with or without their former employees.

38. ILGWU, *Story*, 22.; "Der khazer mark in 'Hester' Park," *Forverts*, September 29, 1907, in Nancy L. Green, ed. *Jewish Workers in the Diaspora* (Berkeley: University of California Press, 1998).

39. Cited in Carpenter, *Competition*, 109. See Susan Glenn's view of the oppressive paternalistic immigrant shop in *Daughters of the Shtetl: Life and Labor in the Immigrant Generation* (Ithaca: Cornell University Press, 1990), passim. In one case, women called an "orphan strike" to protest their boss's "fatherly affection." Nancy Schrom Dye, *As Equals and Sisters: The Labor Movement and the Women's Trade Union League of New York* (Columbia, Missouri: University of Missouri Press, 1980), 67.

40. ILGWU, *The Outside System of Production in the Women's Garment Industry in the New York Market* (New York: ILGWU, 1951), 14; ILGWU, *Report of the GEB* (19th Convention, 1928), 7–8; Carpenter, *Competition*, 116, 132.

41. Cited in Kosak, "Jewish Working Class," 141.

42. Cited in Carpenter, *Competition*, 107.

43. Jacob Loft, "Jewish Workers in the New York City Men's Clothing Industry," *Jewish Social Studies* 2 (January 1940), 76. There is an extensive literature on ethnic entrepreneurs. For a discussion, see Green, *Ready-to-Wear and Ready-to-Work*, 7–8.

44. U.S. Industrial Commission, *Reports of the Industrial Commission*, 19 vols. (Washington, D.C.: GPO, 1900–1902), 15:379.

45. Meiklejohn, "Dresses," 347; OIT, *Réunion tripartite* (1964), 2:20–21.

46. William M. Reddy, *Money and Liberty in Modern Europe* (Cambridge: Cambridge University Press, 1987).

47. OIT, *2e réunion tripartite* (1980), report 2.

48. Marx, *Capital* 1:443. On the notion of "bloc socio-technologique," see Pierre Bouvier, *Le Travail au Quotidien* (Paris: PUF, 1989).

49. New York State Department of Labor, *1st Annual Report* (1901), 1:126–27; *13th Annual Report* (1913), 49–52; *28th Annual Report* (1928), 175; *31st Annual Report* (1931), 18.

50. New York State, Factory Investigating Commission, *2d Report*, 4 vols. (New York: 1913), 2:729; Eileen Boris, "Regulating Industrial Homework: The Triumph of 'Sacred Motherhood,'" *Journal of American History* 71 (Mar. 1985), 746, 760; and idem, *Home to Work: Motherhood and the Politics of Industrial Homework in the United States* (Cambridge: Cambridge University Press, 1994), 168; Miriam Cohen and Michael Hanagan, "The Politics of Gender and the Making of the Welfare State, 1900–1940: A Comparative Perspective", *Journal of Social History* 24 (Spring, 1991), 469–84.

51. New York State Department of Labor, "Report to the Governor and the Legislature on the Garment Manufacturing Industry and Industrial Homework" (New York, 1982), 13.

52. The 20-percent figure comes from Roger Waldinger and Michael Lapp, skeptically quoting two union officials in "Back to the Sweatshop or Ahead to the Informal Sector?," *International Journal of Urban and Regional Research* 17 (1993), 24; "New York Is Fighting Spread of Sweatshops," *New York Times*, November 16, 1987.

53. Eileen Boris and Cynthia Daniels, eds., *Homework: Historical and Contemporary Perspectives on Paid Labor at Home* (Urbana: University of Illinois Press, 1989); Boris, *Home to*

Work; and Stansell, *City of Women*, among others, all argue that outwork was not marginal but central to production.

54. Judith Coffin, "Social Science Meets Sweated Labor: Reinterpreting Women's Work in Late Nineteenth-Century France," *The Journal of Modern History* 63 (June 1991), 230–70, 255–60; Boris, *Home to Work*.

55. Charles Booth, "Sweating," in *Labour and Life of the People*, ed. idem, 3 vols. (London: Williams and Norgate, 1889–91), 1:481–500; Beatrice Webb, "How to Do Away with the Sweating System," in Sidney and Beatrice Webb, *Problems of Modern Industry* (New York: Longmans, Green and Co., 1902), 139–40; James Schmiechen, *Sweated Industries and Sweated Labor: The London Clothing Trades, 1860–1914* (Urbana: University of Illinois Press, 1984). For the United States, see *Industrial Commission*, 15:320; and United States House of Representatives, *Report on the Sweating System*, H. Rept. 3309, 52d Cong, 2d sess, 1893.

56. New York State Office of Factory Inspectors, *12th Annual Report* (1897), 47.

57. Jack Hardy, *The Clothing Workers: A Study of the Conditions and Struggles in the Needle Trades* (New York: International Publishers, 1935), 218.

58. Leichter, "Return of the Sweatshop," 1:4; New York State Department of Labor, *8th Annual Report* (1908), 1:19–20 (measuring carbon dioxide levels in factories); OIT, *Réunion tripartite* (1964), 2:chap. 5, on hygiene and safety in the garment industry; and idem, *2e réunion* (1987), 1:pt. 1, 73–74, on chemical use in the industry.

59. Leichter, "Return of the Sweatshop," 2:3–4; "The New Sweatshops," *Newsweek*, September 10, 1990; *New York Times*, March 6, 1994.

60. Levine, *Women's Garment Workers*, x.

61. Pauline Newman, "We kept the Faith," quoted in Leon Stein, ed., *Out of the Sweatshop* (New York: Quadrangle, 1977), 342. Cf., however, the 1958 newspaper series in the *New York Herald Tribune*, exposing conditions in the industry.

62. ILGWU, *GEB Report and Record of the 38th Convention* (1983), 346.

63. Waldinger and Lapp, "Back to the Sweatshop"; Leichter, "Return of the Sweatshop"; Morrison G. Wong, "Chinese Sweatshops in the United States: A Look at the Garment Industry," in *Research in the Sociology of Work*, Ida Simpson and Richard Simpson, eds. (Greenwich, CT: JAI Press, 1983), 357–79.

64. Piore and Sabel, *Second Industrial Divide*, 264.

65. "The New Sweatshops," *Newsweek*, September 10, 1990; "New York's Terror Taxis, Explained," *New York Times*, August 21, 1994. Not to mention white collar and academic sweatshops: Jill Andresky Fraser, *White Collar Sweatshop: The Deterioriation of Work and Its Rewards in Corporate America* (New York: Norton, 2001); Barbara Garson, *The Electronic Sweatshop: How Computers Are Transforming the Office of the Future into the Factory of the Past* (New York: Simon and Schuster, 1988); special issue of *Anthropology of Work Review*, "Demystifying the Changing Structure of Academic Work," 15:1 (Spring 1994); AHA *Perspectives* (e.g., 33:5 [May–June 1995], 9–18) and in the *OAH Newsletter*, passim.

66. "There has always been a fringe of producers who operate outside the regulatory framework. Since these shops exist in an underground economy, they are almost by definition uncountable." Michael Piore, "The Economics of the Sweatshop," in Andrew Ross, ed., *No Sweat: Fashion, Free Trade, and the Rights of Garment Workers* (New York: Verso, 1997), 135–142, 140.

3
Bringing Sweatshops into the Museum

PETER LIEBHOLD AND HARRY R. RUBENSTEIN

On Sunday, January 23, 2000, an unusual gathering for Beverly Hills took place. A large group of Thai and Latina garment workers used their day off to visit the Simon Wiesenthal Center's Museum of Tolerance. Many of these hardworking individuals had never been to a museum before.

The Center, housed in a handsome red granite building on the edge of Los Angeles's fashionable Beverly Hills, is open to everyone. With active programs for schoolchildren and law-enforcement officers, it normally attracts a wide range of visitors, but Sunday at the Museum of Tolerance is usually a day when Jewish LA Westsiders come to learn more about the Holocaust, the focus of the museum's exhibitions.

But the Thai and Latina garment workers did not come to learn about Jewish history: they came to see their own story featured in the Smithsonian's traveling exhibition, *Between a Rock and a Hard Place: A History of Sweatshops, 1820—Present.* The show prominently featured these garment workers' experience at the notorious El Monte sweatshop. The shop itself had operated just twenty miles away.

The Museum of Tolerance organized this reception to give the El Monte workers, their families, and supporters an opportunity to reunite and to honor their struggles for justice. "You are heroes," proclaimed Julie Su, an Asian Pacific American Legal Center attorney who represented the workers. "You have stirred so many people from apathy and ignorance."[1]

The raid of the El Monte sweatshop in the early morning hours of August 2, 1995, was the end of a surprisingly long story of greed, opportunism, and justice deferred. The illegal sewing operation, located in a seven-unit apartment complex in El Monte, California, began at least seven years earlier in 1988. [2] This large contract sewing shop assembled clothing for numerous manufacturers and retailers. Significantly more egregious than most sweatshops in the United States, the operators of the El Monte shop (at the time of the raid) were holding seventy-two Thai workers in slavery.

The El Monte sweatshop was a family-owned business run by Suni Mana-surangkun, her five sons, two daughter-in-laws, and two additional hirelings. Suni and her eldest son, Sanchai, oversaw the operation. Other sons worked as recruiters, liaisons to manufacturers, and foremen. Added to the shop's management was Rampha Satthaprasit. She started out as a worker, and after becoming romantically involved with one of the sons, was promoted to chief work supervisor and overseer of the company store.[3]

The Manasurangkun family obtained workers for the Los Angeles sweatshop operation in Thailand. Recruiters lured the workers to El Monte with promises that they would be sewing in a clean factory, receiving good pay, and having the weekends off. They even showed photographs of company parties and outings to Disneyland. After workers signed contracts (indenture agreements) committing them to repay 120,000 baht (about $5,000 in 1997 dollars), they were smuggled into the United States using fraudulent passports. The El Monte workers understood that they had made a commitment for a three-year stint and would be returned to Thailand at the end of the term. On arrival in Los Angeles the sweatshop operators confiscated the doctored passports, gave them two days to acclimate, and put them to work. There were no company parties or outings to Disneyland.[4]

The Thai workers were held captive in a two-story apartment building enclosed by a security gate. A five-foot-high cement block wall heightened with corrugated steel panels and topped with rolls of razor wire surrounded it. The operators also partially covered the windows of the apartments with plywood in order to keep the workers from signaling for help. A guard posted outside monitored the workers' movements between the units. The debts owed, a guard force, and threats of physical harm to them and especially their families in Thailand, discouraged the workers from escaping. The operators also intimidated the predominantly female workforce by telling them that if they escaped, Mexicans would rape them, and American authorities would capture them and cut off their hair.[5]

Upon their arrival, new workers were assigned space in one of the crowded upstairs bedrooms, issued a pillow, a blanket, and told to sew their own sleeping pad. The workers slept up to nine in a room, in what one observer described as rooms of wall-to-wall mattresses.[6] The workers sewed sixteen hours a day, seven days a week. The only time off was New Year's Day or when work was slow. Using modern industrial sewing machines, the workers assembled predominantly ladies' and juniors' garments. They sewed in makeshift first floor quarters jammed into what had been the garages, dining rooms and living rooms of the apartments. The workers were constantly being yelled at to work faster. A typical schedule was: wake at 6:00 A.M., begin work at 7:00 A.M., lunch around noon, dinner around 6:00 P.M., and end work around midnight.

The workers received wages based on piece rates, but the rates were set so low that they averaged only 69 cents an hour. The operators of the sweatshop took every opportunity to take back what little money they paid. From their meager earnings, the sweatshop operators deducted money to repay the debt incurred in their journey to the United States. Workers also had to buy, at inflated prices, food and personal supplies from a company store located in the garage of one of the units.[7]

The El Monte sweatshop was a sophisticated operation that produced clothing under contract for major labels such as Clio, Ocean Pacific, and B.U.M. Equipment. Nationally prominent retailers sold the garments in stores around the country. The operators ran two front shops in the Los Angeles downtown garment district to provide a theoretical source of production when representatives from retailers and manufacturers came to inspect facilities and the merchandise they ordered. But even these shops violated wage and safety laws. The downtown shops, employing predominantly Latina workers, finished the garments—pressing them, putting them on hangers, and adding tags in preparation for delivery to manufacturers and stores.

The operators were well aware that they were violating the law and took many precautions to avoid detection. The truck that brought the cut bundles of fabric and delivered the finished sewn goods to the front shop took a circuitous route to throw off possible police tails. The garage doors were only raised high enough to slide the finished bags of clothing under but not enough for police surveillance to see the sewing machines inside. Despite their precautions the sweatshop operation did not go unnoticed. In 1988 another contractor, irritated at having to compete with an operation that did not pay minimum wage, tipped authorities to the El Monte sweatshop. The Immigration and Naturalization Service (INS) wanted to raid the complex but first, according to their legal authority, had to serve notice of inspection. When they showed up later for the inspection, the workers had all been moved and there was no sign of an illegal sewing operation. Finally in 1995 state investigators from the California Department of Industrial Relations took over where the Feds had stopped short. Acting on a tip from the boyfriend of an escaped worker, state investigators staked out the apartment complex and gathered enough information to obtain a search warrant for illegal homework.[8]

On August 2, 1995, law enforcement officers, in a coordinated multiagency action, raided the El Monte sweatshop. They arrested eight of the clandestine garment shop operators and took the seventy-two Thai workers into INS custody. After nine days in detention the INS released the workers and granted them temporary permission to remain in the U.S. as material witnesses to the case against the sweatshop operators. The authorities also raided the front shops. Two of the ten indicted operators avoided arrest.[9]

In February 1996, the eight operators of the El Monte sweatshop pled guilty in Federal court to conspiracy, involuntary servitude (slavery), and smuggling and harboring illegal immigrants. The sentences ranged from two to seven years and a $250,000 fine.[10] With two of the Manasurangkun family members remaining at large, and concern for the workers' safety if returned to Thailand, the federal government granted the Thai workers legal residency with the right to work in the United States. Most expected to apply for citizenship after residency requirements have been met.[11]

During the raid, officers seized labels, orders, and work tickets that showed that a number of manufacturers and retailers were directly contracting with the El Monte sweatshop. By 1999, eleven companies—Mervyn's, Montgomery Ward, Tomato, Bum International, L.F. Sportswear, Millers Outpost, Balmara, Beniko, F-40 California, Ms. Tops, and Topson Downs—while admitting no wrongdoing agreed to pay more than $3.7 million dollars to the 150 workers who labored in the El Monte sweatshop and its front operation. As in most cases of sweatshop production, these companies contended that they did not knowingly contract with operators who were violating the law.[12]

Five years after the raid and three years after the settlement, the reception for the El Monte workers at the Museum of Tolerance provided an opportunity for the workers, their families, and supporters to see the story on display in their hometown. Between the day's formal remarks and catching up with old friends, the El Monte workers quietly toured the exhibition that linked their story to the history of earlier immigrants who had toiled in the tenement sweatshops of another era. One group of workers was heard audibly gasping when they were told that 146 young women perished in the 1911 Triangle Shirtwaist Company fire.[13] For them it was a story not from the distant past, but another example of the horror that they knew too well.

In the museum gallery these workers once again came face to face with the sewing machines over which they labored and the garments which they produced. The razor wire that was impressionistically hung over the machines in the exhibition gave chills to Maliwan Radonphon, who had toiled a year and a half in the El Monte shop making sportswear and other popular youth clothing. "They just showed a little of the wire in the exhibit," she explained, "but it was enough to remind me." There, in the cases before the workers, were the doctored Thai passports used to smuggle in co-workers, letters home that were never mailed by the sweatshop operators, and an assortment of garments seized during the raid. One of the T-shirts on display prominently showed the face of Garfield the cat emblazoned with the slogan "As If I Care". For how many days did the workers have to stare at this cartoon cat's smirking grin while they sewed together the shirts sold under the Garfield label?

But while the public recognized the importance of El Monte, many were surprised that such a topic would become the centerpiece of an exhibition produced at the national museum. A history of sweatshops was not the kind of exhibit that could easily find corporate sponsors. Nor would it please the museum's more conservative critics. Yet, the museum's administrators and staff, once the project began, realized that it was too important not to tell.

The Smithsonian's sweatshop exhibition grew out of a much larger project to examine low-paid labor in America. In 1993, a group of curators at the National Museum of American History, of which we were part, began working on this topic, believing an initiative on low-paid occupations would shed light on how Americans have historically valued work on many levels throughout history. Realizing that the Smithsonian collections had few objects that represented the struggles and successes of working people, we began a search for relevant artifacts.

In November 1995, with the trial of the El Monte sweatshop operators over, a request for material was sent to Jose Millan, Assistant Labor Commissioner for the California Department of Labor Standards. "The History of Technology Division of the National Museum of American History is looking to expand its collections concerning the garment industry, and believes that the El Monte sweatshop raid needs to be recorded as a point of historical and contemporary significance."[14] Realizing the political importance of placing the El Monte story in the nation's museum, the California Department of Industrial Relations was quick to cooperate and donated two sewing machines and half a dozen garments seized during the raid. Eventually the museum collected additional El Monte artifacts from the U.S. Department of Labor, the Asian Pacific American Legal Center, the owner of the apartment complex, and some of the workers enslaved in the shop.

The larger project on low-paid labor soon became a casualty of the "culture wars" (the debate over the direction and control of public history) that were swirling around the Smithsonian and other public institutions in the mid-1990s.[15] Even after the Smithsonian Institution canceled its controversial *Enola Gay* exhibition on the bombing of Hiroshima, some of the museum's staff believed that there was a glimmer of hope that the museum would still support an exhibition on a controversial topic.

With a mixture of boldness and naive self-confidence, by late 1996 we put forward a proposal for an exhibition on the history of sweatshops in the United States. Frustrated at seeing their exhibition program hobbled, the museum's director, Spencer Crew, and Associate Director for Curatorial Affairs, Lonnie Bunch, agreed to support an exhibition on sweatshops, in part, to test the limits (both internal and external) of how far the museum would be allowed to go in presenting controversial material.[16]

Beyond the topic of the history of sweatshop production itself, the exhibition also raised additional questions. Were public institutions, such as the museum, a place to hold this debate over sweatshops? And if educational institutions through exhibitions and other publicly sponsored programs could not address this topic, then how can we expect the public to understand or to care about it?

To allow this project to survive required that we construct an exhibition with demonstrative balance. Balance became the watchword of the project—balance in content, balance in participation, balance in funding. There was never a time that we did not have to demonstrate and defend the exhibition on this point. It was clear to us that this would be the measure of whether the show would be permitted to open. The experience of similar public history endeavors was clear. For large, visible projects, good scholarship by itself was not enough to sustain an exhibition under assault from influential interest groups that often simply did not want the topic discussed. Our challenge was to create this balance and still have a show that would have something to say.

Emerging out of our conversations with numerous consultants and advisors was an exhibition approach that we hoped would present a complex overview of the history of garment industry sweatshops. It also needed to be able to address the anticipated criticism of outside groups and uneasy administrators. [17]

At an early stage in the process we conceived the basic structure of the exhibition. It would include a large historical overview of sweatshops in the United States, a dramatic presentation on El Monte, and an area that we labeled the dialogue section. We planned this last section to include statements and artifacts from organizations and individuals that either were involved or were addressing the sweatshop issue. While the decision to have a dialogue section was easy, the choice of who to invite to participate proved more difficult than we anticipated. In conversations with our advisors, it became apparent that balance meant different things to different people.

When the list of possible dialogue participants grew to twelve individuals, some who had been satisfied earlier asked why their perspective were being diluted (one out of twelve is drastically different than one out of four). At that point, we arbitrarily decided six different people was the most that the space could hold. The participants were selected to represent a range of views: a manufacturer, a community activist, a retailer, a union representative, a government official, and a celebrity endorser. From their own perspective, each would address the topic of sweatshop production in America's garment industry. No restrictions were put on what the speakers would write, other than it could not be libelous.

In November 1996, when work began on the exhibition, it was apparent that the show could become controversial, but not because anyone was in favor of sweatshop labor. Manufacturers and civil rights activists alike decried any occurrence of exploitative work. The controversy, if to come, would center on whether a public educational institution should explore problems in America rather than celebrating the achievements of the nation. While the museum thought it had developed a good approach to addressing the topic of sweatshops, it was by no means certain that it would be able to open such a challenging show. Museum managers did not fear questions on the appropriateness of sweatshops, what they feared was political pressure from Congress and the business community.

In the fall of 1997, our nightmares became reality as newspapers across the nation carried articles about the latest Smithsonian exhibition in trouble. In an all too familiar staccato tone, headlines blared "Plan for Sweatshop Exhibition Draws Fire," "Clothing Makers Cite Bias in Exhibit," "Furor Builds Over Sweatshop Exhibition," and "Clothing Industry Rips into Planned Sweatshop Exhibit."[18] Was this another institutional stumble in the culture wars, where an angry segment of the public and a questioning press would demand that a museum's interpretation be changed? Was the museum's choice of exhibit topic a cheap shot by leftist staff trying to highlight what is wrong with America? Would the acrimony surrounding the project bring it to a stop before the exhibition even opened, or would people want to evaluate the show itself rather than impressions of what it might be?

By the time the controversy exploded, the development of the exhibition was well on its way. The object list was complete, a draft of the script had been circulated to museum management, the designer Mary Wiedeman had largely finished the design, and we were looking for venues for the exhibition to travel. One thing that was consuming a considerable amount of our time was getting national figures for the dialog section. We had commitments from Jay Mazur, President of UNITE!; Maria Echaveste, former Director of the Department of Labor, Wage and Hour Division; Julie Su, attorney at the Asian Pacific American Legal Center; Larry Martin, president of the American Apparel Manufacturer Association (AAMA); and Kathy Lee Gifford, who lent her name to a popular line of clothes sold through Wal-Mart. We were waiting to hear from Tracy Mullin, president of the National Retail Federation (NRF).

We were also very concerned about money. While we had received internal resources for design and some production from the Smithsonian, we still needed about $150,000 primarily for outside production and videos. We had been given some money from the Smithsonian and had a commitment of support from UNITE! and the Department of Labor (from a nonFederal fund). It was clear, however, that we could not accept money from labor without a similar contribution from business. We had asked for support from both the AAMA and the NRF. We were optimistic that the manufacturers would help, but were not as confident about the retailers.

At this point, an old contact, Jose Millan, offered to assist the project. Millan had been the Assistant State Labor Commissioner of California at the time of the El Monte raid and had been instrumental in helping the Smithsonian acquire the El Monte artifacts. Millan, who had recently been promoted to Labor Commissioner, offered to raise political and financial support for the project at the upcoming August 21, 1997, special labor meeting of the California Fashion Association (CFA), a manufacturing trade group. We assumed that the CFA would be more receptive to the news of the exhibition coming from an important insider like Millan. At the meeting Millan went through a laundry list of state apparel industry regulations and closed with an articulate argument for supporting our exhibition. "The industry must denounce El Monte. I think a lot more can be gained by speaking out than by remaining silent."[19]

The audience was not pleased. Almost immediately a suspicious voice called out, "Who is funding the traveling exhibit? We are deeply disturbed at the timing; our industry is under scrutiny as never before, and having it travel throughout California serves no purpose." Others shared the concern. "A troubling aspect is that it is an opportunity for special interests like UNITE! to make it a spectacle." Joe Rodriguez, executive director of the garment contractors association, argued, "Sharing a platform with the union and giving them undue recognition and credibility is something that I do not want to get involved with." Millan tried to turn the tide. "The industry could show leadership by taking a pro-active position. The exhibit is going to happen, and the industry should be out in front! It behooves the industry to speak with its own voice as to how it wants to be portrayed." Bernard Lax, president of the Coalition of Apparel Industries in California, agreed. "It would be better for the industry to take a proactive approach. You take the wind out of the union's sails and they will have nothing to say." But the argument largely fell on deaf ears as the angry mob of garment executives fumed that sweatshops were not their concern. According to an industry trade paper, Lonnie Kane, president of Karen Kane, claimed "the El Monte case was more of an immigration issue than a garment industry issue. '[The El Monte operators] took advantage of our immigration laws. They could have been doing anything. They just happened to be sewing.'"[20]

Back in Washington we didn't know it at the time, but the match had been dropped and our house was on fire. While the national trade association groups, the AAMA, and NRF, seemed to be grudgingly going along with the show, Millan's presentation sparked a national controversy. Soon the fax machines were humming. Following Millan's presentation, the California Fashion Association called a special meeting to consider action. The group decided to oppose the project. Randall Harris, executive director of the San Francisco Fashion Industries, in a letter faxed to Bill Benstrom, chair of the CFA's "Smithsonian Committee," apologized for not being able to attend the emergency meeting and went on to say "A traveling road show is a disgraceful concept. No possible good can come from it. We believe that we must fight the attempts to bring this exhibit to California in every way possible."[21] Indeed the group sent angry letters to California members of Congress and contacted the press.

The newspapers were only too happy to report the controversy du jour, and the next day the *Los Angeles Times* carried the front-page story "Plan for Sweatshop Exhibition Draws Fire." The article reported the industry's anger. Ilse

Metchek, executive director of the CFA announced her plan to bring the Smithsonian down, "We cannot stand idly by. We want to turn this exhibit plan into another *Enola Gay*."[22] And indeed our carefully constructed house of cards began to fall.

Under pressure from California manufacturers, the AAMA rethought their position and pulled their support for the exhibition. "This is a difficult and controversial subject, and we feel that such an exhibit will have the effect of tarring law-abiding companies with the same brush as the sweatshop people," explained the AAMA's Jack Morgan. "There's no way for us to counter that negative image by participating in the exhibit. The only responsible thing to do is to withdraw participation."[23] Without AAMA involvement, the NRF was free to duck, and it decided also to distance itself publicly from the project. Left without industry support, it appeared that Ilse Metchek's prediction would come true and the sweatshop exhibition would be the next victim in the culture wars. Metchek pushed hard for the show to be canceled, saying, "We object to the use of government funding to attack an entire industry under the guise of scholarship."[24]

But instead of applying pressure, Congress saved the day. Representative George Miller from San Francisco began circulating a "dear colleague" letter supporting the show. "We were alarmed to learn that some in the apparel industry are launching a effort to derail the exhibit, arguing that it will be unbalanced and unflattering . . . Censoring this exhibit . . . will only propel the false notion that sweatshops were not part of America's history and are not a problem in today's international economy."[25] Could a nation avoid its sweatshop past, but reform its sweatshop present?

The Smithsonian's secretary, I. Michael Heyman, also sensed the importance of the moment. Feeling he had solid ground on which to stand and wishing to prevent this exhibition from following the path of the *Enola Gay* debacle, Heyman wrote a strong letter of support to the *Los Angeles Times*. "[T]his is a timely subject that deserves our attention. This exhibition on American sweatshops seeks to promote a better understanding of this difficult topic by presenting material from differing perspectives and concerns. . . . The Smithsonian Institution occasionally presents difficult, unpleasant, or controversial historical episodes, not out of any desire to embarrass, to be unpatriotic, or to cause pain, but out of a responsibility to convey a fuller, more inclusive history."[26] But the fight was far from over.

While forty-five members of the House agreed with Representative Miller and signed his letter of support, the feelings were not unanimous. Sam Johnson, a Representative from Texas (and importantly a Smithsonian regent), expressed his concern to a *New York Times* reporter that the planned exhibition was faulty because it focused on the negative aspects of the apparel industry. Justifying his action he explained, "One of the reasons Newt [Gingrich] appointed me was to keep the historical revisionism under control." Luckily for us, other regents (each house of Congress names three members to the Smithsonian board of Regents), came to our rescue. "It is balanced," said Californian Representative Esteben Torres. "We can't sweep things under the rug because they are controversial." Two other Smithsonian regents, New York Senator Daniel Patrick Moynihan and Hanna Gray, former president of the University of Chicago, supported Torres.[27]

But museum management support did not make the matter go away. The bile continued to build and the rhetoric from the industry intensified. In an effort to quite things down, Lonnie Bunch met with the AAMA's Larry Martin. He came on strongly, saying that the show would force American garment producers to go overseas. He wanted the show canceled or at least El Monte removed. Larry Martin was unwilling to talk about compromise or balance. He tried to claim that El Monte was an aberration but backed off saying that there weren't any American sweatshops. Martin was very blunt, saying, "I am a man of influence, I can get fifty congressmen, I control millions of dollars."[28]

Backstage, the pressure from Smithsonian management to get at least a little industry support intensified. Without both financial support from business and their participation in the final dialogue section, the show would be canceled. Early on we had asked Bud Konheim, CEO of Nicole Miller and very visible on the antisweatshop circuit, for support. He gave us advice but no cash. We also went to the Robi Karp, chief counsel for Liz Clairborne and co-chair of the White House Apparel Partnership, but she wanted nothing to do with us. We asked Nordstrom, the retail chain known for their antisweatshop stance, but again got turned down. Finally we asked for a meeting with Jay Mazur, president of the garment worker's union UNITE!. With the Smithsonian's National Museum of American History (NMAH) director, Spencer Crew, sitting in, we pleaded our case, and Mazur said he would make it rain. He promised that he'd make a few calls and raise $50,000 beyond the union's donation of $25,000. Meanwhile, good things were happening at high levels of the federal government.

President Clinton's outspoken antisweatshop Secretary of Labor Robert Reich had stepped down in January 1997, and with his departure went our hopes for high-level help. Alexis Herman, who succeeded him, seemed less interested in the sweatshop issue. But in September 1997, Secretary Herman attended the Social Investment Forum, a coalition of about 400 "socially responsible" investment firms, where they "vowed to use their clout to pressure clothing manufacturers and retailers into taking a tougher stand against apparel industry sweatshops." In her speech Herman criticized apparel industry companies for not doing enough and being too quick to judge projects like the sweatshop show. "The Smithsonian is in the planning stages of this exhibition . . . and these groups are talking about the soup before it's actually cooked."[29] This was not the only good news.

On September 24, we received a call from a high level Department of Labor employee telling us to call Kmart for support. We explained the project to Kmart's vice-president for government affairs, and after a period of consideration they decided to become a major supporter of the exhibition, and agreed to have their CEO, Floyd Hall, become a participant in the exhibition dialogue section. Explaining, Kmart spokeswoman Michele Jasukaitis said, "We have to educate everyone because it's an issue that can't be ignored."[30]

Mazur's efforts to raise money were having an effect, and checks started coming in from industry sources that we had not contacted—Calvin Klein, Maria Rose Fashion, Mauldin Mills, A&H Sportswear, and finally industry giant Levi Straus. David Samson, the spokesman from Levi, summed it up nicely, "The exhibit provides an opportunity for people to learn where progress needs to be made and where progress has been made."[31] Robert Haas, CEO of Levi Straus, also agreed to contribute to the dialogue section filling the slot left open by Martin's departure. The controversy appeared to be over.

Less than a month before the April 1998 opening of the exhibition, with both Kmart and Levi's onboard, the NRF had a change of heart and decided to lend its support to the exhibition. Tracy Mullin, president and CEO of the NRF, explained, "Based on our early discussions, we believed they would point the finger at us and portray us as callous and unethical. Since then, we learned that the exhibit will be much more balanced. . . . It's a chance for us to begin to show the American people how difficult it is for retailers to tackle this problem."[32] But not all industry figures agreed. Right up to the opening, the AAMA held fast in their distaste for the show. In a memo to the curators and published in the exhibition, Larry Martin alleged that "By sponsoring this highly politicized exhibit, the Smithsonian Institution is engaging in a taxpayer-funded smear against the U.S. apparel industry."[33]

On April 21, 1998, Secretary of Labor Alexis Herman opened *Between a Rock and a Hard Place: A History of Sweatshops in America, 1820–Present*, at a well-attended press conference. She complimented labor, business, and activists for their work to combat sweatshops. She went on to state:

> There is a tremendous amount of momentum right now. We need to keep on building on it. I believe the best strategy is the kind that combines education, partnership and recognition. That's exactly what the exhibit does. It marks a true milestone in our effort, and brings us one step closer to realizing our goal. A goal that declares plain and simple: This is where sweatshops belong. In a museum—not in the daily newspapers—and not in the daily lives of our workers. [34]

The exhibition consisted of six sections: Introduction, History, El Monte, Fashion Food Chain, Good Industry Practices, and Dialogue. Visitors entered the exhibition through a walk-in closet. The main label juxtaposed images of a 1900s' tenement shop, the El Monte workers, with clothes that visitors might find in their own closet. The label stated our overt goal to " . . . place the current debate on sweatshops in the garment industry in a historical context and explore the complex factors that contribute to their existence today." The images expressed our other aim, to link the people of the turn-of the-century shops to those of today.

The largest portion of the exhibition was taken up with a historical examination of sweatshop production in the United States (slightly over half of the exhibition's entire 3300 square feet). Focusing on the changing character of the workforce employed in the shops, this section presented the complexity of the issue and how trends in manufacturing, retail, immigration, and reform efforts affected sweatshops production at a particular time.

While the title of the exhibition suggests a history of all sweatshops from 1820 to 1997, in fact, most of the material focused on occurrences only in the apparel industry. By limiting the scope of the exhibition, we were able to provide the depth, focus, and context that the issue demanded. In order to remind visitors that sweatshops are not limited to the apparel industry, there were exhibit cases scattered throughout the history section to illustrate sweatshop conditions in other industries.[35]

The historical overview was followed by material from El Monte. A nine-minute video consisting of interviews with the workers and law enforcement officers who handled the case presented a intimate examination of their experiences. The artifacts displayed nearby made their words all the more real. Every artifact in the El Monte section (from the spools of thread on the sewing machines to the razor wire up above) came from the notorious sweatshop. For many manufacturers and retailers of clothing (particularly from Los Angeles), any mention of El Monte was seen as a frontal assault on the industry. They thought of the case as only an aberration or as an immigration issue, not as an example of an endemic industry problem. Using the voices of the workers and government officials, the exhibition argued that at the very least El Monte represents a dereliction of industry responsibilities.

After the El Monte area were two small sections, the Fashion Food Chain and Good Industry Practices. The Fashion Food Chain section was meant to place American sweatshops into the larger and complex context of current global apparel production. A large map of the world with text blocks explained trade barriers, tariffs, and economic advantages for foreign and domestic production. A listing of the amount of clothing imported from foreign countries to the U.S. and the average wages apparel workers received was provided in a take-away flyer.

The Good Industry Practices video emphasized that there are companies who make affordable clothing without needing to use sweatshops. Representatives from both industry and labor wanted visitors to realize that there were still shops in the United States that pay their employees reasonable wages and produce affordable clothing.

As development of the show progressed, the content of this film became a major point of discussion. No matter how much we assured our business advisors that we were committed to being balanced and fair, disbelief remained. The Good Industry Practices video, created (under our supervision) by an apparel industry production company, helped many interested parties feel that business' point of view was being fairly expressed.

The exhibit concluded with the dialog section. Six individuals answered the question "What should Americans know about sweatshop production in the U.S.?" Each respondent was allowed their own exhibition area—a two hundred–word statement, a thirty-word biography and a 32″ × 32″ display area for artifacts. The six were Maria Echaveste, special assistant to President Clinton and former Director of Wage and Hour Division, Department of Labor; Jay Mazur, president, UNITE!; Robert Haas, CEO, Levi Strauss; Kathie Lee Gifford (in her role as celebrity endorser); Julie Su, attorney at the Asian Pacific American Legal Center; Floyd Hall, CEO, Kmart. Visitors were encouraged to join in the discussion by writing their comments in notebooks that were kept in the exhibition gallery for others to read. Also in this area were notebooks that included articles on the controversy of the exhibition and letters supporting and denouncing the mounting of the show. This section proved essential in helping the show open by demonstrating that business was not collectively unwilling to participate in the exhibition. The involvement of both Robert Haas and Floyd Hall was critical to counter charges leveled by the American Apparel Manufacturers Association that this was simply an "industry smear."[36]

While the exhibition opened to favorable reviews, word came down that Congressman Dan Burton, Republican from Indiana, was concerned. Through Smithsonian management, we were told that he had learned from a staffer that the exhibition might be anti-Semitic. He requested that a copy of the script be sent to him immediately. The Smithsonian managers looked for alternate solutions, fearing that Congressman Burton might distort the exhibition by selectively quoting the script—as others had done during the *Enola Gay* controversy and Burton himself had recently done with the Web Hubbell tapes.[37] The Congressman was invited down to look at the show for himself, but he claimed that his schedule would not allow it. In a brilliant parry, Dennis O'Connor, Smithsonian provost, offered to provide the entire show with objects, graphics, and script to the congressman through the Internet. By doing this, he felt everyone would have a chance to evaluate the labels in context. Within six days the exhibition was put online, and we heard no more complaints from Burton's office.[38]

The one causality of the controversy was the plan to travel the show. With a shortage of money and many potential venues being too nervous to touch such a hot potato, the prospects of a national tour dimmed. After expressing initial interest, the Smithsonian Traveling Exhibit Services (SITES) bowed out, claiming that there was no market for an exhibition that carried so much baggage.

Undaunted we pushed on—asking, imploring, pleading with our peers to host the show in their institutions. We pushed especially hard in the Los Angeles area because we thought we owed the workers imprisoned in El Monte the opportunity to see the show that put their story into a historical context. California State University, Northridge, expressed an interest, but funding shortfalls made the venue seem unlikely. Finally we gave up the search but didn't tell anyone. And much to our surprise, at the proverbial eleventh hour Marcia Choo, from the Los Angeles Museum of Tolerance, called asking for the show.

In an interview with the California Fashion News, Choo explained her motivation: "I'd like to think that this is a gift to Los Angeles. Whether you're a Jewish immigrant—or Korean or Chinese—in most immigrant communities there's someone who has worked in the garment industry as the beginning of the fulfillment of the American dream. It cuts across racial and ethnic lines and has timely references to the headlines of the day." Keenly aware of the concerns of the influential L.A. garment industry, Choo described the exhibition as balanced. "My interest was not to upset or inflame, it was really in helping to push the dialogue in another direction."[39]

Despite pressure from the local Los Angeles garment manufacturers, Marcia Choo pressed forward. Ilse Metchek, executive director of the CFA, once again denounced the show, claiming the Smithsonian "painted the picture of the local manufacturing base with a very negative brush,"[40] To alleviate the CFA's criticism, the Museum of Tolerance agreed to continually play a video, produced by the CFA, highlighting the good civic deeds of the Los Angeles apparel industry.

Triumphing over this last controversy, the exhibition opened in Los Angeles on November 15, 1999. Liebe Geft, director of the Museum of Tolerance, extolled the virtues of the show to a hometown audience, "Experiential learning and environmental exhibitions are very powerful. . . . Sometimes we have to look at the very stark and extreme examples to arouse us into a readiness to engage in debate."[41] The exhibition did not come without costs to the Museum of Tolerance, which had to carefully weigh the support it gave to the exhibition against alienating some of its wealthy supporters who had made their fortunes in the garment industry. At least one employee left as a result of this delicate balancing act.

By the time the exhibition closed in Los Angeles in April 2000, hundreds of thousands of visitors had passed through the exhibition's walk-in closet to be confronted by the lives of workers from mid-nineteenth century seamstresses to today's recent immigrants. The exhibition aimed to remind them that this problem had not disappeared, but, for most of us, is simply out of sight. The exhibition also sought to trace the history of reform efforts, which—while never eliminating sweatshops—did make significant contributions in improving the lives of many workers and their families. An important lesson that we learned from our study was that sweatshop conditions improved at times when the public became concerned over this issue. We hoped that this exhibition served to raise—through the displays, the Web site, associated public programs, publications and the debate over the show itself—a greater awareness of the conditions facing apparel workers today.

This project would not have happened without a committed partnership between the museum and various outside groups that sought to confront this difficult and complex issue. Bringing forth the Smithsonian's sweatshop exhibition demanded considerable trust and respect of the differing perspectives we brought to this project. This required the museum to open itself up and enlist outside groups to contribute in meaningful ways. It also required those— whether government agencies, labor organizations, reform activities or business groups—to understand the roles and limits of public educational institutions.

To some degree, the fears of many apparel-industry groups were warranted. While balanced in content, the existence of a show like this in a public venue created an opportunity for public discourse on an important topic. For those who wanted to sweep the sweatshop issue under the rug, the exhibition was a problem. For others looking for solutions, the exhibition was a success. The Department of Labor used the exhibition to help launch its Anti-sweatshop University program. UNITE! brought in groups of members to educate them on their history and the successes of their predecessors. In Los Angeles, antisweatshop activists stuck stickers with the exhibition's logo on clothing in local stores.

In the struggle over control of public space, it is imperative that activist organizations commit their political and financial resources to projects they see as important, even if the end product is not as partisan as they would wish. Additionally, museums have learned that producing good scholarship on challenging topics is not enough. To survive the inevitable attacks require outside support. *Between a Rock and a Hard Place* demonstrated that a partnership can result in opening up public places for debate and in keeping these precious spaces truly public.

Notes

1. *Los Angeles Times*, January 24, 2000, section B, 1, 3.
2. First amended complaint for injunctive and declaratory relief and damages for peonage and involuntary servitude; violation of the fair labor standards act and California labor code; civil rico; unfair business practices; negligence per se; negligent supervision; and related claims for relief, United States District Court, Central District of California, case no. 95-5958-ABC(BQRx), October 25, 1995, 19.
3. Philip Bonner, Jr., "Operation Robinhood," Report of Investigation, U.S. Department of Justice, Immigration and Naturalization Service, file number 0495053.TH, August 24, 1995; interview with Phil Bonner, INS agent, August 11, 1997.
4. Malinan Radomphon and Praphapan Pongid, El Monte Sweatshop, Video History, December 4–5, 1997 National Museum of American History (NMAH); Indenture agreement between Relax Centre Co. Ltd., of Bangkok and Sirilak Rongsak, Division of History of Technology (DHOT), NMAH.
5. Interviews with Bonner, June 23, 1997; Julie Su, August 11, 1997; Bonner, El Monte Sweatshop Video History, December 4, 1997, NMAH.

6. Declaration of Phitsamai, Baothong, Bureerong, et al. *v.* Uvawas, et. al, United States District Court Case No. 95–5958-ABC(BQRx), p. 1; William Branigin, "Sweatshop Instead of Paradise," *Washington Post*, September 10, 1995, section A, 1, 12.

7. Bonner, "Operation Robinhood"; Declaration of Phitsamai, Baothong, Bureerong, et al., 4.

8. Tongkun Kim, El Monte Sweatshop, Video History, December 4, 1997, NMAH; tip letter; search warrant, DHOT, NMAH.

9. The rush for credit for the raid has led to controversy over who on the enforcement side was involved, when, and why. The initial forty-nine law enforcement officials involved in the raids came from eight different agencies. For more on the controversy, see: Lloyd Aubry, Jr., Director, California Department of Industrial Relations, "Thank California, Not the Feds," *Washington Post*, September 1, 1995; Lloyd Aubry, Fr., Victoria Bradshaw, letter to Janet Reno, Attorney General of the United States.

10. Plea agreement, United States District Court for the Central District of California, United States of America, plaintiff, *v.* Suni Manasurangkun, defendant, February 2, 1996, no. CR95-714 (B)-ABC.

11. Michael Gennaco, El Monte Sweatshop, Video History, December 4, 1997, NMAH; "Seven Thais Enter Guilty Pleas for Detention in Sweatshop," *New York Times*, February 11, 1996.

12. George White, "Sweatshop Workers to Get $2 Million; Labor: Five Firms Settle with 150 Thai and Latino Employees of Notorious El Monte Apparel Facility and Its Sister Plant in L.A.," *Los Angeles Times*, October 24, 1997; "Settlement Agreement and Mutual General Release" between defendants Tomato Inc., David Golombeck and Christopher Wickes and plaintiffs Malee Bureenrong, et al. in claims against Tomato, Golombeck and Wicks in "Bureenrong, et al. *v.* Uvawas, et al.," United States District Court, No. CV 95–5958-ABC (Anx); and "Fangmak, et al. *v.* Uvawas, et al.," United States District Court, No. 96–5238-ABC (Anx), April 22, 1999.

13. *Los Angeles Times*, January 24, 2000, section B, 1, 3.

14. Letter from Anne Petersen to Jose Millan, Assistant Labor Commissioner, California Department of Labor Standards, November 20, 1995.

15. The "culture wars" came to be a term popularly applied to the debate over the direction of public history in the early to mid-1990s. Exhibitions that came under attack included the National Air and Space Museum's *The Last Act: The Atomic Bomb and the End of World War II* (or *Enola Gay*, as it came to be popularly known), the National Museum of American Art's *The West As America*, The Library of *Congress' Freud: Conflict and Culture*, and *Back of the Big House: The Cultural Landscape of the Plantation*, as well as, the heated controversy over the National History Standards. For further readings, see: Martin Harwitt, *An Exhibit Denied* (New York: Copernicus, 1996); Edward Linenthal, "Can Museums Achieve a Balance Between Memory and History?" *Chronicle of Higher Education*, February 10, 1995: B1–B2; Todd Gitlin, *The Twilight of Common Dreams: Why America Is Wracked by Culture Wars* (New York: Henry Holt & Co., 1996); Mike Wallace, "The Battle of the *Enola Gay*," *Radical Historians Newsletter* (May 1995): 1–12, 22–32; Steven Dubin, *Displays of Power: Memory and Amnesia in the American Museum* (New York: New York University Press, 1999).

16. In a discussion with Lonnie Bunch after the show opened, he stated that he believed at the beginning that we at best had a 1 in 3 chance of ever opening.

17. The exhibition's script advisors were Alice Kessler-Harris, Jane McCort, Jean Parsons, Robert Ross, Eileen Boris, Susan Smulyn, and Phil Kahn, Jr. For our examination of the contemporary industry we were fortunate to have the help of a variety of guides who led us into their world of the apparel industry, sweatshops, immigrant communities, and reform organizations. The U.S. Department of Labor; the U.S. Department of Justice, Los Angeles; California Department of Industrial Relations; INS; the Union of Neddletrades, Industrial and Textile Employees (UNITE!); Asian Pacific American Legal Center; the National Consumers League; and the National Labor Committee provided assistance and resources in helping us obtain an understanding of sweatshop production and the efforts to curb their proliferation. We also received considerable help from the industry itself. Though guarded at times, the American Apparel Manufacturers Association (AAMA), The National Retail Federation (NRF), and others (even at some of the most contentious times during the life of this project) continued to make their research departments available for information.

There has been considerable number of historical works on the subject of sweatshops. Among the studies which we relied heavily on were: Eileen Boris, *Home to Work: Mother-*

hood and the Politics of Industrial Homework in the United States (Cambridge: Cambridge University Press, 1994); Nancy Green, *Ready-to-Wear and Ready-to-Work: A Century of Industry and Immigrants in Paris and New York* (Durham: Duke University Press, 1997); Alice Kessler-Harris, *Out to Work: A History of Wage-Earning Women in the United States* (Oxford: Oxford University Press, 1982); Steven Fraser, *Labor Will Rule: Sidney Hillman and the Rise of American Labor* (New York: The Free Press, 1991); Christine Stansell, "The Origins of the Sweatshop: Women and Early Industrialization in New York City," Michael H. Frisch and Daniel J. Walkowitz, eds. *Working-Class America: Essays on Labor, Community, and American Society* (Urbana: University of Illinois Press, 1983); Joel Seidman, *The Needle Trades* (New York: Farrar & Rhinehart, Inc., 1942; and Leon Stein, ed., *Out of the Sweatshop, The Struggle for Industrial Democracy* (New York: Quadrangle/The New York Times Book Co., 1977).

18.   *Los Angeles Times*, September 11, 1997; *Washington Times*, September 27, 1997; *New York Times*, September 20, 1997; *Washington Post*, September 12, 1997.

19.   Kristin Young, "Debate over Smithsonian Exhibit Heats Up," *California Apparel News*, August 29–September 4, 1997, vol. 53, no. 38.

20.   Minutes of Special Labor Meeting: August 21, 1997, 2, DHOT, NMAH; Kristin, "Debate over Smithsonian Exhibit Heats Up."

21.   Letter from Randall Harris to Bill Benstrom, September 19, 1997, DHOT, NMAH.

22.   George White, *Los Angeles Times*, September 11, 1997, A1, A19.

23.   Marcia Stepanek, "Museum's sweatshop exhibit assailed," *San Francisco Examiner*, November 28, 1997, section A, 1, 23.

24.   Ilse Metchek, unpublished letter to the *Los Angeles Times*, September 18, 1997, DHOT, NMAH.

25.   Letter from George Miller to secretary Heyman, September 19, 1997, DHOT, NMAH.

26.   I. Michael Heyman, unpublished letter to the *Los Angeles Times*, September 11, 1997, DHOT, NMAH.

27.   Irvin Molotsky, "Furor Builds over Sweatshop Exhibition," *New York Times*, September 20, 1997, section K, 20.

28.   Notes from meeting between Lonnie Bunch and Larry Martin on October 10, 1997, as related by Lonnie Bunch, DHOT, NMAH.

29.   George White, "Investors Urge Action Against Sweatshops," *Los Angeles Times*, September 25, 1997

30.   George White, "Sweatshop Exhibit Rends Garment Industry," *Los Angeles Times*, December 4, 1997, section D, 3, 11.

31.   White, "Sweatshop Exhibit Rends Garment Industry," section D, 3, 11.

32.   George White, "Trade Group Now Supports Sweatshop Exhibit," *Los Angeles Times*, March 27, 1998, section D, 1.

33.   Memo from Larry Martin to Peter Liebhold, February 9, 1998, DHOT, NMAH.

34.   U.S. Department of Labor press release, April 21, 1998.

35.   At one point, the Smithsonian's administrators asked us to consider cutting the other industries out of the show, fearing that these cases would only increase the number of businesses who would oppose the exhibition. They decided, however, that having other examples would soften the criticism that we were singling out one industry. The cases ultimately remained in the show.

36.   For greater details about the exhibition, see: Peter Liebhold and Harry Rubenstein, "*Between a Rock and a Hard Place:* The National Museum of American History's Exhibition on Sweatshops, 1820—Present," *Labor's Heritage* (spring 1998); Peter Liebhold and Harry Rubenstein, *Between a Rock and a Hard Place: A History of American Sweatshops, 1820—Present*, UCLA Asian American Studies Center and Simon Wiesenthal Center Museum of Tolerance, 1999; and www.americanhistory.si.edu/sweatshops.

37.   George Lardner, Jr., "Democrats Hit Burton over Hubbell Tapes," *Washington Post*, May 4, 1998.

38.   www.americanhistory.si.edu/sweatshops

39.   Kristin Young, "Smithsonian Exhibit Aims for L.A. in November," *California Fashion News*, September 1999.

40.   Joanna Ramey, "Smithsonian Finds Space in L.A. to Show Exhibit on Sweatshops," *Women's Wear Daily*, August 27, 1999.

41.   K. Connie Kang, "Museum Hosts Controversial Factory Exhibit," *Los Angeles Times*, November 15, 1999, section B, 1, 3.

2
Sweatshop Migrations

4

Labor, Liberals, and Sweatshops

RICHARD A. GREENWALD
U.S. Merchant Marine Academy

Sweatshops have been with us a long time. As the essays in this volume demonstrate, the term came into existence in the late nineteenth century and remains with us today because it still resonates. Sweatshops are usually defined by conditions of labor.[1] By the late twentieth century, the term had transcended garment shops and entered into new usage, describing unsavory employment of any kind.[2] Yet the sweatshop remain intricately linked to the garment industry in the public's mind, because it remains a fundamental problem for the industry. This essay looks at the efforts garment unions made to combat sweatshops in the twentieth century. Starting with the strikes of the Progressive Era, the garment union leaders saw worker-organization as an effective means to eradicating sweatshops from the industry. Unions organized the industry, not merely its workers, from the bottom up. By the Great Depression, however, the unions placed increasing faith in the power of federal legislation and regulation. Having placed such trust in the government, they tied themselves closely to the liberal wing of the Democratic Party. Once they latched onto legislation and government action, something they saw as an effective strategy, the garment unions started enlarging the definition of the sweatshop to include runaway shops and, finally, foreign shops.

Clearly, sweatshops and the runaway or "out of town" shop were connected, as manufacturers continually sought out cheap labor and nonunion environments. Recently, scholars interested in economic shifts have given a great deal of attention and ink to the "globalization" of industry. And, in fact, the current antisweatshop movement is intimately connected to the anti-globalization movement.[3] But, as historian Jefferson Cowie has demonstrated, globalism has a history, one rooted in "capital moves," the ability of owners to move production to areas with a weak union culture and an abundance of cheap labor. And, as Cowie and Ken Wolensky's essay in this volume demonstrate, much of the movement took place within the borders of the U.S. How the unions and their reform allies dealt with this is a telling history that informs the current antisweatshop efforts. This essay argues that garment unions and their allies shifted their weapon of choice to combat the combined scourges of—capital

movement and the sweatshop from organizing workers to government legislation and regulation. In the end, garment unions relied on the powers of the
state to curb producers and protect their industry. This worked well for a time.
But ultimately this has been a failed policy. These "international" unions failed
to see the problem in either regional or global terms and thereby, in the end,
resorted to protectionist arguments, which, in an age of growing global trade,
seemed out of step with the current national agenda.[4]

A survey of journalistic coverage on sweatshops in the twentieth century
finds an abundance of material on the period up through the Great Depression. There was a keen sense at that time that the New Deal's federal labor laws,
especially the Fair Labor Standards Act (FLSA), rid the country once and for
all of the dreaded sweatshop. Reformers and the unions heralded the FLSA as
the dawn of a new day.

During World War II, however, with the nation's attention turned to war,
there was concern that the sweatshop was returning. Unions and liberals demanded tighter enforcement of federal and state regulations. They looked to the
War Labor Board, and more importantly, their man in charge, Sidney Hillman,
President of the Amalgamated Clothing Workers Union (ACW or ACWU), to
right all these wrongs.[5] After World War II, it is as if the sweatshop disappeared
from our national radar. In the 1950s and 1960s, the unions' concern shifted to
the issue of "runaway" shops and overseas production, using the same moral
language that they once reserved for sweatshops to denounce these problems.

Economist Michael Piore argues that what accounts for "the sweatshop's return" in recent years is "a more rigorous definition of the sweatshop and a better understanding of the historical forces that led to its decline in the first
place."[6] Surely that is correct, but I believe that the notion of decline and return is a trope, a progressive fallacy. It represents a misplaced faith in legislation alone to solve all labor problems. Twentieth-century liberalism was deeply
connected to and intertwined with labor.[7] Historians of New Deal liberalism
and twentieth-century labor have clearly demonstrated how as liberalism and
the "New Deal Order" fell, so did labor. Therefore, we return to pre–New
Deal–like conditions. Historian Landon Storrs has stated that " . . . reforms
initiated in the turn-of-the-century period known as the Progressive Era and
consolidated during the New Deal . . . curbed the most egregious abuses of
employees in American manufacturing for many decades. In the 1980s and
1990s, however, the weakening of the labor movement, budget cuts for regulatory agencies, and free trade policies blind to labor practices combined to permit a resurgence of the sweatshop and to spread its influences to other kinds of
workplaces." Storrs's solution to the sweatshop, it would seem, would be a return to the New Deal.[8] Part of the reason for the "return" of sweatshops, as I
argue, was the strategy used to originally combat them. Legislation without
corresponding worker organization turned unions into auxiliaries of the
Democratic Party at best, or at worst, into lobbyists for workers.[9] Frances

Perkins, the New Deal Labor Secretary, once expressed this faith in legislation alone as a solution most pointedly when she said, "I'd rather pass a law than organize a union." Perkins was not alone in expressing the belief that enlightened legislation—of the New Deal variety—would solve all the nation's economic and social woes.[10]

The sweatshop did not leave America. Nor did it simply jump the oceans and appear in recreated form on foreign soil. Instead, as recent work by sociologist Elizabeth McLean Petras and others demonstrate, U.S. garment sweatshops have disappeared and reappeared depending on the economic climate and on government attitudes.[11] As for the discourse on sweatshop, I argue, the sweatshop got wrapped up in the larger issues of capital movement (runaway shops) and the relationship between labor and the state (regulation and legislation). When one views the sweatshop only through the veil of traditional production, we miss the complexity of the story. The unions' concern with retaining jobs in unionized settings, and later within the borders of the U.S. is really a continued debate about the sweatshop. So the "rediscovery" of the sweatshop in the 1990s is more than the reemergence of the sweatshop, or more than renewed public interest in an old problem. It is instead a discourse wrapped up in the changing relationship between work and the regulated economy.

Sweatshops in the Progressive Era

Beginning in the Progressive Era, roughly 1890–1917, a discovery of "the labor problem" gripped reform-minded professionals.[12] The fear that miserable working conditions would radicalize the mass of immigrant workers, coupled with humanitarian impulses, combined with worker self-organization to bring the issue of the sweatshop to national attention.[13] The New York City ladies garment industry had, since the mid-nineteenth century, been associated with the worst of industrialization. Low wages, poor working conditions, disease, overcrowding, and the chaotic nature of fashion production rendered the sweatshop the norm. In 1909, in an effort to gain a better working environment and to rid the industry of the sweatshop, at least twenty thousand mostly female shirtwaist makers went on strike. The "Uprising of the Twenty Thousand" was more than the largest strike by women in American history.[14] It was a concerted effort by labor to bring order to chaos in the industry.

Early on in the strike, middle-class reform women became increasingly visible. Many seeing these mainly young immigrant women strikers as "sisters" in the larger women's rights struggle ran to the picket lines as a show of feminist solidarity. Others operated under an older sense of noblesse oblige, an effort to protect these fragile girl strikers. Whatever their motivation, middle-class female reformers stepped up their activity as the strike wore on, becoming a commanding presence. The focus of these reformers' activities was the New York Women's Trade Union League (WTUL). The WTUL was founded at the

American Federation of Labor's Boston Convention in 1903 by the noted socialist William English Walling, labor organizer Mary Kenny, and Hull House's
Jane Addams, along with other social worker types. The WTUL saw itself as
filling a necessary void. The leaders believed in labor unions as a democratic
necessity. But unions had ignored women workers. The WTUL would aid local
and national unions in organizing women. It quickly established branches in
Boston, Chicago, and New York. Unlike the Boston and Chicago Leagues, the
New York League received little support from organized labor. In fact, New
York's unions seemed hostile to the WTUL. Partly because of this, and partly
because of their desire to organize women workers, the New York WTUL saw
the 1909 strike as their opportunity.[15]

As the strike wore on, many of the small and medium shops settled with the
union on all of the wage and hour demands. While these settlements differed
from shop to shop, they had several main features: union recognition, shop committee arbitration for piece rates; union shop or, at least, union preferences when
hiring; and an end to charges for thread, needles, and electricity. The agreements
also instituted a system of fines against management for breaking agreements.
While these fines, the highest being $300, were small, the profit margins were so
close at many shops that even the smallest fine could close down a shop.[16]

The seventy large manufacturers, which dominated the trade, led by Triangle
and Leiserson, however, stayed firm. Rather than go it alone or attempt to negotiate with the union, the owners of Triangle—Max Blanck and Isaac Harris—circulated a letter in early November to all shirtwaist manufacturers
suggesting the formation of an Employers Mutual Protective Association
"...in order to prevent this irresponsible union in gain[ing] the upper
hand ... and] dictating to us the manner of conducting our business."[17]

In late November, members of Local 25 recognized that some of the larger
manufacturers had shifted production to Philadelphia. It appeared as if the
New York strike would be lost because of these "runaway shops." In an effort to
shore up their flanks, Local 25 began to open discussions with the Philadelphia
Shirtwaist Union, a union of some 3,500 members. By mid-December, with
the aid and prompting of Local 25, the Philadelphia waistmakers called their
own general strike. The Philadelphia strike mirrored the New York protest and
was called as a support strike for New York workers, therefore, received little
attention from the ILGWU, AFL, and WTUL. Yet, in establishing working-class
solidarity across geographic boundaries, the Philadelphia strike was an important turning point for the union. Shirtwaist workers of Philadelphia would
also walk out, reaffirming the New York strikers' faith in the union and sig-
nalling a new coordinated militancy to management. Finally, the industrial
workforce was functioning as a *unified* workforce.[18]

Yet on February 15, the ILGWU called off the New York general strike. In
reality, it had all but ended at least two weeks before, having fizzled out. Yet, the
union declared the strike a victory, and, in many ways, it was. What was gained

came from individual shop contracts with small- and medium-sized shops, not the industry-wide agreement union leaders desired. Of the 320 contracts signed, 302 recognized the union. Membership in the local went from 500 members in August to over 20,000 by February. The union had also survived to fight another day. To be sure, without an industry-wide agreement, these shop agreements were weak. However, the strikers were able, at least for now to end the most noxious features of their servitude and begin to claim their rightful place as industrial citizens.

The victory of unionization, however, was accompanied by substantial bureaucratic developments, which limited workers' ability to mount militant protest in the future. Both union leaders and company bosses had come to see that the militancy of the workers and the sheer size of the union necessitated a more formal and bureaucratic organization with which to harness their élan. Simply said, the strike brought significant structural changes to the union. The union in New York divided itself into seven districts, with two divisions per district. A new executive board was created. Because of the nature of the settlements—individual shop agreements—delegates from each district were brought onto the executive board. They were usually older, skilled male workers, recognizing the localized nexus of power within the new ILGWU brought on by the new contract systems. The impact of this agreement was to bureaucratize the union structure and remove rank-and-file workers from industrial relations. The incorporation of local leadership tied the locals to the International in new and curious ways. Most important, the International gained authority in its claim to be the sole legitimate voice of all garment workers. To retain this legitimacy it would expend much time and energy in keeping more radical workers in line. In some ways, then, the ILGWU would increasingly become a police force for regulating workers' militancy.

The cloak makers had reasons to hope for success; their numbers were indeed growing. Local 1, a cutters local, for example, had a mere 200 members in 1908 and yet by 1910, it claimed to be 2,000 strong. Similarly, the Cloak Tailors, Local 9, was saved from the brink of collapse as thousands of Jewish and Italian male tailors filled its ranks. These locals' experiences were not alone, most of the cloak makers' locals swelled. The result, as the unions recognized at the time, was great enthusiasm born for a general strike. The Uprising had convinced many garment workers that their day was near, that they could achieve industrial democracy in their lifetimes.[19]

The union blamed the sweatshop on the presence of nonunion workers and demanded that union members organize the industry. However, without a strong union to protect them, management held tremendous power. The industry was thoroughly antiunion. It was common for shops to fire union members, and some even forbid their workers from joining unions. Many shops required workers to deposit "security," or took regular deductions from their pay. This security would be lost if workers joined unions. This technique keeps the unions out and insured shop owners that workers would stay on the jobs through the busy seasons. Most employers circulated a "blacklist" of union activists. Almost all regularly closed their shops—locking out work-ers—long enough to get rid of all the union members, and then reopened with nonunion workers.[20]

The Cloakmakers Strike of 1910, which quickly followed on the heels of the Uprising, was to use Samuel Gompers apt phrase, "more than a strike [, it was] . . . an industrial revolution" because it created a new system of industrial relations (IR).[21] "The signing of the Protocol," the contract that ended the strike, as historian Louis Levine has noted, ". . . ushered in a new period of constructive experimentation in collective bargaining. . . ."[22] Benjamin Stoll-berg, another earlier historian of the union, believed that "the Protocol of Peace marked a decisive turning point [in part because] . . . its basic idea was later copied by the other needle trades. . . . And in time its influence spread throughout American industry."[23] More recently, Gus Tyler, a retired union of-ficial, asserted that the Protocol "was the beginning of a process that started in the cloak industry . . . and that has continued in America into the closing years [of our century]."[24] In this way, the Protocol has been viewed as *the* watershed event in collective bargaining during the Progressive Era.[25]

Its creators also heralded its significance. As Louis Brandeis, father of the Protocol stated at the time, "it may prove to be a new epic [in labor relations in keeping] . . . with American Spirit and traditions as well as with justice. . . ."[26] And they were all right. The Protocol ushered in a new model of labor rela-tions. The 1910 strike was in many ways the natural result of the 1909 strike. The women shirtwaist makers revitalized the union and brought a host of new allies to the table. What started out as a materialistic relationship between women workers and women reformers became a paternalistic one for the mostly male cloak makers striking in 1910.

To be sure, the Protocol did go beyond hours and wages to the heart of the problems facing industrial America. The settlement rationalized and stabilized an industry known for just the opposite. By standardizing wages, hours, and working conditions, it took away the ability of the smaller manufacturers to undercut the larger ones. In this way, the Protocol created a new labor-man-agement accord. "It introduced the notion," as Benjamin Stolberg observed in 1944, "that labor had a stake in efficient management, continuous prosperity and social responsibility. The Protocol," Stolberg continues, "assumed a benev-olent partnership between capital and labor, a sort of joint industrial syndicate of boss and worker."[27] In essence, the Protocol introduced "regulatory union-ism" to a larger America. This new form, really an added function to industrial unionism, as David Brody has previously noted, was finally accepted by man-agement because it had an added benefit in that it could achieve what the man-ufacturers were unable to by themselves: industrial stability, efficiency and enhanced profitability.[28] Manufacturers agreed to seemingly large gains for previously underpaid workers (hours, wages, improved working conditions and other new benefits) because they gained in productivity. A rationalized industry with efficient production and distribution systems, without periodic work stoppages was simply more profitable than what had gone before. A rationalized industry—with standards of production, wages, and other costs— undercut the smaller manufacturer. These small shops, often referred to as "moths of Division Street," lost the flexibility that made them so competitive. Moreover, the enforcement agency would not be market forces—that never worked—or the industry organization (which, too, was ineffective) but rather, it would be the union itself. Simply by enforcing the Protocol, the ILGWU transformed the industry and increased corporate profits. In fact, larger manufacturers were willing to share a limited portion of these new profits with workers, who received more because they produced more.[29] Jesse Thomas Carpenter, a scholar of industrial relations, has noted how the Protocol rationalized the industry in a short time:

> Since 1910, collective bargaining in the needle trades has been the medium through which the substantial "legitimate" manufacturers, organized into employers associations, have joined hands with their more "reputable" plant workers, organized into labor unions, for the purpose of protecting their mutual interest . . .[30]

The New Deal Sweatshop

After fighting sweatshops for nearly a generation, reformers and unionists alike were horrified when sweatshops seemed to rebound during the Great Depression. Previously, they had been convinced that the sweatshop could be kept at bay through strong unions coupled with state codes. Now, they were not so sure. Reformers close to the National Consumers' League (NCL) spearheaded efforts for national labor standards, building on the experience of state legislation. Efforts to curb the sweatshop during the New Deal, therefore, focused almost solely on the creation of national labor codes, clearly expressed in the passage of the Fair Labor Standards Act.

American reformers had been fighting since the Progressive Era for national labor standards, minimum wage, and maximum hour legislation among other key reforms. Therefore, when the FLSA—a national labor standards code—was passed in 1938, it was seen as nothing short of revolutionary. Reformers saw it as the solution to a host of industrial ills. No one welcomed the FLSA more than the garment unions and their antisweatshop allies who saw it as a device to curb both sweatshops and homework.[31]

The FLSA, when studied at all, is rightly seen as having important gendered implications. Political scientist Suzanne Mettler has argued that, while purporting to be a gender-neutral law, many women found themselves not covered because of the types of jobs they held in domestic service, agriculture, or the service economy. Yet, for women in the garment industry, the FLSA applied. As Mettler states, there was an attitude among New Dealers that saw "trade union participation for men, and struggles for legal protection for women" as the legacy of Progressive Era garment industrial relations.

The New Deal was the most comprehensive attempt to install a national labor code in U.S. history.[32] The National Labor Relations Act of 1933 (NCRA) and the resulting industry-wide codes, albeit imperfect, provided for minimum wage and maximum hour regulations created by tripartite boards—industry, state and labor.[33] While not necessarily always in the workers' favor, the codes did provide a base through which unions could develop. For reformers, who placed more faith in legislative rather than organizational strategies, the NLRA was the solution for all of labor's ills. In addition, because it required administration, it provided reformers with the means to not only influence, but also to direct code administration.[34]

While the FLSA left out many industries (retail, service, and agriculture to name a few), it did cover the garment trades. Through their relationship with Frances Perkins, whose office was drafting the bill, the garment unions ensured that the law would confront the sweatshop. Steven Fraser, biographer of Sidney Hillman, suggests that this personal and political relationship was central to the inclusion of the garment industry and their chief concern, sweatshops. Because of this close relationship between the New Deal and the garment unions, both the ILGWU and the ACWU enthusiastically supported the new law.[35]

The story of the bill's passage is telling because it highlights the antisweatshop roots of the FLSA. According to historian Landon Storrs, Secretary of Labor Frances Perkins asked a key New Deal lawyer, Ben Cohen, to draft a minimum wage bill. Cohen was active in the NCL, which had advocated an antisweatshop stance since its founding during the Progressive Era. Cohen, in fact, had introduced a similar bill for the NCL in 1933. In May of 1937, it was reintroduced as the Black-Connery Bill.[36] The garment unions and the NCL led the push for this bill. By then the unions joined the embrace for legislation. "We supported every kind of bill that was turned out," said the ACWU ". . . on the theory that an unsatisfactory law is better than no legislative protection."[37] Labor's Nonpartisan League, the joint venture of the ILGWU and ACWU, led the labor effort for the bill's passage through Congress. The ILGWU and ACWU used political muscle (their ability to get out the vote in key industrial states) and their connections to key administration officials to influence policy.[38]

It is clear that for the garment unions, the FLSA was part of a larger drive to hold their industry from moving to regions—particularly the South—of cheap labor. "New Dealers, such as Frances Perkins, Tom Cocoran and Sidney Hillman," writes Storrs "had come to share the NCL view that the South was blocking national progress."[39] Reformers and union leaders, therefore, saw the "runaway" shop through the moral lens of the sweatshop. "The advent of the runaway shop," wrote the *Monthly Labor Review* in 1933, "had come to be recognized as a serious evil, embodying the old-time abuses of the sweatshop."[40] In addition, it seemed that New Dealers and their garment union allies lost faith in organizing; or rather they found new faith in legislation. Elinore Herrick, a NCL activist and New York Regional Director of the NLRB stated that "trade unions . . . are just as important as minimum wage laws in the development of our industrial civilization." One can not help but ask if this faith in government regulation, and what Christopher Tomlins has called the "liberal bureaucratic-administrative state," was because of the influence of and the unions' dependence on these reformers?[41] The debates around the sweatshop during the later New Deal and World War II focused on enforcement of federal and state laws. They showed the garment unions increasing use of their political clout to push for stronger regulation. This strategy seemed to work as long as friends of labor were in power. But, when the political ground of liberalism shifted under their feet, the garment unions were left without a comprehensive policy to counter the runaway shop.

Sweatshop Migrations, Invisibility Blues, and the Runaway Shop

While the sweatshop did not disappear in the years after the Second World War, the danger seemed to wane. Over and over again, one can find references that relegated sweatshops to the historic past.[42] To many, the sweatshop became embodied within the battle over homework. When homework was outlawed in the women's apparel industry on December 1, 1942, through the FLSA's Administrator of Wage and Hour Division, the ILGWU announced the death of the sweatshop.[43] In 1944, Sidney Hillman echoed these sentiments. "Many things have happened since that time [the founding of the union]," said Hillman. "Yes, even our people in the *former* sweatshop industries forget what things were like just a little over a decade ago. They take things for granted like the Fair Labor Standards Act."[44]

Sweatshops clearly did not disappear. Nor did the term sweatshop drop from usage. Instead, the sweatshop, too useful as a metaphor for the garment unions and their reforming partners to abandon, was used to describe "runaway" shops, the biggest problem by far that the garment unions faced in the postwar years. In 1954, the ACWU declared that ". . . in many parts of the country today—in the South, in the Southwest, throughout the West and other parts— . . . I say that sweatshops are existing . . . there is no security in these sweatshops of 1954."[45] The unions connected the struggles over capital flight, cheap regional labor, and "right to work laws" through references to the sweatshop.[46]

The unions had been fairly successful in securing better wages and working conditions for the bulk of the garment workers in key areas, particularly New York and Chicago. By the 1950s, however, manufacturers started moving production to regions where the union did not have a strong presence, namely the South. The union's strategy aimed at organizing these regional workers, if only to protect the centers of production.[47] But, it put greater faith in efforts to expand government regulation. The ILGWU repeatedly called on Congress to stop the capital flight.[48]

By 1960, the threat to garment unions was no longer regional; it was international and global. "The competitive advantage of imported apparel is based primarily on the exploitation of sweatshop labor," said the ACWU in 1960:

> The men's and boy's apparel industry was historically a sweatshop industry in this country. Our union was born out of rebellion against the misery and degradation of the sweatshop. The courage and self-sacrifice of our members in the early struggle against sweatshop conditions laid the foundation for the labor and welfare standards which workers in the men's and boy's apparel industry enjoy today. Those standards, in fact, the continued existence of the industry and the jobs of hundreds of thousands of workers, are now in grave jeopardy as a result of the rising tide of apparel imports. we must not permit the evils which we fought against at home destroy us from abroad.[49]

"Let us not make a distinction between sweatshop products," stated the ACWU, "whether they come from the South or from Japan or Hong Kong."[50]

Yet, by the 1970s, garments were increasingly manufactured (or "assembled") overseas. In fact, this trend began decades earlier, as scholar Ellen Israel Rosen makes clear. In the 1950s, during the height of the Cold War, the U.S. began to rethink its long-held protectionist policies. Free trade was the perfect foil to communism, making trade part of foreign aid. Anticommunism united "trade liberalization" with calls for free trade. The garment unions' response was to call for protectionism, which relied on their political clout in Congress to protect their members' jobs. But, by the 1980s, foreign policy (anticommunism) and calls for the free market encouraged increasing importation of garments into the U.S. And labor's friends in Washington were few and far between. In 1983, the Reagan administration created the Caribbean Basin Initiative, which accelerated garment production and assembly in that region. The result was a shift in the industry and a decline for the union. "As the 1980s wore on," writes Rosen, "segments of the apparel and textile industries aligned themselves with apparel retailers to press for a faster increase in imports of textiles and apparel made in low-wage countries." In the go-go economy of the 1990s, few cared about the loss of unionized garment industry jobs.[51]

Conclusion

The sweatshop was tied to the liberal-regulatory state. And the garment unions depended upon the maintenance of that state to keep sweatshops at bay. Cold War political aims combined with the economic advantages of globalism by the 1970s created a great shift in the nation's political economy.[52] This economic and political shift marked the end of liberalism and the New Deal national industrial paradigm.[53] The end of the liberal-regulatory state—a state that the garment unions had come to depend on to offer some control over sweatshop migration—simply left garment unions and their allies without the necessary tools to combat sweatshops or save their jobs. In the years since the 1980s, sweatshops have returned to public attention. UNITE!, the combination of the ILGWU and ACWU, has mobilized with a renewed consumer activist movement to combat sweatshops. But, as history suggests, the key may be to tap into the power of worker organization both here and abroad.

Notes

1. The literature on sweatshops is vast and growing, as this volume attests. For a contemporary start outside of these essays, see Andrew Ross's collection, *No Sweat Fashion, Free Trade, and the Rights of Garment Workers* (New York: Verso, 1997). Also see Laura Hapke, "A Shop Is Not a Home: Nineteenth-Century American Sweatshop Discourse," *American Nineteenth Century History* 2 (Autumn, 2001), 47–66.

2. On sweatshops beyond the garment industry, see Jill Andresky Fraser, *White-Collar Sweatshop* (New York/London: Norton, 2001). Also see Nata Green, "Bike Messengers Call for Crackdown on Sweatshop Courier Companies," *Labor Notes* #286 (January 2003), 6.

3. On this, see Liza Featherstone and United Students Against Sweatshops, *Students Against Sweatshops* (London/New York: Verso, 2002) as well as Featherstone's and Andrew Ross's essays in this volume. Also see Eileen Boris, *Home to Work: Motherhood and the Politics of Industrial Homework in the United States* (Cambridge: Cambridge University Press, 1994).

4. Jefferson R. Cowie, *Capital Moves: RCA's Seventy-Year Quest for Cheap Labor* (Ithaca, N.Y.: Cornell University Press, 1999). On labor internationalism, see Victor Silverman, *Imagining Internationalism in American and British Labor, 1939–49,* (Urbana: University of Illinois Press, 2000).

5. Landon R.Y. Storrs, *Civilizing Capitalism: The National Consumers' League, Women's Activism, and Labor Standards in the New Deal Era* (Chapel Hill: University of North Carolina Press, 2000).

6. Michael Piore, "The Economics of the Sweatshop," in *No Sweat: Fashion, Free Trade, and the Rights of Garment Workers*, Andrew Ross, Ed. (New York: Verso, 1997), 135.

7. On the "lib-lab" connection, see Nelson. Lichtenstein, *The Most Dangerous Man in Detroit Walter Reuther and the Fate of American Labor* (New York: Basic Books, 1995) for the labor side and Michael Wreszin, *A Rebel in Defense of Tradition the Life and Politics of Dwight Macdonald* (New York: Basic Books, 1994) for the liberal-intellectual side.

8. Recently, there has been quite a lot of discussion among progressives for a revival of something like the New Deal. Some of this has been sparked by CUNY historians Josh Freeman and Mike Wallace. See Joshua Benjamin Freeman, *Working-Class New York Life and Labor Since World War II* (New York: The New Press, 2000) and Mike Wallace, *A New Deal for New York* (New York: Bell & Weiland Publishers, 2002).

9. See Mike Davis, *Prisoners of the American Dream Politics and Economy in the History of the U.S. Working Class* (London: Verso, 1986) and Michael Sprinker and Mike Davis, *Reshaping the U.S. Left: Popular Struggles in the 1980s, Year Left* (London/New York: Verso, 1988).

10. Landon R. Y. Storrs, *Civilizing Capitalism: The National Consumers' League, Women's Activism, and Labor Standards in the New Deal Era* (Chapel Hill: University of North Carolina Press, 2000), 1; Also see Gary Gerstle and Steve Fraser, eds. *The Rise and Fall of the New Deal Order, 1930–1980* (Princeton, N.J.: Princeton University Press, 1989), *Frances Perkins' Reminiscences, 1951–55*, Book I, 58. Columbia University Oral History Project.

11. Elizabeth McLean Petras, "The Shirt Off Your Back: Immigrant Workers and the Reorganization of the Garment Industry," *Social Justice* 19 (January 1992), 76–114.

12. Here I am in agreement on periodization for the Progressive Era with Martine Sklar. Sklar traces the beginnings of Progressivism to the economic crisis and economic restructuring

that began in 1890. See Martin J. Sklar, *The Corporate Reconstruction of American Capitalism, 1890–1916: The Market, the Law, and Politics* (Cambridge [Cambridgeshire] and New York: Cambridge University Press, 1988). See also Steve Fraser's essay of the same name in Gerstle and Fraser, op. cit. In addition, see my own *Law and Order in Industry: the Protocols of Peace, the Triangle Fire and the Making of Modern Labor Relations in Progressive Era New York* (Philadelphia: Temple University Press, forthcoming).

13. On workers' self-organization, see Staughton Lynd, Ed., *"We Are All Leaders": The Alternative Unionism of the Early 1930s* (Urbana: University of Illinois Press, 1996). On the fear of sweatshops, see Daniel E. Bender, *Sweated Work, Weak Bodies: Antisweatshop Campaigns and Languages of Labor* (New Brunswick: Rutgers University Press, 2003).

14. Meredith Tax, *The Rising of the Women: Feminist Solidarity and Class Conflict, 1880–1917* (New York: Monthly Review Press, 1980); Alice Kessler-Harris, "Organizing the Unorganizable: Three Jewish Women and Their Union," in *Class, Sex, and the Women Worker*, edited by Milton Cantor and Bruce Laurie (Westport: Greenwood Press, 1977), 144–65; Alice Kessler-Harris, *Out to Work: A History of Wage-Earning Women in the United States* (New York: Oxford University Press, 1982); Joan M. and Sue Davidson Jensen, eds., *A Needle, a Bobbin, a Strike: Women Needleworkers in America* (Philadelphia: Temple University Press, 1984).

15. The literature on the WTUL is vast. See Allen F. Davis, "The Women's Trade Union League: Origins and Organization," *Labor History* 5 (Winter 1964), 3–17; Susan Estabrook Kennedy, *If All We Did Was Weep at Home: A History of White Working-Class Women in America* (Bloomington: Indiana University Press, 1979); Diane Kirby, "'The Wage-earning Woman and the State': The National Women's Trade Union League and Protective Labor Legislation, 1903–1923," *Labor History* 28 (Winter 1987), 54–74; Robin Miller Jacoby, "The Women's Trade Union League and American Feminism," *Feminist Studies* 3 (12/1975), 126–40; Nancy Schrom Dye, "Feminism or Unionism? The New York Women's Trade Union League and the Labor Movement," *Feminist Studies* 3 (12/1975), 111–25; Nancy Schrom Dye, "Creating a Feminist Alliance: Sisterhood and Class Conflict in the New York Women's Trade Union League, 1903–1914," in *Class, Sex, and the Women Worker*, 225–46; Nancy Schrom Dye, *As Equals and as Sisters: Feminism, the Labor Movement, and the Women's Trade Union League of New York* (Columbia: University of Missouri Press, 1980); Elizabeth Anne Payne, *Reform, Labor, and Feminism: Margaret Dreier Robins and the Women's Trade Union League* (Urbana: University of Illinois Press, 1988); Elizabeth Israels Perry, "Women's Political Choices After Suffrage: The Women's City Club of New York, 1915–1990," *New York History* 62, (October 1990), 417–34; and Alice Kessler-Harris, *Out to Work: A History of Wage-Earning Women in the United States* (New York: Oxford University Press, 1982).

16. Charles S. Bernheimer, *The Shirtwaist Strike: An Investigation Made for the Council and Head Worker of the University Settlement* (New York: University Settlement Studies, 1910), 3–5 for model settlement. Also see William Mailly, "The Working Girl Strike," *The Independent*, LXVII, December 23, 1909, 1419.

17. The letter found its way to the *Jewish Daily Forward* who published it. See *The Jewish Daily Forward*, November 4, 1909, 8. See also *New York Herald*, November 6, 1909, 4.

18. For Philadelphia and out-of-town production, see *New York Times*, December 10, 1909, 13; *Jewish Daily Forward*, November 27, 1909, 8; *Call*, December 12, 1909; "The Philadelphia Shirtwaist Strike," *The Survey* 13, February 5, 1910, 595–6.

19. See "Report of Local 1," in *Proceedings of the Tenth Convention of the International Ladies Garment Workers Union* (Boston, ILGWU, 1910), 51–2; and "Report of Local 9," Ibid., 56–7, for examples of this thinking.

20. Joel Seidman, *The Needle Trades* (New York: Farrar and Rinehart, 1942) 133.

21. Ibid.

22. Louis Levine, *The Women's Garment Workers: A History of the International Ladies' Garment Workers' Union* (New York: B.W. Huebsch, 1924), 196.

23. Benjamin Stolberg, *Tailor's Progress: The Story of a Famous Union and the Men Who Made It* (Garden City: Double Day, 1944), 68.

24. Gus Tyler, *Look for the Union Label: A History of the International Ladies' Garment Workers' Union* (Armonk, NY: M.E.Sharpe, 1995), 73.

25. On this, see Bruce E. Kaufman, *The Origins and Evolution of the Field of Industrial Relations in the United States* (Ithaca: ILR Press, 1993).

26. Louis D. Brandeis to Lawrence Fraser Abbott, September 6, 1919, in *The Letters of Louis D. Brandeis: Volume II, 1907–1912: People's Attorney*, Melvin I. Urofsky and David W. Levy, Eds. (Albany: SUNY Press, 1972), 371–72.

27. Stolberg, *Tailor's Progress*, 68.

28. Colin Gordon has astutely argued for just this conception of unions in the political economy of the New Deal years. See Gordon, *New Deals: Business, Labor, and Politics in America, 1920–1935* (Cambridge: Cambridge University Press, 1994). Especially chapter 3 "Workers Organizing Capitalists: Regulatory Unionism in American Industry, 1920–1932," 87–127. And see my review of Gordon (along with three other labor historians), "Present at the Creation: Labor and the New Deal State," *Journal of Policy History* (forthcoming).

29. See David Brody, *Steel Workers in America: The Nonunion Era* (Cambridge: Harvard University, 1960) for an earlier assessment of "regulatory unionism."

30. Jesse Thomas Carpenter, *Competition and Collective Bargaining in the Needle Trades, 1910–1967* (Ithaca: ILR Press, 1972), xix.

31. Clearly, as Eileen Boris demonstrates, the FLSA did not end homework or eradicate the sweatshop. But it went further than any other piece of federal legislation. See Boris, *Home to Work: Motherhood and the Politics of Industrial Homework in the United States* (Cambridge: Cambridge University Press, 1994).

32. Joseph A. McCartin, *Labor's Great War: The Struggle for Industrial Democracy and the Origins of Modern Labor Relations, 1912–1921* (Chapel Hill: University of University of North Carolina, 1998) and Joseph A. McCartin, "Abortive Reconstruction: Federal War Labor Policies, Union Organization, and the Politics of Race, 1917–1920," *Journal of Policy History* 9 (2,1997), 155–83.

33. Irving Bernstein, *Turbulent Years: A History of the American Worker, 1933–1941.* (Boston: Houghton Mifflin, 1970). Also see Lizabeth Cohen, *Making a New Deal: Industrial Workers in Chicago, 1919–1939* (New York: Cambridge University Press, 1990) and Colin Gordon, *New Deals: Business, Labor, and Politics in America, 1920–1935* (New York: Cambridge University Press, 1994).

34. On this larger point, see Clarence E. Wunderlin, *Visions of a New Industrial Order: Social Science and Labor Theory in America's Progressive Era* (New York: Columbia University Press, 1992).

35. Steve Fraser, *Labor Will Rule: Sidney Hillman and the Rise of American Labor* (New York: Free Press; Toronto: Maxwell Macmillan Canada;, 1991), 391 This is a theme that I deal with in my forthcoming book, Greenwald, *Law and Order in Industry.*

36. Storrs, op. cit., 183. On the NCL, see Kathryn Kish Sklar, *Florence Kelley and the Nation's Work: The Rise of Women's Political Culture, 1830–1900* (New Haven: Yale University Press, 1995)

37. ACWU, *Report and Proceedings*, 12th Biennial Convention, 71.

38. Storrs, op. cit., 183–86.

39. Ibid, 186.

40. "Industrial and Labor Conditions," *Monthly Labor Review* 36 (March 1933), 501.

41. Storrs, op. cit., 211. See also Christopher L. Tomlins, *The State and the Unions: Labor Relations, Law, and the Organized Labor Movement in America, 1880–1960* (Cambridge: Cambridge University Press, 1985), 102.

42. The ACWU stated: "In the past twenty five years we have banished the sweatshop." ACWU, "To the Delegates to the Thirteen Biennial Convention of the A.C.W. of A," 9. Also see Leon Stein's 1977 collection: Leon Stein, *Out of the Sweatshop the Struggle for Industrial Democracy* (New York: Quadrangle/New York Times Book Co., 1977).

43. ILGWU, 25th Convention, 1944, 25.

44. ACWU, *1944 Convention*, 19.

45. ACWU, *Convention* (Atlantic City) 1954: 402.

46. The ILGWU equated this much, ". . . the right to work they are trying to get is for low, sweatshop wages . . . ." ILGWU, *30th Convention* (Miami Beach, 1959): 145.

47. ILGWU, *27th Convention*, 1957, 590.

48. See the resolutions of the ILGWU in 1956 for example: ILGWU, *29th Convention* (Atlantic City, 1956): 14, 576–570.

49. ACWU, *22nd Convention*, 1960, 279.

50. Ibid, 283.

51. Ellen Israel Rosen, *Making Sweatshops: The Globalization of the U.S. Apparel Industry* (Berkeley, Calif.: University of California Press, 2002). Rosen's book traces not only trade policy, but also the garment union's inability to counter changes in the industry.

52. Bennett Harrison and Barry Bluestone, *The Great U-Turn Corporate Restructuring and the Polarizing of America* (New York: Basic Books, 1988); Kim Moody, *Workers in a Lean World Unions in the International Economy* (London New York: Verso, 1997); and Kim Moody, *An Injury to All: The Decline of American Unionism*, Haymarket Series (London New York: Verso, 1988).

53. On the Caribbean Initiative, see Rosen, *Making Sweatshops*. On the Post-War liberalism, see Alan Brinkley, *The End of Reform New Deal Liberalism in Recession and War* (New York: Alfred A. Knopf, 1995).

5

"An Industry on Wheels"[1]

The Migration of Pennsylvania's Garment Factories

KENNETH C. WOLENSKY
Pennsylvania Historical and Museum Commission

If American industrial history were summarized in a single text, Pennsylvania's industrial heritage would certainly occupy several pages in each chapter. Steel, coal, lumber, oil, railroads, textiles, and manufacturers of many sorts played prominent roles in the Keystone State's past. So, too, did apparel making. From the Great Depression through the 1960s, the making of clothing in factories, mostly by women, was an important part of the Commonwealth's industrial capacity. When the garment industry peaked in 1969, nearly 200,000 Pennsylvanians earned their living cutting fabric, sewing, pressing, and filling orders in factories that ranged from twelve employees to two thousand or more.

This study, based in part on oral interviews, especially with workers and activists, reviews the history and contemporary state of affairs in the women's apparel industry in a large and populous area of Pennsylvania. It provides a brief history of factory-based apparel making in the United States, the rise of the International Ladies' Garment Workers' Union (ILGWU), and, by the 1930s and 1940s, the emergence of "runaway" garment factories in the northeastern quadrant of the Keystone State whose economy had been solely tied to anthracite coal mining.

Outside of Manhattan's garment district, Northeastern Pennsylvania was a leading locale for the manufacture of women's clothing, as it became the destination for manufacturers fleeing the high costs of production in New York City. Yet the ILGWU did not shun this runaway industry or its workers, desperate for jobs after the decline of the region's coal mining industry. On the contrary, the union's Wyoming Valley District boasted the second largest and most active membership of any ILGWU local in Pennsylvania and the union grew to be an integral part of the community. The oral histories of workers and unionists—rank-and-file and leadership—suggest that they came to believe that the migrations of the industry had ended. Assuming that the industry in Pennsylvania was permanent, they sought to build a strong union community on the foundations of collective bargaining agreements and political ties with the Democratic Party.

Yet the union would come to find that the growth of the runaway industry in Pennsylvania represented just one stop in a larger pattern of sweatshop migrations. By the late 1990s, epitomized by the departure of long-time Pennsylvania manufacturer Leslie Fay, Inc. to Guatemala, the apparel industry in Pennsylvania was in decline. The Keystone State's experience with the garment industry reveals the larger pattern of the movement of capital, and the efforts of labor to respond. In building a union community, workers and ILGWU sought to solve the runaway problem.

An Industry, a Union, and "Runaway" Garment Factories

As the end of the nineteenth-century drew near, New York City had become the prime locale for the American garment industry.[2] Cloaks, suits, dresses, shirtwaists, undergarments, and numerous other items were produced in shops that ranged in size from a few employees to a hundred or more. Early in the twentieth-century, New York garment workers went on strike on several occasions to secure higher wages, shorter hours, union recognition, and an end to contracting. The ILGWU led efforts to restrict contracting and to ensure that wages paid in contractors' shops were the same as those paid to workers in inside shops. Despite the fact that, by the end of World War I the ILGWU had a relatively large membership of 100,000, the union's stability continued to be threatened, in part, by the growth of contracting. A new trend had emerged where contractors set up factories outside the New York metropolitan area. At its 1922 convention, union delegates voted to levy a four-dollar per-capita tax on members to form the Eastern Out-of-Town Department, charged with organizing "runaway" factories that had sprouted in areas removed from Manhattan and its environs. A union survey, conducted prior to the convention, estimated that 270 shops employed 17,000 workers in fifty small towns and villages in New York, New Jersey, Connecticut, and Pennsylvania. By the mid-1920s the Eastern Out-of-Town Department organized 2,500 workers into 29 locals. For the most part, however, Pennsylvania contractors remained unorganized.[3]

By the time David Dubinsky assumed the presidency of the ILGWU in 1932, contracting had grown to be a major problem. As the nation's economy stalled, competition among garment manufacturers—sometimes referred to as "jobbers"—placed tremendous pressure on contractors who were played against one another for even the smallest margins. Contractors responded by ignoring union agreements, paying substandard wages, breaking the union altogether, and seeking the cheapest labor possible by running away to remote areas. The ILGWU described the problem at its 1932 convention:

> The "out-of-town problem" is not a separate problem by itself but is closely tied up with the situation in New York. The number of shops in the suburban terri-

tory grows when it becomes profitable for the New York cloak and dress jobbers to encourage their contractors to move their shops or open shops out-of-town. There are, according to figures obtained by us, not less than 150 dress shops located within a radius of 60 miles from New York employing several thousand workers at unbelievably low wages.[4]

It was relatively easy to establish a runaway factory since apparel manufacturing has traditionally required very little capital investment. The essentials of such a business have historically consisted of sewing machines, a location, workers, and a contract. Labor has remained the largest proportion of ongoing capital outlay. To secure work, contractors engaged in fierce bidding wars where employee wages were a key factor as costs for other capital outlays—such as rent and equipment—remained relatively constant.

As the contracting system expanded in the early twentieth century, an order for women's dresses, for example, often meant that the design and pattern might be "cut" in Manhattan, sent to a contractor in New Jersey or Pennsylvania for assembly, then shipped back to Manhattan for retailing. The exodus of contractors to distant areas was well known to those who followed industry trends. According to Frances Perkins, Labor Secretary to President Franklin D. Roosevelt:

> Since he [manufacturer] cannot hope to meet union conditions or the requirements of labor law, he goes to some outlying suburb where garment factories are not a feature of the local picture and where state inspectors are not on the lookout for him. Or perhaps he goes to a nearby state—New Jersey, Connecticut, Pennsylvania, Massachusetts. The goods he makes up are probably cut in a city shop and "bootlegged" to him by truck. His work force is made up of daughters and wives of local wage earners who have been out of work for months or even years and whose family situation is desperate. The boss sets the wage rates, figures the pay slips, determines the hours of work. His reply to complaints is, "Quit if you don't like it." In the *runaway* shop conditions are usually far below standard and the picture of such a plant is a look back to the sweatshops at the turn of the century.[5]

Garment contractors in Pennsylvania attracted public attention in the 1920s when reform-minded Governor Gifford Pinchot tightened state regulation of what he deemed to be nothing less than "sweatshops" that comprised "the outstanding evil of industrial life of this State."[6] He created a Bureau of Women and Children in the state Department of Labor and Industry to study working conditions and develop legislative remedies. During the Great Depression, the agency surveyed 10,000 workers in runaway factories in Allentown, Doylestown, and Shamokin and discovered that . . .

> pittance wages predominated. For a full week's work more than seventy-five percent received less than $5; nearly one-half earned less than $3 and more than twenty per cent received less than $2. The median average weekly earnings of $3.31 for 14 and 15 years old children in the clothing industry in 1932

was a decrease of sixty per cent from the $8.38 median for the same age group in the same industry in 1926. By 1933 the median had declined farther to $2.76. [7]

Early in David Dubinsky's tenure as ILGWU president, the union knew that more shops of the type found in the Department Labor and Industry's study were sprouting in an area of the Commonwealth that had been long-dependent on the extraction of coal for its existence and survival.

Pennsylvania's Anthracite Region and the Growth of the "Runaways"

Of the three main types of coal—anthracite, bituminous, and lignite—anthracite is the cleanest burning as its content is almost pure carbon. From the mid-nineteenth to the early twentieth centuries anthracite was *the* fuel of choice for tens of thousands of homes, businesses, and railroads throughout the northeastern United States. Another factor distinguishing anthracite, or "hard coal," from bituminous and lignite was that its only deposits in the United States are in a 500-square-mile area of Northeastern Pennsylvania that extends across several counties and comprises an area about the size of Manhattan Island. The area became known as the "anthracite region."

At its peak during World War I, the anthracite coal industry—dominated by a few large absentee-owned corporations—employed over 160,000 workers. In 1917 a record 100 million tons were mined. However, by the 1920s, the industry entered a period of long-term decline from which it would never recover. Decades of conflict between coal operators and the United Mine Workers of America, competition from alternative fuels, inadequate investments by coal companies, and corporate and union corruption perpetuated the decline. By the Great Depression the industry was in deep trouble. As the 1950s drew to a close, anthracite was dealt a fatal blow when the Susquehanna River flooded and destroyed the River Slope Mine of Knox Coal Company in Port Griffith near Wilkes-Barre.[8] With mining in decline, the northern portions of the anthracite coalfield around the cities of Wilkes-Barre and Scranton—with its tens of thousands of people in desperate need of work—became a prime locale for "runaway" garment factories.

The decline of region's single-industry economy left many families struggling to survive. Faced with few alternatives, they turned to public assistance, permanent out-migration, commuting to neighboring states or cities (mainly by fathers and sons), and employment by mothers and daughters in garment factories. An urbanized area known as the Wyoming Valley, with the city of Wilkes-Barre at its center, grew to become a key location for the production of clothing for women and children, virtually all of the work contracted by New York garment manufacturers.

Longtime Wyoming Valley garment-factory owner William Cherkes explained the growth of the area's runaways:

What happened in the thirties and forties, a lot of people [owners] decided that they could do better outside of New York City by not being controlled [by the union]. So they migrated to Connecticut, Pennsylvania, and Massachusetts to open their plants without interference from the ILGWU. And by coming here where there was no unions, or no local branches, you could work independently.[9]

The Wyoming Valley was one of several areas in the anthracite region that attracted garment factories due to a geographically concentrated population, closeness to the consumer, and proximity to Manhattan, where the industry's design base remained. Garment-factory owner Leo Gutstein, who succeeded his father as owner of Lee Manufacturing in Pittston, explained that . . .

[My father] came here in the early 30s. He came out running away from the union that was organizing in New York City. He had a factory in New York City and he came out here with my aunt who ran the factory with him on 23rd Street in Manhattan. He came here, first of all, because there was a large labor force of women. The mines were struggling at that time so there was cheap labor out here and it is not far from New York. People were very reliable, very industrious. In fact, that's how many of the factories evolved in Pittston.[10]

Factory owners benefited not only from a large pool of available labor but also from a strong work ethic among the ethnically diverse residents. According to Cherkes:

They were very industrious, hard-working people because, at that time, to work they would get ahead and do better. And they knew that if they did a better job, you'd respect them and pay them more and do better by them. The man, the miner, had no job, there was no jobs for men. They were the providers—the women.[11]

To complicate matters, organized criminals used garment manufacturing as a legal front for illicit activities. By the 1930s, gangsters had infiltrated the area's garment industry. The town of Pittston, at the northern end of the Wyoming Valley, had long been a seat of organized crime in Pennsylvania, and several of its factories were controlled by organized crime. According to the Pennsylvania Crime Commission:

In Northeastern Pennsylvania, non-union garment centers sprung up to take advantage of the unemployed coal mining population used to low wages and poor working conditions. Major Cosa Nostra leaders from Pennsylvania and New York have dominated the industry.[12]

Though organized crime actually owned, controlled, or influenced a minority of factories in the Wyoming Valley, it occupied a great deal of the ILGWU's attention. Whether or not garment shops were operated legitimately, their rapid growth presented the union with a historic organizing challenge.

According to Pennsylvania Power & Light—one of two suppliers of electric utility service in the Wyoming Valley—between the late 1930s and early 1960s, it serviced more than ninety newly established clothing factories. And, according to the ILGWU, in 1950, forty garment factories—all contractors—existed in Pittston alone.[13]

The ILGWU's Response to the "Runaways"

While it was clear to the ILGWU that New Jersey, Delaware, Rhode Island, New Hampshire, Vermont, and Maine were all potential battlegrounds in the fight to unionize runaway garment factories, it was Pennsylvania, and, in particular, the anthracite region that posed among the most significant challenges. By the mid-1930s, the union estimated that as many as 15,000 garment workers toiled in unorganized shops throughout all of northeastern Pennsylvania. Dubinsky tapped Elias Reisberg, General Manager of the Philadelphia Dress Joint Board, and David Gingold, a Manhattan garment worker, to deal with the situation. Reisberg was appointed head of the union's Cotton Garment and Miscellaneous Trades Department, and Gingold, Pennsylvania State Supervisor. Following a visit in 1936, Gingold reported:

> No other state in the land offers such shocking contrasts as does Pennsylvania. Here beauty and squalor actually lie side by side. Here are filthy mining towns with their warped houses and crooked alley streets where poverty is the byword and death the great emancipator; where thousands are slaving in misery while the abundant gifts of nature, denied to those who toil, are generally heaped upon the countryside.
>
> In recent years the chiseling, runaway garment manufacturer has also come to prey upon the poverty-stricken industrial workers in this setting. Pennsylvania is fertile territory for the garment chiseler who is forever seeking a cheap labor market and to exploit the helpless. One cannot but feel the stirring of the masses, the slow grumbling of the downtrodden whose sisters and wives have become the garment workers in the Kingdom of Coal.[14]

In Gingold's view, much work was to be done where anthracite had once dominated. The area reflected "a wasteland of the unorganized with thousands resigned to grinding exploitation for the sake of a few slices of bread."[15]

In 1937, the union's General Executive Board created several locals in the anthracite region. These included Locals 109 and 131, representing cloak and dressmakers in Scranton as well as Local 249 in the Wyoming Valley. Locals were also established in southern portions of the region, including Pottsville and Shamokin in Schuylkill County. These organizations came under the jurisdiction of the New York Dress Joint Board, the ILGWU affiliate representing various trades associated with dress manufacturing.[16] The unions' goals were simple: recognition and commitment of as many "runaway" employers as possible to a union contract.

By the late 1930s, the ILGWU commenced organizing campaigns in the Wyoming Valley. By the early 1940s, Gingold reported little progress with the thirty or more contractors that had sprouted in the area. He had organized only a few factories, a combined membership of about 250. The passing of Elias Reisberg placed Gingold as head of the Cotton Garment and Miscellaneous Trades Department, later renamed the Northeast Department (Gingold would remain in this position until the 1970s), which retained jurisdiction over organizing in Pennsylvania. To Gingold, the Wyoming Valley and, in particular, Pittston were of nearly constant concern.[17]

In 1944, Dubinsky and Gingold appointed Min Lurye Matheson and Bill Matheson as organizer and educational director, respectively, for the Wyoming Valley local of the ILGWU. In 1946, Min was elevated to director of the newly expanded Wyoming Valley District. Their nineteen years of service yielded among the most active and vibrant ILGWU districts in the nation and represented a largely successful—though temporary—effort to organize an industry that sought to escape organized labor.

Constructing an Activist Union

In addition to addressing "bread-and-butter" such as wages and hours, the Mathesons worked to meet member needs outside of the bargaining table and shop floor. They oversaw the construction of a union health-care center in Wilkes-Barre, the only one of its kind in the anthracite region. With rank-and-file support, Min and Bill initiated workers' education programs and a widely popular ILGWU chorus. By the 1950s, the union became an integral part of the political landscape not only in the anthracite region but in state politics as well. And the ILGWU played an important role in efforts to rebuild the troubled economy of Pennsylvania's single-industry anthracite region.

Matheson described the situation upon her arrival in 1944:

> All the mines were down, men weren't working. We organized in New York and surrounding areas. The wages were getting higher. Employers were looking for low wages and areas where they could produce garments at the lowest level possible so they went to the coal fields of Pennsylvania. At that time things were happening [with organized crime] . . . the big shots in New York, the Genoveses and Albert Anastasia, were having their legal problems. So they wanted a legal front for their illicit activities. They had really set up a [garment] center in Pittston. Whatever they were doing to entice [women] to get them or push them into it. So now they needed a legal front and the dress industry was easy. You need very little capital and all you have to do is have a handful of machines and you're in business. And all these manufacturers in New York who were looking for cheap labor outlets loved it. Work was coming in plentifully and these shops were growing, mushrooming.[18]

As she studied the situation, Matheson was struck by the subordinate positions of women and gendered social, political, and economic divisions:

> The atmosphere in the town was that everything was controlled and the women had no say at all. They did the cooking and the sewing and taking care of the

lunches and getting the men out to work in the mines and the kids out to school. They were active in their churches. Many went to work in garment factories. This was their life. They [shop owners] told the women, for example, "We'll teach you to sew." They worked for weeks for nothing. And the hours! You know there were [labor] laws in the land but they weren't carrying out any of the laws. They made it easy for the women to come in any time of the day or night. Double, triple shifts.

I'd talk to the women at meetings. And the first thing is, "Are you registered to vote?" Yes, they're registered to vote, but they don't vote. "Why don't you vote? Do you go down and vote?" "Well, we do, we do, we go down and we register but we can't cast our vote. Our man has to cast our vote for us." I said, "Why?" "Well, that's the system." That's the system which the Mafia had ordained to control the elections. The women would go in and sign as citizens, but then the man (husband or another male, possibly a shop owner) would go to the polling place and cast their vote. The women were never allowed to vote. Attorneys and judges, a lot of them knew, but they . . . it was all covered up, you know. They could have stopped it.[19]

One way in which the ILGWU reached out to potential members was to communicate with them. In 1945, Bill Matheson's talents as a writer, teacher, and intellectual were channeled into creating a district newsletter which became known as *Needlepoint*. It began as a few mimeographed pages describing the union's purpose, organizing efforts, and positions on such issues as hours, wages, and working conditions. The newsletter was distributed at newly organized garment factories, at the homes of would-be union members, and in various community locales. As the union gained momentum, so did *Needlepoint*. By the late 1940s, the newsletter was produced monthly and contained several feature sections. These included *Our Manager's Column*, used by Min to update workers on the latest issues. Articles regularly discussed political and legislative matters, candidates, upcoming elections, voter registration information, political endorsements, strikes, organizing drives, protests, and rallies. A section entitled "Proverbs" contained poetry, short stories, and literature about life, work, family, and community. Community events, as well as the ILGWU's involvement, were regularly featured. Photographs depicted workers and union members in various settings. And, to provide workers with a voice, a letters-to-the-editor section was added.

By 1963, *Needlepoint* was distributed to all 11,000 union members and proved to be a reliable and comprehensive voice for the ILGWU. Moreover, it furnished a regular and direct link between union leaders and rank-and-file and outfitted workers with a means to connect to the larger organization of which they were a part.

Building an infrastructure also took the form of caring for the health of garment workers, an initiative developed the International. Illness, disease, and on-the-job injury were familiar to garment workers. Contributing to these problems was the nature of the work, the high concentration of workers frequently performing their tasks on crowded shop floors, inadequate enforcement of health and workplace safety standards or lax standards altogether, long hours, insufficient rest, and poor diet. Dating to the emergence of factory-based garment manufacturing prior to the turn of the century, tuberculosis and posture deficiencies were but a few of the routine afflictions among garment workers.

During an era when employee health insurance did not exist and the only access to health care for those who could afford little might be a public hospital or a sympathetic physician, the International set out to address concerns regarding the health of workers in Manhattan factories. The ILGWU became the first union in the country to establish a health center near Manhattan's garment district in 1914.[20] The union's concern for the health and welfare of garment workers extended well beyond New York to areas targeted for organizing, including the Wyoming Valley. The union's Wilkes-Barre health center opened in June, 1948, and attracted numerous union and community officials and the local press.

> A luncheon attended by important union officers, employer representatives and community leaders, and a "Home Town" fashion show will mark the formal opening Friday and Saturday of the $150,000 Union Health Center in Wilkes-Barre to serve 7,000 members of the International Ladies' Garment Workers' Union in the Wilkes-Barre, Hazleton, and Scranton areas.
> Services will be exclusively diagnostic with no charge to ILGWU members. The Center is financed by employer payments into the union's health and welfare fund, as negotiated in union contracts.[21]

The center focused on diagnosing and treating disease, illness, and injury. In addition to routine physical examinations, the center provided X rays, cancer screenings, electrocardiograms, psychiatric consultations, proctology examinations, respiratory diagnostic services, immunizations, and gynecological services.

An equally important goal was to educate rank-and-file members on issues of personal health. As part of its educational and community outreach efforts, the union utilized *Needlepoint*, brochures, and other media to inform garment workers of services and sound health practices. For example, the center advocated twice-yearly examinations for detection and prevention of certain cancers, warned against fad diets, provided information on nutrition and dietary supplements, and conducted routine classes and workshops on health-related topics. Issues of job safety and employer compliance with workplace health and safety standards also became important educational components of the center.

From 1949 to 1958, the center served 16,000 garment workers and their family members, providing over 220,000 examinations, consultations, and testing services. It also supplied countless health-related educational materials and programs. The center provided another means through which the ILGWU established a community presence.

Matheson and fellow organizers recognized the importance of providing the growing rank and file with social outlets that could boost the union's image. In the late 1940s, the district established a highly successful musical chorus of local male and female union members. The chorus promoted themes of worker solidarity, political activism, and community involvement. Clementine Lyons, a founding member of the chorus, explains its history:

> In 1947 we got these shows going. We were, in fact, the first local in the Northeast Department [of the ILGWU] to put on a musical review. In fact, I'll tell you—not because I want to brag because I was part of the show—but the shows began to be part of the social calendar around the area. Shows would be popular shows that were on Broadway at the time, but most of them would be union flavor. We used to go to the Veterans Hospital [in Wilkes-Barre] every Thursday night for years. Around '52, I think, we helped the American Italian Association with their show. We performed at the American Legion, for politicians, rallies, things like that.[22]

Chorus members wrote songs and produced skits and full-scale performances reflecting a political pro-labor message. As it grew in size and popularity, the chorus performed for local and statewide political functions, holiday parties, Labor Day parades, union activities, and other events. Reflective of the union's growing activism, Bill Matheson became the chief lyricist, often crafting political messages into music. His song, "Politics," encouraged garment workers to exercise their right to vote.

Politics

Politics is everybody's business.
Politics is everybody's job.
We've got a job to do,
And it's up to me and you.
Politics is everybody's job.

They must register and vote
'Cause one vote here
And one vote there
Can make us miss the boat.
And many of our friends
Have lost by margins very thin.
Then we wound up with nothing
When the other guys got in.

By 1955, the chorus typically performed at least once per week at clubs, churches, hospitals, and community affairs. Annual districtwide musical reviews were common, with proceeds donated to local charitable organizations.

Holidays were particularly busy times for the chorus. Memorial Day, Labor Day, Fourth of July, and December holiday events resulted in frequent engagements. The chorus enabled garment workers to advocate their growing political activism as it participated in civic events usually involving the Democratic Party. For example, in September, 1956, the group was invited to Harrisburg to perform at a campaign rally and dinner for Democratic presidential hopeful Adlai Stevenson.[23]

The chorus became an important means through which the ILGWU and its members maintained a presence in the community, espoused ideological messages, and delivered their points of view. Chorus performances served as social outlets for members and provided alternatives to the routine of daily life in the factory. Finally, the chorus provided its members with a means to develop skills and talents that might not otherwise be recognized.

In addition to *Needlepoint*, the health-care center, and chorus, the district implemented workers' education programs that reflected the ILGWU's philosophy of educating workers regarding the industrial-capitalist order.[24] Among these programs was the "Union Counseling Class," begun in 1948, in which workers learned of locally available human services and the Community Chest that, like the modern-day United Way, provided umbrella funding and support to human-service agencies. Instructors included college professors, ILGWU officials, representatives of local businesses, and community agency staff. Graduated workers earned designations as union counselors and were responsible for explaining and promoting the availability of local social services to union members in need. By 1961, a total of 495 rank and filers completed this program.

The district also implemented programs to enlighten members regarding political issues. For example, a nonpartisan voting-rights class became part of the agenda in response to the suffrage inequities in towns like Pittston.[25]

The Union created a Political Education Program, or "PEP," in 1954. Partisan in orientation, PEP recruited union members to participate in classes on national, state, and local political issues. PEP advocated positions on issues, endorsed candidates, and encouraged voter registration.[26] Additional programs included "Educational Institutes" that focused on topics such as politics and government, organizing, labor history, garment industry history, economics, and social policy issues. Rank and file participated in the day-long institutes and discussed topics such as current industry conditions, state and federal legislation, and issues in labor history.

Some institutes were held at the ILGWU's Pocono Mountain vacation retreat and conference center, Unity House, near Bushkill, Pennsylvania. The ILGWU operated Unity House from 1919 until 1989 to provide workers with vacation, recreation, and personal renewal opportunities.[27] Wyoming Valley members routinely participated in Unity House institutes. For example, a July, 1953, institute hosted 65 district members to discuss politics, economics, and social issues. Likewise, a September, 1957, institute, focusing on labor movement history and the role of women and minorities, drew fifty district members. An August, 1962, institute featured discussion of federal labor legislation and political issues and drew over sixty district members. Institute guest speakers included union officials, academics, and prominent or up-and-coming public officials such as Eleanor Roosevelt, Pennsylvania governors, and members of Congress.

The district also aligned itself with local institutions of higher education to expand learning opportunities for workers. In the mid-1950s, it partnered with Wilkes College (now Wilkes University) and with the newly formed Pennsylvania State University Extension Campus at Wilkes-Barre. Garment workers attended regularly scheduled classes on topics including factory safety, writing, photography, dance, economics, history, sociology, and labor history. Min was particularly pleased with this achievement program: "Our people went to college. They [educators] gave them [workers] a pretty well rounded view of history. We graduated quite a few. They went to college!"[28]

Education provided workers with the opportunity to ponder the intricacies of the industrial-capitalist order. It altered the isolation frequently associated with routine factory work by enabling rank and file to gather together, fraternize with and learn about each other, their union, and the industry and society of which they were a part. Equally as important, it served as a passageway to develop and promote the maturing political activism of the ILGWU.

When it came to politics the union's infrastructure included various means to educate politically and involve rank-and-file members. *Needlepoint* served as a tool to deliver the union's partisan messages. The chorus acted as a voice to encourage electoral participation and explain publicly the union's partisan views. Another goal of the Mathesons was to grow the union's direct political activism by securing the legally guaranteed right of suffrage for women, supporting politicians friendly to the union's cause, and advocating points of view on issues that effected working people.

Rank-and-file workers learned, through group action, to challenge directly the practice of women deferring their voting rights to men in Pittston—a problem that remained well into the 1950s. Organizers drew upon the support of the growing rank and file who traveled to Pittston to picket for the cause. Local women were educated regarding the voting process then encouraged to pursue their suffrage rights with ILGWU backing at the polling place.

Besides securing the participation of women in the electoral process, political activism also included alignment with labor-friendly politicians. Ideologically, Matheson and fellow organizers linked working-class interests and the philosophy of the progressive wing of the Democratic Party. In the union's view it was Democrats who delivered on "bread-and-butter" issues. As a result, district organizers aimed to influence workers to become politically involved and support Democratic politicians and their policies.

Supporting Democrats, however, was a considerable feat given that Republicans held a three-to-one registration margin in most of Pennsylvania's anthracite region. Beginning in the 1950s, however, with the union's advocacy on behalf of two labor-friendly Democrats, registration patterns began to change. Politicians who earned the support of organized labor were Daniel J. Flood, who served in Congress as Pennsylvania's 11th District Representative for nearly thirty years, and George M. Leader, Pennsylvania's Governor from 1955 to 1959.

Flood, a stage actor turned labor lawyer, established a relationship with the ILGWU in the 1940s by working on behalf of local organizers who ran into trouble with the law as a result of their activities. Flood served as 11th Congressional District Congressman from 1944 to 1946, again from 1948 to 1952, then from 1954 to 1980. The union worked tirelessly to secure his successive elections.

Flood served as the union's educator on complex legislation and policy issues debated in the halls of Congress and on the local impact of federal policy. The ILGWU, in turn, served as Flood's source of grassroots information on issues, concerns, and problems. Flood commonly attended ILGWU events, union meetings, and rallies. For example, he was a regular at the union's annual picnic held at San Souci Amusement Park which, by 1962, drew 15,000 workers and their families.

The union editorialized that Flood proved that he was not shy to take political action to aid his constituents. For the union, politics and politicians, at least in Flood's case, were not beyond the reach of working people:

> We support Dan Flood because Dan helped the garment workers. Yes, it is as simple as that.
>
> Dan worked and voted to raise the Minimum Wage from 40 cents to 75 cents, from 75 cents to $1, and from $1 to $1.15, and to $1.25 one year from now. Each of these raises puts money in the pockets of garment workers. Each of them was won through political action. We support Dan Flood and others like him. We know that the higher wage helped garment workers and that's the purpose of our union—helping garment workers.[29]

The ILGWU worked with Flood to advocate policy and legislation that effected the local community. Championing the passage of the Area Redevelopment Bill provides an illustration.

Flood and Illinois Senator Paul Douglas introduced the measure in the late 1950s to attract industry to economically depressed Appalachian and urban areas. The bill called for federal aid and tax incentives for private enterprise to create new jobs. Flood's district qualified for the proposed aid since, by the 1950s, the demand for anthracite coal dissipated. While garment manufacturing remained a key source of employment—garment contractors were attracted to the area precisely because of the region's depressed economy and the availability of workers—the local economy experienced a continual slide. Wilkes-Barre was designated as one of only two urban areas in the United

States with an unemployment rate exceeding 12 percent. Scranton, the neighboring city, was the other.[30]

Advocating for the Flood-Douglas Bill and working to secure its enactment provided a grassroots public policy opportunity for garment workers. The ILGWU became full partners with a local economic development coalition known as the "Committee of 100" that worked to secure new jobs and economic diversification. *Needlepoint* routinely featured articles on the Flood-Douglas Bill. Accompanied by rank and file, Min Matheson testified before a U.S. Senate committee on the relevance of the measure. Garment workers wrote to senators, congressmen, and the president arguing for federal action. Rallies were held locally and in Washington, D.C., in support of Flood's proposals. The legislation became a regular topic of discussion on the shop floor, in union meetings, and at educational institutes.

Although vetoed twice by President Eisenhower, in 1961, John F. Kennedy signed the Flood-Douglas Area Redevelopment Bill that established the Economic Development Administration (EDA) in the U.S. Department of Commerce and laid the groundwork for creation of the Appalachian Regional Commission. The bill granted millions in aid to distressed areas of Appalachia. Wilkes-Barre was designated as EDA headquarters for the eastern United States.

Building upon this success, ILGWU also backed Flood's views on establishing the federal Medicare and Medicaid programs, advancing minimum wages, lowering social-security retirement age, and other policy and legislative matters important to working people. Their support of him and his policies extended well beyond Matheson's tenure and helped to establish a tradition of working-class support for Democrats in the Keystone State.

The union also aligned itself with Pennsylvania's maverick Democratic governor from 1955 to 1959, George M. Leader. Early in Leader's run for office, Matheson and the ILGWU provided friendly turf for the young, pro-labor Democrat. Though it is impossible to tell the precise influence of the ILGWU when the final votes were cast, Leader carried nearly every anthracite county, meaning that he earned not only Democratic support but the votes of thousands of would-be Republicans. It was quite a feat locally since a Republican majority in countywide vote totals was evident in virtually every gubernatorial election in the twentieth century. It was also an accomplishment statewide as Leader was the second Democrat elected to the one-term, four-year office since 1900, as compared to fifteen Republicans.[31] Leader's election and garment-worker support of him were significant milestones for the ILGWU, according to Matheson:

> This area was Republican. Rock solid Republican. And we, in our fashion, did a great deal to turn it from Republican to Democrat. We worked very hard to elect Governor Leader as a Democrat and that's how we broke the Republican chain-of-command in Pennsylvania. And he gave us a lot of credit for his election. As Governor, he did a lot of good.[32]

Ostensibly, according to Leader, the ILGWU and its alignment with the Democratic agenda played a pivotal role in moving the Anthracite region away from Republican domination.

When I was running [for Governor], the ILGWU was much more powerful than the Democratic organization. Min did a wonderful job for me. She carried a Republican area for a Democratic candidate for Governor. This was unheard of before Min became a real political power. My first encounter with the region was in 1952 when I ran for State Treasurer. The Democratic Party was not terribly strong in the anthracite counties. The party was not terribly strong there. You did not come across a lot of strong Democratic leadership.

The local governments in those Anthracite counties, in most cases, were controlled by Republicans. And the Democratic Party did not have any strength at all. I recall, too, that the state was Republican in terms of registration by about 970,000 voters.

They [ILGWU] were the only Democratic force in the area. The real strength that you felt was the ILGWU. There is no doubt that Min Matheson had mobilized the ILGWU as a political force that had to be reckoned with. The ILGWU was located in other parts of the state, but they weren't a political force like they were [in the anthracite region].

Except for Min, they wouldn't have had that kind of political sophistication. They wouldn't have been informed about what takes place in Washington or how it affects their lives. She had educated them. Min wasn't just a labor organizer. She was a political organizer and educator. Their presence was being felt.[33]

Governor Leader, Min Matheson, and the Wyoming Valley ILGWU maintained a close relationship. Leader was a regular at union events. With Leader in office, the ILGWU realized the opportunity to influence Harrisburg politics and rallied the rank and file to support his policies. They supported and advocated his plans to implement a graduated income tax system, reform the state's unemployment compensation program, implement legislation guaranteeing equal employment rights, and reform the state's mental-health care system. The union also advocated Leader's economic development policies.

While Dan Flood led the charge in Washington for passage of the Area Redevelopment Act, Leader advocated similar legislation at the state level to create the Pennsylvania Industrial Development Authority (PIDA). PIDA (a program that remains in existence) is a low-interest financing program for the development and expansion of manufacturing and industrial facilities in economically distressed areas of Pennsylvania. Seizing the opportunity to advocate for jobs and economic growth in the anthracite region, The ILGWU participated in economic development hearings and meetings sponsored by the governor, testified in the bill's favor at state legislative hearings, lobbied state legislators, and discussed and explained the topic in educational institutes:

Governor Leader is quoted as saying that the new measure will provide for loan assistance to community industrial development groups to construct and lease plants as a means of increasing employment. A program passed by the Democratic House is currently tied up in a Republican Senate. Do you cast your vote for the candidates who will vote for your needs in the House and Senate in Harrisburg?

The Leader Administration introduced a bill authorizing aid to distressed areas in bringing in new industries. We consider that a step in the right direction.[34]

The PIDA bill was enacted during Governor Leader's tenure, demonstrating to garment workers that, in advocating for Leader's policies, they had become part of something larger than themselves for the benefit of the entire community. They experienced, too, the benefits of exercising their growing political clout in the state capital for the welfare of their community.

Combined with Flood's measure, PIDA attracted diversified manufacturing facilities to distressed areas of Pennsylvania including the anthracite region. These measures stimulated a gradual economic recovery. By 1965, the regional unemployment rate dropped to 7.9 percent. By the late 1960s, it fell to 3.9 percent. As one regional historian noted, "In a very real sense the community lived for twenty years—into the 1980s—on the fruits of what was accomplished during the fifties and sixties."[35] Through its grassroots political activism and education, the ILGWU was very much a part of these accomplishments.

The union's influence in altering county voter registration patterns also extended into the following decades. By the late 1950s, Democratic registrants began to outpace Republicans. This trend continued into the 1960s and, by mid-decade, Democrats in several of the anthracite counties represented the majority. Among the factors contributing to this important transformation were the influence of Democratic politicians like Flood and Leader and the enhanced leverage of organized labor, with the ILGWU at the forefront.[36]

By the time Min and Bill Matheson departed for assignments with the ILGWU in New York in 1963, the union's Wyoming Valley District consisted of three locals with nearly 11,000 members in 168 unionized garment factories. The district boasted the largest share of ILGWU members in the anthracite region (Scranton had 5,000; Shamokin 4,000; and Pottsville about 3,100) and the second largest in Pennsylvania. Following a divisive general dress strike in 1958, the union and industry developed a generally amiable relationship. The union had come to believe that it and the garment industry were to remain integral elements in the Pennsylvania economy.

Perhaps ILGWU leaders and organizers didn't foresee early enough the long-term impact of post–World War II changes in U.S. trade policy. It is probable that, in Pennsylvania as elsewhere, the union took comfort in its growth, relative stability, and power after having organized an industry that sought to escape it. When it came to advocating public policies to diversify the regional economy, perhaps few in the ILGWU could foresee that new employers and rising wages in Pennsylvania's anthracite region would serve as incentives for the migration of apparel makers. Maybe the migration of the garment industry simply wasn't seen as perpetual or inevitable. Globalization and international capitalism, after all, weren't yet as prevalent in the 1950s and 1960s as they would be in the 1980s and 1990s. For whatever reason, few in the ILGWU—and perhaps even in the American garment industry—likely recognized that a trickle of Japanese-made scarves that appeared in the New York retail marketplace in the mid-1950s hinted at the near demise of an entire domestic industry before the close of the century.

The ILGWU and Garment Industry in the Post-Industrial Era

Of major concern to garment workers and organized labor in the closing decades of the twentieth century has been impact of overseas-made clothing and the erosion of American jobs. Like other sectors of the U.S. manufacturing economy—from televisions to automobile components to children's toys—the amount of apparel made overseas and sold in the domestic market has grown dramatically. American garment workers, like their counterparts in many other industries, have found themselves downsized, unemployed, underemployed— in short "deindustrialized"—as apparel production moved offshore. Importation of overseas-made clothing and the loss of American jobs have posed unprecedented problems for domestic workers and organized labor.

The impact of imports on the domestic apparel industry and its workers has been prodigious. In 1955, apparel imports amounted to a mere three percent of the total U.S. market. By the mid-1960s they amounted to 12 percent. In the mid-1970s the percentage stood at 31 percent and, by the early 1990s, sales of imports surpassed domestic-made apparel, claiming over 60 percent of the total U.S. market. Put another way, in the early 1960s, about 5 out of every 100 garments sold in the U.S. were made in foreign nations. By the 1990s the number climbed to over 60 out of every 100.

The domestic industry and the ILGWU have been hit hard as a result. When David Dubinsky retired as union president in 1966, the total number of women and children's apparel workers in the United States was 660,000. The number of those workers organized by the ILGWU was 455,000. Twenty years later when Jay Mazur took office as president of the union (a position from which he retired in 2002), employment in this sector of the industry had fallen to about a half-million and ILGWU membership declined by 60 percent to 196,000. In 1995—when the ILGWU merged with the Amalgamated Clothing and Textile Workers Union to form the Union of Needletrades, Industrial, and Textile Employees (UNITE!)—its membership had fallen to 125,000. [37]

Pennsylvania, once a large center of apparel manufacturing, has, likewise, felt the effects. The total number of combined apparel and textile workers statewide peaked at nearly 200,000 in 1969. By 1984, the number dropped to 102,000. In 1998, the Department of Labor and Industry estimated that about 25,000 Pennsylvanians earn a living in some segment of the apparel industry.

The agency also projects that the garment industry will continue to loose more than 5 percent of its workforce annually and that, by 2005, less than 10,000 jobs will remain statewide.[38]

Active membership in what was the Wyoming Valley District of the ILGWU has consistently declined from a height of over 11,000 in the 1960s to a few hundred at the turn of the century. In 1986, the Hazleton and Wilkes-Barre branches of the union merged to form the Hazleton/Wyoming Valley District Council. By the mid-1990s, Scranton area locals were consolidated as well, forming the Northeastern Pennsylvania District Office. By the late 1990s the area—consisting of a few hundred active members and several thousand retirees—was consolidated into the Pennsylvania, Ohio, and South Jersey Joint Board of the UNITE!

As the twentieth century drew to a close, it was clear that garment manufacturers continued to "run away" in search of cheap labor just as they had run to Pennsylvania's anthracite region decades earlier. However, rather than following and organizing, the labor movement was consigned to consolidating, downsizing, and merging and, where possible, encouraging the organizing of overseas apparel workers.

Biennial ILGWU Membership, 1964–1998[39]

YEAR	ILGWU	Wyoming Valley District*
1964	442,318	10,279
1966	455,164	10,901
1968	455,022	11,179
1970	442,333	11,006
1972	427,368	9,634
1974	404,737	8,900
1976	365,346	7,990
1978	348,380	7,374
1980	322,505	7,187
1982	282,559	6,508
1984	247,570	6,055
1986	196,000	4,817
1988	153,000	3,688
1990	145,000	3,570
1992	133,000	2,950
1994	125,000	1,839
1996	245,000**	1,658
1998	217,000**	396

* Data reflects active members in Locals 295-Pittston, 249-Wilkes-Barre, and 327-Nanticoke. From 1946 to 1986 these locals comprised the original Wyoming Valley District.
**Membership numbers reflect the merger of ILGWU and ACTWU in 1995 to form UNITE!

By the late 1970s, the ILGWU recognized that the migratory pattern of the industry was perpetual; it was not merely a phenomenon of the 1920s or the Great Depression. According to Sol "Chick" Chaikin, the union's president from 1975 to 1986;

> Relocating the garment industry was not difficult since it is an industry on wheels. It can be moved overnight because capital investment is low, machines are easily transportable, and materials are comparatively light. Clothes are not steel, not copper, not lumber, not brick.[40]

What accounted for these new "runaway" factories? There are several factors, most of which were not necessarily new. Escape from union contracts is a prime incentive, as is cheap labor. To operate without union interference and with less costly labor, during the second half of the twentieth-century employers established factories in Caribbean, Central and South American, Asian, and Pacific Rim countries. Additional savings are derived by avoiding costly "benefits" such as health care, vacation and sick pay, and workers' and unemployment compensation payments.

Moreover, garment manufacturers have been welcomed by governments in nations who have embraced industrial capitalism. Apparel provides part of the answer to their search for non-capital intensive industries to spur economic development. For example, in the aftermath of World War II, a devastated Japan embraced apparel manufacturing as a relatively quick and easy way to provide employment and grow its economy by exporting products for sale abroad. Scarves were among the first Japanese products manufactured in large quantities then exported to the United States.

The prevailing theory has been that apparel can be made more cheaply abroad. The theory proved true. By 1975, when the pace of imports was growing dramatically, the average U.S. garment worker earned over three dollars per hour. A person doing the same job in Hong Kong received sixty-two cents per hour; in Korea and Singapore, twenty-seven cents; and in Haiti, eighteen cents. By the mid-1980s, when overseas products flooded American markets, the average wage of union and nonunion garment workers in the United States reached $5.75 per hour. By comparison, workers in the People's Republic of China earned the equivalent hourly wage of sixteen cents, in Taiwan fifty-seven cents, $1.18 in Hong Kong, and sixty-three cents in South Korea. Nearly 70 percent of all garments sold in the United States were imported from these countries.

Pressure by U.S. retailers for ever-cheaper garments proved to be another factor behind import growth. Retailers have argued that, in their highly competitive trade, consumers want the best bargain. Overseas-produced clothing is less expensive. Therefore, retailers are obliged to meet demand. An ILGWU study, reported to Congress, discovered that retailers were indeed ordering and purchasing garments from Mexico, Hong Kong, Taiwan, and elsewhere for a fraction of the cost of U.S.-made goods and supplying such apparel to customers. However, customers paid nearly the same price for overseas apparel as they had for items made in the domestic market. Retailers and their shareholders, therefore, were the beneficiaries, not consumers.[41]

Dramatic shifts in U.S. trade policy have also played a role. Clothing produced in foreign countries often benefits from very low or nonexistent U.S. import tariffs, a policy designed to spur free trade. Nations whose exports to the U.S. had been regulated benefit from reductions or total elimination of quotas. In addition, trade agreements have allowed rates of import growth to exceed the rate of growth in the American market. For example, in years when the American apparel market grew by one percent, some trade agreements permitted imports to grow by six percent or more. Finally, major trade policies—such as the North American Free Trade Agreement (NAFTA)—have established new free trade zones and eliminated long-held protectionist barriers that benefited U.S. industries.

As the twentieth century drew to a close, among the most vivid examples of the continued migration of the American apparel industry and the response of organized labor were to be found in Pennsylvania. In the early 1990s, New York–based apparel manufacturer Leslie Fay, Inc. maintained six production and distribution facilities in Northeastern Pennsylvania employing 2,000 workers. Since the company's founding by Fred Pomerantz in 1947, it had grown to be one of the premier producers of women's apparel in the United States. Pomerantz, a New Yorker, relocated to the anthracite region to produce a line of high-quality women's apparel bearing the name of his daughter. By the 1960s, Leslie Fay fashions were commonly recognized and purchased nationwide.

Though the company's corporate headquarters were in Manhattan's fashion district, the anthracite region remained the nucleus of its multimillion-dollar production and distribution network. Its production workers were ILGWU members and the company and union enjoyed generally good relations. In May 1991, Leslie Fay and the ILGWU agreed to a new three-year contract granting workers an average of eight to eleven dollars per hour plus an attractive benefit package.

Leslie Fay was highly regarded as a local employer. On a visit to area in the late 1950s Fred Pomerantz was presented with a Rolls-Royce paid for in part by contributions from local ILGWU members in appreciation for their jobs. The esteem in which the company was held transcended generations. When John J. Pomerantz, Fred's son and the company's chairman, was invited to deliver the commencement address at nearby Wilkes University in 1992, he boasted that its board had recently authorized "the development of a multimillion-dollar, state of the art, dress manufacturing facility here . . . ensuring the continued employment of Leslie Fay personnel in the community."[42]

Less than a year later, however, auditors discovered accounting irregularities at Leslie Fay that were not entirely dissimilar from scandals that would plague corporate America in the early twenty-first century. Overstated revenues, understated expenses, and hidden accounting practices kept the company solvent on paper. Behind the scenes, however, the company's finances differed immensely. Despite the fact that Leslie Fay, Inc. reported record sales of $675 million in 1993, an insolvency amounting to $81 million loomed as its lawyers scrambled to file for federal bankruptcy protection.

As part of its cost-cutting measures, the company announced plans to move all Pennsylvania production jobs to Guatemala when its contact with the ILGWU expired on May 31, 1994. Leslie Fay's proclamation galvanized clergy, social agency representatives, business and labor leaders, local and state politicians, and the ILGWU who formed The Northeastern Pennsylvania Stakeholders Alliance. The group argued that management had an obligation to maintain jobs in the community and that contracting work to Guatemala would devastate the local economy and quality of life while perpetuating the problem of overseas sweatshops.[43]

In May 1994, the ILGWU rejected Leslie Fay's offer to retain the 1,200 local jobs for one year and provide monetary incentives for employees who choose to voluntarily quit. A strike ensued and drew national attention as Leslie Fay workers marched on the company's 7th Avenue (New York) headquarters and on Wall Street and encouraged a consumer boycott at the outlets of leading national retailers. To those sympathetic to the union, the Leslie Fay drama was more than a strike; it was a working-class battle in protest of corporate policy that favored free trade and placed profit above the welfare of communities and people. To those sympathetic to the company, Leslie Fay's decisions were simply a response to its concern over survival in a highly competitive industry that had gone global to reduce labor costs and enhance investor returns.

On July 12, 1994, six weeks after the ILGWU had struck Leslie Fay, both sides announced a tentative three-year agreement. Leslie Fay agreed to maintain 600 production jobs in Pennsylvania for one year. Both the company and union resolved to work toward preserving the jobs for the second and third year of the contract. The company provided $2.3 million in severance to terminated workers, wage increases of 10 percent for those who remained on the job, and increased its contributions to the union's health and welfare fund. Leslie Fay also agreed to adopt a code of conduct to prescribe fair labor standards for its overseas workers.[44]

Most of Leslie Fay's facilities closed permanently. The jobs were moved to factories in Guatemala. As the summer of 1995 drew near, Leslie Fay remained in Chapter 11 and made it clear that its future relied on further reductions in labor costs by moving all production jobs out of the United States. With few choices remaining, the ILGWU subsequently reached an agreement with the company to provide severance pay for about 400 of the 600 remaining workers.

The company promised not to vacate Pennsylvania completely. It retained a warehouse and distribution center and a small plant to produce samples and monitor quality. About 200 union jobs remained.

Within a few months, one of largest and most recognized producers of women's clothing in the United States and a fixture of Pennsylvania's apparel industry since the 1940s padlocked its factories and sent most of its jobs overseas. As Leslie Fay went overseas, a handful of unionized garment factories remained in the Keystone State. With Leslie Fay undone, membership in what was the Wyoming Valley District of the ILGWU dwindled to a few hundred—the vast majority of its roster consisted of retirees.

In the longer term, the ILGWU had lost its struggle with one of the region's most important apparel employers and, indeed, with an entire industry. Capital, free trade, and the global economy had won out over the voices of workers, politicians, religious leaders, labor officials, and members of the community. Within a few years Leslie Fay emerged from Chapter 11 and reported over $200 million in sales. It prospects for future profitability appeared strong. Virtually all of its production originated in low-wage Central American factories.[45]

Pearl Novak, a fifty-one-year member of the ILGWU and a Leslie Fay striker who lost her job, summed it up this way:

> People were really hurt by this. You have to realize that many of them gave their lives to this company. Now they had nothing. Some found work. Some went to school to be retrained. Some are still out of work. Many, like me, were forced into retirement. We had no choice. Sad, isn't it? I was a member of the union when Min Matheson was here. It was different then. The industry was here. Now it isn't. But the union did all that it could have. What else could it have done? What this really comes down to is that we need to educate young people today about why it is so important to keep jobs in the USA, to buy American, to stick with the union, to fight to the end like we did at Leslie Fay. What else is there to do?[46]

The garment industry and its unionized workers are now shadows of what they once were in Pennsylvania. In the northeastern corner of the Commonwealth, the industry provided jobs for thousands in a depressed economy with few employment alternatives. The ILGWU provided not only better pay and benefits, but also a way of life and a culture of its own in communities hard-hit by the decline of anthracite coal mining. Garment factories, like anthracite coal mines before them, have vanished from the industrial landscape in Pennsylvania. They've been replaced by service-sector industries, some high-tech firms, underemployment and unemployment.

The story of the rise and decline of a leading manufacturing industry and that industry's major labor union reveals an important but little-studied piece in the economic and social history of a once-highly industrial state like Pennsylvania. Just as contractors migrated from New York to Pennsylvania in the 1930s and 1940s, so did they later migrate overseas regardless of concerns over sweatshop conditions, low wages, long hours, and larger social and economic implications.

Notes

1. For a thorough historical treatment of the ILGWU in Pennsylvania and its anthracite region, readers should consult Kenneth, Robert, and Nicole Wolensky, *Fighting for the Union Label: The Women's Garment Industry and the ILGWU in Pennsylvania.* (University Park, PA; Pennsylvania State University Press, 2002); "Min Matheson and the ILGWU in the Wyoming Valley," in *Proceedings of the Sixth Annual Conference on the History of Northeastern Pennsylvania: The Last 100 years* (Nanticoke: Luzerne County Community College, 1994); and "Born to Organize," *Pennsylvania Heritage*, XXV (Summer, 1999), 32–39. This article is excerpted from these writings and the author wishes to recognize Robert and Nicole Wolensky and thank them for their important contributions to this research. The title comes from Sol Chaikin, *A Labor Viewpoint: Another Opinion* (Monroe, NY: Library Research Associates, 1980).

2. On the history of the women's garment industry in the United States and unionization efforts, see M. Danish, *The World of David Dubinsky* (Cleveland: World Publishing, 1957); D. Dubinsky, *A Life with Labor* (New York: Simon and Shuster, 1977); P. Foner, *History of the Labor Movement in the United States,* Vol. 9 (New York: International Publishers, 1991); International Ladies' Garment Workers' Union, *ILGWU New History: The Story of the Ladies' Garment Workers* (New York: ILGWU, 1950); L. Levine, *The Women's Garment Workers* (New York: Arno and Company, 1969); L. Stein, *Out of the Sweatshop: The Struggle for Industrial Democracy* (New York: Quadrangle, 1977); G. Tyler, *Look for the Union Label: A History of the ILGWU* (Armonk, N.Y.: M. E. Sharpe, 1995); B. Stolberg, *Tailor's Progress: The Story of a Famous Union and the Men who Made It* (New York: Doran, Doubleday, and Company, 1944); R. Waldinger, *Through the Eye of the Needle* (New York: New York University Press, 1986), and Wolensky, et. al. *Fighting for the Union Label.*

3. *Report of the General Executive Board to the Twenty-first Convention of the ILGWU*, May 2, 1932 (New York: ILGWU).

4. Ibid, 32.

5. F. Perkins (1933), "The Cost of a Five-Dollar Dress," In L. Stein, ed., *Out of the Sweatshop: The Struggle for Industrial Democracy,* (New York: Quadrangle, 1977), 224–225.

6. Commonwealth of Pennsylvania, *Message of Governor Gifford Pinchot to the General Assembly in Joint Session,* January 4, 1927 (Harrisburg, 1927), 67.

7. Commonwealth of Pennsylvania, Department of Labor and Industry, *Pennsylvania Labor and Industry in the Depression,* Special Bulletin No. 39 (Harrisburg, 1934).

8. Robert P., Kenneth C., and Nicole H. Wolensky. *The Knox Mine Disaster: The Final Years of the Northern Anthracite Industry and the Effort to Rebuild a Regional Economy* (Harrisburg: Pennsylvania Historical & Museum Commission, 1999).

9. W. Cherkes, *Oral History Interview.* July 20, 1994, Tape 1, Side 1. Northeastern Pennsylvania Oral History Project, University of Wisconsin, Stevens Point.

10. L. Gutstein, *Oral History Interview.* July 26, 1997, Tape 1, Side 1. Northeastern Pennsylvania Oral History Project, University of Wisconsin, Stevens Point.

11. Cherkes, *Oral History Interview,* July 20, 1994, Tape 1, Side 1.

12. Pennsylvania Crime Commission, *Report on Organized Crime—1970* (Harrisburg: Commonwealth of Pennsylvania, 1970), 8.

13. PP & L data on garment factories in the Wyoming Valley was obtained from a database created by historian Thomas Dublin, State University of New York at Binghamton, to study anthracite region economic revitalization. Data on garment factories in Pittston is derived from a memo entitled "Members of the Greater Pittston Contractors Association," David Dubinsky Papers, 5780/002, Box 297, File Folder 4A, Cornell University School of Industrial and Labor Relations, Kheel Center for Labor Management Documentation and Archives, Ithaca, New York.

14. ILGWU, *Justice,* October 15, 1936, 4.

15. Ibid.

16. *Report of the General Executive Board to the 22nd Convention of the ILGWU,* May 3, 1937 (New York: ABCO Press, 1937).

17. *Report of the General Executive Board to the 24th Convention of the ILGWU,* May 27–June 8, 1940 (New York: ABCO Press, 1940).

18. M. Mathson, Oral History Interview, December 5, 1988, Northeastern Pennsylvania Oral History Project, Tape 1, Side 1.
19. Ibid.
20. Stein, 186–188. Also, on the ILGWU Health Centers, see International Ladies' Garment Workers Union, *News History, 1900–1950: The Story of the Ladies' Garment Workers* (New York: ILGWU, 1950.
21. "Area Garment Workers Open Health Center," *Scranton Times,* 2 June, 1948, 3.
22. Clementine Lyons (July 24, 1993), Oral History Interview, Tape 1, Side 2.
23. "ILGWU Performs at Stevenson Rally," *Wilkes-Barre Record,* 14 September 1956, 4.
24. On ILGWU workers' education, See ILGWU, *News History, 1900–1950.* (New York: ILGWU, 1950) and E. Tarr, "Union based labor education: Lessons from the ILGWU," In London, S., Tarr, E., & Wilson, J., eds. *The Re-education of the American working class* (New York: Greenwood Press, 1990, 63–70.
25. *Needlepoint* (Wilkes-Barre, PA: International Ladies' Garment Workers' Union, May 1955), 2.
26. *Justice,* August, 1954, 6.
27. On Unity House, see Kenneth C. Wolensky, "Unity House: A Worker's Shangri-La," *Pennsylvania Heritage,* XXIV, (Summer, 1998), 20–29.
28. Min Matheson, Oral History Interview, June 28, 1990, Tape 1, Side 2.
29. *Needlepoint,* September 1962.
30. On economic recovery efforts in the northern anthracite region and the efforts of Dan Flood, see Kashatus, "Dapper Dan Flood"; Sheldon Spear, *Wyoming Valley History Revisited* (Shavertown, PA: Jemags Publishing Co., 1994); Kenneth C. Wolensky, "Diamonds and Coal," *Now and Then: The Appalachian Magazine* (Winter, 1997, 20–24); and Thomas Dublin, "After Anthracite: The Attempt to Re-Industrialize and Diversify the Economy After the Decline of Mining" in *Proceedings of the Ninth Annual Conference on the History of Northeastern Pennsylvania,* R. Mittck, ed. (Nanticoke, PA: Luzerne County Community College, 1997), 74–102.
31. Commonwealth of Pennsylvania, *Pennsylvania Manual* (Harrisburg, PA: 1956).
32. Min Matheson, Oral History Interview, December 5, 1988, Tape 2, Side 1, and June 28, 1990, Tape 1, Side 2.
33. George M. Leader, Oral History Interview, May 30, 1995, Northeastern Pennsylvania Oral History Project. Stevens Point, WI: University of Wisconsin, Center for the Small City. Tape 1, Side 1.
34. Spear, *Wyoming Valley History Revisited,* 255.
35. *Needlepoint,* September 1962.
36. "County Was Once Solid Republican Territory," *The Times Leader,* 7 October 1983, 2A, 10A. On voter registration patterns in the Wyoming Valley, see *Pennsylvania Manual,* 1991.
37. Statistics are cited from various sources, including Chaikin, *A Labor Viewpoint 32;* Apparel Industry Caucus—Senate of Pennsylvania, *The Pennsylvania Garment Industry: Foreign Competition Costing Garment Workers' Jobs,* (Harrisburg: Commonwealth of Pennsylvania, 1985), 4–5; K. Miller & S. Smith, *Update on Pennsylvania: The Economy—Jobs, Forecasts, and Telecommunications* (University Park: Penn State University Dept. of Agricultural Economics and Rural Sociology and Bell Atlantic-Pennsylvania, 1997). *Report of the General Executive Board to the Thirty-fifth Convention of the ILGWU,* May 31, 1974 (New York: ABCO Press*); Report of Proceedings, Forty-first Convention, ILGWU,* June 12–19, 1992 (New York: ILGWU, 1992).
38. Commonwealth of Pennsylvania, *The Pennsylvania Garment Industry: Foreign Competition Costing Garment Workers' Jobs,* 1985, 4–5, and; Pennsylvania Department of Labor and Industry, Bureau of Research and Statistics, *Pennsylvania Labor Market Information and Occupational Projection Database* (Harrisburg, 1999), accessible on the worldwide web at www.lmi.state.pa.us/palmids/indprojdata.asp.
39. ILGWU *Census Records-Report #1.* Provided to the author by Lloyd Goldenberg, Auditing Department, UNITE!, 1998.
40. See Chaikin, *A Labor Viewpoint.*
41. For discussion of the migratory patterns of the apparel industry, see Chaikin, *A Labor Viewpoint,* 8, 86: Commonwealth of Pennsylvania, *The Pennsylvania Garment Industry: Foreign Competition Costing Garment Workers' Jobs* (Harrisburg, 1985); *Report of the General Executive Board to the Thirty-fifth Convention of the ILGWU,* May 31, 1974 (New York: ABCO Press, 1974); and *General Executive Board Report to the Thirty-eight Convention of the ILGWU,*

May 27–June 3, 1983 (New York: ILGWU, 1983). Also see Andrew Ross, ed., *No Sweat: Fashion, Free Trade, and the Rights of Garment Workers* (New York: Verso, 1997).

42. "Leslie Fay Goes Astray," *Justice*, October, 1993, 1; "Campaign to save Leslie Fay Jobs: Which side are you on?" *Leslie Fay Workers' Newsletter—ILGWU*, November, 1993, No. 1, 1. "Leslie Fay wants to cut U.S. Thread," *The Times Leader*, March 31, 1994, 1A, 14A.

43. The Leslie Fay bankruptcy, political, social, and union responses, the role of the Stakeholders Alliance, and other issues pertaining to the unfolding saga received wide media attention. See, for example, "Garment Worker arrested in Protest," *Greenwich Times*, May 15, 1994; "Leslie Fay Responds to Claim," *Scranton Tribune*, June 8, 1994, A1, A8; "Kanjorski plans 2d Leslie Fay Hearing," *Women's Wear Daily*, June 15, 1994, 2, 21; "Striking Leslie Fay Workers Protest Big Raises for Bosses," *New York Post*, June 30, 1994, 4; "Leslie Fay Workers Supported by Catholics," *Catholic Light*, June 23, 1994, 10. "Tearing at the Fabric of Women's Lives," *Philadelphia Inquirer*, June 17, 1994, B1, B9; "Leslie Fay to sell some of its Businesses as it Operates Under Chapter 11," *The Wall Street Journal*, March 20, 1995, B6: "Audit Report Details Fraud at Leslie Fay," *Wall Street Journal*, March 28, 1995, B1; "Unionized Leslie Fay Employees Protest Cutbacks in Work," *Times Leader*, March 1, 1994, 1A, 10A; "Furloughed Garment Workers Stage Protest at Leslie Fay," *Wilkes-Barre Citizens' Voice*, March 1, 1994, 3, 33; "Leslie Fay Employees Keep Job Vigil," *Times Leader*, March 2, 1994, 3A; "Leslie Fay to Close its Last U.S. Factory," *New York Times*, May 8, 1995, D3; "Dressmaker to Close Facility in Pennsylvania," *Wall Street Journal*, May 8, 1995, B8.

44. "A Settlement is reached to end Leslie Fay Strike," *New York Post*, July 12, 1994, 6; "ILGWU, Leslie Fay praise tentative Labor Agreement," *Citizens' Voice*, July 12, 1994, 1

45. "Dress Maker to Close its Last U.S. Factory," *The New York Times*, May 8, 1995, D3; "Dress Maker to Close Pennsylvania Facility," *The Wall Street Journal*, May 8, 1995, B8. "Bankruptcy Court Confirms Plan for Reorganization," *The Wall Street Journal*, April 22, 1997, A8; "Earnings Nearly Doubled: Reorganization Costs Drop," *The Wall Street Journal*, May 27, 1997, A4. As of this writing, most of Leslie Fay's products were made in the San Marcos Free Trade Zone in El Salvador.

46. P. Novak, *Oral History Interview*, June 19, 1997, Wyoming Valley Oral History Project, University of Wisconsin-Stevens Point, Tape 1, Side 2.

6

Sweatshops in Sunset Park

A Variation of the Late-Twentieth-Century Chinese Garment Shops in New York City*

XIAOLAN BAO
California State University, Long Beach

On March 12, 1995, the *New York Times* carried a report on the Chinese garment shops in the Sunset Park area of Brooklyn, a neighborhood that houses the new Chinese garment production center in New York City. Unlike most of the Chinatown garment shops in Manhattan, many of the Chinese shops in Sunset Park are not unionized. The weak influence of organized labor and law enforcement agencies in the area had virtually turned the industry there into a safety valve for some Chinese employers to extract quick profits while not complying with any labor laws. Incidents of exploitation increased with the expansion of the Chinese garment shops in the area.

The report in the *New York Times*, written by reporter Jane H. Lii, largely confirmed the above observation. The vivid description of life in the shops, based on the reporter's first-hand experience, gripped the hearts of its readers. According to Lii, the shop she worked in for an entire week was "typical of the small, new shops outside Manhattan":

> The steel doors opened into a dim, dusty warehouse. Red and blue rags covered the four windows, shutting out all natural light. Bundles of cut cloth sat piled in haphazard mounds, some stacked taller than a worker. Under fluorescent lights swinging from chains, rows of mid-aged Chinese women hunched over sewing machines, squinting and silent.

Were the working conditions there as horrific as those that splashed across the headlines in city newspapers? Lii's reply indicated that there was "something more complex at work." What, then, was the complexity? Lii reported that the owner of the shop was "actually benevolent, albeit in a harsh way." "She does not pay minimum wage, but she serves her workers tea. She makes

*This chapter originally appeared as part of a special issue entitled "Sweated Labor: The Politics of Representation and Reform" in *International Labor and Working-Class History*, No. 61 (Spring, 2002). We thank ILWCH and the author for allowing us to reprint the article.

them work until midnight, but she drives them home afterward. She uses child laborers, but she fusses over them, combing their ponytails, admiring their painted fingernails, even hugging them." According to Lii, the boss had opened the business only to save her family's honor, for her brother had, among many things, absconded with close to $80,000 owed to his workers in back wages. The shop also was reopened, according to its present owner, in order to provide jobs for those who came from the same region in China and whom she called "our people."

As Lii reported, the situation of the workers in the shop was also complicated. They "sewed virtually nonstop" because they wanted to make money and had no other alternatives without speaking English. They brought their children into the shop to care for them while working. Several children, however, toiled by their mothers' sides to supplement their incomes. It was said that their mothers wanted to instill in them a work ethic by allowing them to do so.

Lii reported that both the employer and her workers considered American labor laws ideal and laudable, but impractical. The workers considered their employer a good boss "precisely because she was willing to violate labor laws and allow their children to work by their sides." The situation was, therefore, "a miserable complicity born of necessity in an insular, immigrant world" or, simply, "a grim conspiracy of the poor," as the reporter concluded. No wonder that the result of working at Sunset Park was pitiful:

> Seven days later, after 84 hours of work, I got my reward, in the form of a promise that in three weeks I would be paid $54.24 or 65 cents an hour (minimum wage is $4.25). I also walked away from the lint-filled factory with aching shoulders, a stiff back, a dry cough and a burning sore throat.

How representative is Lii's seven-day experience in the shops, and how valid is her analysis? In what ways are the conditions in the Sunset Park Chinese shops similar to the union shops in Manhattan's Chinatown, the hub of the Chinese industry in New York City? In what ways are they different? To what extent are the conditions in Sunset Park similar to those of the city's garment shops at the turn of the twentieth century? What are the factors that have led to these similarities and differences? In the era of globalization, what can the conditions in Sunset Park Chinese garment shops tell us about the impact of globalization in the U.S.? This study attempts to answer these questions.

This article is primarily based on the author's historical research of the Chinese garment industry in New York City over the last ten years, her visits to a number of shops in Sunset Park in the late 1990s, and her interviews with several dozen workers in the area.[1] It gives a brief account of the working conditions in the shops and discusses several highly controversial issues in the Sunset Park Chinese community that relate to the garment industry. By presenting a more differentiated picture of the industry, it argues that while labor organizing and law enforcement remain important ways to address labor abuse in the industry, it is imperative for law enforcement agencies, organized labor, and all concerned individuals to understand the complexity embedded in the highly competitive structure of the garment industry, the multidimensional impact of labor legislation and law enforcement, and the need to develop new forms of labor organizing that are informed and responsive to the challenges of the time. Without such an understanding, any effort to curb the sweating phenomenon is likely to be sporadic and without lasting effect on the industry.

Working Environments

The shop where Jane Lii worked and reported is, in large part, typical of the Chinese garment shops in the Sunset Park area. Many of them are housed in former warehouses or converted garages. Because these shops are often hidden behind a steel door and have no sign on the front, one can hardly tell from the outside the nature of the activities inside the shops or, simply, whether there is any activity at all.

Sunset Park offers the Chinese garment industry many advantages. First, the former warehouses and the converted garages there are spacious. Even though they do not provide comfortable working conditions, they offer much more production space than industrial lofts in Manhattan's Chinatown.[2] The 1983 Chinatown Garment Industry Study reports that in 1981, Chinese shops with about 30 sewing machines occupied an average of 6,070 square feet in Soho. These shops were and are still the largest garment shops in the Chinatown area.[3] However, shops in Sunset Park with a similar number of sewing machines can cover as much as 10,000 square feet.[4] The spacious environment of the shops not only allows an effective flow of production, but also provides shop owners with enough space to expand their businesses.

In addition, rents and maintenance fees for buildings in Sunset Park are relatively inexpensive. In the spring of 1998, for example, the owner of a shop, located between Fort Hamilton Parkway and 43rd Street and covering more than 10,000 square feet, told me that she paid only $2,500 a month for a space that accommodates forty workers. For the same money, she could afford only a 4,000-square-foot shop in Manhattan's Chinatown. Maintenance fees are also low. For an additional yearly payment of $100 to $200, the gas and other equipment and utility lines would be checked by the building owner.[5]

There are, however, many characteristics that Sunset Park shops share with their counterparts in Manhattan's Chinatown. Besides bundles of cut cloth piled up in haphazard mounds in almost any open floor space, there are severe problems with ventilation. Shops that were converted from former warehouses and garages have very few or virtually no windows at all. Conditions are even worse when the employers cover the few windows with rags or newspapers or simply lock the main entrance to conceal operations. In these shops the air is stifling and filled with lint and dust, while workers sew under fluorescent lights in the daytime.[6]

However, unlike Chinatown shops that generally suffer from space limitations, the physical size and working conditions of Sunset Park shops are not all the same. There are shops that have more than thirty workers and cover a space of over 10,000 square feet. There are also shops packed with a dozen sewing machines and piles of cut garments but covering less than 4,000 square feet. These small and big shops are located side by side. However, regardless of the differences, they have something in common. Like their counterparts in Manhattan's Chinatown, there is virtually no space reserved for workers' activities other than sewing. Even in the relatively spacious shops, workers eat their lunch at their sewing machines or at the desks where they work.

Division of Labor

Although the shops in Sunset Park, like those in Manhattan's Chinatown, work on various lines of garments from manufacturers or other contractors, workers mostly produce sportswear and other low-priced women's apparel. The division of labor in the shops varies according to the size of the shop and the line of the garments they produce, but there are in general five kinds of workers on the floor: the sorter, the foreperson, machine operators, pressers, and floor workers.

Garment production starts with the sorter, who separates the cut-up fabrics according to the style of the garments and decides where the work should begin. The cut fabrics are then sent to the machine operators for either sewing or hemming. Machine operators include those workers who sew minor parts of the garments, such as zippers, collars, cuffs and pockets. The garment then passes to the hands of the foreperson, who checks the quality of the sewed or hemmed garments. A quality garment will be sent to buttoners and trimmers who attach buttons, sew buttonholes, and trim extra threads. In its final stage, the garment will be sent to floor workers who hang tags, eliminate irregularities, and put the garments in a transparent plastic bag for shipping.

Like its counterparts elsewhere in the city, the Chinese garment industry in Sunset Park is characterized by its gender hierarchy. The rationale used to justify it is always inconsistent and contradictory. For example, the sorter and pressers, the two highest paid jobs on the shop floor, are almost invariably men. Trimmers, the lowest paid workers, are virtually all women. This arrangement is said to have its basis in women's lack of physical strength to move the bundles of cut-up materials around, and women's intellectual inability to sort the cut-up pieces and to lay out a workable schedule for production. Women are also believed to be too weak to operate the heavy pressing machines and endure the heat generated by them. As a result, they are denied the opportunity to work as a sorter or a presser. What is forgotten in this ungrounded rationale for the gender division of labor on the floor is the duration

of strength, which the Chinese call *yin li*, and the extraordinary wisdom to figure out the way to sew the garments with their ever-changing styles. Both of
these are necessary qualities of machine operators, who are overwhelmingly
women.

It is said that women constitute the majority of machine operators in the
shops because the flexible work hours, made possible by the piece-rate system
and the larger number of operators in the shops, allow them to fulfill their
family responsibilities while working in the shops. This justification ignores
the highly competitive environment among the large number of machine operators that is generated by the piece-rate system. Since garment production is
seasonal and work tends to be limited in most of the shops, in order to make
ends meet, women workers are most likely to utilize every minute available to
compete with one another in seizing work and to produce as many garments
as they can. This work atmosphere is likely to deprive them of the flexibility
that the piece-rate system is supposed to offer.

In addition, as known in the shops, workers' earnings depend not only on
the piece rates and the speed at which they work, but also on the kind of work
they do. The more mechanical and simple the work is, the faster they can produce, and the more money they can earn. There is no denying that pressers
work under extremely stressful conditions, because there are usually only two
or three of them in a shop of thirty or more machines and they have to press all
the finished garments within a given time. However, their work is simpler than
that of machine operators, so they can easily speed up their work after they become used to the structure of the garments and thus increase their incomes.
Because there are only a few pressers in a shop, they are protected from the frenetic competition that is a routine part of the lives of machine operators.[7]

Unlike the pressers, machine operators' incomes fluctuate a great deal.
Since styles are transient due to the unpredictable nature of fashion, it tends to
take much longer for machine operators to get familiar with their work before
they can speed up their production. The unpredictable nature of their work
also creates more opportunities for their employers to keep wages low by constantly changing their piece rates, which are allegedly based on styles.

Family wages are always invoked to justify not only the higher pay of some
traditionally men's work, but also the special payment arrangements in such
sections as buttoning and bagging (putting the finished garments into bags).
Since piece rates in these two sections are much lower than other sections, employers would subcontract the entire workload to one or two married male
workers and allow them to complete the work with the assistance of their families. It used to be said that this arrangement was made to help the men fulfil
their traditional gender roles as "rice winners" and to respect Chinese traditional culture. However, this rationale was cast aside in the early 1990s when
the male workers left for higher paying jobs and women replaced them in these
sections.

As Nancy Green and Susan Glenn have cogently argued, the gender division of labor in the garment industry has never been static.[8] Take the operation of sewing machines for example. Although most sewing machine operators are women, an increasing number of undocumented male workers have taken over these positions in Sunset Park over the last few years. Gender remains at work, however. The recently arrived men could easily take over the traditionally female jobs from women, but the gender identity of their jobs continued to subject them to a position inferior to those in the traditionally men's sections. They are generally believed to be less skilled, physically weak, and hence less manly than the rest of the male workers in the shops.

Fluidity between class and gender lines, generated by the structural flexibility of the garment industry, does not preclude opportunities for upward mobility for female as well as male workers, albeit in different ways and to different degrees. Although most Chinese employers are men and had been workers themselves, an increasing number of women workers have become owners of the garment shops in recent years. This was the case in the shop where reporter Lii worked. Many women employers learned English by attending the free language classes offered by their union or other public institutions. Speaking from fair to good English, they operate their businesses successfully, without the assistance of men. Their past experience as workers and their gender identity may enable them to better understand their women employees. However, this does not guarantee that they will be benevolent bosses, as implied in Lii's report. Recent cases of labor law violations in the Chinese garment shops owned by women have demonstrated that, situated in a highly competitive and marginal position in the city's industry, women employers can be as unscrupulous as their male counterparts.[9]

Wages and Hours

Workers' wages in the Sunset Park garment shops fluctuate greatly, contingent upon the type of work they produce, the level of skill, and the quality and adequacy of work their employer provides. A new hand may earn practically nothing for the first day, while a skilled long-stitch machine operator can earn as much as $600 a week in the high season. In general, as in the case of most Chinatown shops in Manhattan, the sorter, the foreperson, the cleaner(s), and the floor workers are paid by the hour. My interviews show that in 1998 a full-time foreperson or a sorter earned an average of more than six dollars per hour, and the finished garment checkers and cleaners, about three dollars. The rest of the workers in the shops are paid at piece rates. Their incomes vary greatly, ranging from weekly averages of $600 to $700 for a presser; $400 to $500 for a hemmer; $300 to $400 for a single machine operator and buttoner; $250 to $300 for a general machine operator, and $150-$200 for a trimmer. Compared with the union's minimum wages, the above wages of the Sunset Park Chinese garment workers may appear desirable. However, most of these weekly wages are in fact the result of workers' working ten to twelve hours a day. Their work hours are even longer during the busy seasons, with competition mounting in recent years.

Forms of payment are also factors that affect workers' incomes. Like their counterparts in Manhattan's Chinatown, most employers in Sunset Park issue payments in a combination of checks and cash. The portion of the payment received by check is determined by the worker's status or need. For union members, whose number is small in the area, employers tailor the amount of their checks strictly according to the union minimum income requirement for benefit eligibility. However, for nonunion workers, who form the overwhelming majority of the workforce in Sunset Park, the amounts of their checks are either kept below the poverty threshold so that they can maintain eligibility for welfare benefits, or kept in line with the US Immigration and Naturalization Service's basic requirement for financial eligibility for sponsoring the immigration of their family members or relatives into the United States. Working underground, undocumented workers are paid invariably by cash.

Chinese employers argue that workers themselves request various forms of payment. However, my interviews reveal that all workers, regardless of their status, are forced to accept a reduction in their wages, because checks are issued with a deduction of a five to seven percent "handling fee." The same is true for cash payments. Furthermore, piece rates are often not announced before the completion of work and in some shops employers reserve their rights to reduce workers' wages if they consider the wages to be too high.

Researcher Mark Levitan reports that in 1990, 72 percent of the reported incomes of less-skilled blue-collar workers, apparel workers included, were below the poverty threshold for a family of four ($12,674).[10] Underreporting might be a factor in leading to the low-income status of some workers' families. However, what Levitan reported did not appear to be far from reality in the case of Chinese garment workers in New York. My interviews suggest that in the late 1990s the actual average annual income of most Sunset Park Chinese garment workers was only about $20,000.[11] To sustain their families, many have to work long hours, in violation of U.S. labor laws.

In the shops where the employers still bother to concern themselves with the investigations of law enforcement agencies, workers were required to punch their work cards to show that they were working eight hours a day, even before they start their day's work. My interviews, however, reveal that 90 percent of the workers employed in Sunset Park are working ten to twelve hours a day. During the busy seasons or when orders have to be rushed out, it is not unusual for workers to work unusually long hours, or as Lii indicated, even labor around the clock.

Long hours of work, coupled with the hazardous environment of the shops, severely damages workers' health. What happened to Bao Zhi Ni is, indeed, not an isolated case. Her written testimony at a public hearing held by the New

York State Assembly Subcommittee on Sweatshops on October 2, 1997, is illustrative of workers' situations:

> My name is Bao Zhi Ni. I am a garment worker. I have worked in the garment factories for close to ten years. For many long hours, I work without proper safety equipment, and under filthy conditions. I work at least ten to twelve hours everyday, but because the bosses depress the wages so low we can only make $20, $30 a day, even though we're working over ten hours . . .
>
> For many long hours I sit at the sewing machine repeating the same motions. I also have to handle heavy bundles of garments every day. Each day at work is an exhausting day. My eyes are tired, and my vision is blurry. My fingers, wrists, shoulders, neck, back, spine, all these parts of my body are inflicted with pain. I started feeling the pain in my lower back five years ago, but I continued to work in the sweatshops. I have no medical benefits.
>
> My shoulders and back hurt constantly. Because I have been forced to work for such long hours, the cartilage between the bones in my back has rubbed away, and I have a pinched nerve. With the pain and the numbness in my left leg, I know that I have muscular and nervous problems. My fingers and wrists hurt. Now, even after just one or two hours of work, my back aches so much that I can barely stand straight. . . . In order to make a living I have no choice but to force myself to work through this pain. Sometimes I can't do it, but I have no choice but to take one or two days off.
>
> Sometimes I have to take one or two weeks off. When I take this time off to heal just a little, my boss gets angry. The boss will call my house to scold me and say that I'm lazy, tell me that I must go back to work as soon as possible.[12]

My interviews reveal that almost all the garment workers who worked in the industry for more than five years have various health problems. Deng Ying Yi, a longtime labor activist at the Workers Center in Brooklyn run by the Union of Needletraders, Industrial and Textile Employees (UNITE!), is virtually disabled after working in the garment industry for more than ten years, with her nervous system partially damaged. Her case is not unique among workers in Sunset Park. However, most of these nonunionized workers are not covered by any form of health insurance.

To survive in their new homeland, nonunionized workers have to develop their own system to cope with the situation. Many rely heavily on their family ties and community networks. The experience of a Mr. Zhang, who had been a middle-rank official in Guangzhou but who became a finished garment checker in a Sunset Park Chinese garment shop, is indicative of this phenomenon:

> I was already fifty-two when I immigrated to this country. I worked in a garment shop as *cha yi* (Cantonese: a finished garment checker) and my wife *jin sin* (Cantonese: a trimmer). Together, we earned an average of less than $400 a week and we still had to raise a daughter, our youngest daughter who was in her teens and was eligible to come with us when we immigrated to this country. She had to eat, to dress and to go to school. In addition, we had to save money in order to spon-

sor our two older children to come to the United States. How did we manage to do all this? Well, we relied on our family. . . .

I came with my other five siblings under the sponsorship of a brother. Each of us came with his or her own family. Altogether, it was more than twenty of us who came to New York City on the same day on the same plane. We rented three two-bedroom apartments in this part of Brooklyn because the brother who came earlier told us that rents are much less expensive in this area. Each apartment was shared by two families. My family and my brother's family shared a two-bedroom apartment and we paid a total of $700 for rent and utilities but we ate separately. My family spent a little more than $100 each month on groceries. How did we manage to do this? We bought the cheapest possible food at the market, say, the thirty-nine-cent-a-pound chicken on sale at Key Foods and the four-head-for-one-dollar broccoli at the street stands in this neighborhood. In addition, my wife and I also picked up empty soda cans and other stuff on our way home from work. If we were lucky, the monthly income from that part of our labor could cover our groceries for an entire week.

For eight years after we came to this city, we never ate out and never stopped working, eleven to twelve hours a day and seven days a week. Whenever we did not have work to do in our shop my wife and I went to work in another shop.[13]

While family ties are important resources for immigrant workers who came with their families, community networks are the most important assets for undocumented immigrant workers, most of whom did not come with their families. For example, undocumented workers from Wenzhou have contributed money to establish their own "mutual funds." These funds can be used by any member in time of need. This practice has proved to be the most effective way for these workers to survive in time of adversity, since they are denied any social services and benefits in the United States.

As elsewhere in the world, the gendered definitions of roles in the Sunset Park Chinese garment shops, their hierarchical order, and the rationale applied to justify them are shaped by the flexible but highly competitive structure of the garment industry, and have been inherently unstable. This fluidity generates dynamics in the industry, but has also taken a toll on those who labor in the industry. It is by exhausting human resources among the workers and in their community that the nonregulated segment of the garment industry has managed to thrive. Sunset Part is a case in point.

"Co-Ethnic Conspiracy?"

One major aspect of the Chinese garment industry in New York that has generated great interest among some scholars is its co-ethnic nature. Although in recent years more and more garment shops in New York have employers and workers who do not share the same ethnic identity, this is not the case with many of the Chinese garment shops in Manhattan's Chinatown and Brooklyn's Sunset Park. Most Chinese employers continue to hire only workers from major Chinese settlements.

As many studies have pointed out, this co-ethnic nature of the industry has benefited both workers and management.[14] Like their Eastern European counterparts at the turn of the twentieth century, Chinese workers do not have to learn to speak or understand English to work in a garment shop. They can also learn the trade on site and from scratch. In truth, without the industry, many working-class Chinese immigrant families may not have been able to survive.

The co-ethnic nature of the industry is also said to have simplified and humanized management of the shops. Many studies have discussed the particular recruitment pattern of the Chinese shops. Although in recent years a growing number of new immigrant workers have begun to seek employment through advertisements in community newspapers or the help-wanted signs posted in the front of the shops, most employers continue to rely on the recommendations of their workforce for new recruits, and most new immigrant workers obtain their first jobs through their families, friends, and relatives. Some employers also hire job applicants on the spot, without giving them much of a background check. New recruits, especially those who are employed with the recommendations from workers already in the shop, are allowed to use the facilities in the shop to receive on-site training.

Workers can maintain their cultural practices at their workplaces. They celebrate major Chinese festivals in the shops. They also share Chinese food and cooking with one another, listen to the blasting of the closed-circuit Chinese radio broadcasts, and share news about their homeland while working. As Lii noted, although employers in most Chinese shops do not offer their employees overtime payments when they expect workers to work long hours or on weekends, they offer them free rice and water, or even tea in some shops, to eat and drink with their lunch. They also provide lunch or afternoon tea to compensate workers' working on weekends. It is also widely known that most employers in Sunset Park will drive their employees home if their work ends after 11:00 P.M.

Workers who are unfamiliar with the labor laws and their rights in the United States feel obligated to work hard for their employers if their employers are willing to accommodate their needs. The undocumented workers feel particularly grateful to their employers if their employers have offered them any form of protection during immigration or other law enforcement raids. Employers in Sunset Park are known to cover workers up with piles of cut-garments scattered on the floor, or allow them to use the ladder in the shop to climb to the skylight. These gestures foster gratitude on the workers' part, which they feel obligated to reciprocate.

Many workers find it easy to identify with their employers if they are immigrants and have been workers themselves. Workers who desire upward social mobility look up to their employers as role models, a mirror of their future in the land of opportunity. Workers' empathy with their employers' situation, generated by a mixture of gratitude, fear, and admiration, has often led to their acquiescence to their employers' unscrupulous practices on the shop floor. In some cases this relationship of empathy has become so entrenched that law enforcement agents from outside the Chinese community and Chinese union organizers find it difficult to break. No wonder observers of the industry, like reporter Lii, do not hesitate to call the Sunset Park shop "a miserable complicity born of necessity in an insular, immigrant world." However, this conspiracy theory is too simplistic to explain the complex interdependent relationship between the workers and their employers in the ethnic enclave economy of the United States. It also fails to highlight the imbalance of power embedded in this relationship. Failing to locate the ultimate beneficiaries of this relationship, this theory cannot explain fully the causes of sweated labor in the shops.

Clearly, employers' various forms of accommodation benefit themselves rather than the workers. Let's take the special form of recruitment, for example. Since workers' incomes are based on the work they have accomplished, it will only hurt the new recruits if they are slow to learn their routine of work. However, on-site training allows employers to strengthen their personal ties with the newly hired as well as those who are already in the shop. Paying wages in a mixture of cash and checks or simply by cash also enables the employers to avoid paying taxes, the amounts of which are likely to be much larger than their workers'. A closer investigation of the situation in the industry also reveals that accommodations offered by employers are not unconditional. They are given only to workers who follow the rules they set. Those who refuse to do so are fired, blacklisted, physically assaulted, or subjected to other forms of retaliation.

Most Chinese employers do not force their workers to work long hours. However, production is organized in such a way that workers who do not stay as long as the rest will find themselves in an extremely disadvantageous position. Since there is no limit on work hours in most of the shops and workers who are willing to maximize their work hours can work as long as they wish, those who refuse to do so will end up having only "pork neckbones" (a slang in the Chinatown garment industry, referring to garments difficult to sew), or simply no garments to work on the next morning when they return.

Similar situations occur if a worker is ill and takes sick leave, or refuses to work on Sunday. Employers will hire a replacement worker almost immediately after a laborer fails to show up. Employers will also distribute "chickens in soy sauce" (another slang in the Chinatown garment industry, referring to work easy to sew) or paychecks on Sunday. Under these situations, workers who take a sick day are likely to lose their jobs, and those who do not work on Sunday will miss not only an important opportunity to increase their incomes, but also to get paid in a timely manner. Since workers' wages tend to be withheld by their employers for months in Sunset Park, failing to be present on payday will mean another indefinitely long delay in getting paid. It's no wonder that workers in Sunset Park tend to lament, "We have the option to die but we don't have the option to take a sick day or a rest."

Some employers have also blatantly taken advantage of their workers' acquiescence to maximize their profit. Instances of *zhen jia lao ban* (real and fake bosses) and *yi guo liang zhi* (one country, two systems), stories told by labor activist Deng Ying Yi, are indications of how far employers would go.[15] As Deng recalled, one day workers of a shop came to the UNITE! Workers' Center to seek assistance in collecting their wages. It turned out that their employer had closed the shop after owing them several hundred thousands of dollars in back wages and had vanished without a trace. However, when the State Department of Labor finally undertook this case, the department found it difficult to file charges against the real owner of the shop. The owner, an undocumented immigrant himself, had registered the shop with the name and social security number of an elderly worker and had been signing all the legal documents under this worker's name without informing him. Filing charges against owner of the shop would mean charges against this worker, who was not the real owner of the shop.[16]

The story of "one country, two systems" is about a peculiar phenomenon in some unionized shops in Sunset Park. According to Deng, although union contracts stipulate that all workers in a union shop are union members and entitled to union benefits, employers of some unionized shops refuse to register their new recruits as union members and keep their wages in the books. Consequently, there are both union and nonunion members in the same shop who are working under very different systems of employment.

My interviews further reveal other forms of discrimination on the floor. For example, some employers offer different piece rates to workers of different immigration status and from different regions in China. Cantonese immigrant workers, who form the majority of the workforce, tend to receive higher piece rates and work relatively regular hours, while non-Cantonese or undocumented workers are denied all these "privileges." Discriminatory treatments have taken a different form in a small number of shops that hire several skilled workers from other ethnic groups. The non-Chinese workers are offered wages and other working conditions that comply with labor laws, while their Chinese fellow workers, who work side by side with them, have to struggle against the grim reality of low pay and long hours of work.[17]

Chinese employers have been so reckless in exploiting workers in their own community that it reinforces the stereotypical image of Chinese workers as the docile "willing slaves" in the Sunset Park area. This image of the workers subjects them to exploitation not only by Chinese employers, but also by shop owners of other ethnic groups. In 1997, the *Sing Tao Daily* reported that seven Chinese workers from a Jewish-owned garment shop came to seek help from the UNITE! Workers' Center. They complained that they had been discriminated against by their Jewish employer who had closed the shop and refused to pay them according to labor laws, as he did to his Hispanic workers.[18]

The most common problem workers face, however, is the failure to receive compensation for their work in a timely manner. Employers benefit tremendously from withholding their workers' wages. Community labor activists estimate that a shop of average size in Sunset Park has thirty-five workers and the lowest wage of garment workers in the area is about $150 per week. If the owner of a shop withholds his/her employees' wages for eight weeks, which is not uncommon in the area, the employer will have more than $40,000 in hand by the end of the eighth week, even if workers in the shop earned the lowest wage in the area. With this $40,000, an employer can open another shop without having to pay interest as they would if borrowing money from a bank.

Regrettably, as union organizers and law enforcement agencies have pointed out, workers tend not to take any legal action against their employers until their employers close down the shops. The reasons are varied. One major reason is the workers' lack of knowledge about their rights and the political operation in their new homeland. With few employment alternatives, many immigrant workers fear that any form of cooperation with law enforcement agencies or organized labor will cost them their jobs. This was particularly the situation before the signing of the Hot Goods Bill by the New York State governor in 1996.[19] Prior to the adoption of this bill, law enforcement agencies had difficulty in helping workers retrieve their back wages if a shop was closed and the employer was hard to locate. As a result, the longer wages were withheld, the more reluctant workers were to report their cases. They feared that their reporting would lead their employers to close the shop for good.

Workers' reluctance to report labor violations on the floor is also compounded by a lack of understanding about the U.S. income tax system. Many are afraid that the amount of money they receive will be reduced by paying taxes if they seek assistance from law enforcement agencies and have to report their back wages to the Internal Revenue Service. Understandably, undocumented workers have additional concerns. Working underground, they fear that a visit from the Department of Labor to their work place will bring in a raid by the Immigration and Naturalization Service.

While workers are often reluctant to take action against their employers, employers are not hesitant to take advantage of workers' fear. According to longtime observers of the community, many employers in the garment industry engage in speculative financial activities with the money they have withheld from their workers, such as gambling or buying high-return but high-risk stocks. Since most of these activities will not lead to their expected outcomes, the employers close down their shops to avoid payments they owe their employees.

There are also employers who simply try to extract larger profits by closing down operations, absconding with the money they have withheld from their employees, and reopening their businesses under a different name. This was the case where reporter Lii worked. Hence, labor violations are widespread and the turnover rate of many Sunset Park Chinese garment shops is at a record high.[20] This highly unstable situation makes it even more difficult to enforce labor laws in the area, especially in recent years when most of these agencies are understaffed.

Tensions and exploitation in many Chinese garment shops in Sunset Park lay bare the limits of ethnic solidarity in the garment industry. Relegated to the same ethnic economic sector, Chinese employers have to rely on workers in their own community to run their businesses and accommodate workers' needs. However, situated in a marginal position of a highly competitive industry, many employers also do not hesitate to exploit their community ties to maintain their competitive edge in the industry. As in the case with their predecessors in the city's industry, the garment industry offers new Chinese immigrant workers many advantages in working among their own, but it also makes them more vulnerable to exploitation by management on all levels. The degree of labor violation in many Chinese garment shops demonstrates not only the limits of ethnic solidarity but also the devastating impact of the frenetic search for cheap labor on the Chinese community. This impact, as well as the limited nature of ethnic solidarity, will be further explored in the following section.

"The Cantonese vs. the Fujianese"?

One major issue that surfaced constantly during my interviews with workers is their concern about the increasing number of undocumented workers in the industry, most of whom are believed to be from Fuzhou, a major city in the province of Fujian in southeastern China. These newcomers, who speak their own dialect, are often blamed for worsening labor conditions on the shop floor and deteriorating living standards in Sunset Park. They also are charged with undermining workers' solidarity in the industry. Many Cantonese workers believe that there is no way for them to get along well with the Fujianese.

In the course of interviewing workers in Sunset Park, however, I came to know many Cantonese and Fujianese workers who are good friends. I also came to see that although a large number of undocumented workers came from Fuzhou, Fuzhou is not the only place that has sent undocumented Chinese immigrants to the United States. Undocumented Chinese workers also come from Wenzhou, Guangdong, and almost all the coastal areas of China. There are also some from Malaysia and other Southeast Asian countries. Nevertheless, there is a pronounced tendency in New York's Chinese community to identify all undocumented workers as Fujianese. Stories about how fanatically hardworking they are became a recurring theme in the narratives of almost all the non-Fujianese workers. Fujianese workers were said to be so money-crazy that they would bring their rice cookers to the shops, cook and eat there while working, and even spend the night in the shops if they found any work there.

These undocumented workers are also blamed for having eroded the image of the Chinese in the Sunset Park area. It is said that since they spend so many hours at work, they could even do without a place to stay. It is a general belief in the Sunset Park Chinese community that several dozen immigrants from Fuzhou would share a single one-bedroom apartment, either only spending the night there or using it just for bathing and other purposes while spending their nights in the garment shops. I heard little sympathy for their plight in my interviews with non-Fujianese workers.

Anecdotal as these stories are, recycled repeatedly, they have fostered a profound prejudice against workers from Fuzhou. This prejudice is so prevalent that it often blinds non-Fujianese workers to class conflicts on the shop floor. For example, I came across a group of Cantonese workers who had just been fired by their employer for refusing to work as many hours as he wanted. Rather than blaming their unscrupulous employer, they blamed their unemployment on the workers from Fuzhou whom their employer had hired for lower rates and longer hours of work.

Although all prejudices are unjustified, factors that have contributed to the prejudice against Fujianese workers are worth exploring. My conversation with a Mrs. Deng, a Taishanese worker and a staunch opponent of "those hateful Fujianese," is revealing:[21]

A: As you know, the Chinese garment shops in Sunset Park have a bad name as sweatshops these days. Our lives are miserable. It was all because of those hateful Fujianese. They have taken our jobs. The bosses love them because they don't have family responsibilities and can work twenty-four hours a day in the shop. They are very greedy. What is in their eyes is only money, money, money. Recently we Cantonese have been losing ground in my shop. The Fujianese are taking over. They are everywhere in my shop.

Q: Could you tell me how many workers from Fuzhou are exactly in your shop?

A: Well, I never counted them, but, never mind, let me try. There are a total of about forty machine operators in my shop, one, two, three, yes, three are Cantonese, three are Mandarin speaking from Shanghai and Wuhan, and . . . [It turned out that only eight out of a total of thirty-five workers in her shop were from Fuzhou and only five out of the nine undocumented workers in her shop came from Fuzhou.]

Q: So the majority in your shop is not Fujianese and the undocumented workers in your shop are not all from Fuzhou.

A: Yes, you are right. My impression was wrong. But still I am nervous about them. Let me tell you something, actually, there are also undocumented workers from Taishan. A village in Taishan is now almost empty, you know, because they had a smuggler in that village, and he had connections with those snakeheads in New York City. The conditions of the undocumented workers from that village are deplorable. I always think that my situation is already miserable enough. [She was collecting welfare benefits at the time of this interview. Her husband just had a surgery and could not work and she had four schoolchildren to raise.] But theirs are even worse. However, I have been told that compared with those from Fuzhou, they seem to be doing fine because many of them have family members or relatives in New York. Those from Fuzhou don't seem to have this advantage and they owe the snakeheads much more money than those from Taishan. Anyway, I should admit that I don't know very much about them because I don't talk to them and they don't talk to me either.

Q: What then made you so angry with them?

A: They work too hard! Whenever there is some work in the shop, especially the easy jobs, they are there. Very often we don't have any work left when we return in the morning. They have finished all the work at night! But we can't do this. We have to go home at night to take care of our families and to have a little rest. We are human beings, you know. But work is money. They have taken away all our money. They are so hateful!

Q: Did your boss ever close the door of the shop at a time like that?

A: No, how could you expect them to do so? Of course not; for the bosses, the sooner they can get the work done the better. So they love those illegal immigrants from Fuzhou. In the past, many garment shop owners had signs on the gates of their shops, saying "Cantonese only," because they were afraid that they would be harassed by the Fujianese gangsters, who are well known for their fearlessness, if they had Fujianese workers in their shops. But now they don't care. They need workers who can work twenty-four hours a day. So the sign on their gates has also changed. It reads "Fujianese only."

The situation has made me really mad. To be honest, who doesn't need money? I too wish that I could work around the clock, if I did not have a family to take care of. I need money too. I don't mind working hard. I was a peasant in China. Rain or shine, I worked outdoors, under conditions much worst than sewing in a garment shop. I wish I could make more money for my family.

But, wait a minute, I sense something wrong with myself in answering your questions. Haven't I somewhat misjudged those undocumented workers from Fuzhou? Yes, I think I have.

Obviously, tension among the workers, ignited by the highly competitive nature of garment organization and accelerated by the manipulation of management, has led to their misjudgment of reality in the shop.

Ungrounded as the stories about undocumented workers from Fuzhou are, generated by a mixture of myth and reality, they take a toll on all workers from the same place. This can be seen in the response of a Ms. Wong:

I think we immigrants from Fuzhou have been treated very unfairly by our own Chinese community. I am not an illegal immigrant. I came with all the papers as a legal immigrant. In addition, unlike the majority of illegal immigrants from the Fuzhou area, I came from the city and with my family. But still, I am looked at as an illegal immigrant because I came from Fuzhou.

I don't speak Cantonese, so I could not find a job in a restaurant or other place. That's how I ended up working in a garment shop.

My husband and I had a hard time looking for a place for our family to stay when we first came. Landlords from other parts of China refused to rent to us, because we are from Fuzhou. People in the community said we lived like pigs, with several dozen people usually packed in one apartment but registered under only one or two names. So the landlords were scared. Landlords from Fuzhou did not treat us well either. They charged us much higher rents because they knew that we had no choice.

My husband and I finally got to rent this place because we decided to speak Mandarin and pretended to be from other parts of China when we first met our landlady, who is Cantonese. Yes, now, she knows that we are from Fuzhou but she doesn't care anymore because we have become very good friends, and she says we are the best tenants she has ever had.[22]

Many immigrant workers from Fuzhou whom I interviewed shared her experience. Although almost all immigrant workers from Fuzhou have been affected by the prejudice against them, the undocumented ones among them are the most victimized. A Mr. Dong's response was typical:

I don't understand why we should be treated like this! We are human beings too! Yes, we work very hard, because we need money to pay back our debts! Yes, many of us share an apartment, because we want to save money. Do we enjoy our lives in this country? Of course not. We are separated from our families and working underground. We are bullied by our bosses, even including those from Fuzhou. They make us work long hours but pay us much less than other workers in the shops. I don't think anyone would like to live a life like ours! But, still, we are not going to give up because we are working for a better life for our families.

My family lives in a village along the Ming River, and I was a fisherman in the village before I came to the United States. I left my home village because the water there was so seriously polluted that there were no edible fish left. I could not make a living for my family by fishing.

Some people ask, "Why don't you go home if life is so hard for you?" But can we? My family has borrowed a lot of money to send me here. My wife and my kids have pinned their hopes on me, yearning for me to bring them to *meiguo* [the beautiful land, which refers to the United States].

In addition, what will folks in my village say if I return home penniless? I remember when I was in the village, I envied those who returned home from the United States. They looked so successful, squandering money like dirt. I wished I could be like them one day. Of course, after I came to the United States, I got to know that many of them too had been working in a sweatshop, as I do now. If they can make it, I can make it, too. So, I work hard. It is none of anyone's business if I don't eat, don't sleep, and work nonstop.[23]

The strong desire to improve the well-being of their families, reinforced by a degree of vanity for a glamorous return, led the undocumented workers to leave their native land and fall prey to the sweating system in the United States. Although the living conditions of their native land have "pushed" them out of China, it was the underground economy in the United States that has "pulled" them in and lured them to violate U.S. immigration laws.

The experience of the Fujianese garment workers in Sunset Park reminds one of what has happened to each group of newcomers in New York's garment industry. While the constant search for cheap labor brings in different groups of ethnic workers at different points in history, newcomers are always blamed for the cutthroat competition in the industry. This "finger pointing" takes place even within the same ethnic group. As national characteristics were used in the past as a convenient way of explaining the deterioration of working conditions, today regional and dialectal differences, immigration status, and even the location of one's family have become indexes in the Chinese garment industry for differentiating the old from the new, the "human" from the "inhuman," and thereby the excusers from the excused.[24] Labor solidarity in the community is thus undermined by conflicts of interest among workers, as well as elements in the cultural repertoire of the community.

Will Too Much Law Enforcement Kill the Chinese Garment Industry in New York City?

In the late 1990s, a number of Chinese employers in Sunset Park began to react strongly when the New York State Apparel Industry Task Force carried out its mission to enforce labor laws in the city's garment industry. In October 1996, after the task force completed its investigation and charged many Chinese garment shops with labor violations, Chinese employers in Sunset Park launched a massive demonstration to protest the state operation. They called it "adding salt to the wound." Claiming that the law enforcement agency had unjustly labeled all Chinese shops as "sweatshops," Chinese employers held the state investigation accountable for causing the further decline of Chinese garment industry in the city by providing manufacturers with the justification for withdrawing their work from the Chinese community.

According to the Chinese employers, manufacturers should be blamed for the deteriorating working conditions in the Chinese shops. Since they suppressed piece rates to such an intolerable degree and demanded such quick production and delivery of finished garments, Chinese employers were forced to reduce the piece rates they offered to their workers and expect them to work longer hours in order to remain competitive. In addition, since manufacturers frequently delayed payments for finished work, Chinese employers had to withhold wages to their own workers. Labor law enforcement will kill the Chinese garment industry, they asserted, because only by reducing wages and extending work hours could the industry survive in the highly competitive environment of garment production in New York.[25]

The Chinese employers' accusation against manufacturers is not entirely groundless, given manufacturers' frantic efforts to reduce the costs of labor in recent years. However, as many concerned individuals in the community have rightly pointed out, even though the Chinese garment industry has been hit hard by the outflow of garment production from the city, the sweatshop conditions in the industry are what allow the manufacturers to put a human face on their move from the city.[26]

What has happened since the State Department of Labor established its Apparel Industry Task Force in 1987? Did the efforts of the Task Force lead to the decline of the Chinese garment industry in New York City? Did the industry really decline?

Statistics show that despite the shrinking of the city's share in the U.S. garment industry, the absolute numbers of Chinese shops and their workforce in the past decade or more did not suggest any sign of decline; indeed, they grew. In the early 1980s, there were approximately 500 Chinese shops in the city, largely concentrated in Manhattan's Chinatown and employing an estimated 25,000 Chinese workers. In 1998, there was an estimate of more than 800 Chinese shops, scattered in various parts of the city and employing more than 30,000 Chinese workers.[27]

One specific segment of the Chinese garment industry has declined significantly in recent years, however. It is the number of the unionized shops in Manhattan's Chinatown. Between 1992 and 1997 the number of garment shops in Manhattan's Chinatown dropped from 608 to 555 and employment declined from 21,015 to 14,887, a loss of more than 6,000 jobs.[28] The decline in the Manhattan's Chinatown garment industry coincided with the rapid growth of the Chinese garment shops in other parts of the city, in particular, Sunset Park in Brooklyn. Although Manhattan's Chinatown remains the center of the Chinese garment industry in New York, with about 500 Chinese shops still clustered in this area, its importance has been significantly reduced by the rapid growth of the Chinese garment industry in other boroughs.

The decline of Manhattan's Chinatown shops has also led to the weakening of union influence on the entire Chinese garment industry in New York City. In the early 1980s, when shops in Chinatown represented an overwhelming majority of the Chinese garment shops in New York City, more than 90 percent of them were unionized. By the end of the 1990s, it is estimated that the UNITE! Local 23-25 represented only half of the Chinese garment shops in the city.[29] The union's influence has declined even in Manhattan's Chinatown, with the percentage of Chinese union shops dropping from more than 90 per-cent in the early 1980s to fewer than 80 percent by 1997.[30] As a result, member-ship of the UNITE! Local 23-25—the largest local of the union, with an 85 percent Chinese membership—dropped from 28,083 in 1992 to 22,995 in 1996, a loss of more than 5,000 members.[31]

Despite problems embedded in the unionization of the Chinatown gar-ment industry in earlier years, there are still many significant differences in working conditions between union and nonunion shops. The shrinking per-centage of union shops in the Chinese garment industry indicates that more and more Chinese garment workers have been deprived of the benefits and protection to which union members are entitled. It should, therefore, come as no surprise that labor violations are rampant in many nonunion Chinese shops, which have, in turn, undercut working conditions in the union shops.

There is little doubt that manufacturers and retailers should be held ac-countable for the deteriorating working conditions in the city's garment in-dustry. However, many individuals in the community are also correct in pointing out that it is the sweating system in some Chinese garment shops that has provided them with the most convenient excuse to pull production out of New York City. This is particularly true when politicians of all stripes have rec-ognized a political advantage in promoting the elimination of sweatshops in the U.S., and manufacturers and retailers have also been pressured by con-sumer groups as well as labor to distance themselves from contract shops la-beled as sweatshops.

The Chinese employers' argument that "too much law enforcement will kill the Chinese garment industry in New York City" reminds one of the situations at the turn of the twentieth century. As Nancy Green has noted, during that time when progressive reformers, labor leaders, and state legislators endeav-ored to improve labor conditions by passing new legislation and enforcing laws, manufacturers also argued that too many constraints would make the landscape of the garment industry disappear altogether from the city.[32] How-ever, the garment industry remains in New York City, and so will the Chinese garment industry, at least for the decade to come.

Some Reflections

Driven by the search for cheap nonunion labor, runaway shops and sweated labor are not unique to the Chinese garment industry, nor are they new in the history of the city's industry. As early as the 1920s the dispersion of garment shops from Manhattan into various parts of the city already became a peculiar aspect in the landscape of New York's garment industry.[33] The Chinese garment industry, as a major part of the city's industry, is no exception in these regards.

The experience of Chinese workers is in many ways similar to that of their predecessors in the city's garment industry, but there are also differences. Particularly in the 1980s and 1990s, these differences were caused by the challenge of the times rather than simply by the cultural characteristics of the Chinese workers. Garment workers in the first half of the twentieth century were able to enjoy improved working conditions, thanks to the strong influence of labor unions and the continuous growth of the city's garment industry. However, Chinese workers in the late twentieth century were increasingly subjected to abusive labor conditions as the city's industry declined rapidly. Their union, plagued by its entrenched bureaucratic culture, could hardly respond to their needs.

As in the case of the city's garment industry in the early twentieth century, law enforcement and labor organizing remain the two most powerful ways to address the problems in the Chinese garment industry. Both law enforcement agents and labor organizers face the challenge of how to understand the complex reality of the garment industry beyond the highly politicized representations of it in political arenas. However, they also have to address different issues in their own realms.

As Mark Levitan has aptly put it, one of the major factors that has undermined significantly the efforts to eliminate sweated labor in the city is that "there are not enough cops on the beat." Despite the growth of sweated labor in the city's garment industry and the politicians' highly emotional pledges to eliminate it, both New York State and federal investigation teams are severely understaffed. According to Levitan, in 1998, there were only twenty-three investigators in the federal office of the Wage and Hour Division that had responsibility for the entire New York City metropolitan area, and only twenty-three out of thirty-four positions in New York City's Apparel Industry Task Force were filled.[34] As a result, in addition to improving their understanding of the dynamics generated by the highly competitive structure of the garment industry, the history and culture of each ethnic group, and the multifaceted impact of their operations, law enforcement agents still have to battle the shortage of hands in carrying out their tasks, a difficult situation that is indeed not of their own making.

Organized labor faces another type of challenge. Never before has UNITE!, the major labor union of the U.S. garment industry, been under so much pressure to reform itself. The parochialism and the culture of business unionism that UNITE! shares with other traditional trade unions have proved to be impotent in this new age of the global economy. Today, with the impressive growth of the community-based labor organizations in New York's Chinatown and other ethnic communities, the question UNITE! faces is no longer whether it is willing to change but whether the change is adequate to maintain its legitimacy as a labor union in the industry.[35] In this era when capital has already globalized its search for inexpensive labor, how can we develop effective organizing strategies that are not only responsive to the needs of U.S. workers but also allow them to join forces with workers in other parts of the world?

This is a question very much on the agendas of trade unions as well as concerned individuals in the Chinese community and the city.

Notes

1. Unless otherwise noted, the following discussion is primarily based on these sources and the information provided by Liang Huan Ru, the former veteran union organizer in Brooklyn.
2. I use "Manhattan's Chinatown" because new Chinatowns have recently emerged in other boroughs of New York City, such as Queens and Brooklyn.
3. Abeles, Schwartz, Haechel & Silverblatt, Inc., *The Chinatown Garment Industry Study* (hereafter *Study*) (New York: International Ladies' Garment Workers' Union Local 23–25 and the New York Skirt and Sportswear Association, 1983), 55. For the sizes of the shops in Manhattan's Chinatown, see *Study*, 49–59.
4. See for example, the weekly special issue of the *Sing Tao Daily* (hereafter *STD*), March 8, 1998, 7.
5. My visit to the shop and interview with the shop owner.
6. One woman worker told me in an interview that it was so hot inside her shop in summer that sometimes she simply could not help crying while trying to rush out her work.
7. Experienced pressers began to lose this advantage in more and more Chinese garment shops in recent years, largely due to the increased competition from undocumented male workers. Unable to compete with the low wages accepted by the latter, they too had to face economic insecurity in the industry. I am indebted to a reminder from Liang Huan Ru, an organizer of UNITE! Local 23–25, and May Ying Chen, vice president of UNITE!, for this piece of information. What, however, must be kept in mind is that while competition has mounted among pressers in recent years, women machine operators also faced competition from undocumented workers.
8. See Susan Glenn, *Daughters of the Shtetl: Life and Labor in the Immigrant Generation* (Ithaca, New York: Cornell University Press, 1990), 90–131, and Nancy Green, *Ready-to-Wear and Ready-to-Work: A Century of Industry and Immigrants in Paris and New York* (Durham: Duke University Press, 1997), 161–87.
9. The most recent case was the one at 446 Broadway in November 1997, in which a young woman employer closed her shop after withholding a large sum of money in back wages from her employees. The case was covered by most major newspapers inside and outside the Chinese community. See, for example, *New York Times*, December 14, 1997.
10. See "Opportunity at Work: The New York City Garment Industry" (New York: Community Service Society of New York, 1998), 39.
11. This observation has been supported by recent coverage in Chinese community newspapers. For example, as covered in *World Journal* (hereafter *WJ*) in 1996, the monthly income of an elderly couple who worked in a Chinese garment shop was $1,800 and $2,200, respectively. Given the depressed piece rates in the last two years and the seasonal nature of the industry, this observation, based on interviews with workers in Sunset Park, does not seem to be far away from reality.
12. Directly quoted from "Behind Closed Doors: A Look into the Underground Sweatshop Industry," a report by the New York State Assembly Sub-Committee on Sweatshops (New York, November 1997), 59–61.
13. Interview by the author on April 13, 1998.
14. See, for example, Bernard Wong, "The Role of Ethnicity in Enclave Enterprises: A Study of the Chinese Garment Factories in New York City." *Human Organization* 46 (2), 1987: 120–9.
15. "One country, two systems" is the Chinese state policy in Hong Kong after the former British colony was returned to China in 1997.
16. Cases like this are not unheard of in the Chinese garment industry in Manhattan's Chinatown as well as other boroughs of the city. See, for example, The Chinese Staff and Workers Association, *Zhi Gong Zhi Sheng* (January 1994).
17. I was told that this small number of workers from other ethnic groups were likely to have worked for the former owner of the shop and the Chinese employer employed them as part of the deal when he/she purchased the business. I was also told that some Chinese employers deliberately kept these workers to protect their businesses from harassment by Chinese

gangsters, who tended not to attack shops with non-Chinese workers for fear that their illicit activities would be known beyond the Chinese community.

18. *STD*, December 19, 1997.
19. The "Hot Goods Bill" was signed into law on July 2, 1996. This bill has established "additional methods of obtaining restitution for unpaid apparel industry workers from contractors, manufacturers, and retailers." For a further discussion of this bill, see "Behinds Closed Doors," 4.
20. The *Study* has reported that at the end of 1981, 28 percent of all Chinese shops in Chinatown had been in business for less than one year and close to half of them had been in operation for less than two years (p. 68). However, in the late 1990s, as many workers have pointed out, the Chinese garment shops in Sunset Park are often opened and closed down within months.
21. Taishan is a county in Guangdong Province. Immigrants from this county are also generally called "Cantonese."
22. Interview by the author on July 2, 1998.
23. Interview by the author on June 21, 1998.
24. Immigration status and whether one is living with their family have become important indexes because much of the Chinese community has chosen to believe that legal immigration and family life are the norms throughout the history of the community, however invalid this belief is.
25. For a summary of their arguments, see *STD*, April 22, 1998.
26. For different voices in the community, see, for example, the weekly special issues of *STD*, May 17, 1998 and June 28, 1998.
27. The estimate of 800 Chinese shops is based on an adding of the approximate 500 shops in Manhattan and the more than 300 shops in Brooklyn and other boroughs. More than 30,000 workers were estimated by the community press in the end of 1997. See *STD*, December 22, 1997.
28. These statistics are provided by the Research Department of the New York State Department of Labor.
29. In 1997, when the union signed a new contract with Chinese employers, the three Chinese contractors' associations represented only 406 shops in the city. This was later reported in most Chinese community newspapers. See, for example, *STD*, February 23, 1998.
30. This percentage of Chinatown union shops in 1997 is based on a comparison of the number of garment shops in the Chinatown area provided by the state labor department, which is not classified according to ethnicity, and the estimate of Chinatown union organizers and the Chinese newspapers. See, for example, *STD*, December 22, 1997 and April 29, 1998 and *WJ*, February 28, 1998.
31. These statistics are provided by the UNITE! Research Department. The estimated percentage of the local's Chinese membership in this study is consistent with the numbers provided by the local.
32. Green, *Ready-To-Wear*, 50.
33. See Nancy Green, "Sweatshop Migrations: The Garment Industry between Home and Shop," in *The Landscape of Modernity: Essays on New York City, 1900–1940*, eds. David Ward and Olivier Zunz (New York: Russell Sage Foundation, 1992), 213–32.
34. Mark Levitan, *Opportunity at Work: the New York City Garment Industry* (New York: Community Service Society of New York, 1998), 59.
35. One of the most active community-based labor organizations in New York's Chinatown in the last two decades is the Chinese Staff and Workers' Association.

7
Offshore Production[1]

EDNA BONACICH
University of California, Riverside

RICHARD P. APPELBAUM
University of California, Santa Barbara
(with **KU-SUP CHIN, MELANIE MEYERS,**
GREGORY SCOTT, AND GOETZ WOLFF)

In January 1997, Guess? Inc., the largest apparel manufacturer in Los Angeles, announced that it was moving 40 percent of its production to Mexico.[2] That same month, the California State Employment Development Department reported that apparel employment had grown in Los Angeles County by more than 6 percent over the past year, continuing a pattern of growth over the past few decades. How are we to understand these contradictory facts? Is Los Angeles an exception to the general pattern throughout the United States of erosion of employment in the apparel industry? Or is it, too, succumbing to the lure of lower wages offshore, especially in nearby Mexico, now that the North American Free Trade Agreement (NAFTA) has eased restrictions on imports from that country and will entirely eliminate them by 2004?

There are some indications that the industry in Los Angeles has a special vitality, as shown in its exceptional pattern of employment growth in comparison with substantial decline in the United States as a whole. Most jobs have been lost in the northeast. No other state besides California shows robust employment growth, and southern California accounts for four-fifths of the California apparel industry. But despite the continuing growth of apparel-related employment in Los Angeles, the region faces an uncertain future.

There are compelling reasons for design and marketing to remain in the region, but not necessarily for assembly. Throughout the world today, there is a global race to the bottom for labor-intensive production as capital seeks out the cheapest possible workers. For southern California'a apparel industry, the temptations are obvious. Mexico, now unfettered thanks to NAFTA, provides workers at a tenth the cost of those in Los Angeles: Few independent unions are organizing workers there, few muckracking journalists are eager to expose sweatshops, and few citizens' groups are scrutinizing the industry.

The Growth of Global Production

Beginning with the move from the relatively high-wage, unionized northeast to the low-wage, nonunionized south in the 1920s and 1930s, United States apparel manufacturers have for a long time relocated production in search of cheap labor.[3] The movement offshore did not begin, however, until well after World War II. In 1956, offshore sourcing was pioneered in the menswear industry in Los Angeles, when Ben Kurtzman, the owner of Sportsclothes Ltd., then a leading manufacturer of inexpensive suits "for the the people who live between New York City and Los Angeles," began sourcing in Japan.[4] In the 1950s and 1960s, governments in east Asian countries such as Hong Kong, Taiwan, and Korea, with financial and technical assistance from United States aid programs, encouraged the growth and expansion of textile and garment production. By the early 1970s, the three countries were running massive trade surpluses in those goods and had greatly surpassed Japan in apparel exports.[5] By the end of the decade, nearly three-quarters of all United States apparel imports came from east Asia.[6]

The shift accelerated in the 1980s, leading to a massive increase in imports. These imports have not increased because other countries have decided to produce clothing for the United States market; they consist of goods made by United States companies overseas. Both retailers and manufacturers have become significant importers of garments that are produced more cheaply in developing countries around the globe. This has created a rift in the industry: Those who produce locally find themselves in competition with the importers. In 1987 the United States had already become the world's leading apparel importer, accounting for 27 percent of global imports in clothing.[7] Between 1988 and 1992, United States imports of clothing grew by 50 percent, to $30.5 billion; in 1992, 92.4 percent of all clothing imports were from the developing economies.[8]

By now United States apparel manufacturers, scouring the globe for the cheapest labor they could find, were followed by retailers seeking off-shore production of their own private-label lines. In 1991 Greater China (Hong Kong, Taiwan, and the People's Republic of China) accounted for 40 percent of United States apparel imports.[9] By the early 1990s the apparel export industries in Thailand and Indonesia had surpassed the $3 billion mark, and India, Sri Lanka, and Malaysia topped $1 billion in apparel exports.[10] By this time manufacturers in the garment business in the United States, Hong Kong, and South Korea made it clear that such far-flung sites as Vietnam, Guatemala, Burma, North Korea, and Mongolia were either targets of planned investment in export-oriented garment factories or had already gone on line.

Since the passage and implementation of NAFTA in 1994, Mexico has surpassed Hong Kong and approaches China in terms of the dollar value of combined textile and apparel exports to the United States. As recently as 1990, United States imports of textiles and apparel from Mexico totaled only $678 million, in comparison with $3.8 billion from Hong Kong and $3.6 billion from China. By 1997, United States apparel and textile imports from Mexico, 40 percent higher than they had been the previous year, had grown to $5.9 billion, far greater than imports from hong Kong ($4 billion) and approximating imports from China ($6 billion).[11]

Since the early 1960s, when garment imports and exports were roughly in balance, the trade deficit in apparel and related textiles has grown at an increasing rate, more than doubling in each of the last three decades. By 1996, imports exceeded exports by nearly $40 billion.[12] In that year, imports comprised more than half (57 percent) of wholesale apparel consumption in the United States.[13]

The push by United States companies to produce abroad found a welcome in many developing countries seeking to industrialize. Garment production is relatively labor intensive, requiring little startup capital. It is, thus, one of the first industries that newly industrializing countries enter. They welcome the orders from United States firms, which boost their exports. In exchange, they offer the United States companies a docile and controlled labor force, typically composed of very young women. The offer may be backed by the creation of special export processing zones and, frequently, by repressive regimes that provide guarantees against labor unrest.

Offshore apparel production is usually the result of arm's-length transactions. Rarely do garment firms establish manufacturing subsidiaries abroad. Instead they contract with independent firms to produce the goods to their specifications. The offshore contractors fall into two broad categories: what's called full-package production (sometimes called Original Equipment Manufacturing, or OEM), for which the contractor takes complete charge of the entire production from the purchase of textiles to the completion of garments, and offshore assembly plants (or *maquiladoras* as they are called in Latin America) that assemble cut cloth and provide only the labor for sewing. This latter category is often called 807 production, after the paragraph in the United States tariff regulations that allow the reimport of goods assembled offshore with a tariff charge only on the value added, that is, the cost of labor.[14]

The flood of imports led to attempts by the segments of the domestic apparel industry to regulate the flow of trade. Although world trade during the postwar period was to have been liberalized under the 1947 General Agreement on Tariffs and Trade (GATT), textile and apparel trade was never entirely included. As textile and apparel trade with Japan grew during the 1950s, for example, a number of so-called voluntary export restraints, the result of pressures by the United States textile and apparel industry, restricted United States imports of selected categories of goods from Japan. European countries followed suit, fearing Japanese penetration into their traditionally strong textile and apparel industries. The restraints imposed on Japan did not affect the growing imports from other Asian countries, such as Hong Kong; moreover, European restrictions were seen by United States trade officials as violations of GATT. Accordingly, a more comprehensive approach to regulating global trade in apparel and textiles was sought. The Multifiber Arrangement (MFA), reached in 1974, provided for bilateral agreements between trading nations that would regulate trade in apparel and textiles.[15] Its principal vehicle was an elaborate quota system, whereby each country established import quotas for detailed categories of goods from each major trading partner (for example, the United States might allow 300,000 women's wool sweaters from Hong Kong in a given year).[16] Subsequent versions of the MFA became increasingly reactive as global textile and apparel trade exploded during the 1970s and 1980s. Nonetheless, imports to the United States have continued to grow steadily. In fact, one of the effects of quotas has been to disperse apparel production throughout the world, as United States companies have sought new sources of production in countries where quotas are unfilled or even nonexistent.[17]

United States firms, supported by the United States government, began to use *maquiladoras* in the Caribbean, Mexico, and Central America, as a way of gaining access to "their own" cheap labor. Special programs, such as those for 807 production, were created, in part, to make offshore production easier in the Western Hemisphere and compete with the rising Asian tigers. The Caribbean Basin Initiative, enacted in 1983 to eliminate tariffs on most Caribbean exports to the United States, did not initially apply to textiles and apparel. In 1986, such exemptions were provided in the 807A ("super 807") provisions, which liberalized quotas for apparel assembled in the Caribbean from fabric made and cut in the United States.

But far from the important trade agreement affecting textiles and apparel has been NAFTA, which calls for complete elimination of all tariffs on industrial products traded between the United States, Canada, and Mexico within ten years of the treaty's implementation, which occurred on 1 January 1994.[18] The treaty immediately removed barriers on about 20 percent of United States textiles and apparel exports to Mexico, with most of the remaining tariffs scheduled to be eliminated by the turn of the century. (Prior to NAFTA, Mexican tariffs were 20 percent on apparel and 15 percent on textiles.) In order to qualify under NAFTA rules, clothing must be made from North American yarn that has been spun into fabric in North America.

At the time of this writing, the Clinton administration was making efforts, in the face of some opposition, to extend NAFTA to other countries, and was also attempting to pass legislation liberalizing trade (and offshore production) in Africa. Moreover, under GATT, international trade is to be deregulated and the entire quota system for apparel imports dismantled. The World Trade Organization, which emerged out of GATT, is now overseeing the dismantling; under current provisions (adopted in 1994 as a result of the so-called Uruguay Round), quotas under the MFA will be eliminated within ten years and textile and apparel trade will then be governed by the trade rules for other sectors.[19]

Offshore Production (Profiles of Four Large Firms)

Los Angeles is the gateway for apparel imports from Asia and Mexico. Each year, billions of dollars' worth of clothing comes in through the ports of Los Angeles and Long Beach, loaded in containers and piled high in ships. Los Angeles is also conveniently close to Mexico; precut goods are easily driven across the border to be sewn in Mexican factories. Los Angeles is thus situated at a global crossroads, so the transfer of the industry offshore is not logically difficult. (In speaking of the apparel industry moving offshore, we are referring only to production.) The apparel firms that are based in Los Angeles are likely to maintain their headquarters and design facilities there because, as Bent Klopp, the senior vice president for production planning for Bugle Boy Industries, commented in 1991, "We see ourselves as merchandise managers rather than manufacturers. We have 700 factories throughout the world, including Taiwan, Hong Kong, China, the Philippines, Indonesia, Korea, Singapore, Malaysia, Pakistan, Bangladesh, Sri Lanka, Mexico, Honduras, the Dominican Republic, Turkey, and, to a limited extent, Guatemala. We are looking at Oman and Dubai for future production. In the United States, we use factories in Los Angeles and the Carolinas. Five years ago [1986] we only produced in Taiwan. Now it represents 18 percent of our production. China is 22 percent. Mexico and Central America are six percent, while Los Angeles accounts for one percent."[20]

Bugle Boy Industries

Bugle Boy, one of the region's largest firms and a well-know manufacturer of young men's clothing, represents one end of the import continuum. At the time of this interview, Bugle Boy had nearly all of its clothing made in Taiwan, China, and elsewhere in Asia and claimed to be the number one receiver of containers in the Port of Long Beach. Bugle Boy initially produced in Taiwan because the company's founder and chief executive officer, Bill Mow, had strong personal ties in that country, where he was born. The firm has since diversified geographically, and its reasons provide some understanding of the considerations that go into a firm's source decisions. According to Klopp, Bugle Boy initially began spreading its operations to obtain a larger quota to raise the ceiling on the number of garments it could import, but there were other reasons as well. "When we go into a country, we don't want to dominate. We just want to get a piece of the action. Given our volume, we could distort the economy, and would find ourselves competing against ourselves. You also avoid risk by spreading around, for example, fluctuations in exchange rates, political upheavals, and national disasters. We never have production in Bangladesh during June and July because of the monsoon season. And it is important to know what is going on politically."

Bugle Boy evaluates each country in terms of what is called its needle capability. Can it make fancy pants or basic pants? "Asia," said Klopp, "is flexible," that is, capable of making a variety of products. "The rest of the world is cookie cutter," meaning that, "outside of Asia, if you ask for a small change in the product, labor costs can shoot up from $1 to $5. Mexico and Central America, as well as the Europeans, suffer from being too mechanical. They are too automated and can't be flexible. Mexico and Honduras have had too many joint ventures with the United States. They are not being trained to do flexible work." Despite these reservations concerning Mexico, by 1998, Bugle Boy's production in that country had increased fivefold during the previous three years, to 15 million units.[21]

Chauvin International Ltd.

Another manufacturer with almost all of its production offshore in the mid-1990s was Chauvin International Ltd., a $100-million company that made the once-popular label B.U.M. Equipment. (The firm went bankrupt in April 1996, and has since moved to Rhode Island.[22]) The garments were what is called fashion basics, namely T-shirts and sweatshirts, and they were made offshore and then dyed, screen-printed, embroidered, and otherwise finished in Los Angeles. According to the production manager, Jeff Richards, who we interviewed in 1994:

> We have everything cut and sewn overseas by contractors. It is all CMT [Cut-Make-Trim: the garments made in their entirety, from cutting through assembly]. We only buy finished garments. A tiny percent of our production is done domestically, less than one percent. We use buying agents overseas and work through them, though we are involved in the selection of factories they use. In the past, 60 to 70 percent of our production was in Hong Kong, but now it is down to 30 percent. We also have agents in India. What we do locally is finishing. We bring in the sewn garment and have it dyed, printed, and embroidered locally. The finishing comes to 30 to 35 percent of the total production cost. Producing in Asia is definitely slower than producing locally. You need a ninety- to one-hundred-twenty-day lead time. We try to allow for more time than that. The truth is, the quality is much higher for imports. We have had low success with United States–made goods.

Los Angeles offers numerous finishing establishments, including several hundred local dye houses, but Richards predicted that local finishing was doomed, because the cost was not competitive with that in low-wage countries. "It costs 25 cents per 1,000 stitches to embroider [the company logo] here. In India it costs 6 to 8 cents. That means if you have a 10,000 stitch embroidery, you have $1.80 per garment difference. Finishing abroad requires the lead time by thirty to sixty days. The technology is moving overseas. We get some of our production from Israel. They couldn't embroider finished goods, so they came here, bought the appropriate equipment, and now can do it."[23]

Chorus Line, Inc.

At the other end of the continuum, Chorus Line, Inc., one of the well-established and venerable manufacturers of fashionable junior sportswear in Los Angeles, had long prided itself in producing virtually all of its garments in southern California. According to the senior vice president, Gene Light (whom we interviewed in 1994), all that began to change in the early 1990s: "We have been in business for almost twenty years. For seventeen of them, everything was produced domestically and by that I mean in southern California. About three years ago we started looking into Mexico, under the 807 program. Last year we began dabbling in the Pacific Rim. Now we have set our projections for 1995. We have six divisions, each with somewhat different plans. Some will increase their work in Mexico, and some in the Orient."[24]

By 1995, Chorus Line was planning to have as much as a quarter of its production done offshore, including between 5 and 10 percent in Mexico and much of the rest in low-wage Asian countries such as the Philippines, Indonesia, Sri Lanka, Dubai, and possibly Bangladesh. Light reported that the firm was shifting its production offshore for several reasons.

> One is that we are increasing our volume and we can't increase it here because of price. The price pressure is coming from the retailers. If we remained in the United States, we would have no growth pattern. We wouldn't be competitive anymore. The retailers are vicious. They come to us and say they want to buy a garment for $10. We say we can't make it for $10. They say they can get it from so-and-so for $4.10, and so-and-so is making it in north China. Here the minimum wage is $4.25 an hour. How can you compete with $2.50 a day? A second reason for moving offshore is that the government and the state are becoming zealots in invoking the labor laws. They are invoking 1938 labor laws and using them to put the onus on the manufacturer because they don't have the money to enforce the laws. You should realize that we don't endorse child labor or nonpayment of minimum wage. But we have our own business to run. Our position is: If we continue to face pressure, we will move offshore or to Mexico.

Production offshore is not without its costs, especially in Chorus Line's fashion-sensitive market niche. Longer lead times and higher transportation costs risks requiring the firm to carry more inventory than might be sold. As a result, Chorus Line is more inclined to go with tried-and-true styles that have proved successful over the years. Nonetheless, Light predicted that Chorus Line will end up producing half of its goods offshore, although half would be made locally because retailers were demanding ever quicker delivery from the time of ordering. If Asia had a four-month cycle and Mexico a two-month cycle, orders could be turned around in Los Angeles in a single month. Light observed that "so long as the stores need a quick turn, a large segment of the industry will remain in Los Angeles." Even so, "if we are forced to move everything to Mexico, we will." This prediction appears to be coming true: By early 1997, Chorus Line had shifted 70 percent of its production to Mexico, the rest remaining in Los Angeles. According to Barry Sacks, the chairman and chief officer, because of tough price competition, the company had no choice.[25]

California Fashion Industries (Carole Little)

In 1994 we also interviewed Kenneth Martin, the production manager of Carole Little, the principal label of the largest manufacturers of fashionable women's clothing in Los Angeles. At that time, nine months after NAFTA went into effect, the firm employed between 1,100 and 1,200 workers in-house, including designers, product engineers, sample makers, and distribution workers. "The garment industry," said Martin, "does have a future here, but the government needs to give the industry a break, on worker's comp[ensation], and to offer tax breaks and incentives, because this industry employs a lot of people, especially those who don't have much education. I think we may see a short-term exodus, but we're also likely to see fluctuations. Some firms will come back after they discover that they face problems with cycle time, quality, and control. Many are looking at Mexico right now, and some may try it out for a while. The industry will always be there, I think. But you can't take that for granted."

At the time of this interview, in September 1994, the firm was increasing its production in Asia, because much of its work required labor-intensive beading and hand embroidery, which was too costly to do domestically. The company was already importing up to half of its clothing from Asia and was planning to increase that figure to two-thirds. Less than 15 percent of the work was being done in Mexico but, with the passage of NAFTA, said Martin, "we are looking to expand our [Mexican] production if we can develop quality production in Mexico. We tried using the Dominican Republic for a few months, and now we are looking at Guatemala, Costa Rica, and Honduras. We've also looked at Columbia. These places have a problem of logistics. Delivery takes ten days to two weeks, and even air freight provides poor service. Producing there makes more sense for the east coast than for us. We've been in Mexico for four years. Our hope is to reverse percentages, so that 10 to 15 percent will be produced in the United States and the remainder in Mexico. We are planning to complete this shift in five years. We recognize that, when you get out of Los Angeles, you need to assign more managers to oversee production. There are many more experienced sewing machine operators here."[26]

In sum, four of the largest apparel manufacturers in Los Angeles rely on offshore production for at least some of their contracting. With the passage of NAFTA, more and more films are looking south, rather than across the Pacific. NAFTA offers the advantages of proximity, low wages, and fewer trade restrictions.

The Consequences Of NAFTA

In our 1992 survey of the 184 largest apparel manufacturers in Los Angeles, about 30 percent (fifty-six firms) reported that they were producing offshore. Only 25 percent of the firms doing offshore sourcing (fourteen firms) reported that all of their production was done offshore. Thirty-one firms (17 percent of the total) reported sourcing from Mexico. Yet many manufacturers expressed concerns that NAFTA, which was implemented in 1994, would harm local production. The opinion of Mitch Glass, the vice president of production of Cherokee Inc., is typical of sentiments expressed before NAFTA's passage. "If they open the border with Mexico, the immigrants will go away and so will the contractors. The government needs to work out a special deal for this industry like they have in agriculture. NAFTA will kill the local industry. Only the high-priced fashion items will stay. Los Angeles will become a ghost town. Five years from now, we will be in Mexico. I am opposed to NAFTA; it isn't fair to contractors in Los Angeles. They can't compete. The industry will definitely move to Mexico, but a cost in terms of start up, training, quality, supply of materials, trim, and zippers. I've been looking at shops in Mexico. I saw fabulous textile goods being made there. I'm thinking of cutting there, and have looked at eight or nine sewing shops near Mexico City."[27]

In late 1997 and early 1998, using our list of 184 large companies, Judi Kessler reinterviewed sixty-seven firms, and found that about 75 percent were having some of their production done in Mexico. Most expected to increase their Mexican production in the future.[28] Kessler also found that about 25 percent of the firms interviewed were sending production to Asia and other countries, suggesting that they were developing global sourcing strategies. She concluded that the companies moving to Mexico tend to be larger or to be engaged in high-volume, private-label production. Smaller firms, she reported, lacked the financial and personnel resources to move as easily as the bigger companies can.

The movement of the apparel industry to Mexico predates the passage of NAFTA. Between 1989 and 1993, apparel imports from Mexico to the United States grew at an annual rate of about 30 percent, increasing from about $535 million in 1989 to $1.3 billion in 1993. After NAFTA passed, the rate of growth of apparel imports from Mexico jumped to 45 percent per year. The value of these imports grew from $1.8 billion in 1994 to $5.2 billion in 1997, just three years after NAFTA took effect. These statistics in themselves do not prove that the Los Angeles apparel industry is shifting its production to Mexico. Some of the growth in Mexican exports could be accounted for because companies (in Los Angeles and elsewhere) that are already engaged in offshore sourcing are moving some of their Asian and Caribbean production to Mexico. Nevertheless, the statistics reveal the rise in importance of Mexico as a source of garments produced for the United States market.

Melanie Myers, co-author of this chapter, conducted in-depth interviews with ten firms, including two suppliers of apparel inputs such as textiles, five apparel manufacturers, one manufacturer of a related product, one sewing contractor, and one industrial laundry. She received tours of these factories and was able to get a clear picture of the impact of NAFTA upon them. Two high-end manufacturers reported feeling no effects of NAFTA, positive or negative; others were clearly enthusiastic or discouraged.

The owner of one of the supply firms reported that, unless he receives some sort of low-interest financing, he would close his operation in Los Angeles and move to Mexico within the next six months. He had already purchased a building in Mexico and was preparing to move all of his production down there. Moving to Mexico would reduce his labor costs from about $80 a day per person to about $5 a day per person. In addition, in Mexico he could purchase cheaper supplies, face less regulation, and pay lower taxes. Even if this firm receives financial assistance from the city, it will still open its Mexican facility, but will retain the more technologically advanced production in Los Angeles, keeping some jobs here.

The sewing contractor was one of the larger of such firms, with over 200 employees. The owner reported that her business has been hit hard by NAFTA. The company's principal manufacturer, a private label producer for J.C. Penney and Wal-Mart, used to supplement in-house sewing by employing seventeen contractors around the Los Angeles area. Now, that manufacturer has moved most of its production to Mexico and employs only two remaining local contractors. The manufacturer suggested to the contractor that she, too, move her business down to Mexico, but she did not want to do that and was planning to close down in May 1999. The manufacturer will, however, continue to use its other local contractor for quick-turn production.

The vice president of a large manufacturer with annual revenues of about $150 million and about 325 employees stated that the need to be located in or around the garment district for production work has been declining over the past ten years. Until five years ago, this manufacturer sourced all of his production in Los Angeles. Now every year the percentage spent abroad rises. Retailers, he feels, are placing contradictory demands on apparel manufacturers. On the one hand, they require prices that can be met only by offshore production. On the other hand, they require quick turnover for certain products, which generally means local production. This firm is a licensee for a local design establishment and needs to remain close to the design teams, so its headquarters, at least will remain in the greater Los Angeles area.

The industrial laundry, which is also a dye-house, employed around one hundred workers. The owner reported that many laundries previously based in Los Angeles have already moved to Mexico. She stated that, although labor costs are much lower, transportation, time lags, and quality of work continue to be problems in Mexican production. Moreover, water is scarcer than it is in California and the quality is different. For these reasons, dye-houses, as distinguished from laundries, are unlikely to leave Los Angeles. Moreover, dye-houses need to be close to the designers. Laundries tend to locate close to the sewing contractors, so follow them as they move. The firm has opened a laundry in Mexico, but still retains a laundry and dye-house in Los Angeles.

Not all of the stories were as bleak as these. One major manufacturer, with $120 million in annual sales, had a sourcing plan that included local and offshore production. This company has a large inside shop that employs six hundred people and uses the latest technology. It also employs between thirty and seventy local contractors, owns a factory in Mexico, and employs contractors there, in Central America, and in China. The president felt that NAFTA has been good for business, allowing the company to combine sourcing strategies.

These interviews suggest that apparel firms have mixed responses to NAFTA. Some firms, especially small contractors competing in the moderate market, have been harmed by competition from low-wage areas offshore. Other firms, particularly large manufacturers, welcome the opportunity to have freer access to those same low-wage areas. The interviews suggest that a firm's sensitivity to NAFTA is, in part, a function of its size, the type of market it produces for, and other industry-specific factors, such as the need to be near designers or the need to retain some local employment for quick-turn production.

Until recently, the southern California apparel industry has appeared to live a charmed life. Running counter to the rest of the nation, employment in the industry increased every year, despite the obvious fact that individual firms were moving some of their production to Mexico. Then in 1998, for the first year since 1993, the number of apparel and textile jobs in the County of Los Angeles fell, from 111,900 at the end of 1997 to 110,000 a year later, according to statistics provided by the Employment Development Department. This represents a drop of less than 2 percent, after years of more or less steady growth. Nevertheless, it could signal the beginning of the end. Ted Gibson, the chief economist at the California Department of Finance, saw no cause for alarm, but Joe Rodriguez, the executive director of the Garment Contractors Association said, "For a while, we've been able to hold our own. But maybe NAFTA has finally caught up with us."[29]

Guess? Inc. Moves To Mexico

In January 1997, Maurice Marciano, the chairman and chief executive officer of Guess? Inc., announced that the quantity of Guess garments sewn in Los Angeles would drop from 75 percent in August 1997 to 35 percent by February 1998. Because Guess is the largest apparel manufacturer in the Los Angeles area and had previously boasted that 90 percent of its production was in Los Angeles, Marciano's announcement gave a special urgency to debates about the effect of NAFTA on production in Los Angeles.

Some blamed the move on stepped-up enforcement efforts. Or example, a prominent local apparel attorney, Richard Reinis, who heads the Compliance Alliance, a group of firms that polices its contractors for compliance with minimum wage and overtime laws, explained the Guess move as partly the result of "tremendous pressure from a very effective Department of Labor Wage and Hour division. It's causing a sea change in an industry that has operated virtually untouched for sixty years."[30] In response to the move, Bernard Lax, then the president of the Coalition of Apparel Industries of California, commented that price was not as much of an issue as was liability related to labor law enforcement. "They have created a bad environment in California," he said.[31]

Others blamed the exodus of Guess on the fact that it had been targeted by UNITE!, the garment industry union, for an organizing campaign. "For the most part, manufacturers and contractors believe UNITE! is one of the biggest threats to the apparel community in L.A.," stated an article in *California Apparel News.*[32] Some feared that unionization would drive up the cost of labor, pushing production offshore. Although Marciano had stated that the shift was mainly "a commercial decision," to "stay competitive" and "lower costs," it was widely believed in the industry that there were other reasons for the firm's decision: UNITE!'s efforts to spotlight the firm's use of sweatshops in Los Angeles and embarrassing state and federal investigations of the firm's practices. Guess was the first company in the United States to be targeted by the Department of Labor to develop a compliance agreement, earning it a short-lived place on the Department's Trendsetter list, until investigations in late 1996 led to the company's being removed from the list and placed on "probation." Marciano's emphasis on the economic reasons for the move were partly the result of legal considerations: UNITE! had filed a complaint with the National Labor Relations Board, claiming that Guess was moving to Mexico in order to evade unionization.[33] Such a move would be illegal under the terms of a settlement agreement that Guess had just signed with the NLRB, which included a provision that the company would not intimidate unionizing workers by threatening to move to Mexico rather than allow its workers to join a union.[34]

Guess had already begun to move some production to Asia in 1993, but none to Mexico because it felt that Mexican factories could not deliver the quality required. According to Marciano, since the passage of NAFTA, Mexican factories had invested in automatic equipment, and many of Guess's competitors were already moving there.[35] He therefore announced a production shift of several million units a year with a wholesale value of between $300 and $325 million. Marciano claimed the Guess would save between $1.50 and $2 per garment by sending cut fabric to sewing plants in Mexico, Peru, and Chile.

Guess? Inc. moved production to Tehuacán, Mexico, which is fast becoming a center of denim production for manufacturers in Los Angeles and elsewhere. A city with an exploding population of some 300,000 people, Tehuacán is a few hours' drive southeast of Mexico City. It is the second-largest city in Puebla, in an impoverished region populated mainly by indigenous peoples who provide a large and hungry source of labor. Tehuacán's estimated 400 sewing factories reportedly sew and stonewash jeans for such major labels as Polo, Lee, Bugle Boy, Cherokee, and Levi's, and for Guess, since it decided to move out to Los Angeles.[36]

In February 1998, a delegation of human rights observers, including one of the authors (Rich Appelbaum) among them, heard evidence from local workers of many forms of exploitation and mistreatment in the factories, and of a pervasive atmosphere of fear.[37] For example, guards at one of the factories pulled guns on local human-rights workers who were attempting to interview workers on a public sidewalk outside one of the largest factories a few days before the delegation's arrival. Wages ranged from $25 to $50 (United States) for a forty-eight-hour workweek, with forced (and unpaid) overtime often used to meet production quotas. Sometimes overtime involved all-night shifts, with workers prevented by security guards from leaving the factories. Minors as young as thirteen years of age were reported to be working alongside adults under unsafe conditions that sometimes resulted in accidents. The enormous, prosperous-looking, and frequently windowless factories (surrounded by high walls and locked gates) stood in stark contrast to the sprawling *colonias*, where workers lived in makeshift, dirt-floor shacks, typically without access to running water, electricity, sewage, schools, or other basic urban amenities. The final report stated, "What the delegation found in Tehuacán, Mexico, is that worker rights are not respected and codes of conduct are not enforced; instead they are subordinated to the global search for cheap labor. Humane treatment of *maquiladora* workers and respect for their rights are traded off for the mass production of on-time and high-quality clothing."[38]

Tehuacán provides cheap labor far from the eyes of union organizers, mackracking journalists, and antisweatshop activists. Its location far from the United States border, in a rural, semifeudal area, helps to assure that it remains largely out of view. It typifies the opportunities available to United States manufacturers in the wake of NAFTA, opportunities that seem to force a choice between exploitation at home and exploitation abroad.

Who Will Stay—and Who Will Leave?

Is Guess's departure indeed the beginning of the end, the start of NAFTA's "giant sucking sound," that Ross Perot predicted? Jack Kyser, the director of research for the Economic Development Corporation in Los Angeles County, clearly thought so. Saying that Guess's move "could be the thing that turns the tide," Kyser suggested that other apparel makers might conclude that, if Guess were satisfied with Mexican production, why shouldn't they be? The *Los Angeles Times* article containing Kyser's observations contributed: "Typical of the trend is J. Michelle of California, a woman's sportswear and dressmaker, which says it has shifted about half of its production to Mexico since December 1995. Richard Tan, the company's president, said that Mexico has long offered low labor costs but that the difficulties of doing business kept him away. But now that Mexican contractors have improved production quality and delivery time, he said, it has become an attractive place to do business. 'The bottom line is prices. If I don't go to Mexico, I won't get the business, because I've got to be competitive,' Tan said."[39]

The doomsayers looked at the statistics on the continued growth in local apparel industry employment and, quite simply, didn't believe them. For example, the day following Guess's announcement, the *Wall Street Journal* reported Richard Reinis's estimate that 50,0000 apparel jobs had been lost in Los Angeles between mid-1995 and early 1997, even though official statistics were later to show an increase of some 9,000 jobs during that same period. Reinis based his figures on the fact that three members of the Compliance Alliance (L'Koral Industries, Toni Blair of California, and Little Laura of California) had shifted production to Mexico.[40] Bernard Lax also disbelieved the official figures. He claimed that more than 20,000 jobs had been lost in Los Angeles County from September 1996 to February 1997 and that as many as 40,000 jobs would disappear in 1997.[41] Economists at the University of California at Los Angeles were somewhat more circumspect; although they did not claim that jobs had been hemorrhaging to Mexico, they did worry that the industry had added only 1,000 new jobs in 1996, instead of the 11,000 it had added in each of 1994 and 1995.[42]

How is it possible to reconcile official statistics showing a growing industry, with the insiders' belief that it is in a state of imminent collapse? According to Bernard Lax, the increase in official employment was an artifact of enhanced enforcement effort, which "brought companies that were operating underground onto the books, generating misleadingly strong numbers."[43] Others argued that, while the major firms were leaving, smaller firms were expanding to take up the slack.

For most manufacturers, Mexico remains a mixed blessing for production. In our interviews, manufacturers complained about poor quality, unpredictability, bribery, excessive bureaucratic red tape, late deliveries, and hijacked shipments of goods. "In Mexico, the border patrol charges to let your goods pass. This happens as you move from one province to the next, each one having different rules."[44] Labor accounts for only about 12 percent of the wholesale cost of making a garment, and savings on labor can be offset by the other costs of doing business in Mexico. Goetz Wolff, a professor of Urban Planning at the University of California at Los Angeles, and expert on the apparel industry, concurred. "There are going to be significant amounts of production remaining here," he said. "The low wage in Mexico is not as low as it appears—once you start looking at the other costs involved."[45] After interviewing a number of manufacturers and other persons knowledgeable about the industry, Larry Kanter concluded that a massive move to Mexico was unlikely. "Frustrated by the high cost of labor and encouraged by the North American Free Trade Agreement, L.A. clothing manufacturer Tony Podell decided two years ago to try his luck in Tijuana. He located a large factory and began hiring Mexican crews to produce some less expensive lines of shirts, dresses, and pants. 'I've yet to make a profit,' said Podell, whose Podell Industries Inc. makes high-end women's wear. 'I've found very few large factories down there that can produce consistently.' Podell makes the Laundry by Shelli Segal label."[46]

These sentiments were echoed by Jeff Mowdy, the production manager for Francine Browner, Inc., one of the ten largest manufacturers in Los Angeles, with annual sales of $100 million. In August 1996, when we interviewed Mowdy, 90 percent of the firm's production was domestic, with the remainder done in Mexico. Although Mowdy complained about the costs of the compliance programs required by the Department of Labor and of the difficulty of finding legitimate shops, his experience with Mexico was not encouraging: "We don't produce in Mexico because of NAFTA. We began talking about moving there before NAFTA passed. We went there solely because of price points [lower costs]. We contracted in Tijuana. Typically you start at the border and move inland, where the better production is done. It's been a nightmare and now we are moving back to the U.S. It's worth doing stuff there if you have a big volume because they can do it cheaply. But we don't do programs [large volumes of unchanging styles that can be mass-produced], and the learning curve there is very different from here. In order to succeed in Mexico you have to have your own shop. But then you have to be able to feed it. And you can't keep changing the styles because of the slow learning curve. I hate doing work there."[47]

Gus Leonard, the production manager for Paul Davril, Inc., a firm whose products included licensed men's and boy's wear for brands such as Bugle Boy and Guess, expressed similar sentiments: "We don't produce in Mexico. I'm looking at Ecuador, Honduras, Guatemala, and Costa Rica. There is a problem with Mexico. The factories don't have middle management. So if the owner is out of town, or having a two-hour lunch, you can't get decisions made quickly enough. There is a sense of arrogance among Mexican producers. They have the attitude: 'You can't just come into my place and tell me how to run things.' You need to have your own people living there and working for you. If I used Mexico, I'd have to send someone to live there. This hasn't only happened to us, but to other companies as well. NAFTA hasn't improved it."[48]

Ilse Metchek, the executive director of the California Fashion Association (the major organization of manufacturers), argues that small firms cannot afford to shift production out of Los Angeles. She estimates that nine out of ten apparel firms are too small to move, and that these firms employ most of the region's garment contractors and workers. "They cannot afford to make 100,000 [items] at a clip, which is what is required to go to Mexico. You can't do small runs of high fashion [in Mexico]—and that's what the majority of the firms here do."[49] Metchek's viewpoint is supported by Mark Lesser, the president and co-owner of Wearable Integrity, Inc. a smaller company that makes women's casual dress under the Barbara Lesser label. He pointed out that companies with sales between $1 million and $40 million would have a hard time moving textiles and garments back and forth across the border, especially if they are dealing in small quantities.

Some of the confusion in these contradictory predictions stems from sectoral differences. Certain types of clothing are more easily manufactured in Mexico than are others. According to Tony Podell, "You can make T-shirts for Kmart or Wal-Mart [in Mexico], but for our product you just can't do it."[50] Marcus Sphatt, the owner of Bepop Clothing, a company that opened a new facility in January 1997 near Tecate, Mexico, where it will eventually employ 1,000 workers, and will be able to do cutting, sewing, washing, and finishing, says that this company will maintain fashion production in California and source basics from Mexico. Turnaround times in Mexico, he said, range from eight to ten weeks, compared to the four to five weeks in California.[51] Obviously, this is a factor that helps to keep the production of fashion local.

Lonnie Kane, the president of Karen Kane Co., Inc., a producer of expensive, fashionable women's wear, does not plan to move to Mexico. High-end companies with shorter runs rely on the contracting base in Los Angeles; it is the manufacturers of high-volume junior, moderate, and budget clothing that, he said, are prime candidates for Mexico.[52]

Writing in the *Los Angeles Times*, business analyst Joel Kotkin drew similar conclusions. He argued that companies such as City Girl, Inc., concentrated in the fashion end, want to stay in Los Angeles because of the skilled labor base, the textile suppliers, the design community, and the large number of contracting firms that enable quick turnarounds. "The large-scale economics," he write, "that drive larger producers of relatively standardized goods to Mexico often turn out to be unsuitable for smaller, specialized producers. As L.A. manufacturers learned in the 1970s and '80s with respect to production in Asia, the delays and lead times associated with outsourcing, not to mention quality control, often prevent firms from seizing the initiative on fast-changing fashions. A product sewn in Mexico, for example, can take up to six weeks to return to the states, compared with a turnaround as quick as two weeks in Los Angeles.[53]

There is a pattern in these and similar comments made by experts and manufacturers. The consensus seems to be that the production of basics, for which there are big runs of the same line and styles do not constantly change, are likely to leave Los Angeles. The smaller companies and those that specialize in fashion, for which runs are short and styles constantly changing, will remain. These companies need a quick turnaround, and they need the smaller factories characteristic of the industry in Los Angeles. Joe Rodriguez, the executive director of the Garment Contractors Association in southern California, summarized the situation. "We are the last holdouts because of the niche market we're in. We do work nobody else wants to do—low-volume fashion stuff, small, unmanageable lots with an ungodly mix of styles."[54]

The Attractions of Los Angeles

Although it is evident that apparel firms will increasingly shift production to Mexico, so far at least, employment has remained high and has shown only a minor downturn. Something is keeping the industry in Los Angeles. What are the factors that lead apparel companies to continue to source at least some of their production locally?

One obvious factor is the availability of low-wage, immigrant labor. Yet, if that were the only reason for the success of Los Angeles as an apparel center, the local industry would clearly be doomed, because much cheaper labor is available just across the border. Other regions of the country also have low-wage, immigrant labor pools, yet have experienced a decline in apparel production.

Two other factors help to account for the presence of a thriving garment industry in Los Angeles. The first is the region's national (indeed, global) cultural significance, which helps assure a ready market for what have been called its "cultural products." The second is the existence of a well-developed infrastructure that provides exceptional support for the apparel industry. We must also consider a third factor, the efforts of local government to keep the industry from leaving.

"Cultural Products"

Allen Scott and David Rigby of the Geography Department at the University of California at Los Angeles have proposed that the synergy within the apparel industry in Los Angeles extends to a larger complex of what they call "cultural-products industries."[55] They see a propensity in Los Angeles for industries to specialize in the creation of cultural products: apparel, textiles, furniture, printing and publishing, leather products, prerecorded records and tapes, jewelry, toys and sporting goods, advertising, motion picture production and distribution, entertainers, and architectural services. These industries produce "small batches of output for specialized market niches and [their] competitive strategy typically entails constant product differentiation and/or significant levels of customization."[56]

Involved in so-called hyperinnovation, which tends to be associated with small, labor-intensive firms, these industries produce high-quality, constantly changing goods and benefit from identification with a particular place, the goods being associated with the locale. The mystique of the location of origin adds to the value of the goods, which assume in the popular imagination the reputation of the place and its characteristics. The words "California" and Los Angeles conjure up images of sun and surf, of people who are wealthy and glamorous, of Beverly Hills and the beach. Cultural-products industries both benefit from these images and help to create and maintain them.[57] The movie and music industries help to define Los Angeles and at the same time benefit from being associated with the city. Similarly, the fashion industry has helped to define an "L.A. style," and that style is, in turn, a product of preexisting and constantly evolving images of Los Angeles.[58]

The fashion and entertainment industries provide synergy for each other. The Annual Academy Awards demonstrate this vividly, as the stars showcase the work of prominent fashion designers. The movies and television employ fashion designers, some of whom are part of the Los Angeles fashion industry, and whose work sometimes creates new consumer tastes. Moreover, at a social level, fashion and entertainment often intersect. Both *Women's Wear Daily* and *California Apparel News* report on the rich and famous, the people from both industries who attend social events and are seen. Both industries provide wealthy celebrities who comprise an important sector of the glitterati of Los Angeles.

It All Comes Together Here

Once an industry becomes established in a region, a critical mass is achieved, after which numerous supporting components of the industry provide a crucial infrastructure for further development. The industry becomes self-sustaining; future growth becomes a self-fulfilling prophecy. Economic geographies refer to such regions as industrial districts and to the results of geographic concentration as agglomeration effects.

A large body of literature suggest that successful industries are more likely to thrive in geographical areas that have firms, factories, supporting infrastructure, and specialized labor markets.[59] Geographically dense industrial concentrations minimize the cost of doing business by providing proximity to markets, the ability to acquire goods and services quickly, lower transportation and communications costs, access to suppliers, and in general the rapid exchange of information and knowledge. A strong support infrastructure—business services, training schools, and research and development facilities—can also benefit competitive firms. Such geographical concentrations can reinforce personal contacts that may be rooted in family connection, ethnic ties, and other long-standing connections and give rise to social networks that provide informal economic relationships with a structure. The ability to have face-to-face, handshake connections is especially important in industries that are based largely on trust and personal knowledge. Geographical concentration also tends to intensify competition, motivating the participants to outshine one another, thereby improving the quality of goods.[60]

The apparel industry in Los Angeles provides a textbook example of the benefits of concentration because everything one needs to "make it all happen" is close at hand. Sydney Morse, a former owner and director of the CaliforniaMart, maintains that a downtown location is crucial for the industry because "we're an information business—the faster and better the information, the more significant the sale."[61] Los Angeles is a generator of fashion: Designers the world over watch the kids there to spot the latest trends. Los Angeles also boasts numerous textile converters, companies that specialize in altering fabric by dyeing and printing it, creating the colorful, fashionable, sometimes fanciful garments for which Los Angeles is known. In addition to design and fabric, every other need of apparel manufacturers can be found within a few miles of the downtown garment district: financial, accounting, and legal services; zippers bindings, threads, sewing machines, and other supplies and equipment; schools that provide training in everything from design to machine operation; and more than a thousand manufacturers' showrooms hosting a year-round stream of buyers. In addition, Los Angeles itself, consuming the very fashion that it generates, is a major market for clothing.

To illustrate how these elements work together to provide its unique vitality, we describe briefly three important components of the apparel industry in Los Angeles: the CaliforniaMart, various business services, and schools that train fashion designers and would-be manufacturers.

The CaliforniaMart

The CaliforniaMart, in the center of the garment district on Ninth Street between Los Angeles and Main Streets, was built by Harvey and Barney Morse. The Morse brothers moved to Los Angeles from New York City, getting their start as manufacturers of women's lingerie. During the 1950s, according to Harvey Morse's son, David, buyers would come to Los Angeles with their checkbooks in hand, yet wind up spending days wandering throughout the sprawling Los Angeles basin in a sometimes futile search for suitable manufacturers. The Morse brothers saw an opportunity, figuring that they could actually "create a marketplace to capture buyers' dollars."[62] They acquired the land in 1952, opened the first Mart building in 1964, the second two years later, and the third in 1973. Barney Morse's son, Sidney, emphasized the entrepreneurial nature of this venture: "No government financing, tax incentives, nothing. My father and my uncle did this by their balls."[63] The Mart was envisioned as providing one-stop shopping for buyers who came to Los Angeles to view the samples of California manufacturers, along with those of their United States and even international firms.

Today the Mart's buildings contain more than three million square feet of space, devoted primarily to some fifteen hundred showrooms representing more than ten thousand collections. Showrooms are staffed by either independent manufacturers or independent representatives who receive commissions for showing lines for manufacturers who do not want to maintain a showroom themselves. The Mart also provides travel programs, apparel-related directories, meeting rooms, event management, shows and conferences, a print shop, a fashion office responsible for producing fashion shows, and a department that organizes trade shows, not to mention a food court and underground parking. It houses buying offices, trade associations, major trade publications and libraries. Unlike apparel marts in other cities, the CaliformiaMart, because of its proximity to the country's largest concentration of manufacturers and contractors, has buyers visiting year-round, rather than only in response to periodic trade shows. Buyers are also attracted by the Mart's many special events: Each year it produces more than fifty fashion shows and twenty specialty markets for particular types of apparel.[64]

All told, an estimated one hundred thousand buyers were visiting the Mart annually around 1990, when the facility was reportedly running at nearly full occupancy and plans were being laid to construct another building specializing in men's wear.[65] At that time the Mart claimed to generate over $8.5 billion in annual wholesale sales and was the largest apparel mart in the United States.[66] Those halcyon days were not to last. By the early 1990s, ownership and management of the Mart had passed down to Harvey Morse's son and daughter, David Morse and Susan Morse-Lebow, and Barney Morse's son, Sidney. The brother, sister, and cousin shared responsibilities in an informal basis, although over time each came to specialize, David in leasing, Susan in finance, and Sidney in overall operations. By 1992, the Mart was experiencing financial and administrative difficulties, caused partly by a downturn in the economy and partly by an overall weakening of the position of the independent manufacturer in the face of consolidation among retailers. Increased price competition from discount stores such as Price Club and Wal-Mart plus private-label production by large retailers were squeezing the manufacturers who comprised the Mart's tenant base. By the mid-1990s, according to the Mart's owners, occupancy had declined to between 80 to 85 percent. The tenants were also displeased with rising rents and declining service, which many attributed to the debt service incurred in 1987 when the property had been refinanced by Equitable Life Assurance and the owners had taken $250 million in cash out of their property. Rising rents and space reconfigurations that were done without their consent contributed to a tenant's revolt.

In response to these difficulties, Sidney Morse, who had given up full-time duties in 1990, assumed full control.[67] Morse attributed the Mart's financial difficulties not only to the changes mentioned in retailing above, but also to such misguided government policies as the maintenance of high interest rates, which he viewed as squeezing out credit for small business.[68] Under these unfavorable conditions, the mart's owners were drawing the conclusion that devoting a valuable piece of downtown real estate exclusively to manufacturers' showrooms might not be its best possible use. Alternative uses, including office space for other industries and increased cash-and-carry operations, were all under consideration.[69]

Business Services

Within a short walk from the CaliforniaMart is a host of business services such as banks, factors, lawyers, buying offices, and accountants who specialize in apparel manufacturing. For example, Union Bank shares a long history with the industry, as well as a plaza with CaliforniaMart. In the immediate vicinity there are several buying offices, companies that arrange purchases (or place orders directly) for retailers, thereby providing an important link between retailers and manufacturers.

There are approximately fifteen Certified Public Accountants (CPAs) in Los Angeles who specialize in apparel manufacturing, although fewer than half a dozen dominate the industry.[70] A brief discussion of their role will illustrate the importance of nearby business services to the industry. Marty Josephson, a partner in Stonefield Josephson, one of the leading apparel accounting firms, reported to us that the firm's average client did between $15 and $20 million in annual sales, and the largest, $200 million, and that Stonefield Josephson provided some specialized services for even larger firms. He told us that the CPAs sometimes serve as the chief financial officers for manufacturing firms, providing them with a wide array of financial services that most manufacturers could not otherwise afford, among them, the preparation of financial statements and tax returns, the provision of compliance checks and other audits, accounting for inventory flow, reconciling factor accounts and business ledgers, forecasting, and advising on long-term planning. The very largest firms are more likely to have their own accounting and financial services; the very smallest are likely to be too risky to be taken as clients by the principal CPAs in the garment industry.[71]

The fact that the CPA is independent of the firm helps to assure the manufacturer's creditworthiness. A particular CPA typically manages the books of many competing manufacturers, providing an important cross-cutting linkage in the industry. For example, one of the largest apparel accounting firms in Los Angeles, Moss Adams, in 1992 managed the accounts of more than 200 apparel firms nationwide, half of whom were in Los Angeles County; Stonefield Josephson had 100 clients in apparel.[72] The relationship between the manufacturing firm and its CPA is extremely close. The fact that the CPAs have access to the books of competing firms means that confidentiality, and trust, are key attributes of this relationship.

Schools

Los Angeles County is home to several colleges and universities that prepare students in fashion design and other aspects of the apparel business. These schools are significant for continually producing new generations of designers, many of whom enter the local apparel industry. The schools also train people in the various aspects of running apparel firms, from both a technical ad and a business point of view. In recent years, they have worked closely with city and other public agencies to help promote the image of Los Angeles as a major design center.[73]

The four major apparel-related schools on Los Angeles are the Fashion Institute of Design and Merchandising, Otis College of Art and Design, and California Design College, which are private, and Los Angeles Trade-Technical College, a public school that is part of the statewide community college system. The American College of the Applied Arts and Woodbury University are smaller private schools.[74]

The Fashion Institute of Design and Merchandising was founded in 1969. This school offers an associate-of-arts degree in fashion design, interior design, merchandise marketing, and apparel manufacturing management. Its principal campus is in the garment district, and there are branch campuses in San Francisco, Orange County, and San Diego. The institute is a significant force in the apparel industry in Los Angeles, and its founder and owner, Tonian Hohberg, is extremely influential. The school links its programs to the entertainment industry by providing programs that combine fashion and entertainment, another example of the synergy generated by being located in Los Angeles. Karen Kane is one of the school's graduates.

Otis College of Art and design offers a four-year degree in fine arts. It has close connections to many industry leaders. California Design College, which graduates about 100 students a year, specializes in computer-aided design, and is expanding its curriculum to cover advanced professional fashion design.

Los Angeles Trade-Technical College provides technical training and apprenticeship in fashion design for those willing to settle or hours of technical classes in plain, concrete-block buildings located in the industrial downtown. Among the school's better-known graduates are Carole Little, Karl Logan, Robin Piccone, Dorothy Schoelen of Platinum Clothing Co., Inc., and Sue Wong. As with other design programs, the emphasis is strictly practical: Classroom education is shunned in favor of a hands-on approach to learning the specifics of apparel manufacture, from sewing to fabric selection, from advanced design to merchandising. As part of the statewide community college system, Trade-Tech is able to offer an inexpensive, two-year associate-of-arts degree. For California residents, fees run a few hundred dollars a year; the private schools are much more expensive. The college provides aspiring designers who could never afford the more upscale schools with an opportunity to find jobs with local manufacturers, even if the starting rung is a patternmaker rather than designer. About half of its thousand students attend daytime classes full-time; the remaining half are older, working students who attend evening and Saturday classes.[75]

Several public community colleges, including Trade-Tech, make up the California College Fashion Consortium.[76] Offering training in various aspects of the apparel industry, these schools throughout California ensure that talent can be recruited by the industry irrespective of class background. Once they graduate, alumni form a network that helps to recruit the next generation of graduates.

The Los Angeles apparel industry faces a critical dilemma. On the one hand, much of the industry wants to retain production here for all the reasons cited above. On the other hand, the intense competition and the fragmentation generated by the contracting system tend to produce illegal and abusive sweatshops. The fact that government agencies have cracked down on sweatshops drives some industry leaders to recoil at what they define as government overregulation and an antibusiness climate, developments that drive them, they maintain, to move offshore. This threat is credible because labor costs are even lower in countries such as Mexico and China. And the lower the wages they find offshore, the more the pressure on local firms to lower their own wage bills, increasing the number and proportion of sweatshops in Los Angeles.

Some will argue that this movement ultimately benefits everyone. Countries such as Mexico will develop economically, and wages there will gradually rise, as has happened in the newly industrializing countries of East Asia. Meanwhile, consumers in the industrial economies benefit from ever-lower prices, and fashionable garments become accessible to everyone. But the argument can equally be made that the movement offshore ratchets down wages in the industrial world, while the workers in poor countries find that they must operate under regimes in which their efforts to raise wages are crushed. Instead of benefiting, the workers lose.[77] Meanwhile, industry profits and executive salaries remain high, reflecting the fact that businesses are able to use offshore production to take most of the gains for themselves.

Lowered wages for workers cause problems down the line. The less workers make the less they can buy, leaving apparel manufacturers to chase fewer consumer dollars. How can NAFTA hope to increase United States exports to Mexico if Mexican wages are too low to sustain an increase in consumption at least equivalent to that lost from United States workers who are no longer employed as a result of capital flight? The rich winners in the system can only buy so many clothes; they cannot sustain a mass market. By continually trying to push labor costs ever lower, the apparel industry kills the goose that lays its golden egg. Meanwhile, the industry's threats to move offshore in the face of overregulation by the Department of Labor and other government agencies puts it in the unconscionable position of appearing to condone the exploitation of an oppressed workforce, both here and abroad. No fancy words about entry-level jobs providing immigrants with a toehold on the first rung of a ladder that leads inevitably into the middle class can veil the ever-lower wages that characterize the industry.

For now, we can expect that the production of basics, namely, garments that do not reflect the rapid changes in fashion and can be produced in bulk for the continual replenishment of a predictable market, will gradually find a way to

Mexico and elsewhere. But the part of the apparel industry that generates cultural products is likely to remain, and to keep growing, as new firms with innovative ideas keep emerging. It is possible that the continued growth in employment statistics already reflects this reality, that is, even as the industry loses one sector, another continues to grow and pick up the slack.

Notes

1. Originally published and reprinted in Edna Bonicich and Richard P. Appelbaum et al., *Behind the Label: Inequality in the Los Angeles Apparel Industry* (Berkeley: University of California Press, 2000). Reprinted by permission of the University of California Press.
2. Rhonda L. Rundle, "Guess Transfers Manufacturing to Mexico amid Labor Charges," *Wall Street Journal*, 14 January 1997. Stuart Silverstein, George White, and Mary Beth Sheridan, "Guess Inc. to Move L.A. Work South of the Border," *Los Angeles Times*, 15 January 1997, A1; Elena de la Cruz, "Firma Guess traslada operaciones a Mexicó," *La Opinión*, 15 January 1997.
3. Roger Waldinger, *Through the Eye of the Needle: Immigrants and Enterprise in New York's Garment Trades* (New York: New York University Press, 1986), 54–56.
4. Sally Kurtzman, interview by authors, 3 March 1992.
5. See, for example, Chung-In Moon, "Trade Frictions and Industrial Adjustment: The Textiles and Apparel Industry in the Pacific Basin," *Pacific Focus* 2, no. 1 (1987): 105–33.
6. United States Department of Commerce data presented in Gary Gereffi, "Global Sourcing and Regional Divisions of Labor in the Pacific Rim," 51–68 in Arif Dirlik, ed., *What Is in a Rim? Critical Perspectives on the Pacific Region Idea* (Boulder, Colo.: Westview Press, 1993).
7. GATT data; cited by Kitty G. Dickerson, *Textiles and Apparel in the International economy* (New York: Macmillan, 1991), tables 6–12 through 6–14.
8. Data from *Demand, Production and Trade in Textiles and Clothing: Statistical Report to the Secretariat*. Textiles Committee, General Agreement on Tariffs and Trade (GATT); United Nations Statistical Division, 1993.
9. United States Bureau of the Census, *United States General Imports* (Washington, D.C., 1992).
10. General Agreement on Tariffs and Trade (GATT), Textiles Committee, *Demand, Production and Trade in Textiles and Clothing: Statistical Report to the Secretariat* (New York: United Nations Statistical Division, 1993).
11. United States Department of Commerce, International Trade Commission, Office of Textiles and Apparel, "Major Shippers Report: Section One: Textiles and Apparel Imports by category"; http://otexa.ita.doc.gov/msr/catvo.htm [30 May 1998]. Imports of apparel only from Mexico in 1997 reached $5.1 billion, from China were $4.5 billion, and from Hong Kong were $3.9 billion; ibid., http://otexa.ita.doc.gov/msr/catvI.htm [30 May 1998].
12. In 1996, the value of imports of apparel and related textiles totaled $48 billion; the value of exports was $1.8 billion. United States Department of Commerce, Office of Trade and Economic Analysis, "Trends Tables: Apparel and Other Textile Products (SIC 23)" in United States Industry Sector Data; http://www.ita.doc.gov/industry/otea/usito98/tables/23.txt [30 May 1998].
13. American Apparel Manufacturers Association, *1997 Focus. An Economic Profile of the Apparel Industry* (Arlington Vt.: AAMA, 1997), chart A, 4.
14. Subsequently, paragraph 9802, but still commonly referred to as 807.
15. The MFA followed several earlier multilateral restrictive agreements among the major trading nations, the most important of which was the so-called Long-Term Agreement, which was in force from 1962 until it was superseded by the MFA. For a detailed history of the regulation of textiles and apparel, see Vinod Aggarwal, *Liberal Protectionism: The International Politics of Organized Textile Trade* (Berkeley, Calif.: University of California Press, 1985); also, see chapter 10 (on which much of the present discussion is based) of Kitty G. Dickerson, *Textiles and Apparel in the International Economy*, 2nd ed. (New York: Macmillan, 1995).
16. Currently United States quota restrictions are triggered when exports to the United States exceed one percent of a country's total trade.
17. Another effect of quotas has been to encourage the illegal transshipment of goods from low-wage countries with limited quotas (such as China) through higher-wage countries with large quota allocations (such as Hong Kong and Taiwan). Such "submarined" goods

constitute a large volume of global apparel trade, providing much work for United States customs officials. Authors' interview with Thomas Gray, Special Agent, United States Customs Office, Hong Kong, 29 November 1991.

18. United States Department of Commerce, International Trade Administration Office (NAFTA), "NAFTA Key Provisions"; http://iepntr.itaiep.doc.gov/nafta/3002.htm [May 30 1998].

19. Both authors have written on this topic in the past, so we refer our readers to those works of more extensive treatment. See Richard P. Appelbaum, David Smith, and Brad Christerson, "Commodity Chains and Indistrial Restructuring in the Pacific Rim: Garment Trade and Manufacturing," 197–204 in *Commodity Chains and Global Capitalism*, ed. Gary Gereffi and Miguel Korzeniewicz (Westport, Conn.: Grrenwood, 1994); Edna Bonacich, Lucie Cheng, Norma Chinchilla, Nora Hamilton, and Paul Ong, eds., *Global Production: The Garment Industry in the Pacific Rim* (Philadelphia: Temple University Press, 1994); Richard P. Appelbaum and Brad Christerson, "Cheap Labor Strategies and Export-Oriented Industrialization: Some Lessons from the East Asia/Los Angeles Apparel Connection," *The International Journal of Urban and Regional Research* 21, no. 2 (June 1997), 202–17; Brad Christerson and Richard P. Appelbaum, "Global and Local Subcontracting: Space, Ethnicity, and the Organization of Apparel Production," *World Development* 23, no. 8 (1995), 1363–74.

20. Brent Klopp, senior vice president for productions planning, Bugle Boy Industries, interview by authors, 11 October 1991. All information concerning Bugle Boy is from this interview.

21. Don Lee, "Fashion Forward," *Los Angeles Times*, 26 April 1998, D, 1.

22. "B.U.M. moves to Rhode Island," *California Apparel News*, 2 October 1997, 7.

23. Jeff Richards, production manager, B.U.M. Equipment, interview by authors with the assistance of Edward Tchakalian, 19 August 1994.

24. Gene Light, senior vice president for manufacturing, Chorus Line Corp., interview by authors with the assistance of Edward Tchakalian, 25 August 1994.

25. Silverstein, White, and Sheridan, "Guess Inc. to Move."

26. Interview with Kenneth Martin, senior vice president for manufacturing and sourcing, Carole Little, interview by authors with the assistance of Edward Tchakalian, 1 September 1994. Martin was murdered in December 1994, in a string of killings and attempted murders of Carole Little personnel that occurred between 1993 and 1995.

27. Mitch Glass, vice president for production, sourcing and scheduling, Cherokee, Inc., interview by authors, 14 August 1991.

28. Judi Kessler, "Southern California: Transition Takes Hold," *Bobbin*, October 1998, 30–38.

29. Larry Kaner, "Levi's Move Overseas Paralleled in L.A. Apparel Trade," *Los Angeles Business Journal*, 8 March 1999, 5.

30. Cited in Larry Kanter, "Guess Defection Unlikely to Spark Garment Exodus," *Los Angeles Business Journal*, 20 January 1997, 1.

31. Cited in Kristi Ellis, "The Southern Draw," *Women's Wear Daily*, Los Angeles Fall I, March 1997, 26–29. See also Kristin Young, "Guess Move Begs Question: Is California Business Friendly?" *California Apparel News*, 17–23 January 1997, 3.

32. Young, "Guess Move."

33. "Union Files New Charges against Guess," *Los Angeles Times*, 18 January 1997, D2.

34. This issue is complicated by the contracting system, under which Guess can shift its contracting offshore without moving its headquarters out of Los Angeles. Because the contractors, both here and in Mexico, are ostensibly independent, Guess can claim that it has not moved offshore, even though its production has.

35. Rundle, "Guess Transfers Manufacturing."

36. This is the number of licensed factories; there are reportedly at least as many "underground" factories.

37. The delegation included representatives of the National Interfaith Committee for Worker Justice, the National Association of Working Women, the Women of Color Resource Center, the Commission on Social Action of Reform Judaism, the Los Angeles Jewish Commission on Sweatshops, the Rural Organizing Project of Oregon, UNITE!, and the Highlander Research and Education Center.

38. National Interfaith Committee for Worker Justice, "Cross-Border Blues: A Call for Justice for Denim Workers in Tehuacán Maquiladoras" (pamphlet), National Interfaith Committee for Worker Justice, Chicago, Ill., June 1998, 5.

39. Silverstein, White, and Sheridan, "Guess Inc. to Move."
40. Rick Wartzman, "Apparel Data Look Great (But Don't Count on It)," *Wall Street Journal*, 15 January 1997.
41. Ellis, "The Southern Draw." In fact, the number of jobs between September 1996 (112,700) and February 1997 (112,800) was virtually unchanged; in 1997 some 7,300 jobs were added (from 109,700 in December 1996 to 117,000 in December 1997); State of California, EDD.
42. Silverstein, White, and Sheridan, "Guess Inc. to Move."
43. Quoted in Wartzman, "Apparel Data Look Great."
44. Jeff Mowdy, production manager, Francine Browne, Inc., interview by Edward Tchakalian, 22 August 1994.
45. Kanter, "Guess Defection."
46. Ibid.
47. Mowdy, interview. In mid-1996 Francine Browner, Inc. was bought by BCBG Max Azria, a growing fashion powerhouse, leaving unclear what future sourcing policies of the company will be; Kristin Young, "BCBG Acquires Francine Browner," *California Apparel News*, 28 July to 1 August 1996, 4.
48. Gus Leonard, interview by authors, May 1995.
49. Kanter, "Guess Defection."
50. Ibid.
51. Ellis, "The Southern Draw."
52. Ibid.
53. Joel Kotkin, "Is Having a Garment Industry Worth All the Trouble? *Los Angeles Times*, 19 January 1997, M6.
54. Don Lee, "Fashion Forward."
55. Allen J. Scott, "The Craft, Fashion, and Cultural Products Industries of Los Angeles: Competitive Dynamics and Policy Dilemmas in a Multisectoral Image-Producing Complex," *Annals of the Association of American Geographers* 86 (1996), 306–23; Allen J. Scott ad David L. Rigby, "The Craft Industries of Los Angeles: Prospects for Economic Growth and Development," *CPS Brief*, California Policy Seminar, 8 July 1996, Berkeley; David L. Rigby, "The Apparel Industry in Southern California," Geography Department, University of California at Los Angeles, 1995.
56. Allen Scott, "The Craft, Fashion, and Cultural Products," 307.
57. For an interesting discussion, see Harvey L. Molotch, "Art in Economy: How Aesthetics and Design Build Los Angeles," *Competition and Change: The Journal of Global Business and Political Economy* I, no. 2 (1995), 145–85; and "L.A. as Product: How Design Works in a Regional Economy," 225–75 in *The City: Los Angeles and Urban Theory at the End of the Twentieth Century*, ed. Allen J. Scott and Edward W. Soja (Berkeley, Calif.: University of California Press, 1996).
58. See Edna Bonicich and Richard P. Appelbaum et al., *Behind the Label: Inequality in the Los Angeles Apparel Industry* (Berkeley: University of California Press, 2000) for a brief discussion of the history of the apparel industry in relation to Hollywood.
59. See, for example, Michael E. Porter, *The Competitive Advantage of Nations* (New York: The Free Press, 1990); Allen J. Scott, "Flexible Production Systems and regional Development," *International Journal of Urban and Regional Research* 12 (1988), 171–86; Michael J. Piore and Charles F. Sabel, *The Second Industrial Divide: Possibilities for Prosperity* (New York: Basic Books, 1984); Michael Storper and Richard Walker, *The Capitalist Imperative: Territory, Technology, and Industrial Growth* (New York: Blackwell, 1989). For a case study of the importance of agglomeration in the electronics industry of southern California, see Allen J. Scott, *Technopolis: High Technology Industry and Regional Development in Southern California* (Berkeley, Calif.: University of California Press, 1993).
60. H. Hakansson, ed. *International Marketing and Purchasing of Industrial Goods*, 2nd ed.(Chichester, England: John Wiley, 1982); T. H.Willis and C.R. Hutson. "Vendor Requirements and Evaluation in a Just-in-Time Environment," *International Journal of Purchasing Management* 10 no. 4 (1990), 41–50; Mark Granovetter, "Economic Action and Social Structure: The Problem of Embeddedness," *American Journal of Sociology* 9 no. 3 (1985), 481–510; Richard Walker, "The Geographical Organization of Production Systems," *Environment and Planning* 6 no. 4 (1988), 377–408.
61. Sidney Morse, interview by authors, 28 October 1992.

62. David Morse, at the time managing partner of CaliforniaMart, interview by authors, 7 January 1992.
63. Sidney Morse, interview.
64. CaliforniaMart; http://www.californiamart.com/About/cm_profile.html [11 June 1998].
65. Susan Morse-Lebow, at the time responsible for financial operations, interview by authors, 27 August 1992. The projected building was never undertaken, although millions of dollars were invested in it. "Thank God we didn't do it," said Susan. "We cut our losses."
66. This description of CaliforniaMart comes from its promotional materials, including a press fact sheet, a history, and the regularly released directories.
67. Susan had just had a child at the time of interview, and was pregnant again, which limiter her involvement in the family business. David decided to devote his full energy to Mart Management International, becoming the sole partner of what had initially been another family venture to develop an Asian version of the CaliforniaMart. The Trade Mart Singapore billed itself as the region's first integrated resource center for the wholesale fashion trade by linking Hong Kong, Indonesia, Malaysia, the Philippines, South Korea, Taiwan, Thailand, and Singapore in an effort to become "the centre of Asia's fashion business." The $140-million project was a joint venture between Mart Management International and Parkway Holdings of Singapore. In 1998, Trade Mart Singapore offered some 300 wholesale fashion showrooms and offices; Trade Mart Singapore; http://www.tmsinfo.com [11 June 1998].
68. Sidney Morse, interview. This assertion was contested by Bruce Corbin, the regional vice president for administration of Union Bank, who claimed that the high interest rates of the early 1980s had long since declined, and that money was available, but that the difficulties in the industry (which he characterized as "treacherous") made most manufacturers bad credit risks (Bruce Corbin, interview by authors, 2 September 1992).
69. Cash-and-carry refers to the production of goods that are already manufactured and are available for immediate sale to retailers; conventionally, garments are manufactured only on specific orders from retailers.
70. Corbin, interview; Ronald Jones, CPA and managing partner, Moss Adams LLP, interview by authors, 9 November 1992.
71. Marty Josephson, interview by authors, 4 November 1992.
72. Jones, interview; Josephson, interview.
73. For example, in May 1997 representatives of the Economic Development Corporation in Los Angeles met with leaders in art and design education, including representative of Otis College of Art and Design and the Fashion Institute of Design and Merchandising to investigate the feasibility of hosting an annual international *L.A. by Design* show that would feature the apparel, entertainment, furniture, toy, and food industries; *California Apparel News*, 16 May 1997, 4.
74. "Education: How Do You Keep the Apparel Industry Stocked with Talent?" *California Apparel News*, 3 to 9 July 1998, A1.
75. S. J. Diamond, "Designing the Future," *Los Angeles Times*, 15 November 1992, E1.
76. These include El Camino College in Torrance, Fullerton College, Glendale College, Long Beach City College, Los Angeles Valley College in Van Nuys, Orange Coast College in Costa Mesa, Palomar College in San Marcos, Pasadena City College, Rancho Santiago College in Santa Ana, Saddleback College in Mission Viejo, and San Diego Mesa College; *California Apparel News*, 18 to 24 June 1993, 10.
77. For a more detailed discussion, see Bonacich et al., *Global Production*.

The turn-of-the-century sweatshop and its Jewish immigrant workers through the lens of a social reformer. This photograph of a sweatshop in a Ludlow Street tenement, New York City, c. 1889 highlights ideas of the sweatshop as a disorganized, dirty and diseased, cramped, ethnic workplace. Photographer, Jacob Riis, Courtesy Library of Congress.

We would like to thank Barbara Briggs, Kitty Krupat, Kenneth Wolensky, Peter Liebhold, and Harry Rubenstein for their help in putting together these images.

"Between Pharaohs." In this cartoon from the Yiddish newspaper *Der Groyser Kundes* (April 18, 1913), the Egyptian Pharaoh tells the sweatshop boss: "I had Jews working for me but never like this." Immigrant sweatshop workers, like those caricatured in the cartoon, often pointed to their physical pain and disfigurement as evidence of the injustice of the system. Courtesy, Smithsonian Institution, National Museum of American History.

" . . . the Sweatshop is virtually gone today." In showing two "garment workers at play," *Life* magazine printed this obituary for the sweatshop at the height of the New Deal. The New Deal coalition of unions, reformers, and government officials combated the sweatshop by focusing on regulation and factory inspection. *Life*, August 1, 1938. Hansel Mieth/TimeLife Pictures/Getty Images.

Organizing a runaway industry. When garment manufacturers left New York for places like Pennsylvania beginning in the 1920s, the garment unions, like the International Ladies' Garment Workers' Union (ILGWU), followed. Here, ILGWU rank-and-file and union leaders picket Jenkins Sportswear in Pittson, Pennsylvania, 1958. Courtesy Kenneth Wolensky, Photo by Steve Lukasik.

The return of the sweatshop. The operators of a sweatshop in El Monte, California, after a raid by the California Department of Industrial Relations on August 2, 1995. The exposure of conditions in this factory, perhaps more than any other event, highlighted the reality of the global sweatshop for the American public. This sweatshop, owned by a Chinese-Thai family, produced clothing for popular American brands and held 72 illegal Thai immigrant workers in slavery. The raid spurred a controversial Smithsonian exhibition about sweatshops and catalyzed a new wave of antisweatshop activism. Courtesy, Smithsonian Institution, National Museum of American History.

The façade of a global industry: the textile center in contemporary Los Angeles. On the one hand, the passage of the North American Free Trade Agreement has encouraged many Los Angeles manufacturers to seek cheap labor in Mexico. On the other hand, the proximity to United States markets and the culture industries of Hollywood and the arrival of Asian and Latino/a immigrants has sustained employment. Courtesy, Smithsonian Institution, National Museum of American History.

The global American sweatshop: a knit-goods sweatshop in Queens, New York, 1997. Such small shops are organized around the labor of recent immigrants and dependent on complex ethnic and family networks. They often escape the overextended gaze of factory inspectors. At the same time, labor unions have found it increasingly difficult to organize such small shops. Courtesy, Smithsonian Institution, National Museum of American History.

The contemporary reformer and the global sweatshop. The National Labor Committee's (NLC) Charlie Kernaghan visits the Mandarin International factory in El Salvador that made clothing for American companies like the Gap and Eddie Bauer. In the 1990s, American-based activist and consumer campaign emerged around forced birth control, harsh conditions, and firings of union activists at Mandarin. The campaign concluded with the signing, in Brooklyn, New York, of an agreement between the NLC and the Gap allowing for independent monitoring of the factory. Courtesy Kernaghan/NLC.

8

Globalization and Worker Organization in New York City's Garment Industry

IMMANUEL NESS
Brooklyn College, City University of New York

For the better part of the last century, garment and textile industries have been a mainstay of the New York City regional economy, providing manufacturing jobs at decent wages for many urban residents. Even as manufacturing in general declined in the city since the 1950s, the industry remained a strong presence in the city through the 1960s, reaching a high of 250,000 workers in the 1970s, most of whom were members of the two leading unions—the International Ladies Garment Workers Union (ILGWU) and the Amalgamated Clothing and Textile Union (ACTWU). As other industries declined, garment and textile workers accounted for over half of all manufacturing jobs in New York.

Beginning in the mid-1970s, garment production in New York began a more precipitous decline, falling to an estimated low of 82,500 workers in 1996. The primary cause of this decline was the relocation of garment production to lower-cost regions in the U.S. south and southwest and, more recently, offshore. Despite the decline, New York remained the fashion capital of the United States as designers continued to value its standing as a center of communications, the arts, and finance.

New York's growing importance as the preeminent global fashion center led to a small recovery of the garment industry in the 1990s, as rapidly paced changes in women's styles created a demand for quick turnaround that could not be met by low-wage offshore competitors.[1] To meet the growing need for rapid production, hundreds of small sweatshops sprouted up in neighborhoods throughout the city, employing thousands of recent immigrants at wages well below the legal minimum. By 1998, union officials and demographers estimated that employment in the garment industry had rebounded to some 140,000 workers, a full half of whom labored in the informal underground economy. But this growth would be short-lived.

9/11 and Its Aftermath

The fragility of employment in the New York City garment industry—poignantly and most dramatically revealed by a steep decline in jobs in the immediate aftermath of the terrorist attacks of September 11, 2001—suggests an important characteristic of the globalization of production. Production migrates *and* it remains. But globalization continues to effect the production that remains, in this case, in the old garment center of New York City. Sometimes garment producers uproot production in the search for cheap labor; sometimes cheap labor comes to the producers, in the extreme case as illegal immigrants. Such workers can hardly depend on governmental or nongovernmental agencies and groups, from factory inspectors to activist groups, for help in transforming spontaneous outbursts of resistance and resentment into enduring kinds of protection. At the same time, the looming threat of relocation is a trump card in the hand of employers—even those with every intention of remaining in New York. Globalization affects workers in the old garment centers and in the new. Thus, activists in New York in recent years find themselves seeking local answers for the decline in employment and conditions, problems fundamentally rooted in global patterns of production. Different and hostile groups, like UNITE!—the leading AFL-CIO garment and textile workers union, established through the merger of ILGWU and ACTWU—and the Chinese Staff and Workers Association (CSWA) have suggested new models of organizing, like workers' centers. In the end, though, such local strategies have run up against the reality that when production is easy to move, the labor of those who have moved to find work is hard to defend.

In one day—September 11, 2001—the already shaky garment industry suffered a dramatic blow. The catastrophic consequences of the World Trade Center attacks included economic aftershocks that will take years to overcome. Garment and apparel production was hit harder than any industry in the city. According to UNITE! nearly 40 percent of an estimated 25,000 members will permanently lose their jobs in the city in the wake of the attacks. This estimate does not include the 50,000 nonunion garment workers whose jobs have been placed in jeopardy.

Chinatown, the hub of New York's garment industry, is situated just a few blocks from the World Trade Center site. Garment shops there proved especially vulnerable, since they are dependent on trucking for the shipping of materials and products. When, in the weeks and months following September 11, traffic in the Chinatown area was restricted to emergency vehicles, thousands of garment workers lost their jobs.

Unlike restaurants, the retail trade, tourism, and other service industries, which gradually recover over the years from disaster, garment production is acutely vulnerable because manufacturers can easily shift production to other locations, in the city and elsewhere, where low-wage garment workers can be found. Chinatown's garment industry was the epicenter of job loss in New York, as 14,000 apparel workers were laid off or permanently lost their jobs. An area survey by the Asian American Federation of New York reported that nearly 40 percent of garment factories shut down in the three months following September 11, as production declined by 60 percent.[2]

Average wages in the apparel industry in Chinatown fell nearly a hundred percent, from $207 to $112 a week. The same study reported 2,641 temporarily dislocated workers. By 2003, as economic conditions in Chinatown continued to deteriorate, federal promises of assistance and redevelopment seemed stillborn. A UNITE! official reports that half of the unionized garment jobs have been lost in Chinatown, and union leaders remain doubtful the industry will recover to pre-9/11 levels. Meanwhile, manufacturers flee and promised government assistance falls well short of the needs of local producers. The closure of apparel manufacturing shops in Chinatown has hit low-wage immigrant workers from mainland China, Hong Kong, and Taiwan especially hard, though thousands of workers in other centers of local garment production—Manhattan's Fashion District, Long Island City, and Sunset Park, Brooklyn—have also been affected. To make matters worse, workers in the sizeable underground segment of the industry are typically paid under the table, and so are not eligible for federal unemployment insurance relief.

New York's Garment Industry in the Global Economy

The massive garment shop closures in the wake of 9/11 have taken an extraordinary toll on both union and nonunion workers, but 9/11 by itself cannot explain the hemorrhaging of garment production in New York City over several decades. To understand this decline, we need to examine the garment industry through the lens of globalization; over the last thirty years, production has shifted increasingly to low-wage regions of the world. Large retailers that dominate the industry have chosen to cut costs and increase profits by outsourcing garment production to regions where workers are paid a fraction of the low wages paid garment workers in New York. If the young women who predominate in New York garment production cannot support themselves and their families on their meager earnings here, their counterparts in China, Guatemala, Haiti, Indonesia, the Philippines, Sri Lanka, and Vietnam find themselves at least equally strapped. Cost cutting in New York is but an extension of the free trade policies initiated by the U.S. in support of these large merchandisers. The exploitation of workers in the city is facilitated by the ability of retailers to go global.

When the New York garment industry began its precipitous decline in the 1970s, production was shifted mainly to the low-wage U.S. south and economically-depressed areas in the north; only later, with the relaxation of trade restrictions in the hemisphere and elsewhere, did it move offshore. Today unionized garment workers in New York City, even those earning just above the U.S. minimum wage, cannot compete with workers in Latin America and East Asia who are paid as little as eight cents an hour for producing identical products. Still, the fashion industry's need for rapid turnaround has kept some production in New York, but under significantly worsened conditions.

How were major retailers able to cut labor costs in New York? Globalization is not simply the transfer of production and technology throughout the world. One of its primary features is the growing international mobility of labor and the creation of a transnational migrant workforce.[3] Nonunion garment manufacturers in New York have replaced low-wage labor in the formal sector with tens of thousands of transnational migrants employed at even lower wages and enjoying no health benefits. This transnational workforce, which today accounts for the majority of garment workers in the city, is employed in sweatshops that compete for retail contracts against the declining unionized sector. The resulting wage competition causes a vicious cycle of spiraling cost-cutting, as union shops lower their prices to compete for work against nonunion workers.

International migration is perhaps the single most important demographic trend in contemporary New York City, having added over one million newcomers in the last decade alone.[4] As a vital entryway for international capital, the city has experienced a growing demand for a large and differentiated labor force in all sectors of the regional economy. Immigrant workers are employed both in the state-sanctioned legal economy and in the informal economy unregulated by federal or state law.[5] Recent demographic research suggests that immigrants enter specific labor-market niches on the basis of formal and informal referral networks that tend to emerge through familial, kinship, and community bonds of association. Educated and higher-skilled workers (particularly those with some command of English) tend to be employed in scientific, technical, and professional positions, while those without skills—including the urban poor and displaced peasantry—are typically employed at the low end of the underground economy, in garment, jewelry, and toys and trinket manufacturing.

In the global marketplace, the nation-state has become increasingly subordinate to international capital flows. Workers' rights have been undermined precipitously as national labor and social welfare laws have been superseded by neoliberal policies underlying globalization.[6] To improve the living conditions of migrant workers, it is necessary to assert their rights as global citizens and workers. This is a formidable task in a post-9/11 political environment of nationalism and xenophobia.

The growth of a transnational labor force with greater labor mobility has brought migrant workers from developing nations to New York City and other urban centers in the developed world. The early-twentieth-century garment-worker mobilizations led by European immigrants have today been replaced by equivalent mobilizations by new immigrants.[7] The United Nations Organization for Migration estimates that the number of transnational workers from developing nations has doubled worldwide from 75 million in 1965 to 150 million in 2000.[8]

Worker Power and Organizational Failure

It would be a serious mistake to conclude that garment workers employed under extreme forms of exploitation are unwilling to organize to defend their interests. Indeed, struggles occurring between workers and owners appear regularly today in forms starkly reminiscent of struggles a century ago. What is different from the situation at midcentury is a decreased capacity to translate worker power and militancy into enduring improvements in the conditions of work. Largely responsible for this change is a restructured industry in which retailers call the tune and work is parceled out to jobbers, many of them fly-by-night.

The dramatic erosion of wages and working conditions presents significant problems to workers seeking to organize. In this hostile environment, do garment workers have any hope of improving their conditions? Have they the power to overcome the forces of globalization? At first blush it seems that unions clearly do not possess the power they once did. Globalization of the industry over the last twenty years or so, and the resulting outsourcing of production has dispersed standardized garment manufacturing to low-wage areas (domestic and foreign) and so has diminished the bargaining power of medium-wage garment workers represented by unions.[9] Thus, unions and other labor institutions appear to have a limited ability to respond effectively to these changes. Trade unions and new immigrant workers have always had a problematic relationship. Unions representing native-born workers have often ostracized immigrants, despite their prominent role in the history of the labor movement. In late nineteenth- and early twentieth-century America, immigrants were crucial to the formation and growth of an industrial labor movement. They have since become a driving force in the success of unions in the growing service and public sectors of the economy. Still, established unions frequently regard immigrants as outsiders and as unfair competitors at home and abroad, a xenophobic attitude that has contributed to organized labor's declining membership and consequent loss of political influence.[10] While immigrants (like native workers) resist employer abuses today as in the past, the policies and practices of established unions often dampened whatever interest they might have in becoming members. However, as union presence recedes in low-wage industries, some unions—notably garment, building maintenance, and transport unions—have become more receptive to new immigrants. Yet despite the welcoming rhetoric, unions continue to have a checkered relationship with these workers. Though immigrants are often viewed as integral to the survival and growth of unions, extensive resources are required to help them organize. They are also viewed at times as posing a threat to union leadership, a serious concern to entrenched labor bureaucrats.

Top-Down and Bottom-Up Organizing Strategies

A debate rages among labor organizers in New York over who is to blame for the failure to promote and sustain worker organization. Two explanations are advanced for the failure to organize garment workers in New York City despite the dramatic erosion of wages and working conditions. One is put forward by UNITE!; the other by critics of the union and by competing independent labor organizers. Noteworthy is that both sides agree that globalization of production is the primary cause for the growth of sweatshops.

The Union Position

UNITE! and its affiliate locals place the blame for the rise in sweatshops on giant retail clothing chains: Wal-Mart, Kmart, Target, Federated Department Stores, the GAP, and others. To produce apparel at the lowest possible cost, these chains outsource production to the lowest possible bidder. Thus, in New York City, sweatshop conditions have proliferated in the underground informal economy and even in union shops, which increasingly must struggle to stay in business. Owners of these shops find themselves whipsawed by jobbers demanding lower-priced goods and a union seeking to improve wages.

Wages in the New York City apparel industry are calculated by piecework in which jobber, contractor, and worker are paid according to the number of units produced. In union shops, a contract is negotiated specifying piecework rates intended to ensure wages above the legal hourly minimum. Moreover, the contract includes health insurance for workers and their families. The added costs involved make it in the interest of jobbers to place work in nonunion shops that pay workers below minimum wage, so long as quality goods are produced.

The disincentive to contract work to union shops tends to increase production in nonunion firms and thus leads to the proliferation of sweatshop conditions. Particularly during economic slumps, the union frequently has been compelled to accept lower piece rates lest jobbers and retailers shift production elsewhere. In the struggle to retain work in their shops, unionized firms are often forced to lower bids just to remain competitive; the result is that in some cases workers are paid less than the negotiated rate. When violations occur, the union maintains workers are often afraid to file grievances for fear the shop will close, costing them their jobs.

The union claims that although wages have stagnated and occasionally declined to sweatshop levels, workers still prefer union representation, if only for the health insurance and the right to grieve. Acknowledging the decline in wages and conditions in unionized shops, the union adamantly insists that even the lowest-wage union shop pays piecework rates higher than those prevailing in nonunion sweatshops. In turn, the union ruefully notes, workers employed in nonunion shops are under intense pressure to shun unionization lest higher piece rates and the cost of health benefits will pit them against even more exploitative nonunion shops, at times set up by their employer at a nearby location. Higher wages also raise the cost of garments made in New York and so encourage retailers and jobbers to contract work not sensitive to time constraints out to foreign producers. As a result of these pressures, the unionized apparel firm in New York City is threatened with extinction. In this climate, the union laments, it is discouraged from organizing new shops even when workers want a voice.

UNITE!'s Detractors

Although the union has a range of critics, those who condemn it for failing to defend workers tend to focus on corruption among union officials, including mob ties, and a general torpor and climate of negligence.[11] These critics argue that a systemically corrupt union leadership cuts deals behind the backs of workers, allowing bargaining agreements in its own shops to go unenforced and permitting sweatshop conditions and wages to fall to as low as $1.00 an hour. According to this argument, UNITE! officials work with organized crime organizations to dominate the manufacture and transport of garments in the region. The union, they contend, in effect collaborates with employers in the subordination of workers by its failure to enforce agreements, and in turn receives kickbacks, a share of the profits at expense of workers.

Parts of the industry, it must be admitted, are indeed tied to organized crime, particularly in the realm of transportation. Some UNITE! locals have themselves been implicated in racketeering. However, the national union has placed into trusteeship several locals found to be involved in schemes to defraud workers. Leaders of these locals are dismissed, and the national assigns officials to rehabilitate the affiliate. Moreover, it is noteworthy that UNITE!, unlike several national unions, has never faced federal charges of corruption.

In response to declining conditions, both independent labor organizations and the garment unions have also tried to organize workers to improve wages and conditions in the industry. The most common tactic is the establishment of workers' centers intended to recruit, educate, and organize these undocumented immigrants. Rather than focusing on union recognition and collective-bargaining agreements, workers' centers stress the enforcement of minimum-wage laws and labor standards, thereby fighting the proliferation of sweatshops.

The first workers' centers in New York were established by independent labor organizers outside union auspices. The CSWA, founded in 1979 by Wing Lam, a former organizer for ILGWU, is the most prominent workers' center in the industry. Based in Lower Manhattan's Chinatown, CSWA has since opened an office in Sunset Park, Brooklyn; both neighborhoods have a high concentration of garment sweatshops and Chinese workers. The organization claims a membership of over 1,000, mostly Chinese-Americans, and concentrates on garment, domestic, restaurant, and construction workers. CSWA considers its workers'-center model the basis for a new labor movement independent of the AFL-CIO.

CSWA considers most unions, including UNITE!, to be corrupt organizations more concerned with advancing institutional concerns than serving the needs of workers in workplaces and communities. The organization tries to mobilize its members to fight for improved workplace conditions and to mobilize community supporters around issues of affordable housing and racial discrimination.

CSWA's most notable organizing campaign has been its efforts to improve conditions in Chinatown's exploitative restaurant industry, where workers are paid well below minimum wage—even counting tips, which management often takes for itself—and work long hours. At the Silver Palace Restaurant, the most notorious of Chinatown's banquet halls, CSWA established 318 Restaurant Workers Union as a vehicle to advance the interests of workers. CSWA, workers, and community supporters engaged in mass pickets in the early to mid 1990s to force the employer to comply with labor law and respect the workers' right to organize. In 1995, to avoid unionization of the 900-seat restaurant, the Silver Palace filed for bankruptcy; in May 1997, the establishment was closed. When in August 1998 it reopened as the New Silver Palace, organizers of the union were denied reinstatement by the new employers. The organizing effort continues to this day.[12]

Against this background it might be asked, Why is UNITE! so disdained by CSWA? A particular concern of CSWA is that the workforce of recent female immigrants that dominates in Chinatown garment shops is subject to discriminatory treatment and sexual harassment. CSWA echoes the UNITE! position that workers are afraid to complain, and that "unethical employers and garment manufacturers and retailers exploit the vulnerability of these passive and submissive workers."[13]

CSWA estimates that 20,000 Chinese immigrant women are employed in garment sweatshops in Chinatown. Since 90 percent of these sweatshops are represented by UNITE!, CSWA concludes that no advantage attaches to working in unionized shops. Irrespective of unionization, CSWA contends, working conditions are intolerable in both Chinatown and Sunset Park: "Regardless of whether or not these women are union or non-union, documented or undocumented, they are forced to work 12–16 hours a day, six or seven days a week, with no overtime pay, benefits or even minimum wage."[14] In Sunset Park, where recent immigrants are drawn by lower housing costs, wages and working conditions are even more oppressive than in Chinatown, CSWA estimates that some 10,000 women earn no more than $1 an hour, given prevailing piecework rates.

Failure Explained

What is intriguing about CSWA's analysis of the wages and working conditions in New York sweatshops is how much it shares with UNITE!'s explanation.

Both organizations have stated that inadequate labor law, the nonenforcement of existing labor law, and anti-immigrant laws such as employer sanctions lead to the oppression of workers.[15] Moreover, both would agree that the system of subcontracting undermines wages and working conditions.

Both organizations argue that the system is close to impossible to change without fundamental changes in the system of global garment production; this would mean providing standards at or above the living wage for workers throughout the world. The sweatshop conditions of New York's garment industry, both maintain, are the extension of a globalized system that exploits workers. CSWA explains that the subcontracting of garment production "allows firms to seek out and exploit the most vulnerable pockets of labor, . . . [R]acism and economic exclusion help to cultivate the notorious sweatshop underground in which Chinese immigrant workers are trapped."[16] UNITE!, too, asserts that globalization and subcontracting have contributed to the deterioration of working conditions and a growing inability to enforce union contracts and labor law.[17] Unfortunately, despite reasonably earnest attempts by both CSWA and UNITE! to improve wages and working conditions, neither organization has managed to change the system.

Despite a demonstrable agreement in their analysis, a relentless dispute rages between the two organizations. CSWA and its network of supporters are responsible for most of the accusations hurled at UNITE! of sweatshop conditions in its shops. In a widely publicized exposé of UNITE! in the *Village Voice*, Robert Fitch found a union shop at 446 Broadway where workers had not been paid for almost twelve weeks. He argued that though some two-thirds of garment contractors operate under sweatshop conditions, fully three-quarters of the shops organized by UNITE! are in violation of wage, hour, and safety regulations.[18] Still, the closure of garment shops that once paid wages above the legal minimum fuels realistic fears of job loss among workers in sweatshops and so makes it more difficult to improve working conditions. And though some local union leaders have been implicated in corrupt activities, the flight of garment production to offshore low-wage competitors is the major reason for the desperate situation that prevails.

In 1993, UNITE! established the Garment Workers' Justice Center, a workers' center designed to draw immigrant workers in sweatshops dispersed throughout the Fashion District to a central location.[19] The Justice Center offered unorganized immigrant workers associate membership in the union, job training, English language education, and assistance in disputes with employers. In 1995, UNITE! claimed to have organized 1,500 associate members in the Fashion District. This community-based outreach strategy was intended to be the step toward eventually organizing 25,000 low-wage garment workers dispersed throughout the midtown area.

The short-term objective of the workers' center was to organize political and ideological support for unionization among the disenfranchised Chinese and Mexican immigrant workers who make up the majority of workers in the industry. The long-term goal was to sustain union-organizing campaigns among these communities. The latter would have entailed the mass organization of immigrants in Fashion District sweatshops and beyond, a task successfully undertaken by garment unions in the first three decades of the last century. But by the late 1990s, not even one worker had become a member of the union as a result of the organizing drive. The only recognition and bargaining agreement the union succeeded in winning was quickly rendered meaningless when the owners filed for bankruptcy and moved production elsewhere.

Case Study of Spontaneous Strike

Workers from time to time do challenge corporate power. Yet, even then, their success is tempered by the realities of the global system of garment production. An episode of worker organization and militancy that occurred in 1996 demonstrated both the power of workers and the difficulty of solidifying hard-won gains in a system of globalized production. The workers involved had come together under the auspices of UNITE!'s midtown Justice Center.

In December 1996, a majority of workers employed at a garment sweatshop in the Fashion District petitioned the shop owner for union recognition. The firm had habitually failed to pay workers on time—in some cases not at all—and had accumulated hundreds of thousands of dollars in outstanding claims for back wages. Workers also complained of excessively onerous working conditions; management had harassed, disrespected, and physically abused workers, and had employed child labor. The shop, a subcontractor that produced garments for major clothing retailers, employed a workforce of about 300, mostly undocumented young women from Mexico and Ecuador.[20]

When the owner refused to recognize the workers' petition to join a union, they initiated a sit-down strike demanding back wages and union representation. Demands by supervisors that they end the strike were refused until managers promised immediate payment of back wages. When the workers left the factory, suspected union sympathizers were interrogated, threatened with dismissal, and physically intimidated by management. When the owner reneged on the promised back wages, the workers organized public demonstrations in the days before Christmas, targeting a primary customer for the sweatshop's apparel—a large New York department store catering to trendy, upscale shoppers.

Amid growing public awareness of the workers' oppressive conditions, the demonstrations were embarrassing to the retailers, several of whom canceled orders for garments subcontracted to the sweatshop. To keep its remaining contracts, management finally relented and agreed to recognize the union and negotiate a contract. The owners agreed to pay workers $40 a week toward back wage claims until paid in full. The contract required managers to treat workers respectfully, discipline them with just cause only, and refrain from threatening or hitting them. It also specified hours and provided seniority rights.

The reluctant decision by management to recognize the union was made because workers gained the upper hand by threatening to withhold their labor and by exposing abusive conditions to the public. Unfortunately, the conflict did not end there. Shortly after workers and management agreed to the contract, the owner failed to live up to its terms. The demonstrations had caused retailers to cancel orders, and others followed, shrinking both from the negative publicity and from the prospect of lower profits occasioned by higher labor costs. With no state or federal regulations to prevent retailers from switching from one subcontractor to another, production was transferred to less visible local sweatshops or to offshore producers operating where working conditions are not monitored. These decisions by retailers at the top of the global food chain placed an impossible financial burden on sweatshop management. In early January, the sweatshop failed to pay both current weekly wages and the installment payment against back wages. At that point, the union uncovered evidence that management was secretly transferring work to a sweatshop in nearby Long Island City to avoid the union contract while producing apparel for contractors it had retained.

The power that workers in the Manhattan sweatshop thought they had gained evaporated very quickly. Workers had no say in making sure that government regulatory agencies enforced the laws. They had no say in decisions by global corporate retailers to cancel the orders that provided them work. Finally, they had no say in management's decision to transfer work to another facility.

Because the industry is structured to operate in ways so contrary to the interests of workers, the union came to conclude that the effort was hopeless. The lesson to be drawn is that now, more than ever, power in the workplace is not simply a dynamic between workers and their immediate employers. Though workers had a direct voice in the decision to withhold their labor, protest abuses, and negotiate a contract, their voice was absent in the subsequent actions (and nonactions) taken by management, jobbers, retailers, and government agencies.

Conclusion

Global industrial restructuring and the growth of subcontracting to jobbers and to small shops unorganized by unions have over the last two decades encouraged a rapid expansion of low-wage jobs in the New York garment industry. As a result, unions experienced in industrial organizing techniques increasingly require strategies for reaching workers in this changed environment. Globalization and increased capital mobility require organizing strategies that target smaller, spatially dispersed firms employing relatively few workers.[21]

Fundamentally, CSWA and UNITE! share the position that globalization has eroded working conditions in New York City and given rise to sweatshops. But if UNITE!'s failure to reverse this trend is to be explained primarily by its corruption, as CSWA claims, why has it proved so hard for the latter to improve conditions? It must be admitted that the problem has deeper roots, patterns in the industry that go back thirty years.

Although immigrant garment workers frequently mobilize to defend their interests, and will continue to do so, the power of global retailers makes it all but impossible to successfully transform conditions in New York City sweatshops. This power imbalance is the primary factor in the failure to mobilize workers to improve conditions. What is remarkable is that undocumented immigrant workers protest on their own through sit-down strikes, usually without the support of unions or other labor organizations.[22]

Every day, thousands of workers in New York's garment industry resist unfair wages, oppressive conditions, and harassment. Their efforts take many forms—from slowing the pace of work to finding shortcuts to get through the day, from disparaging the boss to organizing into membership organizations. In the New York garment industry, immigrant workers with no backing at all engage in sit-down strikes. Resistance never stops. The big question is how labor institutions can translate workers' anger, energy, and self-activity into a force that can challenge the political and economic power of global retailers. The answer lies in a sustained social protest movement outside the bounds of labor law, a movement that encompasses the broader working class (or not) in all sectors of a restructured economy.

Notes

1. For an examination of New York's garment industry in historical and contemporary perspective, see Mark Levitan, *Opportunity at Work: The New York City Garment Industry* (New York: Community Service Society of New York, 1998); Gus Tyler, *Look for the Union Label: A History of the International Ladies Garment Workers' Union* (Armonk, N.Y.: M.E. Sharpe, 1995); Roger D. Waldinger, *Through the Eye of the Needle: Immigrants and Enterprise in New York's Garment Trades* (New York: New York University Press, 1986), 97.
2. Asian American Federation of New York, *Chinatown After September 11th: An Economic Impact Study* (New York: Asian American Federation of New York, April 14, 2002), 18–31.
3. For an examination of the development of a transnational labor force, see Nancy Foner, ed. *New Immigrants in New York* (New York: Columbia University Press, 2001). See also Héctor R. Cordero-Guzman, Robert C. Smith, and Ramón Grosoguel, eds., *Migration, Transnationalization and Race in a Changing New York* (Philadelphia: Temple University Press, 2001); Nigel Harris, *The New Untouchables: Immigration and the New World Worker* (London: I. B. Tauris Publishers, 1995); and Peter Stalker, *The Work of Strangers: A Survey of Labour Migration* (Geneva: International Labor Office, 1994).
4. Robert C. Smith, Héctor R. Cordero-Guzman, Ramón Grosoguel, "Introduction: Migration, Transnationalization and Ethnic and Racial Dynamics in a Changing New York" in Héctor R. Cordero-Guzman, Robert C. Smith, and Ramón Grosoguel, eds., *Migration, Transnationalization and Race in a Changing New York* (Philadelphia: Temple University Press, 2001), 1–32.

5. One of the most well-known examinations of the informal economy is Saskia Sassen, *The Global City: New York, London, and Tokyo*, (Princeton: Princeton University Press, 2000), 197–319. For an examination of the specific affects on New York, see also Saskia Sassen, "The Informal Economy" in John H. Mollenkopf and Manuel Castells, eds., *Dual City: Restructuring New York*. (New York: Russell Sage Foundation, 1991), 79–109.

6. This analysis, central to Hardt and Negri's argument regarding the changed nature of the global capitalist system, asserts that the nature of imperialism has fundamentally shifted from direct territorial control to one of economic domination, see Michael Hardt and Antonio Negri, *Empire* (Cambridge: Harvard University Press, 2000).

7. For a historical examination of immigration to the U.S. and the growth of undocumented immigrants in the contemporary era, see Nancy Foner, "Transnationalism Then and Now: New York Immigrants Today and at the Turn of the Twentieth Century," in Héctor R. Cordero-Guzman, Robert C. Smith, and Ramón Grosoguel, eds., *Migration, Transnationalization and Race in a Changing New York* (Philadelphia: Temple University Press, 2001), 35–57.

8. International Organization for Migration, *World Migration Report 2000* (Geneva: United Nations, 2001).

9. See Edna Bonacich, Lucie Cheng, Normal Chinchilla, Nora Hamilton, & Paul Ong, eds., *Global Production: The Apparel Industry in the Pacific Rim* (Philadelphia: Temple University Press, 1994); Laurence Mishel and Paula B. Voos, eds.; *Unions and Economic Competitiveness* (Armonk, NY: M. E. Sharpe, 1992); Fred Rosen and Deidre McFadyen, *Free Trade and Economic Restructuring in Latin America* (New York: Monthly Review Press, 1995); Roger D. Waldinger, *Still the Promised City? African Americans and New Immigrants in Postindustrial New York* (Cambridge, MA: Harvard University Press, 1996).

10. Peter Stalker, *The No-Nonsense Guide to International Migration*. (London: Verso, 2002).

11. See Robert Fitch, "Union Reformation." *Tikkun* 15 (March/April 2000), 21–23; Peter Kwong, *Forbidden Workers: Illegal Chinese Immigrants and American Labor* (New York: The New Press, 1997), 91–99, examines the rise and fall of the ILGWU and the rise of a rank-and-file garment-workers' movement in Chinatown.

12. In Chinatown, it should be noted, there is particularly virulent opposition among restaurant and garment-shop owners to the legitimate organization of workers, see Leon Lazaroff, "Chinatown's Union Debate: In New York, a Chinese Restaurant Joins the Ranks of Garment Sweatshops in a Heated Labor Dispute," *Christian Science Monitor*, June 29, 1998, 3.

13. See Chinese Staff and Workers Association Web site, www.cswa.org/garment.htm ,2000.

14. www.cswa.org/garment.htm, 2000.

15. Muzaffar Chishti, "Employer Sanctions Against Immigrant Workers," in *Working USA: The Journal of Labor and Society* 3 (March–April 2000), 71–76, demonstrates that employer sanctions—devised to penalize employers—fall more heavily on immigrant workers.

16. www.cswa.org/garment.htm, 2000.

17. Union of Needletrades Industrial and Textile Employees Web site: www.uniteunion.org.

18. See Fitch, 2000.

19. Immanuel Ness, "Organizing in Immigrant Communities: UNITE!'s Workers' Center Strategy," in *Organizing to Win*. Kate Bronfenbrenner, Sheldon Friedman, Richard Hurd, Rudy Oswald, and Ronald L. Seeber, eds. (Ithaca, NY: Cornell University Press, 1998), 87–101.

20. Though undocumented immigrants are not legally able to work in the U.S., employers who hire them are nonetheless required to comply with federal and state minimum-wage laws, the forty hour work week, and legislation that protects workers from discrimination and oppressive conditions. In practice, federal and state government authorities rarely enforce labor and antidiscrimination laws.

21. An examination of efforts to organize undocumented workers and their willingness to be organized in California is described by Héctor L. Delgado, *New Immigrants, Old Unions: Organizing Undocumented Workers in Los Angeles* (Philadelphia: Temple University Press, 1993).

22. For specific historical studies of immigrant workers in New York, see Melvyn Dubofsky, *When Workers Organize* (Amherst, MA: University of Massachusetts Press, 1968), 40–85; M. P. Fernandez-Kelly and Saskia Sassen, *A Collaborative Study of Hispanic Women in Garment and Electronics Industries* (New York: Unpublished Monograph, 1991); David G.

Gutiérrez, *Between Two Worlds: Mexican Immigrants in the United States* (Wilmington, Delaware: Scholarly Resources Inc, 1996); Philip Kasinetz, *Caribbean New York: Black Immigrants and the Politics of Race* (Ithaca, NY: Cornell University Press, 1992), 90–110; Sarah J. Mahler, *American Dreaming: Immigrant Life on the Margins* (Princeton, N.J.: Princeton University Press, 1995); Patricia R. Pessar and Pamela M. Graham, "Dominicans: Transnational Identites and Local Politics" in Foner, *New Immigrants in New York,* 251–273.

3
Sweatshop Resistance

9

Sweatshop Feminism

Italian Women's Political Culture in New York City's Needle Trades, 1890–1919

JENNIFER GUGLIELMO
Smith College

On January 19, 1913, over 4,000 striking Italian women garment workers gathered at Cooper Union in New York City to learn that the International Ladies' Garment Workers' Union (ILGWU) had signed an agreement with manufacturers without their approval. With jeers and the stomping of feet, the women rejected the union leaders' instructions to return to work. Several women rushed to the stage, forcing speakers off the platform with cries of "a frameup," and urged workers to abandon the ILGWU in favor of the more militant Industrial Workers of the World (IWW). A "storm of protest," as the *New York Times* called it, spread to the streets. Thousands of Italian women workers hurled stones at the windows of a nearby shirtwaist factory and sat in the center of Third Avenue. The next day, in an icy snowstorm, 20,000 workers, mainly Italian, marched through the city's garment districts.[1]

The 1913 rioting erupted after unprecedented numbers of first- and second-generation Italian-American women spent months on a mass organizing campaign in New York City's clothing trades. Alongside other immigrant workers, they had organized picket lines, convinced others to abandon their sewing machines, and withstood arrest and beatings. Although skeptical of the ILGWU (an American Federation of Labor affiliate), they hoped the union would bring them better wages and safer working conditions. By late January, 150,000 workers in four sectors of garment production had walked off their jobs. Yet, at the height of the strike, Italian women argued, the ILGWU had sold them out. The new settlement assigned women to the lowest paid jobs, and set their minimum wage lower than men who held the same jobs. The agreement had won union recognition but no greater voice for women. The ILGWU leaders, workers argued, "preferred to deal with the employers rather than with their own members."[2]

The 1913 riot was the first of several turning points in the history of Italian women workers in the United States. The history of New York City female garment workers in this period focuses instead on the first major garment strike in the city, the famous 1909 "Uprising of 20,000," in which Jewish women workers responded to the reluctance of the ILGWU's male leadership by aligning themselves with middle-class progressives and feminists in the Women's Trade Union League (WTUL). Scholars have been quick to assert that Italian women were unorganized and unsympathetic to the union movement because only 6 percent (approximately 2,000) of the strikers were Italian women, while they comprised a third of the shirtwaist industry labor force.[3] Unlike the Jewish women who earlier dominated the garment industry rank and file, Italian women did not join the New York garment unions en masse until the Great Depression. Prior to that decade, however, they were neither docile nor bound by patriarchal families: their political struggles were more often waged outside of and in opposition to "mainstream" labor and political organizations. However, by the time African-American, Puerto Rican, Chinese, and other Asian and Caribbean women and men began to enter the garment trades in the years following World War II, Italians held a relative monopoly over the higher-paying jobs and enjoyed their own ethnic locals. This essay examines the journey Italian women garment workers made from waging oppositional struggles from the margins to occupying the privileged spaces at the center of U.S. labor institutions.

The Roots of Resistance

Italian women needleworkers first became a discernible part of New York City's garment labor force in the 1880s, and they came to occupy the second largest group of workers in the industry, after Jews from Eastern Europe and Russia, before the First World War. The garment industry was stratified rigidly by gender, ethnicity, and race, and Italian women were initially assigned to the lowest paid "women's work," as finishers, operators, sample makers, shirtwaist and dressmakers, and as home- or piece-workers. As historian Miriam Cohen has documented, the numbers of Italian women garment workers continued to grow during the first half of the twentieth century. In 1925, 64 percent of all Italian women in the U.S. worked in the fashion industry. By the 1930s, Italian women were the majority of garment workers in New York City, just as African-American, Chinese, Puerto Rican and other women began entering the clothing industries in larger numbers. By 1950, 77 percent of first-generation, and 44 percent of second-generation Italian-American women in New York City were factory operatives, the majority of them in the needle trades.[4]

Various factors account for the presence of Italian women in the garment trades, but significant among them is that Italian women had acquired skills in needlework before migration. Tina Gaeta's story is somewhat typical: She learned to sew from her mother and grandmother, both seamstresses in Salerno, before migrating to New York City in 1902. She also recalled that the *sarta* (seamstress) held a distinguished position in her community; the scissors that dangled at her waist symbolized her status. In New York, a young Tina and her siblings helped their mother with piece-work in the men's clothing trade; when they became skilled, they entered the factories in their neighborhood. In fact, New York City's garment trades contained large percentages of southern Italian women who had previously earned wages in sewing in Italy. Those who did not have such skills turned to the simple work of finishing men's and women's tailored garments and were trained in other, less-skilled tasks.[5]

Italian women also brought with them a history of protest and rebellion. As historians such as Donna Gabaccia and Jole Calapso have well documented, women played critical roles in Italy's turn-of-the-century popular movements, and their collaborative activities often helped them to carve out autonomous political spaces.[6] Throughout southern Italy and Sicily, in regions with the highest percentages of migration to the U.S., women often emerged as the most militant activists in popular demonstrations and neighborhood movements among farm workers and urban laborers. Gender differences were also important; while men focused on employers, women targeted the state and resorted more frequently to direct action strategies such as looting and rioting. In Sicily and in cities throughout Italy, women participated in tax revolts, occupied government-owned land, and destroyed municipal offices, demanding that "All should have bread for themselves and their children." After 1900, Italian women turned to collective action in trade unions and radical political parties, participating in organizing drives and strikes in textile, tobacco, clothing, rice, and hemp industries.[7] Such stories, experiences, and political lessons were a vital part of what Italian women carried into the U.S. labor movement; their activism, as historian Rudolph Vecoli observes, "did not simply spring from the American soil" but was "in many ways an extension of the labor movement in Italy."[8]

Women's Revolutionary Proletarian Culture before the First World War

From the moment Italian women entered the United States, they united to alleviate poverty and exploitation. The hardships of work in the garment industry are well known. Employers monitored women closely to maximize production and discourage collective action. They fined workers for being late, talking, singing, and taking too much time in the bathroom. Italian immigrant women became highly critical of what they termed the "*rigorosa sorveglianza*" (rigorous surveillance) of garment employers, the dangerous work conditions, and the low quality of work they were forced to produce rapidly.[9] Italian women also lived in communities rife with protest. In cities such as Hoboken, Paterson, Newark, Lowell, Passaic, Little Falls, Boston, Hopedale, Rochester, Lawrence, Lynn, Chicago, Tampa, Cleveland, and Providence, Italian women were central actors, if rarely leaders, in workers' movements, and were regularly portrayed in the Italian immigrant radical press as "*le più ardenti nella lotta*" (the most ardent in the struggle).[10] Indeed, Italian women often entered politics in the U.S. via labor militance. They became pivotal to workplace actions, where they drew on communal protest traditions from Italy and the urban female neighborhood networks they developed in the United States. For example, when clashes between workers, police, and factory owners grew violent in Paterson, West Hoboken, and elsewhere, Italian women used a tactic from Italy—they protected their children by sending them to stay with *compagne* (women comrades) further away. The "exodus of children" in turn strengthened ties among Italian women in the New York metropolitan area.[11] In addition, as in their homelands, women's direct action tactics involved entire communities, as demonstrated in the 1912 Lawrence Strike and 1913 ILGWU strike, where the female mob was at the heart of workers' strategies.[12]

Neglected by mainstream labor organizations, Italian women in New York City pursued collective forms of protest and resistance that, like in Italy, were independent of formal organization but embedded instead in women's neighborhood and kinship networks. Since most of them found jobs through family and friends, and worked in factories located within or near their neighborhoods, the garment shop was at the center of informal systems of female networking. Through such relationships, Italian women learned transportation systems, how to communicate with English-speaking employers and co-workers and, if they had children, how to find care for their young while they worked.[13] In her 1919 study, Louise Odencrantz found that Italian immigrant women relied on these networks to learn "the rudiments of the trade, so she did not feel as 'strange' as if she had been plunged into the midst of work," and "to make her clothes more presentable according to American standards, so that she will look less like a new arrival."[14] Ginevre Spagnoletti's dress shop in the Bowery was "full of Italian women bending over their machines and peering at the needles," as the El trains roared by, but also a place where the women were always "singing and joking together to escape the monotony and beat back the gloom."[15] Like other workers, Italian women also colluded to steal time for themselves on the job by slowing down the pace of work and using any opportunity to talk about family, neighborhood, work conditions, and politics.[16] For their part, Italian-language workers' papers chronicled such stories to encourage oppositional activism.[17] Stories of women's collective action were also retold on the shop floor, around kitchen tables, and on tenement stoops, and passed from one generation to the next. These daily, unorganized, seemingly spontaneous actions formed an important part of Italian American women's political strategies, as they did for all workers.

Italian seamstresses in New York City also used more formal organizational strategies to build solidarity and political consciousness. Especially important were workers' *circoli* (clubs); modeled on the mutual-benefit societies that in Italy had become a popular strategy for extending radical movements, these groups spread throughout the Italian diaspora. In the U.S., they also forged alliances with radical Spanish, Eastern European and Russian-Jewish, Cuban, Puerto Rican and other Caribbean immigrant workers' groups, which were also transnational in nature. This network was the heart of New York City's revolutionary working-class subculture in this period. In the handmade cigar industry, such groups coalesced into unions and jointly published radical newspapers. And in Brooklyn, Italian shoe and garment workers built coalitions with Spanish-speaking and Jewish neighbors through a *circolo* called Club Avanti, which was founded by Sicilian anarchists and free-thinkers.[18]

L'emancipazione della donna (the emancipation of women) was a regular topic of conversation within these circles because women kept the issue on the agenda; they invited prominent Italian women radical intellectuals and activists to speak on women's activism in transnational labor movements and to help them mobilize Italian women workers in the U.S.[19] Angela and Maria Bambace, for example, were drawn into labor activism in 1916 by attending meetings sponsored by Italian socialists and anarchists in their neighborhood in Harlem, where they also met IWW organizers and learned syndicalist strategies.[20] Tina Cacici, a textile worker who would become a notorious leader of a radical faction in the Lawrence strike of 1919 and an organizer for the Amalgamated Clothing Workers of America (ACWA), first became known for her fiery speeches on women's emancipation at a local socialist club in Brooklyn.[21]

Women also organized their own *gruppi femminili di propaganda* (women's propaganda groups), where mothers and daughters could debate and produce revolutionary theory and strategy.[22] The *gruppi femminili* also reflected Italian women's desire to assert their commitment to the labor movement and confront those male comrades who believed a woman could never "elevate herself from subservience."[23] In response, they argued, "You believe that a woman, who takes care of the entire home and the children, is not concerned with education, that she cannot find the time in her long day, to dedicate herself to her emancipation? . . . Women also have the capacity, tenacity, and perseverance to confront obstacles and elevate themselves. . . . We agitate, we organize to prove to the world that accuses us, that we too are capable of these things.[24] The core group of women active in the *gruppi femminili* embraced revolutionary socialist and anarcho-syndicalist ideas, and advocated working-class mobilization and collective action in the context of the industrial union movement. For example, Italian women textile workers in Paterson formed one of the earliest *gruppi femminili*, and one of the first IWW locals alongside men in 1906, laying the groundwork for collective action in the years that followed.[25]

Workplace agitation increased dramatically among Italian workers in New York City overall after the founding of the IWW in 1905. The centrality of international working-class struggle and revolution to the *circoli* and the "virtually disenfranchised status" of Italian workers in relation to the exclusionary and nativist unions of the American Federation of Labor, helps to explain why many Italian workers joined "a militant organization that made unskilled workers the primary subjects of its revolutionary program." The IWW drew its membership from many Italian immigrant radical circles, and assisted with major organizing drives among Italian shoemakers, hotel workers, barbers, piano makers, textile, garment, construction and dock workers throughout New York City.[26]

Given the richness of this culture, it seems unlikely that Italian women failed to join the 1909 "Uprising of 20,000" because they were isolated from radical political and social movements, lacked militant traditions, or suffered from weak community networks and restrictive families.[27] Rather, they did not join en masse because they were not convinced that either the ILGWU or the WTUL were committed to their struggles. Moreover, evidence of their activism appears almost exclusively in Italian-language sources. If the Italian-language dailies such as *Il Bollettino della Sera* and *Il Progresso Italo-Americano* covered the 1909 Manhattan shirtwaist strike only briefly, they gave considerable attention to another strike that occurred that same month, just across the Hudson River, in Hoboken, New Jersey. There, Italian women textile workers engaged in a month-long strike for livable wages, shorter work hours, and improved working conditions, and they did so alongside Italian men, and Armenian, Russian, German, Polish and other immigrant women and men.[28] Yet both WTUL and ILGWU leaders routinely described Italian immigrant women as "hopeless" labor activists, "absolutely under the dominance of men of their family, and heavily shackled by old customs and traditions."[29]

The vast majority of Italian garment workers in New York City did not join the ILGWU in the 1909 strike, but they were visible and active participants in the "Great Revolt" of 50,000 cloakmakers one year later. That strike helped to make the ILGWU the third-largest member of the AFL (1914). More than 2,800 Italian workers—many of them inspired by the gains made in the 1909 uprising—joined the ILGWU in the first three days of the 1910 strike. Three of the strikers, Catherine Valenti, Anna Canno, and Sadie La Porta, organized a separate local to mobilize the unprecedented numbers of Italian women that began attending union meetings and joining picket lines, often with their children. Three weeks later, an additional 20,000 Italian workers walked out, including large numbers of Italian women finishers who went on strike in solidarity with the mostly male cloakmakers.[30]

Why did Italian women begin to organize in garment unions at this time? Their dramatic shift from "scabs" to ILGWU strikers speaks less of their sudden politicization than of an important change in strategy that was then taking form. First, Italian women were willing to join a strike orchestrated by the more moderate, reformist, AFL-affiliated union because it had become increasingly impossible to organize separately from them. As historian Annelise Orleck has argued, the 1909 shirtwaist uprising produced mixed results, but it "breathed new life into a struggling immigrant labor movement and transformed the tiny ILGWU into a union of national significance."[31] In the next decade, the ILGWU would become more effective than the IWW in forcing garment employers to the bargaining table, and so began to attract many revolutionary leaders in the Italian immigrant community. Second, the ILGWU became willing to invest time and funds to recruit Italian organizers. Unlike the 1909 uprising, Italians had been involved in planning and executing the 1910 strike.[32] The ILGWU also granted Italian workers financial and institutional support and, moreover, self-governing spaces crucial to developing their own activism and to building internal leadership.

The ILGWU subsequently drew the energies of many Italian men, including prominent radicals, but it was Italian women who at all times composed the majority of workers in the garment industry and unions. From the outset, workers such as the Bambaces, Susanna Angretina, Rosalina Ferrara, Rose De Cara, Giordana Lombardi, Anna Coocha, Laura Di Guglielmo, Lina Manetta, Maria Prestianni, Anna Squillante, Millie Tirreno, Rosalie Conforti, and countless others, created the first organizing teams that brought thousands of *compagne* into the ILGWU.[33] These teams of women were formed during and after the 1910 strike, and included both immigrants and the American-born. Indeed, union meetings, demonstrations, and picket lines were often multigenerational. Tina Gaeta remembered how her mother, who "was always against homework" encouraged her daughters "to carry the picket sign when her shop went on strike."[34] Giuseppina Bambace not only let her daughters attend union meetings and participate in organizing activities but she sometimes joined them on their union rounds with a rolling pin tucked under her arm, just in case there was trouble.[35] A buttonhole maker and mother of six, Ginevre Spagnoletti, joined the union after she started reading the newspapers and pamphlets of an Italian anarcho-syndicalist *circolo* in her Greenwich Village neighborhood. Each evening after work, she read them aloud to her children and encouraged political debate at her kitchen table.[36] Families were a central site where Italian women developed oppositional ideologies and strategies of resistance, and the union culture they created would be grounded in such relationships.

The women who formed the first ILGWU organizing teams differed from the rank and file in one significant respect: Most did not have children. But they often worked in the same "women's jobs" as their sisters, as operatives, drapers, finishers, hemstitchers, and examiners. They also became radicalized by the deteriorating labor conditions in the factories, exemplified most dramatically by the 1911 Triangle Shirtwaist Factory fire in New York City, which claimed the lives of 146 Italian and Jewish women and girls. Similarly, the highly publicized and violent labor uprisings in the 1910s—in Lawrence, Paterson, Chicago, Ybor City, and other cities where Italian women were major components of the labor force—further politicized Italian immigrant women.

After the 1910 strike, Italian women formed the majority in the newly formed Organizational Committee of the Italian Branch of the ILGWU, which became the Italian Branch, Local 25 after the 1913 strike. With their own organizational space, they consolidated their activism. Women in shops across the city contacted the committee daily, reporting on their struggles, methods of resistance, and their need for assistance. Organizers met with workers in community meetings and by finding work in garment shops that were nonunion. They visited women and listened to their grievances, brought them into the union, and encouraged them to shape and direct the movement—all at the risk of arrest and violent beatings from employers and police. They planned workplace committees, distributed leaflets, ran educational and publicity programs, cultural activities, demonstrations, strikes, picket lines, soup kitchens, and theater troupes.[37] Organizers used newspapers, such as the popular socialist Italian-language weekly *L'Operaia* (to which thousands of women garment workers were subscribers by 1914) to create a community of "*lavoratrici cosciente*" (politically informed or "conscious" women workers).[38] They carried the message that "the inferiority of women is not physiological or psychological, but social," and advocated instead a "*femminismo*" that was based on "the spirit of solidarity between women." This feminism, they asserted, was not "a movement against men, but one that is primarily interested in developing intelligence among women." Rather, it was "the belief that the woman is exploited doubly, by capitalism and by her companion. . . . In the labor movement, women can find the opportunity to become a militant force for humanity with a clear vision of the world."[39]

These tactics paid off when unprecedented numbers of Italian women joined the large-scale uprisings among garment workers in 1913 and 1919. It was also due to such efforts that women joined the ILGWU once Italian members had their own autonomous language-locals in 1916 and 1919. Colomba Furio's groundbreaking research on this topic showed that "an overwhelming majority" of Italian women and girls joined the ranks of striking workers during the 1919 strike wave, and "distinguished themselves on picket lines, at strikers' meetings, and on organizational committees."[40] As one older Italian woman recounted, she joined the union in this period because "me sick of the boss, me sick of work, me sick of go hungry most time." She then raised her deformed finger, the bone worn down into the shape of a hook, and revealed the space where her front teeth had once been. With a body damaged from decades of quickly twisting cotton and biting buttonholes to save time and keep her factory job, she concluded, "me sick, me tired, me can stand no longer, that's why me all strike."[41] The first administration of the Italian Dressmakers' Local 89 of the ILGWU (chartered in 1919) included many women "who had shown particularly outstanding abilities during the strike" that won the 40-hour work week.[42]

The transition from revolutionary industrial unionism to the reform socialism of the ILGWU was neither straightforward nor accomplished quickly. In the Italian-language radical press of the U.S., male activists routinely asked, "Is it compatible for an industrial socialist to also become a propagandist for the AFL?"[43] Although male political leaders dominate the newspapers and the historiography, Italian-American women were at the center of these community struggles, and they made themselves highly conspicuous. When ILGWU organizer Pasquale Di Neri tried to speak to a group of Italian women garment workers before the 1913 strike, he was met with the "loud cynical laughter" of an older Italian woman who yelled out, "Ha! Ha! You want more 15 cents to pay you fakers!" She then proceeded to "make [him] look ridiculous in the presence of the other finishers." Several weeks later, the same woman led an independent strike in her shop when employers demanded an impossible work pace.[44] Support for the "new unions" was at first tenuous. In 1913, for instance, several thousand Italian American women joined the ILGWU strike, but one week after the union settled without a vote and the female "rioting" in Cooper Union took place, close to one thousand of them in twelve factories across New York City abandoned the ILGWU and declared a strike (for better pay and shorter hours) under the auspices of the IWW.[45] Only when repression in the aftermath of World War I against the left destroyed the IWW and threatened foreign-born radicals with deportation did Italian women fully focus their energies on building the ILGWU. And even then, they continued to combine activism in the union with other community movements.

The Red Scare, Fascism, and Italian-American Women's Radicalism in the Interwar Period

Reform-oriented socialist labor organizations like the ILGWU were adopted more fully by Italian workers in the 1930s only as these immigrants came to terms with what was possible in the U.S. Historians are only beginning to tell the story of how the repression of immigrant radicals and their prewar movements like the IWW, preceded the incorporation of Italian American workers into the mainstream U.S. labor movement and contributed to the making of their national identities—both as Americans and Italians. Yet, scholars generally agree that "the New York clothing industry [was] the theater of a significant political recomposition within the Italian American left."[46] Ironically, there are virtually no studies of the Italian-American women who ran the organizational departments and composed the majority of the rank and file in garment unions during this period. This is true even though American Studies scholar Michael Denning has argued that by the 1930s the "symbolic center of Popular Front womanhood was the garment industry."[47] By shifting our focus to the culture of struggle in the interwar years, we can assess the dramatic impact that shifting organizational strategies had on gender and inter-ethnic relations for Italian-American women workers.

Italian-American historians generally agree that during and after World War I, the federal government's push for national unity and the repression of radical campaigns caused a massive dislocation in the Italian-American labor movement. As Vecoli writes, the political climate of the First World War "dealt the first debilitating blow to Italian radicalism. Smashing their presses, shuttering their offices and meeting places, and arresting thousands, federal and state agencies instituted a reign of terror against the *sovversivi* [subversives]."[48] According to historical sociologist Salvatore Salerno, these "red scare" campaigns targeted those Italian American radicals who publicly challenged U.S. racist and imperialist ideologies, and thus resulted in the muzzling of a critical oppositional practice developing within Italian America.[49] In addition, during the 1920s, the racism and anti-Catholicism of the Ku Klux Klan, nativist movements for immigration restriction, and the eight-year struggle of anarchists Nicola Sacco and Bartolomeo Vanzetti made it clear to Italian Americans that they were perceived by native-born European Americans as inherently inferior and undesirable.[50]

Italian-American women responded to this repression by "uniting around a common ethnic identity" in the Italian-language locals of the reformist socialist unions less targeted by the government, such as the ILWGU and the newly formed ACWA. As Vecoli reminds us, this was not just a tale of assimilation. Demographic changes also mattered. With Italian immigration to the U.S. drastically limited by restrictive legislation in 1921 and 1924, the economic strategies of many Italian families shifted from seasonal labor migrations and temporary settlement to the expansion of community support systems. Regional loyalties and diasporic identities began to give way to Italian and American nationalisms, as "ethnic identity, class-consciousness, and workers' demand for respect as 'citizens' fused." Nationally, unionism was also at a low tide; the number of women in garment unions plummeted by almost 40 percent between 1920 and 1927.[51]

In the ILGWU, women's membership dropped even further when "civil war" broke out in the 1920s, and the General Executive Board expelled communists and unaffiliated women activists struggling for more democratic representation. Since Italian garment workers in the ILGWU had established their own language locals just before this confrontation, the 1920s were spent consolidating and safeguarding ethnic autonomy. Furthermore, to protect their new jurisdiction over Italian-American workers, the Italian locals supported the actions of the ILGWU leadership. This placed Italian-American organizers "in an ideal position to negotiate theirs and their constituency's ethnicity within the broader labor and political context."[52] But it came at a great cost. By the late 1920s, the Italian Dressmakers' Local 89 (the largest of the two Italian-language locals in the ILGWU) was heavily bureaucratized, with men in leadership positions over a primarily female rank and file. On the eve of the stock-market crash, this "progressive" union (which unlike other AFL unions, had sought to organize women workers) had become deeply stratified along gender lines.[53]

The response of Italian-American women organizers to these developments varied. Some organizers, such as Angela Bambace and Albina Delfino, opposed the direction taken by the Italian locals and became active in Communist Party meetings and strikes, where they formed alliances with Jewish anarchist and communist insurgents, some of whom were Wobblies (IWW members). For such actions, both women were denounced by the Italian locals. For the rest of the 1920s, Bambace assisted the ACWA's organizational campaigns in Elizabeth, New Jersey, and then accepted a position to unionize garment workers in Baltimore for the ILGWU. Delfino became a labor organizer for the Communist Party, traveling between Lawrence, Providence, Boston, Paterson, and New York City, with Frances Ribaldo, a Sicilian-American woman organizer in the party, to assist workers on the verge of, or already on strike, and to combat racial and ethnic antagonism within these working-class communities. Other organizers, such as Margaret di Maggio and Grace de Luise, became virulently anticommunist and committed to the ethnic-based organizing strategy of Local 89. Ironically, these women came together in the antifascist movement.[54]

In the 1920s and 1930s, as Italian-American garment workers became increasingly sympathetic to Mussolini's claims for a "New Italy," anarchists, syndicalists, communists, socialists, and other radicals joined the movement to fight fascism. Margaret di Maggio, who entered the garment trades at the age of thirteen and joined the ILGWU because of the Triangle Fire, and who became a renowned organizer of Local 89, was also well known in her Sicilian family for challenging those who "felt drawn by Mussolini's promise of grandeur to the Italian people." Di Maggio's niece recalled how "she and my grandfather were always arguing. . . . She wanted to buy him a round trip ticket to go back to Italy and see how things were."[55] While large numbers of Italian-American women participated in the spectacle of sending their wedding rings to Mussolini's coffers, smaller numbers crowded antifascist rallies, many of them sponsored by the garment unions. Throughout the 1920s and 1930s, Angela Bambace, Margaret di Maggio, Lucia Romualdi, Lillie Raitano, Josephine Mirenda, and other leading ILGWU organizers were active in antifascist circles in New York City. They joined the interethnic coalition of radical groups that united for the release of Sacco and Vanzetti and to support for Republican Spain. The union remained one of many sites of activism.[56]

The garment unions became central to the lives of the majority of Italian-American women garment workers during the dramatic labor mobilizations of the 1933–34 Depression-era strike wave. In August of 1933, 60,000 dressmakers in New York, New Jersey and Connecticut walked off their jobs and into the streets. Joined by African-American, East-European Jewish, Puerto Rican and other women dressmakers, Italian-American women filled strike halls to capacity, stormed nonunion shops calling workers to join them, marched through the streets of their neighborhoods, and formed picket lines outside shops demanding decent wages and working conditions and an end to sweatshops once and for all. Activists included both veterans from earlier labor struggles and new recruits, immigrants and the American-born. Together they ushered in what many Italian garment workers would later call *l'alba radiosa* (the radiant dawn).[57]

Italian-American women were the overwhelming majority of strikers during this five-day ILGWU-led strike. For the first time, they held a measure of power in the industry and union. Many Italian garment workers also associated the strike with becoming American. Frank Liberti, a presser and organizer for the Italian Dressmakers' Local 89 recalled, "I became a Citizen . . . during the 1933 Strike."[58] In March of the following year, Margaret di Maggio, Minnie Badami, Dorothy Drago, Yolanda Liguori, Angelina Farruggia, and other prominent organizers of Local 89 traveled to Washington, D.C., to present President Roosevelt with a bronze plaque and pledge the support of Italian-American garment workers to the National Industrial Recovery Act. By then, Italian women were almost 80 percent of Local 89 (whose 40,000 members made it the largest local in the nation), and the majority in other large locals.[59]

The acquisition of mainstream organizational space and authority in the U.S. labor movement reconfigured Italian-American women's activism in several significant ways. Following the uprising in 1933, the garment unions became a central site of Italian-American women's community activism. Since they composed the majority of the rank and file, they were called upon by the union leadership to consolidate the gains of the strike. They continued to run the organizational drives and struggled with Italian and Jewish men for a voice in union affairs. Yet, the sheer magnitude of new members propelled the Italian locals into "an important center around which Italian American life in New York City revolved."[60] As tens of thousands of women poured into the local's district offices, spread throughout New York City's Italian neighborhoods, veteran organizers were needed to mentor and train those new to the movement. The movement thus remained multigenerational.[61]

As in earlier periods, women socialized their own children within union culture by bringing their families to workers' halls and meetings. Margaret di Maggio, the manager of Local 89's organizational department, was not only described as a mother figure by the newest recruits, but her twelve-year-old niece was literally at her side during many union meetings. The atmosphere in the local's offices also reaffirmed a sense of family. Di Maggio's niece recalled that in "the thirties and forties you couldn't get through the halls for the mobs that were there." "They would work on their lunch hours," she added, "they would run to the union at 5:00. At 8:00 the halls would still be mobbed . . . You become so involved, it's home."[62] Indeed, during the 1930s, while male leaders of the garment unions emphasized ethnic nationalism in their appeals to Italian-American workers, women organizers of Local 89 more often referred to the union as *nostra grande famiglia* (our large family), thereby drawing attention to the union as a central community institution based on the labor of women.[63] They also took the malleable social ideal of *la famiglia* and infused it with political purpose to justify making their union work a priority over their commitments to kin. Indeed, the great flood of new members demanded a new kind of commitment from women organizers. As di Maggio's niece remembered, since union women "worked until the wee hours of the morning," and on weekends, "few knew whether they had families."[64] Actually, many organizers came from union families; they often delayed marriage, and most left organizing or took a sabbatical during child-rearing years. While some women did their union work in defiance of a husband or parents (and thus talked of being disowned or of "broken marriages"), most who did marry chose partners within the movement. As Albina Delfino stated, "you cannot be active, unless your mate has the same opinion."[65] Such sentiments were prevalent earlier, but during the massive Depression-era organizing drives, more women than ever chose to devote their lives to the movement and to redefine their responsibilities to kin in ways that included community activism. Women were drawn to the ILGWU for many of the same reasons that they joined workers' *circoli*. The union provided a space for them to combine political activism and intellectual pursuits, and as with the *circoli*, the union offered classes in political strategy, including Marxist theories of working-class revolution, vocational and technical training, and social events. Labor organizing also provided women with a rare opportunity to achieve both personal and collective advancement, earn an income, and get the education most missed when they entered wage work as children.

Investing in Whiteness: Concluding Comments

As women breathed new life into the labor movement and made careers out of union organizing, they also struggled with increased union bureaucratization. After the civil war of the 1920s, the union offered few avenues for democratic representation and those women who drew attention to inequalities were marginalized, if not removed, from union offices. Women were excluded not only from positions of power in the union, but also from the dominant symbolic system of labor in this period.[66] Ironically, their more common response to this marginalization would be to unite with men around the practice of racialized exclusion, rather than work with other women to democratize the union.

Why did Italian-American workers come to see their interests as against rather than in solidarity with the industry's newest recruits? While the 1933 strike had dramatically affirmed the logic of working-class solidarity, Italian-American women confronted a society obsessed with the ideology of racial differences. Pronouncements of white racial superiority were widely disseminated in popular culture and used to justify lynchings, immigration restriction, and segregation. In the ILGWU, leaders sometimes espoused the ideology "We are all minorities"; at other times, they sought to avoid the issue of race altogether and drew attention instead to the "culture of unity" offered by a multiethnic socialist union.[67] Despite repeated demands by Puerto Rican seamstresses, only Italian workers were permitted the autonomy of their own language locals, enabling them to acquire leadership positions in the International.[68]

Italian-American women did not possess the formal power to exclude workers from the union, but they did work to exclude women and men of color from their workplaces by opposing Puerto Rican membership, treating Puerto Rican women with open hostility in the shops, and refusing to work alongside them. It also appears that those Italian-American women who remained in Local 89 throughout their lives rarely initiated or joined class-based, interethnic coalitions. Instead, they used their political stature in the union to counter the nativism and racism that cast *them* as undesirable citizens and members of an "inferior race," and distanced themselves from the newcomers.[69]

The types of coalitions that Italian garment workers had forged with other Latin workers in the decades before the First World War were no longer a central part of their workplace organizing strategies. Rather, alliances with Latino and African-American workers more often developed outside the union, in local neighborhood movements that developed to confront the devastation of the Great Depression. In grassroots struggles for better housing, education, and health care, in Popular Front groups such as the United Council of Working Class Women, the International Workers' Order, Congressman Vito Marcantonio's Harlem Legislative Council, and in the few remaining anarcho-feminist circles, Italian-American women continued to collaborate with African-American, Puerto Rican, Cuban, Jewish, and other working-class women.[70] Yet, in the 1940s, they also mobilized to keep African-American and Puerto Rican children out of "their" schools and "their" public housing. Decades later, community activists would recall that tensions between Italians and their Puerto Rican and African-American neighbors increased so dramatically in these decades that it led to new organizing strategies. Vito Magli remembered that in the 1930s "we had a situation where we had to intervene and explain to the brothers and sisters about racism in the Italian-American community. . . . We had to combat racism, a problem in the progressive movement."[71] Historian Robert Orsi has suggested that increased tension occurred in part because Italian immigrants and their children learned that "achievement in their new environment meant successfully differentiating themselves from the dark-skinned other."[72] His observation also applies to Italian-American women garment workers, whose claims to being different from their African-American and Puerto Rican co-workers grew more insistent at precisely the same time that these groups entered the industry in larger numbers. Yet, Italians lived alongside both groups for decades, sharing neighborhoods, schools, and workplaces. The 1930s and 1940s, then, were a critical turning point for Italian immigrants and their children. It is no coincidence that they began to distance themselves from racialized "others" at the same time they achieved numerical and political power in the garment unions, and gained access to the higher-paying jobs. As historian Thomas A. Guglielmo's research on Italians and race-making in Chicago well demonstrates, "protecting this powerful and privileged position required that Italian Americans grow increasingly vigilant about policing the color line."[73] This racial privilege too was the site of continual dialogue and contestation, as Italian Americans confronted and debated the costs of a white identity.[74]

Italian-American women garment workers entered the age of the Congress of Industrial Organizations—a period historians commonly associate with increased interethnic working-class unity—with few spaces in the heavily bureaucratized garment unions for a revolutionary, multiethnic, working-class feminist movement. Italian immigrant women's "sweatshop feminism"—their collective struggle to reenvision the world according to the priorities of those most marginalized by industrial capitalism—would diminish as they acquired national and racial identities as white Americans. The journey Italian-American women made, from workers of the world to white workers, demonstrates the considerable power of nationalism and racism to mobilize those with transnational working-class and subaltern identities in the early twentieth century. It also enables us to locate the challenges and alternatives this group of sweatshop workers developed to contest such processes, and their own role in both sustaining and challenging institutionalized privilege.

Notes

Acknowledgment   I am deeply grateful to Donna Gabaccia, David Roediger, Salvatore Salerno, and Franca Iacovetta for commenting on earlier drafts of this essay. Very special thanks to Donna for her editorial expertise in helping me shorten the original version to fit this collection. A longer version of this essay was originally published in *Women, Gender, and Transnational Lives: Italian Workers of the World*, Donna Gabaccia and Franca Iacovetta, eds. (Toronto: University of Toronto Press, 2002).

1. *New York Evening Post*, January 20, 1913; *New York Times*, January 19, 20, and 22, 1913; *New York Call*, December 30, 1912; January 1, 7, 9, 13–16, and 19–20, 1913; February 2 and 5, 1913; *The New-York Sun*, January 4, 1913; *Il Bolletino della Sera*, January 3, 4, 10, and 16, 1913; *L'Era Nuova*, January 11 and 25, 1913; *Il Proletario*, January 18 and 25, 1913; February 1, 1913; *Il Progresso Italo-Americano*, January 10, 1913 to February 3, 1913.

2. *New York Times*, January 19 and 20, 1913; Annelise Orleck, *Common Sense and a Little Fire: Women and Working-Class Politics in the United States, 1900–1965* (Chapel Hill: University of North Carolina, 1995), 76.

3. Orleck, *Common Sense and a Little Fire*, 41–50, 57–63; Susan A. Glenn, *Daughters of the Shtetl: Life and Labor in the Immigrant Generation* (Ithaca: Cornell University Press, 1990), 177, 213.

4. Miriam Cohen, *Workshop to Office: Two Generations of Italian Women in New York City, 1900–1950* (Ithaca: Cornell University Press, 1992), 53; Table 12, 167; 47.

5. Colomba Furio interview with Tina Gaeta, November 22, 1976, reprinted in Furio, "Immigrant Women and Industry: A Case Study, The Italian Immigrant Women and the Garment Industry, 1880–1950" (Ph.D. diss., New York University, 1979), 449–50; Louise Odencrantz, *Italian Women in Industry* (New York: Russell Sage Foundation, 1919), 38, 41, 51, 313–14; U.S. Immigration Commission, *Immigrants in Industries*, Senate Document 633, 61st Congress, 1st Session (Washington, D.C.: Government Printing Office, 1911), 376.

6. Jole Calapso, *Donne Ribelli: un secolo di lotte femminili in Sicilia* (Palermo: S. F. Flaccovio, 1980); Donna Gabaccia, *Militants and Migrants: Rural Sicilians Become American Workers* (New Brunswick: Rutgers University Press, 1988), 150–1; Camilla Ravera, *Breve storia del movimento femminile in Italia* (Roma: Editori Riuniti, 1978).

7. In addition to sources in previous citation, see Elda Gentili Zappi, *If Eight Hours Seem Too Few: Mobilization of Women Workers in the Italian Rice Fields* (Albany: State University of New York Press, 1991).

8. Rudolph J. Vecoli, "Pane e Giustizia," *La Parola del Popolo* 26 (September–October, 1976), 58.

9. *Il Bolletino della Sera*, December 17, 1909; Odencrantz, *Italian Women in Industry*, 41.

10. Quote from *L'Era Nuova*, May 13, 1913. See, for example, Ardis Cameron, *Radicals of the Worst Sort: Laboring Women in Lawrence, Massachusetts, 1860–1912* (Urbana: University of Illinois Press, 1993); and Nancy A. Hewitt, *Southern Discomfort: Women's Activism in Tampa, Florida, 1880s-1920s* (Urbana: University of Illinois Press, 2001).

11. *L'Era Nuova*, February 17 and March 2, 1912; May 10 and 17, 1913; *Il Proletario*, February 16, 1912. See also Furio, "Immigrant Women and Industry," 176–7; and Cameron, *Radicals of the Worst Sort*, 142–43, 154.

12. Cameron, *Radicals of the Worst Sort*, 111–6.

13. Furio interviews with Gaeta, Lazzaro, "Mrs. D," in "Immigrant Women and Industry," 453, 473, 397; Josephine Roche, "The Italian Girl," in *The Neglected Girl* (New York: Russell Sage Foundation, Survey Associates, 1914), 95–98.

14. Odencrantz, *Italian Women in Industry*, 43, 25.

15. Patrick Watson, *Fasanella's City: The Paintings of Ralph Fasanella with the Story of His Life and Art by Patrick Watson* (New York: Ballantine Books, 1973); Paul S. D'Ambrosio, *Ralph Fasanella's America* (Cooperstown, N.Y.: New York State Historical Association, 2001).

16. Watson, *Fasanella's City*, 99–100.

17. *L'Operaia*, April 18, 1914.

18. Julia Blodgett interview with Antonino Capraro, September 11, 1969, tapes 4, 6 and 7, Capraro Papers, Immigration History Research Center, University of Minnesota (hereafter IHRC); Edwin Fenton, *Immigrants and Unions A Case Study: Italians and American Labor, 1870–1920* (New York: Arno Press, 1975), chap. 9; Bruno Ramirez, "Immigration, Ethnicity, and Political Militance: Patterns of Radicalism in the Italian-American Left, 1880–1930," in *From the "Melting Pot" to Multiculturalism*, Valeria Gennaro Lerda, ed. (Rome: Bulzoni Editore, 1990).

19. For example, the activist-intellectual Bellalma Forzato Spezia came to the Bronx; Concenttina Cerantonio went to Newark. See also *L'Era Nuova*, May 27, 1911, and many other postings in this Paterson-based, Italian-language anarchist newspaper; and *Il Proletario*, December 1, 1907.

20. "Notes to interview," February 18–20, 1975, Bambace Papers, IHRC.

21. Blodgett interview with Capraro, September 12, 1969, tape 5, Capraro Papers, IHRC; *Il Proletario*, February 17, 1911.

22. *La Questione Sociale*, September 15, 1897; May 5, 1900; November 6 and 23, 1901; December 14, 1901; January 4 and 11, 1902; April 5, 1902; May 10, 1902; July 12 and 26, 1902; August 16, 1902.

23. *La Questione Sociale*, October 5, 1901; November 6, 1901.

24. *La Questione Sociale*, September 15, 1897. See also, for example, *La Questione Sociale*, August 24, 1901; October 15, 1901; November 23, 1901; December 8, 1906.

25. Salvatore Salerno, "No God, No Master: Italian Anarchists and the Industrial Workers of the World," in *The Lost World of Italian American Radicalism*, Philip Cannistraro and Gerald Meyer, eds. (Greenwood Press, forthcoming).

26. Ramirez, "Immigration, Ethnicity, and Political Militance," 128; Gabaccia, *Militants and Migrants*, 140; Salvatore Salerno, *Red November, Black November: Culture and Community in the Industrial Workers of the World* (Albany: State University of New York, 1989), 48–9, 58, 89.

27. For an excellent discussion of this stereotype see Glenn, *Daughters of the Shtetl*, 191–94.

28. *Il Bolletino della Sera*, November 2, 23, 24, 26, and 27, 1909; December 4, 8, 9, 10, 14 and 17, 1909; February 2, 1909; *Il Progresso Italo-Americano*, November 25, 1909.

29. Quotes reprinted in Glenn, *Daughters of the Shtetl*, 190–93; and Furio, "Immigrant Women and Industry," 99–104.

30. *New York Call*, July 5, 1910; *L'Araldo*, July 21, 1910. See also Furio, "Immigrant Women and Industry," 154–56, 162.

31. Orleck, *Common Sense and a Little Fire*, 63.

32. Fenton, *Immigrants and Unions*, 495.

33. "Notes to interview," February 18–20, 1975, Bambace Papers, IHRC; *L'Operaia,* September 13, 1913; April 4, 1914; August 13, 1914; September 3, 1914; October 17, 24, and 31, 1914; January 2, 1915; February 27, 1915.

34. Furio interview with Gaeta, "Immigrant Women and Industry," 456.

35. Jean A. Scarpaci, "Angela Bambace and the International Ladies Garment Workers Union: The Search for an Elusive Activist," in *Pane e Lavoro: The Italian American Working Class,* George E. Pozzetta, ed.(Toronto: The Multicultural History Society of Ontario, 1980), 103.

36. Watson, *Fasanella's City,* 137.

37. *Lotta di Classe,* December 27, 1912; April 13, 1912; *L'Operaia,* September 13, 1913; April 4, 18, and 23, 1914; August 13, 1914; September 3, 1914; October 17, 24, and 31, 1914; January 2, 1915; February 27, 1915; April 24, 1915.

38. Circulation figures are estimated in *The Message,* December 25, 1914.

39. *L'Operaia,* July 4, 1914; April 24, 1915.

40. Furio, "Immigrant Women and Industry," 94–95.

41. Theresa Malkiel, "Striking for the Right to Live," *The Coming Nation* 1:124, January 25, 1913.

42. *Guistizia,* December 6, 1919.

43. *Il Proletario,* March 31, 1911.

44. P. Di Neri, "When is the Next Meeting," *The Message,* October 15, 1915.

45. *Il Progresso Italo-Americano,* January 1, 1913.

46. Ramirez, "Immigration, Ethnicity, and Political Militance," 137.

47. Michael Denning, *The Cultural Front: The Laboring of American Culture in the Twentieth Century* (New York: Verso, 1996), 4, 138.

48. Rudolph J. Vecoli, "The Making and Un-Making of an Italian Working Class in the United States, 1915–1945," in *The Lost World.* See also Fiorello B. Ventresco, "Crises and Unity: The Italian Radicals in America in the 1920s," *Ethnic Forum* 15:1–2 (1995): 12–34.

49. Salvatore Salerno, "*I Delitti della Razza Bianca*" (The Crimes of the White Race): Italian Immigrant Anarchists' Racial Discourse as Crime," in *Are Italians White? How Race Is Made in America* Jennifer Guglielmo and Salvatore Salerno, eds. (New York: Routledge, forthcoming).

50. Vecoli, "The Making"; John Higham, *Strangers in the Land: Patterns of American Nativism, 1860–1925* (New Brunswick: Rutgers University Press, 1963), 264–330; Paul Avrich, *Sacco and Vanzetti: The Anarchist Background* (Princeton: Princeton University Press, 1991).

51. Elisabetta Vezzosi, "Radical Ethnic Brokers: Immigrant Socialist Leaders in the United States between Ethnic Community and the Larger Society," in *Italian Workers of the World: Labor Migration and the Formation of Multiethnic States,* Donna Gabaccia and Fraser Ottanelli, eds. (Urbana: University of Illinois Press, 2001).

52. Ramirez, "Immigration, Ethnicity, and Political Militance," 139.

53. Alice Kessler-Harris, "Problems of Coalition-Building: Women and Trade Unions in the 1920s" in *Women, Work and Protest: A Century of U.S. Women's Labor History,* Ruth Milkman, ed. (New York: Routledge & Kegan Paul, 1985).

54. Scarpaci, "Angela Bambace"; Furio, "Immigrant Women and Industry"; Ruth R. Prago interview with Albina Delfino (January 9, 1981), Oral History of the American Left, Wagner Archives, Tamiment Collection, New York University (OHAL).

55. Furio interview with Diane Romanik, "Immigrant Women and Industry," 417–26.

56. Scarpaci, "Angela Bambace," 104–7.

57. *New York Times,* August 16 and 17, 1933; Fannia M. Cohn, "The Uprising of the Sixty Thousand, The General Strike of the Dressmakers' Union," *Justice,* September 1, 1933; *Daily Worker,* August 17, 18 and 19, 1933; *Il Progresso,* August 16–20,1933. See also materials on 1933 strike in Boxes 28 and 45, Papers of Charles Zimmerman; Box 69, Papers of David Dubinsky; and Box 8, Papers of the Research Department, ILGWU Archives, Labor-Management Documentation Center, Cornell University (hereafter LMDC). "*L'alba radiosa*" is from Serafino Romualdi, "Storia della Locale 89," in *Local 89 Fifteenth Anniversary Commemoration Pamphlet* (1934). For similar sentiments see Speech by Antonino Crivello, 1937, Box 1, File 1, Papers of Antonino Crivello, IHRC; Address by John Gelo, April 2, 1937, Box 15, File 8, Antonini Papers, ILGWU Archives, LMDC; Local 48, *Libro Ricordo;* Local 89, *We the Italian Dressmakers Speak* (New York, 1944); *Giustizia* (October, 1933).

58. Letter from Frank Liberti to David Dubinksy (1962), Liberti Papers, Botto House National Landmark, Haledon, New Jersey.

59. *Giustizia,* April 1934; "Administration of Local 89, 1934" in *Local 89 Fifteenth Anniversary Commemoration Pamphlet* (1934), and "Administration of Local 89, 1944–46" in ILGWU, *Jubilee, 1919–1944* (1944). See also "New York: Our City-Our Union," (1940), Box 1, Crivello Papers, IHRC; and Furio interviews with Catania, de Luise, and Gaeta, "Immigrant Women and Industry," 427–35, 436–45, 446–457.

60. Charles Zappia, "Unionism and the Italian American Worker: A History of the New York City 'Italian Local' in the ILGWU, 1900–1933" (Ph.D. diss., University of California—Berkeley, 1994), 87.

61. *Giustizia* (October, November, and December 1933; February, March, and April 1934); ILGWU, "Administration of Local 89," *Commemorative Pamphlet, Local 89* (New York: ILGWU, 1934); Romualdi, "Storia della Local 89."

62. Furio interview with Romanik, "Immigrant Women and Industry," 425.

63. Romualdi, "Storia della Locale 89," 63.

64. Furio interview with Romanik, "Immigrant Women and Industry," 423.

65. Letter from Maria Rosaria Cimato to Antonini (June 9, 1939), Box 16, File 6; Letter from Lucia De Stefano to Antonini (February 9, 1940), Box 15, File 9; Letter from Lina Richeri to Antonini (March 19, 1942), Box 16, File 7; Letter from Lucia Romualdi Lupia to Antonini (August 18, 1942), Box 16, File 7, all from Antonini Papers, ILGWU Archives, LMDC. Quotation is from Prago interview with Delfino (OHAL).

66. Elizabeth Faue, *Community of Suffering and Struggle: Women, Men, and the Labor Movement in Minneapolis, 1915–1945* (Chapel Hill: University of North Carolina Press, 1991), 20.

67. Romualdi, "Storia della Locale 89"; Antonino Crivello speech, (1937), Box 1, File 1, Crivello Papers, IHRC. See also Nancy L. Green, *Ready-to-Wear and Ready-to-Work: A Century of Industry and Immigrants in Paris and New York* (Durham: Duke University Press, 1997); and Lizabeth Cohen, *Making a New Deal: Industrial Workers in Chicago, 1919–1939* (Cambridge: Cambridge University Press, 1990).

68. Altagracia Ortiz, "'En la aguja y el pedal eché la hiel': Puerto Rican Women in the Garment Industry of New York City, 1920–1980," in *Puerto Rican Women and Work: Bridges in Transnational Labor,* Altagracia Ortiz, ed. (Philadelphia: Temple University Press, 1996), 58.

69. Ortiz, "En la aguja y el pedal eché la hiel"; Altagracia Ortiz, "Puerto Rican Workers in the Garment Industry of New York City, 1920–1960," in *Labor Divided: Race and Ethnicity in the United States Labor Struggles, 1835–1960,* eds. Robert Asher and Charles Stephenson (New York: State University of New York Press, 1990); Will Herberg, "The Old-Timers and the Newcomers: Ethnic Group Relations in the Needle Trades' Union," *Journal of Social Issues* (Summer 1953); Roy B. Helfgott, "Puerto Rican Integration in the Skirt Industry in New York City," in *Discrimination and Low Incomes,* New School for Social Research, ed. (New York: Studies of New York State Commission Against Discrimination, 1959); http://historymatters.gmu.edu/d/121/.

70. Letter from Esta Pingaro to Vito Marcantonio (October 5, 1941), Box 67, File 6; and Letter from John W. Sutter to Vito Marcantonio (October 24, 1938), Box 3, File 3, Papers of Vito Marcantonio, New York Public Library; Paul Buhle interview with Vito Magli, March 15, 1983 (OHAL). See also Letters from women to Constantino Lippa, Box 10, File 14, Papers of the International Workers' Order, LMDC. For evidence of *circoli,* see, for example, "Communicazioni: New York, NY," *L'Adunata dei Refrattari* (April 26 and 30, 1932).

71. Paul Buhle interview with Vito Magli (OHAL).

72. Robert Orsi, "The Religious Boundaries of an Inbetween People: Street *Feste* and the Problem of the Dark-Skinned 'Other' in Italian Harlem, 1920–1990," *American Quarterly* 44 (September 1992), 317.

73. Thomas A. Guglielmo, *White on Arrival: Italians, Race, Color, and Power in Chicago, 1890–1945* (New York: Oxford University Press, 2003).

74. See, for example Buhle interview with Magli and Prago interview with Delfino (OHAL); "Notes re Civil Rights Meeting, July 9, 1963"; "Radio Address, WBMD" (May 10, 1964); and "Statement by Mrs. Angela Bambace," (n.d.), all in Bambace Papers, IHRC.

10

Consumers of the World Unite!
Campaigns Against Sweating, Past and Present

EILEEN BORIS

University of California, Santa Barbara

The "return of the sweatshop" generated international outrage at the end of the twentieth century, as it had at its dawn. The low wages and exploitative working conditions throughout Asia and the Americas provided by brand-name manufacturers and retailers like Nike, Gap, Target, and Walt Disney aroused public indignation. Human rights groups and trade unions—notably the National Labor Committee, Global Exchange, Sweatshop Watch, and UNITE! (Union of Needletrades, Industrial and Textile Employees)—sought to turn purchasing power into a weapon for social justice. They created graphic exhibits, filed class-action lawsuits, and instigated boycotts, appealing to consumers to reject goods produced under "unfair" conditions. A worldwide movement pushed the International Labour Organization (ILO) to pass a convention that applies labor standards to home-based workers. A revival of student activism emerged in support of worker rights, staging sit-ins to force universities to contract for logo bearing clothing with only those apparel manufacturers who meet stringent codes of conduct.[1]

The competitive dynamics of today's global garment industry, abided by the deregulatory politics of the Reagan era, has trumped the labor-standards regime forged at the beginning of the twentieth century. Then a vibrant women's reform movement appealed to the moral power of consumers to improve the laboring conditions of women and children who toiled. Middle-class women not only exhorted consumers to demand products made under decent working conditions, but also sought legislation to outlaw the sweatshop. Joining with the nascent garment unions, they gained minimum-wage, maximum-hour, child-labor, and industrial-homework laws first on the state and then on the federal level. Recognizing that "regulation of working conditions through organized persuasion was not enough," as reformer Florence Kelley explained,[2] they further lobbied for enforcement mechanisms, including state labor standards inspectors. New Deal labor laws, especially the 1938 Fair Labor Standards Act, codified these gains. After World War II, the sweatshop seemingly belonged to an industrial Dark Age. But, by 1980, it had swept back into view.[3]

This essay analyzes campaigns against the sweatshop during three key periods: the early twentiety-century Progressive Era, following the rise of Industrial America; the New Deal, responding to the economic crisis of the 1930s; and the 1990s struggle of social justice coalitions against a new global economy. In each period, opponents of sweated labor relied on a set of inter-related tactics: codes of conduct embodied by union, "white," Blue Eagle, and "No Sweat" labels; unionization resulting in collective bargaining agreements and worker self-organization; and labor standards legislation. While appeals to the consumer dominate much of this history, including current efforts, such strategies alone were unable to stop sweating. Neither could labor standards legislation without enforcement, which has required independent monitoring by unions, women's, human rights, religious, solidarity, and other advocates. The larger political economy—including such factors as the political power of trade unions and overall labor market segmentation by gender, age, and immigrant status—has proved central to the health of sweatshops past and present. Without unionization and state-guaranteed worker rights, the sweatshop has reigned.

The definition of "sweatshop" remained fairly constant throughout the century. The U.S. Department of Labor in 1896 defined sweating as "a condition under which a maximum amount of work in a given time is performed for a minimum wage, and in which the ordinary rules of health and comfort are disregarded."[4] Then, as now, the garment industry provided the template for sweated labor, with its system of subcontracting, reliance on immigrants and homeworkers, cutthroat competition, and dependence on fashion or consumer whim. Middlemen "earned their profit from the margin between the amount they received for a contract and the amount they paid workers with whom they subcontracted. The margin was said to be 'sweated' from the workers because they received minimal wages for excessive hours worked under unsanitary conditions."[5] In the late twentieth century, two or more violations of wage, child-labor, hour, and safety/health laws defined sweatshops in the United States. Sweatshops appeared in restaurants and meat processing as well as in the traditional apparel trades.[6] The global sweatshop consisted of workplaces, often in nations with undemocratic regimes that banned trade unions that paid less than a living wage, employed the underaged, coerced workers, and forced them to labor for excessive hours under unhealthful conditions.[7]

"Right Goods, Rightly Made": The Origins of Ethical Consumption[8]

During the late nineteenth-century era of laissez-faire, besieged by the vicissitudes of capitalist instability and a judiciary bent on protecting "freedom of contract," working people sought middle-class allies in their fight against the sweatshop. They fashioned images of contagion, fanning moral outrage through portraits of "SICK BABIES . . . LYING ON UNFINISHED GOODS," young women "bare-armed, some with their bosoms half bare and bathed in perspiration," and "machines rattling" amid "dirt, overcrowding, and . . . disease."[9] Sweated laborers were to be pitied as stunted beings; their products, feared as harbingers of illness. Still such appeals to health and morality existed alongside economic rationales. Workingmen urged their fellows to have families consume only union-made goods in the struggle to organize garments and related industries. This call often rested on self-interest; unionists would exclude immigrant and female labor, maintaining a breadwinner's wage for adult white or Northern European men. But such discourses appeared less effective with the general public than scare stories of tuberculosis lurking in tobacco or cloth. With prohibitions against tenement-house manufacturing overruled by courts, in 1888 the Cigar Makers' International Union appealed to "an enlightened and humane public opinion" through the Working Women's Society of New York City to end labor exploitation.[10]

New York workingwomen themselves already had approached noted charity reformer Josephine Shaw Lowell two years before for aid in their own efforts at organization. Searching for bargains, consumers generated "some of the worst evils from which producers suffer," Lowell explained. Thus consumers had the duty "to find out under what conditions the articles they purchase are produced and distributed, and to insist that these conditions shall be wholesome and consistent with a respectable existence on the part of the workers." Lowell combined elite concern for the masses with calls for protective labor laws for women and children. She also demanded living wages. Investigation, education and publicity, mobilization, and legislation would become weapons of choice as reformers politicized consumption, turning to legislatures for relief against sweating. Lowell's testimony proved crucial, for example, in passing the 1896 New York Mercantile Inspection Act, which shored up state inspection of department stores.[11]

In 1891, the Consumers' League of New York had formed to assist such department store clerks. It developed "a list which shall keep shoppers informed of such shops as deal justly with their employees, and so bring public opinion and public action to bear in favor of just employers, and also in favor of such employers as desire to be just, but are prevented by the stress of competition, from following their own sense of duty."[12] Over the next few years, groups met in other cities; they created the National Consumers' League (NCL) in 1899 to tap the moral righteousness of prosperous women. As the energetic National Secretary Florence Kelley explained: "If the people would notify Marshall Field . . . and others that they would buy from them no clothing made in sweatshops, the evil would be stopped."[13]

A decade before, Kelley, who became a socialist while studying in Europe, laid out the theory of ethical consumption that shaped their course. This was a philosophy also rooted in the moral environmentalism of the Victorian sage John Ruskin that would become central to a new generation of economists who were beginning to theorize on the significance of consumption for modern life.

Through their power as consumers, Kelley argued, middle-class and elite women could end child labor, "unit[ing] with the wage-earners to control the conditions under which the things they purchase are produced." Kelley grounded her ethical appeal in the economics of garment production. Denying that sweating cheapened goods, she argued that lower prices actually came from use of cheap materials, mechanical power, and improved industrial organization. Child labor and homework actually added to the human cost of industry, jacking up the final price of products, and discouraging mechanization. The moral power of consumers, then, could aid the laws of economics and speed technological change. But her ethical appeal also was a material one. Self-protection was to join reason, sentiment, and guilt to motivate the ethical shopper. "Rights of Purchasers" included freedom from diseased and dirty products. These rights merged into the duties of citizenship. "Before the individual purchaser can vindicate his own personal rights, the whole body of purchasers are constrained to save childhood for the children, and home life for the workers who dwell in tenements," Kelley proclaimed. Rights became socially based and collectively obtained. Eschewing individual solutions to removing the germs thought lurking in clothes, the program of the NCL would guard the consumer by improving the conditions of producers. It not only would protect less fortunate women and children, but also eventually would secure "ethical gains through legislation."[14] During a time when the sexual division of social life first engendered consumption as female, suffrageless women could excise citizenship through their choices as consumers.

Kelley derived the idea for "a national alliance of women which would furnish its label to all manufacturers of women's clothing" made under decent working conditions from the label campaigns of the cigar makers and other trade unionists, including the Knights of Labor, but over the years made this strategy her own.[15] Introduced in 1899 for women's white muslin undergarments, the "white label" (drawing upon the racialist association of white with purity) distinguished the NCL. The label went to manufacturers who met the League's labor standards—obedience to state factory laws, production on the premises, no overtime, and no children employed under sixteen—and passed inspections conducted by the League or by state departments of labor. By 1904, sixty factories had earned the white label, which emphasized production "under clean and healthful conditions." The League even entered into a "partnership" with one department store magnate, John Wanamaker, who also manufactured his own line, much as major retailers do today. As historian Kathryn Kish Sklar has concluded, "for him the White Label campaign offered a perfect opportunity to give his commercial leadership a moral aura and at the same time consolidate his economic power." Thus the campaign actually benefited those manufacturers who could achieve economies of scale.[16] Relying on the technique of the industrial exhibit, a reform tactic perfected by the National Child Labor Committee through photomontages shot by documentarian Lewis Hine, Wanamaker fashioned window displays that compared sweatshop to model-factory conditions and showed off his products adorned with white labels. Reformers developed such material culture lessons out of the belief that facts would precipitate social action. A marriage of social investigation and exposé distinguished the NCL approach to reform and generally marked Progressive era campaigns against the sweatshop.[17]

Commitment to minimum wages superceded an initial concern with sanitary working conditions that had attracted many members. In the 1890s, unionists and reformers had won state licensing laws that restricted who could manufacture specified items in tenements. At best, early regulatory legislation improved "surface conditions" or pushed work into the surrounding countryside and out of states like New York and Massachusetts, which had the most developed labor departments, to form the first "runaway" shops. Even with mandated inspection of tenements, enforcement proved difficult as families moved, employees lacked knowledge of their rights, and the laws could only monitor the surroundings of workers, not the manufacturers, subcontractors, or retails who profited from their labor. Licensing against sweated labor stressed perils to the consumer rather than rights of workers; it focused more on conditions in workers' homes than on particularities of the labor contract.[18]

The white label, in contrast, offered a symbol around which the League organized to win government-enforced labor standards. Through numerous state campaigns, it secured maximum-hour and minimum-wage laws for women and curbs on child labor, though courts restricted most legislative limits on men's "right to contract." The League also helped develop state enforcement agencies, staffing such agencies with its members. It defended these laws in the courts, researching and writing legal briefs that defined the field of sociological jurisprudence. The League's brief in *Muller v. Oregon* provided justification for the Supreme Court to uphold maximum hours for women in 1908. Between 1912, when Massachusetts established the first minimum wage board and 1923, when the Supreme Court struck down the District of Columbia's law in *Adkins v. Children's Hospital*, fifteen states, the District of Columbia, and Puerto Rico provided minimum wages for women. The NCL spearheaded this drive, aided by the National Women's Trade Union League, other trade unionists, social workers, settlement residents, and male industrial relations specialists.[19]

By 1915, the NCL boasted 89 locals in 19 states, of which thirty-four were in universities, colleges, and schools. A year later, membership stood at 23,000. On the eve of World War I, France, Germany, Belgium, and Switzerland had consumers' leagues, all of who sent delegates to international conferences that foreshadowed the modern International Labor Organization.[20] By that time, unions had brought some order to the chaotic garment industry. The 1910 "Protocol of Peace" had not only solidified unionization of women's garments, but also initiated the Joint Board of Sanitary Control to monitor conditions.

Three years later, the International Ladies' Garment Workers Union (ILGWU) and the Joint Board asked the NCL to help them draw up a new label agreement. But during the strike-torn war years, manufacturers who sought to stymie unions promoted the NCL label, whose standards by then lagged behind those negotiated through collective bargaining. Kelley recommended that the League drop the white label, the effectiveness of which had passed. It did so in 1918.[21]

During the war, Kelley herself served on the Board of Control of Labor Standards for Army Clothing, the first real attempt by the federal government to regulate sweating. (The House of Representatives had considered taxes on goods made in sweatshops during late-nineteenth-century hearings, but in the end failed to recommend such legislation.)[22] In November 1917, the War Labor Policies Board issued "General Orders" mandating labor standards—daily hours, overtime, wage standards, health, and safety—that previously had proved impossible to obtain through legislation because judicial interpretation of "freedom of contract" had limited such laws to women and children. The Board of Control, created a year later by Secretary of War Newton D. Baker (who happened to be serving as the NCL's titular president), directly intervened against sweatshops. Along with protégé Sidney Hillman of the Amalgamated Clothing Workers of America (ACWA), Kelley attacked the practices of Quartermasters as being more concerned with production on time than with working conditions. The Board of Control called for the eight-hour day, a wage scale acceptable to unions, no subcontracting, and investigation of employer premises prior to awarding contracts. In the process of banning exploitative conditions in the making of army uniforms, the Board of Control also built up Hillman's union. Even as the union played a key role in putting political pressure on the Wilson administration for establishing labor standards, once in place those standards proved crucial for its own development. [23]

Blue Eagles and Fair Labor Standards

Depression conditions jeopardized the modest gains won by "the new unionism" of the 1920s.[24] Amid the general breakdown of labor standards, the NCL marshaled reform and labor forces in December 1932 to mobilize for state interference in the labor contract. This larger coalition—including state labor officials, the National Child Labor Committee, the League of Women Voters, garment unionists, National Council of Jewish Women, and the National Organization for Public Health Nursing, among others—resolved to work for union labels in the needle trades by pressuring retail stores not to sell goods produced under "substandard conditions," a return to the label strategy. But they also endorsed shortening hours and raising wages to fight the economic crisis. By 1934, the new Division of Labor Standards within the Department of Labor would call for gender-inclusive standards, whenever possible, though some advocates for wage-earning women still feared that courts would end protections for women by striking down ones that also covered men.[25] Throughout the decade the NCL acted on "the conviction that consumers have a far-reaching responsibility to use their buying power and their power as citizens to advance the general welfare of the community," then executive secretary Mary Dublin explained in 1940. "What is not paid in wages, the community is called upon to pay in relief; in wage subsidies; in contributions to meet the cost of illness, dependency, delinquency, and numerous other social ills which these conditions produce," she claimed.[26]

The New Deal fought the sweatshop on two fronts: it legislated national labor standards and promoted trade unionism. Under the 1933 National Industrial Recovery Act, tripartite industrial boards, composed of representatives of business, labor, and government (representing the public or consumer), created hundreds of codes of fair competition (known as NRA codes) to regulate and encourage business activity. Section 7(a) of the act mandated inclusion of labor standards and encouraged collective bargaining. Here codes of conduct became federalized. State power backed the codes of conduct and labels, but volunteerism still dominated enforcement. Businesses abiding by codes developed for their industry by representatives of their industry could display the "Blue Eagle," symbol of the NRA that they "did their part" for industrial recovery. Consumers were to purchase goods with "Blue Eagle" tags from merchants who displayed the "Blue Eagle" sign. Emphasizing the importance of consumers, Eleanor Roosevelt titled her defense of the NRA, *It's Up to the Women*. NRA head General Hugh S. Johnson explained, "It is women in homes—not soldiers in uniforms—who this time will save our country."[27]

Drafted and enforced by code authorities, usually under the control of the major manufacturers' associations, NRA codes bypassed antitrust rules to protect against price chiselers. They went around existing networks of state factory inspectors and labor standards experts. But, dependent on power relations in a given industry, enforcement could be both unfair and sporadic; as one member of the Labor Advisory Board to the NRA complained, the "standard Chamber of Commerce type executive who is typical on the code authorities is not equipped to enforce labor provisions."[28] Where unionized employers controlled the code-making process, they incorporated collective bargaining provisions. But most workers were unorganized, ninety percent of those outside of agriculture in 1935.[29] Codes also expressed distinctions based on the identity of the worker, rather than the nature of the work. Differentials existed on the basis of region, leading to lower pay in the South, especially for African Americans. Rates based on the characteristics of the worker also generated lower pay for women, learners, the "handicapped," and homeworkers. Moreover, the codes failed to cover domestic service, agricultural labor, and public employment, industries disproportionately consisting of white women and men and women of color. The NCL and the women's reform network sought to end racial and gender differentials, but with only meager success.[30]

After the Supreme Court in May 1935 declared the NRA unconstitutional and blocked other labor-standards legislation, including New York's new minimum-wage law for women, New Dealers hoped to bypass the Court's narrow interpretation of the commerce clause. Political pressure—Roosevelt's stunning reelection, the court packing threat, and the persistence of the Depression—led the Court to finally sustain labor standards. In upholding a Washington State minimum-wage law nearly identical to New York's, *West Coast Hotel vs. Parish* of 1937 demolished the myth of freedom of contract and thus opened the way to sex-neutral wage and hour legislation. So did *National Labor Relations Board v. Jones and Laughlin Steel Corporation*, which not only affirmed the National Labor Relations Act of 1935 (which in its origins sought to aid unionization), but also most significantly reinterpreted the meaning of commerce. After this case, activities that might be considered intrastate when taken separately could come under Congressional jurisdiction "if they have such a close and substantial relation to interstate commerce that their control is essential or approach to protect that commerce from burdens and obstructions."[31]

The Fair Labor Standards Act (FLSA) of 1938 was to fulfill the state's responsibility to provide "the minimum standard of living necessary for health, efficiency, and general well-being of workers."[32] Though designed to aid the newly formed Congress of Industrial Organizations (CIO) to organize the South, FLSA initially legislated a minimum wage of twenty-five cents an hour, too low to bother Southern detractors. It set a maximum standard workweek of forty-four hours, required time and a half for any additional hours, and prohibited child labor (under sixteen). White men in basic industry, and most unionized workers, made a higher wage. Sidney Hillman lobbied successfully to insure inclusion of garment sweatshops, but as political scientist Suzanne Mettler points out, "the masses of low-paid women in nonunionized service occupations were, by contrast, excluded . . . laundries, hotels, hairdressing, restaurants, retailing, and domestic service. These became defined as "intrastate commerce."[33] Executive, administrative, supervisory, and professional labor, and adult agricultural work also remained outside the law. Though gender and race neutral, FLSA in fact perpetuated racial and gender hierarchies. Still women in textile and garment sweatshops, as well as men in other low-waged occupations like sawmills and furniture, obtained real wage increases. And because it was national, FLSA put a break on runaway shops, the tendency for manufacturing to leave states with effective labor law enforcement for those without laws even on their books.[34] Here the platform of Florence Kelley, who died in 1932, became realized.

The success of FLSA again depended on enforcement. The symbiotic relationship between labor standards legislation and unionization lay behind both its enactment and subsequent history. NLRA encouraged the growth of the CIO, which in turn worked for national labor standards. Women reformers in and outside of the state also served as midwives. Secretary of Labor Frances Perkins, Clara Beyer of the Division of Labor Standards, and Lucy Randolph Mason and Dublin of the NCL (Perkins and Beyer also belonged to the League) pushed for the FLSA along with the garment unions and other progressive groups. The AFL initially opposed passage and then remained neutral at best. Reformers and unionists then sat on industry boards that raised the initial minimum wage for a number of substandard industries, the majority of which belonged to apparel, such as knitted outwear and embroidery. Their vigilance became necessary because the Wage and Hour administration never had enough inspectors to police all sites.[35]

The Consumers' League and reformers had become, as historian Landon Storrs has aptly noted, "agents of the New Deal."[36] Though often disappointed by restrictions on coverage, enforcement mechanisms, and the general meagerness of standards, the NCL pushed a Rooseveltian laborite platform in the states as well as in Washington. During WWII, it briefly changed its name to "the National Consumers' League for Fair Labor Standards" to differentiate itself from those who focused on the rights of consumers, like Consumer Union and Consumer Research. These product-oriented groups, along with the hold on policymakers of Keynesian theories of underconsumption, had moved the consumer closer to the center of the economic question.[37]

During the leftward shift of the thirties, however, another group of organized women consumers emerged. The League of Women Shoppers (LWS) sought to fill a space vacated by the NCL's lobbying and legislative strategy and the inability of the National Women's Trade Union League—whose leaders were even closer to the Roosevelts—to replicate an earlier emphasis on unionization.[38] The LWS belonged to a broad Popular Front, with Communists prominent among its leaders. In its early years, membership somewhat overlapped with the NCL, particularly in New York where Frieda Miller and Mary Dublin [Keyserling]—both future directors of the U.S. Women's Bureau—belonged. One NRA official, Elinore Herrick, was also a joint member.[39] It claimed 24,000 members.[40]

Among the banners of the LWS, one proclaimed "Fair Labor Standards," but another suggests a linguistic shift that distinguished its tone, more than its program, from the NCL: "Use Buying Power for Justice." The LWS embraced direct action in focusing on strike support, stressing "the right of unionization." Thus *The Woman Shopper* announced in its initial August, 1935, issue: "[W]omen can be a force in solving one of the fundamental problems of our times. Many employers in stores and factories are imposing sweat shop conditions on their workers. Labor can only remedy its condition by uniting to present its demands. Labor can only reach the employer through a union." In contrast to the defiance that "unscrupulous employers" displayed before Labor Boards, the LWS claimed that "store and factory owners compete to satisfy our desires." They would listen to women consumers. Similar to the Consumers'

League, the Shoppers would investigate "the facts" before voting support of workers in a labor dispute. "Support" consisted of picket duty as well as publicity and "withhold[ing] patronage" or boycotting.[41]

Newsletters highlighted numerous disputes in which the LWS participated to win for labor. These were not limited to garments and related trades. From retail shoes in New York City to restaurants in Los Angeles to the Hearst newspaper chain, the Shoppers fought for higher wages, better hours, and worker organization. The New York branch alone participated in 155 support actions between 1935 and 1940. By the Second World War, commitment to "justice" would embrace "rectify[ing] undemocratic practices against race, creed, color or sex which militate against fair living standards" and supporting the Fair Employment Practice Committee (FEPC), whose continuation the League also demanded. Under Lucy Randolph Mason, the NCL had defended African-American rights to equal pay vigorously before NRA code committees, recognizing that the low wages of the South undermined national conditions. While the NCL relied on its insider status to influence those with political or administrative power, the LWS stood outside, literally on picket lines. It would fade in the atmosphere of Cold War hysteria. In contrast, supported by trade unions, foundations, and anti-Communist liberals, the NCL would turn into a Washington lobby group. But its grassroots locals atrophied. [42]

From Fair Trade to Worker Rights

The national consensus that historians now name the New Deal Order ushered in union growth, legislative labor standards, and consumer preference for union-made goods. But even before its demise in the 1980s, runaway shops and import substitution undermined the economic health of the US garment industry. From the 1920s, manufacturers had headed South to escape labor laws and unions. In the post–World War II era, they took advantage of export-processing zones in Hong Kong, Taiwan, Korea, and Singapore as well as government tax breaks that encouraged investment in the Caribbean, Central America, and Mexico. From 4 percent in 1961, the percentage of imports grew to 31 percent in 1976 to over 60 percent by 1997. Meanwhile federal legislation and international rules facilitated corporate globalization. After 1963, Item 807 taxed only the value added to garments cut in the United States but exported for assembly; other provisions over the years maintained this loophole. The Caribbean Basin Initiative of 1983 ended tariffs for many goods made in that region. In 1993, the Clinton administration won passage of the North American Free Trade Agreement (NAFTA), while a renegotiated General Agreement on Tariffs and Trade (GATT) rewrote international rules to drop barriers. Such promotion of "free trade" contributed to the undermining of labor standards and the inhibiting of the right to unionize.[43]

Worried about imports as early as 1959, the ILGWU kicked off a "Look for the Label" campaign that relied on economic nationalism to prod the consumer to "Buy American." The union label represented "decency, fair labor standards and the American way of life." As one advertisement in the *New York Times* explained:

> The label means more than better workmanship. More than better styling. It has a deeper value. The knowledge that somewhere a human being who sewed the garment you will wear earns a living wage, and has a decent place to work. Look for this ILGWU label. It feels good to support democracy.[44]

By the 1970s, even manufacturers with union contracts found it cheaper to pay "liquidated damages" to the ILGWU (a fee to compensate for removing work from union shops) than continue production in the United States. ILGWU membership began to plummet, while domestic apparel manufacturers closed up shop.[45] The ILGWU in the 1980s, however, maintained enough political clout to stop the Reagan administration from removing prohibitions on industrial homework in ladies' garments, although all other homework bans incorporated into the FLSA in 1949 ended. Yet Reagan managed to undermine the entire labor standards regime by underfunding wage and hour inspection.[46]

By the early 1990s, the ILGWU's "rate of liquidated damages sank below the level at which it was punitive and prevented a shift overseas, and became merely a payoff," historian Dana Frank has charged. With less power, the union entered the "Crafted With Pride in the USA" coalition dominated by textile manufactures, which sought to block cheaper imports.[47] And too often "Made in the USA" labels hid the presence of sweatshops.[48] But activism reemerged in this century-old union when in 1995 it merged with the Amalgamated to form UNITE!, an act that brought a renewed commitment to organizing. Soon afterward, it initiated the Stop Sweatshops Campaign, with the NCL as co-chair, which sought to mobilize middle-class consumers, especially religious groups and women's clubs, to demand that local retail stores reject sweatshop-made goods. As geographers Rebecca Johns and Leyla Vural have concluded, "UNITE! relies on consumer politics as a lever to pry open space for organizing, but such production-based goals are at least partially masked behind the politics of consumption."[49]

The 1980s fight against lifting the homework bans had publicized a new generation of sweatshops where immigrants from the Americas and Asia—most of them here without official papers—labored in conditions reminiscent of the turn of the century. The competitive dynamics of the fashion trades required flexibility and quality control, leading to "just-in-time" and small-batch production that brought manufacturing back to the United States. Retailers, themselves concentrated into a few major chains (Wal-Mart, Kmart, Sears, and Dayton Hudson) had the economic clout to control manufacturing. This further atrophied the chain of responsibility that ran from manufacturer to worker. Final assembly began to occur in the underground shops of New York, Miami, and Los Angeles. The discovery in August 1995 of the El Monte,

California, "slaveshop," where seventy-two Thai women bent over machines behind barbed wire producing clothes for Nordstrom, Sears, Montgomery Ward, and other brand-name stores, dramatized the human consequences of garments global marketplace.[50]

The El Monte revelations stimulated an end of the century campaign against the sweatshop orchestrated by trade unions and NGOs (nongovernmental organizations) that relied on public scrutiny to force corporate compliance with "human rights" and labor standards. Dependence on mass marketing and reliance on logos and corporate image had made business vulnerable to reformer appeals to ethical consumption in ways only dreamed of by the NCL in the past.[51] Consequently, in the 1980s and early 1990s some brands, like Levi-Strauss and Nike, sought to ward off exposure of the conditions under which their goods were made. They established firm-based codes of conduct monitored by their own employees or accounting agencies, like Ernst & Young.[52] The American Apparel Manufacturing Association in October 1998 created its own plan to inspect and certify factories. But, as Charles Kernaghan of the National Labor Committee (NLC) charged, "they never even translated these codes of conduct into foreign languages. . . . It was meant for public relations, the Congress, for advertisements, and for some concerned consumers."[53]

Formed by trade unionists to oppose U.S. intervention in Central America (at a time when the AFL-CIO was still under the control of old Cold Warriors), the NLC turned into an independent labor-rights group after the Salvadoran peace accords in 1990. Drawing upon close relationships with Central American trade unionists, grassroots activists, churches, women's groups, and human-rights organizations, it had the credibility to gather workers' own stories. It has been able to expose conditions inside factories too easily hidden from government inspectors and corporate-backed monitors, neither of whom have been able to break through layers of intimidation and fear. Through campaigns against the personal label of television personality Kathie Lee Gifford, sold by Wal-Mart and made in Honduras but also in New York City's garment center, or against Gap clothing sewn in El Salvadoran sweatshops and Disney logos produced in Haitian ones, the NLC has perfected the politics of disclosure. "A huge believer in social movements," Kernaghan deploys publicity as a tool to force Congressional action and open up factories for unionization. Like other "solidarity" groups, the NLC personalized facts by sponsoring tours by *maquiladoras* workers. A meeting with fifteen-year-old Wendy Diaz, it claims, led Kathie Lee to ask "forgiveness." Gifford's subsequent testimony against sweatshops generated publicity for the cause, even if performed to rehabilitate her image as a supporter of children.[54]

In the wake of the exposure of Kathie Lee, in August 1996 Secretary of Labor Robert Reich created a Presidential taskforce of apparel and footwear makers, trade unions, the NCL, and religious and human-rights groups.[55] Already the Department of Labor (DOL) had revived use of the "hot goods" provision of the FLSA to seize products manufactured in violation of wage, hours, child labor, and health and safety regulations. The DOL had begun to issue a "No Sweat" label and a "Fashion Trendsetters List" of retailers and manufacturers who "pledge to help eradicate sweatshops in America and to try to ensure that their shelves are stocked with only 'No Sweat' garments." The reliability of this list, however, was questionable. First caught straying was Guess, Inc., which in early 1997 began moving 70 percent of its operations to Mexico. By joining the taskforce or Trendsetters, companies—especially those "outed" by the NLC and Central American solidarity groups like US/LEAP, (United States/Labor Education in the Americas Project) such as the Gap, Phillips-Van Heusen, and Starbucks—tried to disassociate themselves from pictures of child laborers and stories of starvation wages and brutality while still reaping the financial benefits of offshore production.[56]

Over the next two years, the White House Apparel Industry Partnership (AIP), co-chaired by Linda Golodner of the NCL and Roberta Karp of Liz Claiborne Inc., struggled to forge a system of self-regulation for U.S. companies. With a Republican Congress hostile to unions and a Democratic administration committed to free trade, volunteerism under the mantle of the White House offered a half a loaf that the NCL could embrace. Human-rights terms could trump a generalized hostility to unions, it believed.[57] In the ensuing controversy, the NCL parted from its trade union allies to work with the possible rather than striving for the better. This choice of strategies alienated it from the growing grass roots and university-based protest, the latter fanned by students returning from Union Summer and then offered an opening by the AIP's courting of university participation.[58]

Activists led by Medea Benjamin of Global Exchange harshly judged the AIP's "Code of Conduct" and governing body, the Fair Labor Association (FLA). The Code permitted a 60-hour workweek and a minimum working age of fourteen, lesser standards than in the United States. It was structured so that the corporate delegates essentially had a veto over decertification of companies; monitoring appeared tied to accounting firms that had created their own market niche out of this demand; and disclosure succumbed to bureaucratic layers of secrecy. Monitors would check only 30 percent of member factories the first year, with another 5 or 10 percent in subsequent years. The Code of Conduct tilted so blatantly toward the corporate partners that UNITE! and the Interfaith Center on Corporate Responsibility refused to sign the final agreement. Tepid commitment to the right to organize and rejection of living wages led unions and faith-based NGOs to drop out of the Partnership in November 1998. The Code emphasized fairness rather than worker rights, with employers ultimately interpreting the definition of fairness.[59] UNITE! leaders were also skeptical over independent monitors. As one explained, "the very concept of 'independence' indicates a sense of superiority, of being above class and class struggle," while another asked, "Doesn't independent also mean independent of the workers. . . . This is a classless good government group idea that is often used against us. Unions as some outside group instead of unions as the real voice of workers."[60]

The weak standards of the FLA, however, proved too stringent for most manufacturers, including one original AIP member, Warnaco (a conglomerate holding Calvin Klein among its labels). Needing to expand the initial group of signatories to gain credibility, the FLA turned to universities, reserving for them a single seat on its fourteen-person board. For over a year, students had been calling upon schools to end logo and athletic-licensing agreements with companies who produce apparels and sneakers under substandard conditions. Among hip politicos, steeped in techniques of deconstruction and cultural studies, the tradition of ethical consumption had morphed into a critique of branded imagery.[61] But most students' views resembled those of one University of Wisconsin woman: "White kids who've never been involved in political or social justice activity before, but who recognize that our clothes shouldn't be made by people who are treated like slaves—it's an easy thing to understand."[62]

Duke University, the site of the first Students Against Sweatshops, lead the way in March 1998 with a "code of conduct" that included the right to unionize, disclosure of factory locations, inspection by independent monitors, bans on child labor, workplace safety, and minimum wages. The summer before, Duke student Tico Almeida, along with other interns and staff at UNITE!, had come up with the idea of a student antisweatshop movement.[63] Soon students were demanding living wages and women's rights, not only for equal pay and maternity leave but also bodily integrity, that is, freedom from sexual harassment and forced birth control. From California to the Ivy League, from small liberal arts schools to sports-centered state universities like Wisconsin, Arizona, and Michigan, students forged a network where listservs and Web sites became preferred means of communication. Forming United Students Against Sweatshops (USAS) in the summer of 1998, they elected supporters to student councils, staged protests at homecomings, and took over buildings.[64]

Initially membership in the FLA promised administrators a way to pacify student demands without disrupting university routines. By the summer of 1999, over 100 universities had joined. But USAS judged FLA undemocratic and its code, inadequate. Georgetown University became the first to withdraw from the FLA following a "sleep-in" in November 1999.[65] USAS formed a rival organization, the Workers Rights Consortium (WRC), committed to independent monitoring and full disclosure of manufacturing sites. WRC assumed "that work conditions will not be changed by codes and monitors that come from industry, but by involvement of workers, through collective bargaining with management," explained one activist in the *New York Times* after Nike CEO Phil Knight's retaliatory withdrawal of a $30 million donation to the

University of Oregon.[66] Four affiliated schools in February 2000—Brown, Loyola University New Orleans, Haverford College, and Bard College—had grown to 57 by the summer of 2000, when the hostile *Times* correspondent Thomas L. Friedman argued, "the FLA was formed to make a difference. The WRC was formed to make a point." [67] By January 2003, the number of affiliated schools had nearly doubled to 112.[68]

Rather than call for boycotts and plant closures, the students demanded improvement of working conditions. Rather than privatize labor law enforcement through a permanent system of factory policing, they sought to "open up the space for workers and their allies to advocate on their own behalf." Sitting on the WRC Advisory Council was the Director of the Corporate Affairs Department of the AFL-CIO, the Director of the Industry Development Department of UNITE!, representatives from South African, Asian, and Nicaraguan labor unions, and the Director of the Trade Union Program of Harvard University. Its governing board consisted of six members selected by the Advisory Council, three from universities, and three from USAS. Responding to Nike's decision in April 2000 to release "the complete audits" and locations of 600 plants, *Business Week* declared, "Who Says Student Protests Don't Matter?" The WRC challenged in its very name, with its focus on "workers" and "rights," the meaning of "fairness" embraced by the FLA.[69] Over the next two years, its investigations and support aided union victories at the Kukdong factory in Puebla, Mexico, BJ + B factory in Villa Altagraica, Dominican Republic and the New Era Cap factory in Derby, New York.[70] The WRC planned on expanding the number of investigations threefold (from three to ten to fifteen) during 2003.[71]

Meanwhile, FLA in April 2002 revamped its monitoring process in response to criticisms over corporate control of its investigations. It would select factories to monitor through random sampling, choosing monitors whom it would pay directly, and make its visits unannounced. Companies no longer would be privy to the monitor's report before the FLA and would be required to present a remediation plan. FLA would post monitoring information on its Web site but, while the name of the company using a monitored factory would appear, the factory's name would not. They also would add suppliers and agents to their purview. WRC proponents, however, rejected these changes as inadequate because the FLA still relied on for-profit accounting firms, did not reveal actual factories under investigation, and accepted internal corporate monitoring. Its inability to involve NGOs or the workers they represent limited the credibility of the FLA among those seeking global solidarity.[72] But whether even truly independent monitoring will be enough to promote worker power remained questionable. Thus some called for labor rights as part of a "social clause." The regulatory regime of global institutions, including the WTO, could be used as a means to raise labor standards within nations of the "South." Labor standards, if enforced, then would offer a more friendly terrain to conduct unionization.[73]

By the summer of 2001, USAS had broadened its concerns beyond the over-seas garment industry to become a vehicle for student/labor solidarity. New "Principles of Unity" announced: "We consider all struggles against the systemic problems of the global economy to be directly or by analogy a struggle against sweatshops."[74] The antisweatshop movement became redefined:

> Workers, people of color, and students are routinely dis-empowered in garment factories, computer factories, strawberry fields, fast food restaurants, hotels, prisons, and even our own universities. . . . Our opposition to sweatshops and what they embody enables us to build a larger organization that addresses the social justice concerns of students outside our progressive circles.

They strove to reach the student who felt "uncomfortable with the cultural norm that says she or he needs to wear $150 Nike sneakers and unaffordable designer clothes in order to be cool." [75] They would associate the marketing of cool with the production of clothes and other goods. By early 2003, it had chapters in over 200 universities. At its national conference in Los Angeles that February, over a hundred students met to strategize not only how to stop sweatshops and fight the institutions of global capitalism (the WTO, IMF, and Free Trade Association of the Americas) but also how to provide solidarity for farmworker struggles, win living wages in their communities and on campuses, and support immigrant rights.[76]

The Problems of Solidarity

"In a world economy increasingly dominated by giant retailers and manufacturers who control global networks of independently owned factories, organizing consumers may prove to be a precondition for organizing production workers," WRC Advisory Council member Richard Appelbaum has concluded.[77] From Allentown, Pennsylvania, to Los Angeles to North Olmsted, Ohio, cities passed ordinances that forbid contracting for services or goods made under sweatshop conditions. Bangor, Maine, declared that "ordinary people should have something to say about the behavior of businesses, large or small, that operate in our community. We would never permit local vendors to sell us rotten meat, or stolen property, or illicit drugs because such behavior offends our community values. Likewise, we do not condone international corporations supplying our retailers with items made under conditions that equally offend our sense of decency." It resolved that no clothes sold in the city come from sweatshops. By1999, legislators had introduced antisweatshop bills in New Jersey and New York as well as before Congress.[78] Rudolph Giuliani, however in 2001, vetoed the measure passed by the New York City Council. But the Defense Department's PX stores planned to established new rules to hold suppliers to a code of conduct. In September 2002, labor, religious, and other activists launched the Campaign for the Abolition of Sweatshops &

Child Labor to regain media attention through testimonies of workers and the drafting of legislation to prohibit government purchase of sweatshop goods.[79]

Consumer organization was itself an international phenomenon, with numerous European "clean clothes" campaigns, although few truly transnational organizations existed. Instead, solidarity groups, many of which developed out of 1980s' campaigns against U.S. intervention in Central America, linked activists around the globe and introduced U.S. consumers to their struggles. The U.S./LEAP, for one, sponsored the tour of a former *maquiladoras* laborer on "How We Clandestinely Organize Sweatshops" with STITCH (Support Team International for Textileras), whose steering committee was dominated by trade unionists and had a representative from USAS. Just like the tours sponsored by the NLC, these testimonial speeches before meetings of students or liberal church groups or women's organizations could appear as performances of sweatshop exploitation, maintaining the distinction between the laboring woman and the woman consumer. Nonetheless, at a time when the gendered dimensions of sweating either disappear or manifest themselves only in victimized portrayals of women, STITCH consisted of women who support "Central American women who are organizing to improve their lives." Updating the appeal of Florence Kelley, feminist activist Barbara Ehrenreich solicited funds for this group by reminding more prosperous U.S. women that they "reap the benefits of an unfair economic system that exploits and degrades women." The National Organization for Women, the Ms. Foundation, and other feminists condemned Nike for supporting "Women in Its Ads but Not Its Factories." Eleanor Smeal of the Feminist Majority argued, "just like the feminists at the turn of the century fought them [sweatshops], it's incumbent on us to do the same." [80]

Meanwhile, the National Mobilization Against Sweatshops, a project of the Chinese Staff and Workers Association of New York, launched in 1999 the "Ain't I a Woman?" campaign against Donna Karan to have the designer "correct the problem of sweatshop labor *inside* New York City rather than simply shutting down," explained Miriam Ching Yoon Louie in *Sweatshop Warriors: Immigrant Women Workers Take On the Global Factory*. This book itself was a product of the movement, written by the former national media director of Fuerza Unida and Asian Immigrant Women Advocates. In recording the local struggles of Chinese, Mexican, and Korean women, it challenged the reader to listen to the stores of those "who clothe, feed, and care for us, who take risks and lead resistance on our behalf," not as "an act of consumerism" or "voyeurism" but as a step toward action.[81]

Despite the surge of protest that greeted the new century, grassroots activists worried "whether we see ourselves merely as enlightened reformers or as true allies of labor." Rejecting the "reform" model that "makes workers the objects of reform, rather than the agents of their own liberation," that "sees change emanating from above," student radicals have opted for the "solidarity" model in which "activists respond to workers' calls for solidarity and they take their direction from those workers." But, as the national coordinator of the Campaign for Labor Rights noted, "If only life were that simple!"[82] With production increasingly located in countries where the state suppresses freedom of speech and association, solidarity movements have to create conditions for unionization as much as support already existing efforts. Similarly, USAS leaders, like staffer Marion Traub-Werner, worried that the movement's emphasis on the point of consumption reinforced the very corporate hegemony that antisweatshop activists hoped to undermine. "When we began," she confessed in 2002, "we never challenged the idea that students should consume and we never questioned the university athletic industry as a whole or the university as a marketing machine."[83]

Like campaigners whose visits abroad taught that sweatshop sewers were young people who also laughed and loved, one student participant in a retreat with Mexican workers concluded: "I don't want to run a corporate campaign unless it's attached to real people."[84] The extent to which the denizens of sweatshops were real people remained as problematic as they did a century ago, however. As cultural critic Laura Hyun Yi Kang has shown, even opponents of capitalist and patriarchal exploitation reinscribe racialized and nationalist gender identities through representations of the third world woman worker, especially the Asian woman with her "nimble fingers." In the new transnationalism, the U.S. consumer/protester retains superiority, while the "third-world woman," reduced to a pathetic body, remains victim.[85]

USAS leaders have considered this potential pitfall. Pitzer College student Evelyn Zepeda explained, "Because USAS does not reflect the constituency it works on behalf of, it really needs to continue seeing its role as an ally."[86] To the extent that subjects of solidarity turn into objects of reform, creating a movement of allies but not of equals, today's antisweatshop crusaders face a risk not so dissimilar to their counterparts in the past, whose class position and standpoint differed from the Jewish and Italian immigrants of their concern. But if they can open spaces for worker organization, if independent monitoring becomes a means to an end but not the end itself, the distinction between producer and consumer might fade as both lay claims to global citizenship.

Notes

Acknowledgment I would like to thank Ralph Amburster-Sandoval for sharing his research and Daniel Lichtenstein-Boris for his updates on USAS—and his commitment to social justice.

1. For a good summary, Andrew Ross, ed., *No Sweat: Fashion, Free Trade, and the Rights of Garment Workers* (New York: Verso, 1997). See also "Homeworkers Win Vote at ILO Convention," *Outworkers News: Newsletter of the West Yorkshire Homeworking Unit & the Homeworkers Association*, Issue 21 (Autumn 1996), 1.
2. Florence Kelley, "The Problem of Sweating in America," *The Chautauquan* 60 (Nov. 1910), 414–21.

3. See Eileen Boris, *Home to Work: Motherhood and the Politics of Industrial Homework in the United States* (New York: Cambridge Univ. Press, 1994). This essay relies on my previous work to reanalyze the history of campaigns against sweated labor in light of developments since the early 1990s.

4. Henry White, "The Sweating System," in *Bulletin of Department of Labor* 4 (Washington, D.C.: GPO, 1896), n.p. See Daniel E. Bender, "Sweatshop Subjectivity and The Politics of Definition and Exhibition," *International Labor and Working-Class History* , 61 (Spring 2002), 13–23, and Bender, *Sweated Work, Weak Bodies: Anti-Sweatshop Campaigns and Languages of Labor* (New Brunswick: Rutgers University Press, 2003).

5. Quoted in U.S. General Accounting Office, *"Sweatshops" in the U.S: Opinions on Their Extent and Possible Enforcement Options*, Briefing Report to the Honorable Charles E. Schumer, House of Representatives, GAO/HRD-88–130BR (August 1988), 11.

6. *Ibid*, passim.

7. Michael Piore, "The economics of the sweatshop," in *No Sweat*, 135–42. See, for example, Dan La Botz, *Made in Indonesia* (Boston: South End Press, 2001).

8. I'm indebted to Landon R.Y. Storrs, *Civilizing Capitalism: The National Consumers' League, Women's Activism, and Labor Standards in the New Deal Era* (Chapel Hill: Univ. of North Carolina Press, 2000), 18–23, and her use of Jacqueline K. Dirks, "Righteous Goods: Women's Production, Reform Publicity, and the National Consumers' League, 1891–1919," (Ph.D. diss., Yale University, 1996), 163.

9. Quoted in Boris, *Home to Work*, 56–57.

10. Boris, *Home to Work*, 45.

11. Lowell quoted in Storrs, *Civilizing Capitalism*, 19; Joan Waugh, *Unsentimental Reformer: The Life of Josephine Shaw Lowell* (Cambridge: Harvard Univ. Press, 1997), 197–202.

12. Maud Nathan, *The Story of an Epoch-Making Movement* (New York: Doubleday, 1926), 22, also quoted by Storrs, *Civilizing Capitalism*, 14.

13. Kathryn Kish Sklar, *Florence Kelley and the Nation's Work: The Rise of Women's Political Culture, 1830–1900* (New Haven: Yale Univ. Press, 1995), 221.

14. Boris, *Home to Work*, 88–89; Florence Kelley, *Some Ethical Gains Through Legislation* (New York: Macmillan, 1905), 230.

15. Sklar, *Florence Kelley*, 63–68, 151–52; "Work for the Women," unidentified clipping, Nov. 1888, microfil vol.2, Thomas and Elizabeth Morgan Papers, Illinois Historical Society; Boris, *Home to Work*, 83–93.

16. Kathryn Kish Sklar, "The Consumers' White Label Campaign of the National Consumers' League, 1898–1918," in *Getting and Spending: European and American Consumer Societies in the Twentieth Century*, Susan Strasser, Charles McGovern, and Matthias Judt, eds. (Washington, D.C.: The German Historical Institute with Cambridge Univ. Press, 1998), 17–35, esp. 23–4, 31.; Boris, *Home to Work*, 82.

17. Sklar, "The Consumers' White Label Campaign," 31; Maren Stange, *Symbols of Ideal Life: Social Documentary Photography in America, 1890–1950* (New York: Cambridge Univ. Press, 1989), 1–87.

18. Boris, *Home to Work*, 64–65, 164, 166.

19. Vivien Hart, *Bound by Our Constitution: Women, Workers, and the Minimum Wage* (Princeton: Princeton University Press, 1994), 63–86.

20. Boris, *Home to Work*, 86.

21. Boris, *Home to Work*, 92; Sklar, "The Consumers' White Label Campaign," 32–33.

22. House of Representatives, Committee of Manufactures, 52nd Congress, 2nd Session, Report No. 2309, "Report on the Sweating System under House Resolution, February 13, 1892;" see Boris, *Home to Work*, 65–67.

23. Eileen Boris, "Tenement Homework on Army Uniforms: The Gendering of Industrial Democracy During World War I," *Labor History* 32 (Spring 1991), 231–52.

24. See Steven Fraser, *Labor Will Rule: Sidney Hillman and the Rise of American Labor* (New York: Free Press, 1991), 146–237.

25. Boris, *Home to Work*, 206–7.

26. Dublin quoted in Linda F. Golodner, "Apparel Industry Code of Conduct: A Consumer Perspective on Social Responsibility," Paper presented to Notre Dame Center for Ethics and Religious Values in Business, Oct. 6, 1997, 2, available on www.nclnet.org.

27. Johnson quoted in Storrs, *Civilizing Capitalism*, 98; Mrs. Franklin D. Roosevelt, *It's Up to the Women* (New York, Frederick A. Stokes Co., 1933).

28. Quoted in Storrs, *Civilizing Capitalism*, 113. For a summary of the NRA, Boris, *Home to Work*, 201–12.

29. Figure from Robert Zieger, *The CIO, 1935–1955* (Chapel Hill: University of North Carolina Press, 1995), 18.

30. Storrs, *Civilizing Capitalism*, 90–123; Suzanne Mettler, *Dividing Citizens: Gender and Federalism in New Deal Public Policy* (Ithaca: Cornell University Press, 1998), 179.

31. See Hart, *Bound By Our Constitution*, 138–50; Mettler, *Dividing Citizenship*, 180–83; 298 U.S. 587 (1936); 300 U.S. 379 (1937); 301 U.S. 1 (1937). On *West Coast Hotel*, Julie Novkov, *Constituting Workers, Protecting Women: Gender, Law, and Labor in the Progressive Era and New Deal Years* (Ann Arbor: University of Michigan Press, 2001).

32. Fair Labor Standards Act, *Statutes at Large*, 52, sec. 2 9a, 1060. See Deborah M. Figart, Ellen Mutari, and Marilyn Power, *Living Wages, Equal Wages: Gender and Labor Market Policies in the United States* (New York: Routlege, 2002), 91–119.

33. Mettler, *Dividing Citizenship*, 186.

34. Mettler, *Dividing Citizenship*, 196–205; Boris, *Home to Work*, 274; Phyllis Palmer, "Outside the Law: Agricultural and Domestic Workers under the Fair Labor Standards Act," *Journal of Policy History*, 7 (Fall 1995), 416–40.

35. Boris, *Home to Work*, 273–301; Storrs, *Civilizing Capitalism*, 177–203.

36. Storrs, *Civilizing Capitalism*, 153.

37. Meg Jacobs, "'Democracy's Third Estate': New Deal Politics and the Construction of a 'Consuming Public,'" *International Labor and Working Class History* 55 (Spring 1999), 22–51; see also Lizabeth Cohen, "The New Deal State and the Making of Citizen Consumers," in *Getting and Spending*, 111–25; Lawrence B. Glickman, "The Strike in the Temple of Consumption: Consumer Activism and Twentieth-Century American Political Culture," *Journal of American History* 88 (June 2001), 99–128.

38. On the League and its evolution, see Annelise Orleck, *Common Sense and a Little Fire: Women and Working-Class Politics in the United States, 1900–1965* (Chapel Hill: Univ. of North Carolina Press, 1995).

39. Storrs, *Civilizing Capitalism*, 35, 237, 114; Special Committee on Un-American Activities, *Investigation of Un-American Propaganda Activities in the United States*, House of Representatives, 78th Congress, 2nd Session (Washington: GPO, 1944), 1002–23 contains membership lists. See also Elinore Morehouse Herrick, "A Sister Organization," *The Woman Shopper*, 1 (November 1935), 3, on the activities of NCL appeared in the newsletter of the LWS.

40. There is no history of the Shoppers, but see Helen Sorenson, *The Consumer Movement* (New York: Harper and Brothers, 1941), 127–28, and Kathleen Banks Nutter, "Jessie Lloyd O'Connor and Mary Metlay Kaufman: Professional Women Fighting for Social Justice," *Journal of Women's History* 14 (Summer 2002), 132–35

41. Christmas Card, 1942, in Box 1, Papers of the League of Women Shoppers, Sophia Smith Collection, Smith College; "Editorial," *The Woman Shopper*, 1 (August 1935), 1, 3, in Box B–24, Folder 424, Consumers' League of Massachusetts Papers, Schlesinger Library, Radcliffe.

42. Minutes of the Seventh Annual Membership Meeting of the League of Women Shoppers, Inc., May 9th and 10th, 1944—New York City, 5, 9, Box 1, LWS Papers; for strike support, see *The Woman Shopper*, 1 (August, October, November 1935), Box 25, folder 424, B-24; *The Woman Shopper* {Los Angeles}, 2 (Jan.–Feb. 1938) , Box 1, LWS Papers; Sorenson, *The Consumer Movement*, 127–28; Storrs, *Civilizing Capitalism*, 104–8, 244–51.

43. Elizabeth McLean Petras, "The Shirt on Your Back: Immigrant Workers and the Reorganization of the Garment Industry," *Social Justice* 19 (Spring 1992), 76–115; Dana Frank, *Buy American: The Untold Story of Economic Nationalism* (Boston: Beacon Press, 1999), 148–50. Import figures from Alan Howard, "Labor, History, and Sweatshops in the New Global Economy," 156; Ross, "Introduction," 17–25, both in *No Sweat*. For a full history of these efforts, see Ellen Israel Rosen, *Making Sweatshops: The Globalization of the U.S. Apparel Industry* (Berkeley: University of California Press, 2002).

44. Quoted in Pamela V. Ulrich, " 'Look for the Label'—the International Ladies' Garment Workers' Union Label Campaign, 1959–1975," *Clothing and Textiles Research Journal*, 13, #1 (1995), 52. For economic nationalism, see Frank, *Buy American*, especially 131–59.

45. ILGWU membership went from 457,517 in 1969 to 308,056 in 1980 to 146,506 a decade later. Frank, *By American*, 132. Los Angeles alone saw a drop of 4,000 companies from 1986 to 1996, when the number of companies reached more than 20,000. James Flanigan, "Much-Needed Change May Finally Be Starting," *Los Angeles Times*, Aug. 4, 1996, D1. The

number of garment workers has dropped from a peak of 1.4 million in early 1970s to 800,000 in 1999. Expansion has come among the immigrant and undocumented. Richard Appelbaum and Peter Dreier, "The Campus Anti-Sweatshop Movement," *The American Prospect* (September 1999), 72.

46. Boris, *Home to Work*, 337–61; Petras, "The Shirt on Your Back," 106.

47. Frank, *Buy American*, 146–47, 187–92.

48. See, for example, "Stop Saipan Sweatshops/Protest The Gap," *Global Exchanges*, Issue #38 (Spring 1999), 1, 14. Goods made in Saipan qualified for "Made in the USA" labels.

49. Rebecca Johns and Leyla Vural, "Class, Geography, and the Consumerist Turn: UNITE! and the Stop Sweatshops Campaign," *Environment and Planning Annual*, 32 (2000), 1198–1200.

50. Julie Su, "El Monte Thai Garment Workers: Slave Sweatshops," in Ross, *No Sweat*, 143–49, esp. 147.

51. Naomi Klein, *No Logo: Taking Aim at the Brand Bullies* (New York: Picador, 1999).

52. Randy Shaw, *Reclaiming America: Nike, Clean Air, and the New National Activism* (Berkeley: Univ. of California Press, 1999), 13–96. For the aversion of Levi Strauss to "transparency" and its global search for cheap labor, see Karl Schoenberger, *Levi's Children: Coming to Terms With Human Rights in the Global Marketplace* (New York: Atlantic Monthly Press, 2000).

53. "Charlie Kernaghan: the Labor Activist Who Made Kathie Lee Cry," *WorkingUSA* 2 (July–August 1998), 37; Paula L. Green, "Industry to Oversee Textile Factories," *Journal of Commerce*, Nov. 6, 1998, 8A; for the emergence and discourse of the movement, Rebecca De Winter, "The Anti-Sweatshop Movement Constructing Corporate Moral Agency in the Global Apparel Industry," *Ethics & International Affairs*, 15 (October 2001), 99–117.

54. *Ibid.*, 38–39; Kitty Krupat, "From War Zone to Free Trade Zone: A History of the National Labor Committee;" Charles Kernaghan, "Paying to Lose Our Jobs;" National Labor Committee, "An Appeal to Walt Disney," all in *No Sweat*, 51–112. See their Web site, www.nlc-net.org. For the history of cross-boarder labor solidarity and campaigns involving a wide array of actors during the 1990s, see Ralph Armbruster-Sandoval, *Globalization and Cross-Border Labor Solidarity in the Americas: The Anti-Sweatshop Movement and the Struggle for Social Justice*, manuscript in author's possession, 2002.

55. Schoenberger, *Levi's Children*, 220–4. Members included Liz Claiborne, L.L. Bean, Nike, Reebok, Karen Kane, Nicole Miller, Tweeds, Patagonia, Phillips-Van Heusen, Warnaco, Interfaith Center on Corporate Responsibility, International Labor Rights Fund, Robert E. Kennedy Memorial Center for Human Rights, Business for Social Responsibility, Lawyers Committee for Human Rights, National Consumers League, Retail, Wholesale and Department Store Union, and UNITE! "Labor Standards to Get Broad Input," *Journal of Commerce*, Nov. 5, 1996, 3A; Appelbaum and Dreier, "The Campus Anti-Sweatshop Movement," 74.

56. Ross, "Introduction," and "Postscript," in *No Sweat*, 27–28, 294–95, 298; Eyal Press, "Breaking the Sweats," *The Nation*, 264 (April 28, 1997), 5.

57. Johns and Vural, "Class, Geography, and the Consumerist Turn," 1199.

58. The ALP is listed among League accomplishments in National Consumers League, "100 Years of Advocacy, 1899–1999," NCL, 1999, 11. In an attempt to end a rift with the student movement, NCL Golodner was a signatory to "Open Letter to the University Community," Feb. 28, 2000, issued by the Fair Labor Association that reaffirmed workers' rights. www.lchr.org/sweatshop/commit.htm

59. "Pact Signed for Plant Workers Abroad," *The Boston Globe*, A9; Press, "Breaking the Sweats," 6; Steven Greenhouse, "Banishing the Dickensian Factor," *New York Times*, July 9, 2000, D, 5; Jill Esbenshade and Edna Bonacich, "Can Conduct Codes and Monitoring Combat America's Sweatshops?" *WorkingUSA* 3 (July–August 1999), 26–29. See also, Alan Howard, "Why Unions Can't Support the Apparel Industry Sweatshop Code?" *WorkingUSA* 3 (July–August 1999), 34–50.

60. Johns and Vural, "Class, Geography, and the Consumerist Turn," 1206–7.

61. Ross, *No Sweat*; Klein, *No Logo*.

62. Simon Birch, "Sweat and Tears: A Vast Protest Movement Is Sweeping US Campuses," *The Guardian* (London), July 4, 2000, 12.

63. Kitty Krupat, "Rethinking the Sweatshop: A Conversation About United Students Against Sweatshops (USAS) with Charles Eaton, Marion Trub-Werner, and Evelyn Zepeda," *International Labor and Working Class History*, 61 (Spring 2002), 113.

64. Appelbaum and Dreier, "The Campus Anti-Sweatshop Movement," 71–78; Shaw, *Reclaiming America*, 81–86. Lisa Featherstone and United Students Against Sweatshops,

Students Against Sweatshops (New York: Verso, 2002) recounts the history of the group. For updates, go to http://www.people.fas.harvard.edu/~fragola/usas/index.html (last accessed 2/14/03).

65. L. Kim Tan, "Rights Group Losing Student Backers," *The Boston Herald*, Nov. 16, 1999, 31; see Web site, www.workersrights.org.

66. Sarah Edith Jacobson, "Dialogue: Nike's Power Game," *New York Times*, May 16, 2000, A23.

67. Workers Rights Consortium, "Companion Document,"2; Workers Rights Consortium, "Members," at www.workersrights.org, Thomas L. Friedman, "Knight Is Right," *New York Times*, June 20, 2000, A25.

68. http://www.workersrights.org/as.asp, last assessed 2/14/03.

69. Worker Rights Consortium, "Enforcement of University Licensing Codes of Conduct," 7, at http://www.workersrights.org/ (last assessed 2/14/03); listserv of the Committee of Labor Rights chronicled the student sit-ins from 1998, E-mails in author's possession; Louise Lee and Aaron Bernstein, "Who Says Student Protests Don't Matter?" *Business Week*, June 12, 2000, 94, 96.

70. Featherstone, *Students Against Sweatshops*, 80–91; "Worker rights consortium update: still kicking corporate ass," *Active Work: A Newsletter of the United Students against sweatshops* (winter 2002), 2, available at http://www.people.fas.harvard.edu/~fragola/usas/index.html, last accessed 2/14/03.

71. United Students Against Sweatshops, "New Changes to the FLA: Explanation and Renewed Criticism," July 2002, report, n.p., at http://www.people.fas.harvard.edu/~fragola/usas/resources.html, last assessed 2/15/03.

72. New Changes to the FLA: Explanation and Renewed Criticism," July 2002, report, n.p., at http://www.people.fas.harvard.edu/~fragola/usas/resources.html, last accessed 2/15/03.

73. Robert J.S. Ross and Anita Chan, "From North-South to South-South: The True Face of Global Competition," *Foreign Affairs*, 81 (September/October 2002), 8–13; Joshua Cohen and Joel Rogers, eds., *Can We Put An End to Sweatshops?: A New Democracy Forum on Raising Global Labor Standards* (Boston: Beacon Press, 2001).

74. http://www.people.fas.harvard.edu/~fragola/usas/about.html, last accessed on 2/14/03; Featherstone, *Students Against Sweatshops*, 2.

75. Krupat, "Rethinking the Sweatshop," 114–5.

76. Personal communications, Daniel Lichtenstein-Boris, January 30, February 3, 2003. See flyer, "Save the Date: Global to Local: Making Connections in the Student/Labor Movement," http://www.people.fas.harvard.edu/~fragola/usas/conference/index.html, last accessed 2/14/03.

77. Appelbaum and Dreier, "The Campus Anti-Sweatshop Movement," 72.

78. Golodner, "Apparel Industry Code of Conduct," 8–9; Johns and Vural, "Class, Geography, and the Consumerist Turn," 1203–4.

79. "Giuliani vetoes bill aimed at sweatshops,"*New York Times* (March 31, 2001), B6; "The PX Is Going PC," *Business Week* (April 8, 2002), 10 ; Aaron Bernstein, "Remember Sweatshops?" *Business Week* (September 30, 2002), 14.

80. Linda Shaw, "The Label Behind the Label: Clean Clothes Campaigns in Europe," in *No Sweat*, 215–20; Marion Traub-Werner, "Marina Gutierrez in Honduras: How We Clandestinely Organize Sweatshops," *Labor Notes*, #255 (June 2000), 6; Krupat, "Rethinking the Sweatshop," 117; Letter from Barbara Ehrenreich to Dear Activist for Social Justice, n.d.. c.1998; Shaw, *Reclaiming America*, 70–77, Smeal quoted on 76.

81. Miriam Ching Yoon Louie, *Sweatshop Warriors: Immigrant Women Workers Take On the Global Factory* (Boston: South End Press, 2001), 231, 253.

82. E-mail communication from clr.igc.apc.org, "Student Activism Continues," posted May 6, 1999: Trim Bissell, "Waiting for the Other Shoe."

83. Krupat, "Rethinking the Sweatshop," 119.

84. Krupat, "Rethinking the Sweatshop," 119; Featherstone, *Students Against Sweatshops*, 72.

85. Laura Hyun Yi Kang, "Si(gh)ting Asian/American Women as Transnational Labor," *Positions: East Asia Cultures Critique* 5 (Fall 1997), 403–37; see also Ethel Brooks, "The Ideal Sweatshop?: Gender and Transnational Protest," *International Labor and Working Class History*, 61 (Spring 2002), 91–111, reprinted in this volume.

86. Krupat, "Rethinking the Sweatshop," 126, 122.

11
The Rise of the Second Antisweatshop Movement*

ANDREW ROSS
New York University

The legions who have contributed to the antiglobalization movement in recent years have been driven by many different struggles: against genetically modified foods, structural adjustment programs, undemocratic World Trade Organization (WTO) decision-making, economic privatization, to name a few. Yet there has been one staple, enduring, target of activist attention in all quarters of the movement, and that is the global sweatshop. Indeed, the sweatshop has become a byword for globalization, even though its origins predate, by more than a century, the moment when production (as opposed, merely, to capital) became internationalized, and when offshore locations became much cheaper than unionized, high-wage sectors of the industrialized West.

Jack Welch, former CEO of General Electric, the largest multinational corporation in the world, once described the optimum manufacturing model for his company: "Ideally, you'd have every plant you own on a barge." The barges, of course, would move periodically to an anchorage offshore whichever country or regional labor market was offering the best investment climate at any one time. Welch's barges are an investor's fantasy and a union organizer's nightmare. Two decades of prescribed free markets and trade liberalization have brought them much closer to reality. Yet the extensive damage wrought by such trade policies—economic stagnation, currency crises, stock market crashes, political collapses, environmental degradation, and acute income polarization—has taken its toll on the Washington consensus. The antiglobalization movement that broke the surface of public awareness at the WTO's Third Ministerial in Seattle in 1999, and registered its presence at every world economic meeting since then, has shaken the confidence of global elites in their ability to go on making decisions through institutions that are nontransparent and undemocratic.

*Some portions of this essay were originally published in *No Sweat: Fashion, Free Trade, and the Rights of Garment Workers* (New York: Verso, 1997).

One of the chief tributaries of antiglobalization action has been the anti-sweatshop movement itself, loosely but effectively coordinated among a network of groups: trade unionists, interfaith organizations, college and high-school students, human-rights groups, and local NGOs. This movement has surprised battle-weary activists, long resigned to seeing their causes treated with indifference. After all, most citizens of the North, however much they themselves are hurting, are not known for their discomfort at evidence that workers in poor countries are suffering too, and, more often than not, on their behalf. Most consumers don't want to know that the goods they are purchasing may have been made by workers with no rights or contracts, slaving through a 90-hour workweek, in unsafe, unsanitary factories, with abusive supervisors. When they learn about these conditions, however, they generally want something done about them.

As a result, activists have been successful not only in generating widespread outrage at the conditions they have exposed at home and abroad, but also in seeing follow-through on the part of a broad spectrum of institutions. Public attention was guaranteed early on in the campaign by revelations about the likes of basketball prince Michael Jordan, who earned more ($20 million) in 1992 for endorsing Nike's running shoes than Nike's entire 30,000-strong Indonesian workforce did for making them. Or Disney's CEO, Michael Eisner, who earned over $200 million from salary and stock options in 1993, which, at $97,600 per hour, amounted to 325,000 times the hourly wage of the Haitian workers who made Pocahantas, Lion King, and Hunchback of Notre Dame T-shirts and pajamas, and who sewed on Mickey Mouse's ears. Highly visible inequities on this scale opened the way for a decade of exposés, targeted at big-name retailers, manufacturers, and their subcontractors.

The tug of war between corporations, activists, and government agencies has produced several outcomes: sweat-free city ordinances, corporate codes of conduct, global monitoring groups like the Fair Labor Association (FLA) and the Workers Rights Consortium (WRC), SA8000, and other corporate/trade union/NGO alliances like the Ethical Trading Initiative. Pressure to include fair labor standards in world-trade agreements has generated a full-blown debate about the impact of these standards on the development opportunities of poor countries. Will these provisions hamper the ability of developing nations to compete for trade and investment, or are they the only way to ensure that fair labor prevails throughout the global economy? Are core, or universal, labor standards the most equal way of reforming a chronically unequal system? Are they a high price poor countries are asked to pay to appease the ethical conscience of activists in the North, or are they justifiable costs to be borne by the transnational firms that exploit cheap labor pools wherever they can find them?

Whatever the outcome of this debate, the antisweatshop movement will have forged the first paths toward the establishment of ground rules for labor in the global economy. One hundred years earlier, the first crusade against sweatshops challenged corporations and trusts who exploited the creation of a national market to escape local and state regulations. National labor and safety standards, worker rights, and environmental protections were introduced as a result. This time around, the map is much larger, the potential to hide abuses is much greater, and so the tactics of activists have had to be more makeshift, even experimental. This essay reviews the ground conditions that gave rise to this movement, and analyses some of its achievements.

The Garmento's Mixed Legacy

The apparel industries are a showcase of horrors for the global economy. Here, the gruesome face of neo-liberal free trade is all too apparent as the corporate hunt for ever cheaper labor drives wages down in entire subcontinental regions where countries compete to attract foreign investment. Historically, apparel is where underdeveloped countries start their effort to industrialize. The barrier to entry is very low because apparel requires a minimum of capital investment and machinery, and the operations of sewing and assembly are labor-intensive. Indeed, not much has changed in the way of technology since the invention of the sewing machine. In the period of the European empires, primary commodities were shipped from the colonies, and goods manufactured in industrial centers like Manchester were exported back. Since the 1970s, a new international division of labor has allowed poor countries to enter the export market by competing at the low end of the production chain. Yet their participation in the global market and their capacity to attract capital are governed ultimately by the demands of those who control the retail markets in high-wage countries and who take the lion's share of the profit from the garment trade. Structurally, U.S. retail giants who command the world's largest internal market are in a position to call the shots globally. It is under their price pressure and concerns about inventory risk that local contractors and suppliers are forced to pursue ever-tighter profit margins in the enterprise zones and assembly platforms of the developing world.

Because the textile and apparel industries have seen some of the worst labor excesses, they have also been associated with historic victories for labor, and hold a prominent symbolic spot on the landscape of labor iconography: from the Luddite weavers' resistance to the introduction of power looms, to the mid-nineteenth century protest of the "factory girls" in New England mills, the early twentieth-century garment workers' strikes against the sweating system, the unions' roles in forging pioneer labor-capital accords, and the recent rise to prominence of workers' struggles against the far-flung production empires of Nike, the Gap, and other leading brand names. In the public mind, the strongest association is with labor's successes in "eradicating" the sweatshop in the first two decades of the century. Of course, it never disappeared. Severely restricted in its zone of operations, the sweatshop dropped out of view, and lived on in the underground economy. But the repugnance attached to the term "sweatshop" commands a moral power, second only to slavery itself, to rouse public opinion into a collective spasm of abhorrence. For some, the public will to eliminate sweatshops from the labor landscape can designate a significant level of moral development on the part of a national community. It symbolizes a state of civilization that other nations cannot yet afford. Even in the U.S., which has routinely refused to ratify most of the labor standards proposed by the International Labor Organization (ILO), and where extensive commercial use is made of prison labor, the recognition of core labor rights in safe and sanitary workplace is understood as a requisite of membership in the First World.

This claim to moral superiority on the part of developed nations is one of the reasons why the much-hyped "return of the sweatshop" to the North has provoked such revulsion in these countries. Few aspects of the corporate roll-back of the postwar social contract have been greeted with the public outcry that followed revelations that sweatshops are thriving at the heart of most major North American cities, and that items of clothing on sale at family-brand stores like J.C. Penney, Sears, Wal-Mart, and Kmart were made by young immigrant mothers and their teenage daughters toiling in inhuman conditions only a matter of miles away from the point of purchase. These disclosures summon up the misery and filth of turn-of-the-century workplaces—tenements, lofts, attics, stables—plagued by chronic health problems (tuberculosis, the scourge and signature sickness of the sweatshop, has also made a return of late), and home to the ruthless exploitation of greenhorn immigrants.[1]

The dingy Victorian archetypes notwithstanding, sweatshops today come in all shapes and sizes. In Central America, they are brand-new, brightly lit factories, with armed guards patrolling a barbed-wire Free Trade Zone. In Los Angeles, they are in ranch-style, suburban compounds and dwellings. A 1994 General Accounting Office (GAO) report estimated that over a third of New York's 6,500 garment shops are sweated, as are 4,500 of LA's 5,000 shops, 400 out of 500 in Miami, and many others in Portland, New Orleans, Chicago, San Antonio, and Philadelphia. In the LA basin, $1 an hour is not an uncommon wage in Orange County's Little Saigon, while the New York City wage floor hovers around $2 an hour in Sunset Park's Chinatown. Government deregulation, a weakened labor movement, import competition, the contracting system, and the increased availability of immigrant workers with few other labor options have all combined to create and sustain these conditions. Much of U.S. production is concentrated in fashion-forward women's wear, subject to seasonal volatility and therefore requiring fast turn-arounds, yet more and more basic and sportswear lines are becoming fashion-conscious and time-sensitive. There are now five or six industry seasons instead of two, and products are kept on retail shelves for less and less time.[2] One of the results of the accelerated fashion changes and reduced lead time is that domestic manufacturers are increasingly encouraged to compete with the south at the low end. The typical immigrant firm can maintain a competitive advantage through its proximity to market and its production of short runs.

But what exactly is a sweatshop? The GAO defines a sweatshop as "an employer that violates more than one federal or state labor law governing minimum wage and overtime, child labor, industrial homework, occupational safety and health, workers compensation, or industry registration." Holding to this definition, however, means that we are more obliged to accept the existence of labor conditions that cover the legal standards, but only barely. Sweatshops are seen to be morally and politically apart from the lawful low-wage sector, which is condoned as a result.[3] Virtually every low-wage job, even those that meet minimum wage requirements and safety criteria, fails to provide an adequate standard of living for its wage-earner, let alone his or her family. In most respects, it is the systematic depression of wages, rather than conscious attempts to evade labor laws, that is the structural problem. Installing proper fire exits may turn a sweatshop into a legal workplace, but it remains a low-wage atrocity. All the more reason to define and perceive the "sweatshop" as a general description of all exploitative labor conditions, rather than as a subpar outfit, as defined by existing laws in whatever country the owner chooses to operate. Edna Bonacich and Richard Appelbaum argue for a broadening of "the definition of sweatshops to include factories that fail to pay a 'living wage,' meaning a wage that enables a family to support itself at a socially defined, decent standard of living." [4]

Historically, "sweating" refers to the system of subcontract, the farming out of work by competing manufacturers to competing contractors. Sweating was indigenous to garment production because of its division of labor, separating the craft processes of design, marking and cutting, from the labor-intensive sewing and finishing, and organized around a three-tier system of small producers—the inside shop, the contractor, and the home. In this industry on wheels, neither the jobber nor the manufacturer nor the contractor was responsible for each other's conduct.[5]

Today's U.S. garment industry shows many similarities. In 1996, the Bureau of Labor Statistics showed that, with the exception of the fast-food industry's burger-flippers ($11,920), and apparel and accessory store employees (at $13, 971), apparel and textile workers in the *legal* sector earn the lowest average annual wage among U.S. industries, at $19,225. Ethnic entrepreneurship is as crucial as ever. Asian and Latino immigrants, often undocumented, are denied access to the mainstream labor economy through racial labor segmentation, and are thereby forced into ethnic enclaves where labor laws are routinely neglected.[6] Where patterns of family labor are relevant, the obligations of youth to the immigrant culture of apprenticeship and to patriarchal cohesion add greatly to the degree of exploitation.[7] Women still make up the majority of sweated labor, their sewing skills traditionally undervalued, and their home-work sustaining the most underground sector of an industry. The system of subcontracting is alive and well, ever driving wages and profit margins down.

But there are differences. Decades of industrial regulation have left a raft of labor laws on the books, even if they are patchily enforced. The rise and ero-sion of union power has left an uncertain legacy, especially among new immi-grants drawn from countries with the modern equivalent of the Russian Pale's "Czarist repression." The apparel industry is now global in scope, with hun-dreds of countries producing for a small number of importing nations. The runaway shops are no longer in Trenton, New Jersey, or Scranton, Pennsylva-nia, or in antiunion states in the south. They are in the *maquiladoras* of the Caribbean basin, and their equivalent in Indonesia, Vietnam, China, and Thai-land, often in live-in labor compounds that make the company towns of yore look like Pleasantville.

The balance of power has shifted decisively towards the giant vertically in-tegrated retailers, who increasingly produce their own private brand labels in many of these countries, bypassing the manufacturer, the union shop, and the domestic worker. The big players are no longer industrial patriarchs, account-able to workers' communities through co-religionist ethics. They are anony-mous corporate executives, solely accountable to their boards or stockholders. Subcontracting, disdained by early twentieth-century apostles of scientific management, has become a standard principle of all post-Fordist production, used in auto parts, building maintenance, data processing, electronic assem-bly, public-sector work, and every other industry restructuring itself away from central economies of scale and mass production. Last but not least, pop-ular fashion is now a mainstay of mall retailing, both at the high-end and dis-count end. The globalization of the youth fashion revolution has increasingly defined the terms on which the industry has had to respond through restruc-turing, adjustment, and rationalization. The worst manifestations of the global sweatshop are all the more tragic when adolescents in poor countries are toiling to meet the style demands of their age peers in the North who are fortunate enough to have disposable income.

Politics of Trade

Globalizations's race toward the bottom of the wage floor poses a challenge for the survival and rekindling of the labor movement in an industry that has ben-efited from an unusual degree of domestic protections. That story dates to the very beginning of the Industrial Revolution, when the British imposed tariffs on Bengali textiles (for centuries previously, the leader in international trade) in order to protect its own rising industries in Lancashire and the West of Scot-land. The U.S. initiated its own protectionist tradition through import substi-tution and developed an effective system of tariffs and embargoes in the course of the nineteenth century. Powerful enough to impose voluntary restraints upon Japan's textile export trade in the 1940s, the American industry—in cahoots with European producers with whom it has shared a "gentleman's agreement" to waive all import duties—succeeding in exempting textile and apparel trade from many of the key rules of the General Agreement on Trade and Tariffs (GATT). From its 1947 inception to the Uruguay Round in 1994, the GATT's rules against discrimination (most favored nation treatment), tariff protectionism, and quantitative restrictions on imports were all relaxed for textile and apparel. A series of international accords culminating in the 1973 Multi Fiber Arrangement (MFA) sought to manage the trade flow from developing countries to Western markets through an elaborate system of bilateral agreements regarding import quotas and trade routes. This protectionist agreement was promoted in order to give developed countries time to adjust to the massive increase in exports from the south. Yet the competitive challenge of Asian producers has been so powerful that the developing countries succeeded, in the most recent GATT round, in winning a global agreement to eradicate the tangle of trade restrictions that have protected industries in the north for so long. The MFA is now being phased out, and in 2005, the final 49 percent of trade will be quota-free.[8] At that point, it is estimated that China's share of the global garment market will jump to 44 percent, and, with its vast post-WTO army of unemployed, its labor costs will undercut all other producers in the region.

The post-MFA free-trade order is likely to intensify patterns established over the last thirty years. In each of the world's spheres of influence—Asian, European and American—the respective cores are now serviced by discount-labor regions. As industries matured in the Asian Big Four (Hong Kong, South Korea, Singapore, and Taiwan), and unions drove domestic wages up, suppliers in these countries established assembly operations in the least developed Asian countries—Vietnam, Bangladesh, Sri Lanka, Indonesia, and China. For the Western European industries, textiles, design, and cutting are mostly domestic, while the sewing occurs in Northern Africa, and increasingly in Eastern Europe. Because of its proximity to the largest internal market, the situation in the American hemisphere is the most complex. In response to the first wave of Asian imports, from 1961 to 1971, the U.S. industry struggled to meet its first test of structural adjustment. Manufacturers were advised to "automate, relocate, or evaporate."[9] Because the physical limpness of fabric precluded the spread of automation to labor-intensive sectors, the push for increased productivity through mechanization was supplanted by the promise of cheap labor markets offshore. Thus began the hemorrhaging of jobs in the domestic industry.

From 1963, manufacturers could take advantage of a special provision (Item 807, now 9800.62) in the U.S. Tariff Schedule that allowed cut garments to be exported for assembly and reimported into the US. Duties were paid only on the value added to the garment through low-cost assembly. In conjunction with the creation of *maquiladora* free-trade zones as part of the Border Industrialization Program, offshore production skyrocketed. In 1983, the Reagan administration expanded the pool of sourcing countries through the creation of the Caribbean Basin Initiative (CBI), extending special trade privileges to 22 Caribbean countries (later increased to 27, and enhanced under Clinton to embrace benefits similar to those afforded Mexico under the North American Free Trade Agreement (NAFTA)) that afforded tariff-free access for many export products.

Anticommunism drove the CBI as much as the need to compete with Asian imports. Aggressive neo-liberal penetration of state economies, backed up by low-intensity military conflict, was adopted as the most efficient way of combating Caribbean socialism. In the wake of the land- and labor-reform movements of the 1970s, which gave rise to the Sandinista revolution in Nicaragua, Manley's socialist government in Jamaica, the New Jewel Movement in Grenada, and rebel-peasant insurgencies in many other nations, President Reagan announced a "state of danger" in the nation's backyard and began to pour money into the region in order to secure its economic and political dependency upon U.S. needs and interests. Offshore facilities owned by U.S. firms multiplied in the export-processing zones set up by loans and grants from USAID and other government agencies. Preferred trading arrangements ensured that class alliances between foreign investors and local elites were preserved; in countries like Haiti, Guatemala, and El Salvador, the *maquilas* are partly owned and managed by ex-members of military juntas, while the lure of industrial employment takes peasant reformist pressure off traditional landholding elites.

So, too, the gender division of labor was consciously exploited to preserve power and maximize profit. As Cynthia Enloe points out, the hemispheric free-trade market built by CBI, NAFTA, and now President Bush's thirty-two-nation Free Trade Area of the Americas, "stretching," in the words of his father (who envisioned it), "from Port Anchorage to Terra del Fuego," has been built on low female wages in the "unskilled" sectors of garment-making, food-processing, and electronics assembly. As women moved into the export industries (making up 90 percent of export zone labor) traditionally male manufacturing sectors like sugar, oil, and bauxite, with double the going wages of women, went into decline. Undervalued female labor also undergirds the U.S. domestic workforce, especially in the immigrant economy that supports sweatshops. Women and children's labor are on the frontline of the new industrial investment all over the world, just as it was in the mills of Manchester at the dawn of the Industrial Revolution.[10] Their entry into the industrial workforce allows them more freedom of movement in the public sphere, and the potential for an independent income. Yet the labor regime they enter can be as patriarchal and coercive as the familial one from which they are escaping.[11]

The consequences of offshore production for the populations of Central America and the Caribbean have amounted to a disaster by several criteria: human rights, environmental, economic, and political. The CBI failed to deliver improved trade earnings, and with the exception of the export zones cranking out profit for their foreign owners (many of them from Korea, Hong Kong, and Taiwan) to the tune of heavy subsidies from host governments, almost every other region has been hit hard. Local economies produced less and less for local consumption, economic nationalism and political sovereignty were severely eroded, and any chance of sustainable development was stillborn. Structural adjustment created a legacy of undiversified economies acutely vulnerable to every mild recession in the U.S.[12] By contrast, export promotion has yielded a bonanza for U.S. transnational firms (and for those Asian suppliers outsourcing in the region for proximity to the U.S. market) where wages as low as 12 cents an hour in Haitian or 31 cents in Honduran and Salvadorean *maquilas* can be freely maximized, and where local regulations against child labor, subminimum wages, and union repression are routinely waived by governments so hungry for foreign investment they will pay the companies' telephone and utilities bills. The offshore apparel industry remains the most notorious illustration of a free-trade economy: twenty-hour workdays forced on workers to fill their quotas, widespread sexual harassment, coercive birth control, brutal suppression of labor organization, and starvation wages.

These conditions are the result of programs designed to make U.S. apparel companies competitive. But, they have done little to help North American workers, now in competition with their *maquila* counterparts or with immigrant workers in the core centers. Pitting first-world against third-world workers drives wages down on both sides, and allows businesspeople to portray labor-rights advocates as domestic protectionists bent on depriving *maquila* workers of their industrial wage ticket out of poverty. (The same arguments are now cropping up in Asia, where the Chinese wage floor is undercutting the labor market in countries throughout the region). But the high-reward strategy, for companies, also carries some risks—poor quality control, inadequate managerial supervision, political instability. Few risks are greater than the potentially humiliating exposure of human-rights violations in the factories of companies that cannot afford to have the names of their designers, endorsers, or merchandising labels publicly sullied.

Tactics and Strategies

Indeed, it is the counter-strategy of public exposure that has fired the energies of labor and human rights activists in the last few years.[13] In the wake of the publicity scandals, companies have been pressured to implement codes of conduct and facilitate monitoring of labor conditions in their contractors' plants. Why has this strategy been necessary and why has it worked? By 1996, the four largest retailers in the U.S. commanded two-thirds of the market value of apparel sales.[14] Their chief point of vulnerability is their good name, susceptible to bad publicity and to consumers' boycotts. Equally, the weak link in the global chain of design, subcontracting, and merchandising is the willingness of first-world consumers to pay huge markup prices. Nike was able to move its factories from South Korea and Taiwan to Indonesia, China, Thailand, and Vietnam to exploit lower wages, but the comparative advantage means nothing if consumers are not willing to pay $125 for a shoe assembled for 70 or 80 cents. If consumer abhorrence for sweatshops has a decisive impact on sales patterns, all is lost.

Accordingly, the leading edge of activism shifted away from labeling ("Made in the USA" labels don't tell us very much anymore, and are often sewn on in Asia or Central America), toward the high-end publicity strategy of targeting the image of large, well-known companies. The groundwork for this tactic was established through the research on Indonesian export-sector factories undertaken by Jeff Ballinger, a former textile union organizer, in the late 1980s at the Asian-American Free Labor Institute. In an extensive study that showed a majority of export producers paying well below the minimum wage (their workers earned under 14¢ per hour), Nike's subcontractors emerged as among the worst offenders. Phil Knight's company had just begun to enjoy its mercurial rise to the merchandising forefront of popular culture. With its celebrity endorsers and hotshot "Just Do It" advertising campaign, targeting Nike was a perfect publicity vehicle for exposing the inequities of offshore export production. Ballinger's famous annotated blowup of the pay stub of one of Nike's Indonesian employees ("The New Free-Trade Heel") appeared in *Harper's* in 1992, and Press for Change, his one-man NGO, became the company's perennial gadfly, helping to establish Nike as the number-one villain in activists' demonization of corporate-led globalization.[15]

While media-driven targeting pays large dividends, its shortcomings are legion. In some export sectors, the worst offenders are producers for regional markets who do not have a globally recognizable brand name. So too, a high-profile fight with a brand name runs the risk of being declared passé once the villain is perceived to have changed its policies. Thus, both Nike and the Gap have benefitted from the public perception that they have reformed their ways. In a thoughtful article on the antisweatshop movement's use of media-driven politics, B. J. Bullert distinguishes between public-relations activists—who "adopt" causes and frame them in terms of "heroes and villains" to fit with media templates—and long-term activists, like Ballinger, whose enduring focus on the unspectacular lot of workers cannot be so easily served up for public consumption. Both are needed, she concludes, though the difference between them illustrates the gulf between those for whom the movement is a potent weapon in the anticorporate crusade and those for whom the daily survival of workers is all.[16]

In the contribution of a group like the National Labor Committee (NLC), we can see a healthy fusion of these tendencies. As with Ballinger's work, the NLC has produced invaluable research on workers' conditions in the field, but it has also succeeded most effectively in capturing the public's attention through media-driven campaigns. Founded by three union presidents in 1980 to combat the assassination of Central American union organizers, the NLC helped organized labor in the region survive Reagan's war, and began to concentrate its efforts on publicizing the ravages of the *maquila* system. Its 1992 report, *Paying to Lose Our Jobs* (based on an undercover operation in which NLC members posed as a small apparel company looking for an offshore opening) documented the promotional activities and the economic support (to the tune of $1 billion) offered by U.S. government agencies to induce American corporations into *maquila* production. The report was released amid widespread anxiety about a new round of domestic job losses, and its profiling on CBS's *60 Minutes,* followed by two *Nightline* programs, broke the news that U.S. taxpayers were funding, often through illegal channels, the transfer overseas of their jobs. Legislation was immediately passed to outlaw USAID from funding EPZs, and while the funding continued, the NLC's model of seeking high-level publicity for its exposés was established.

The NLC has turned to specific corporate targets. The GAP, a hugely profitable nonunion company with a progressive, hip streetwear image, was the object of a highly successful NLC campaign in 1995. Two *maquiladora* workers were featured on a national speaking tour: Judith Viera from the infamous El Mandarin plant in El Savador producing for the GAP, as well as Liz Claiborne, Eddie Bauer, J. Crew, and J.C. Penney, and Claudia Molina, from Global Fashions in Honduras. Top newspaper columnists (most notably, Bob Herbert, at the *New York Times*) were energized, and a coalition of groups, from universities, unions, human rights and consumer organizations, and churches and temples, were mobilized to pressure the Gap to remedy its labor abuses. Despite threats like the one issued by the owner of the San Marcos Free Trade Zone, former Salvadorean Army Colonel Mario Guerrero, that "blood will flow," the coalition prevailed. An agreement reached with the Gap was unprecedented, and sent a chill throughout the industry's corporate offices. Under the agreement, codes of conduct would be translated into Spanish and posted inside every factory, and independent monitors would be allowed to conduct regular inspections of labor and safety conditions.

In the summer of 1996, the NLC hit the publicity jackpot when, following Charlie Kernaghan's testimony at a Congressional hearing, TV celebrity Kathie Lee Gifford's Wal-Mart clothing line was linked to child-labor and human-rights abuses, first in Honduras, and then in New York City. Gifford's saccharine TV personality, and her precious association with childrens' charities were a perfect foil for revelations about the child labor behind her label. Gifford was caught in a media maelstrom over which she had no control until it was stage-managed by

New York's most highly paid spin publicist, Howard Rubinstein. Each step of her painful public progress was dissected in the national press and TV as it segued from fierce denial and resentment toward her accusers to slapstick self-vindication (when she started endorsing, for Kraft at the age of seventeen, she "didn't think she had to go check out the cows") to humanitarian sympathy with sweatshop workers and righteous anger at their bosses. The instant butt of jokes, and cartoons featuring "Sweatshops of the Rich and Famous," or "Tours of the Stars' Sweatshops," Gifford still took only three weeks to ascend to the saintly rank of labor crusader. Vowing to "shine a light on the cockroaches," she provided a photo-opportunity for Governor Pataki's signing of a Retailers Responsibility Bill to outlaw sweated products in New York State, testified in further congressional hearings, and co-starred in Labor Secretary Robert Reich's fashion industry summit conference in Washington in July 1996. Her decision to mandate independent monitoring for her line obliged Wal-Mart, the world's biggest retailer and seller of the Kathy Lee line, to announce new codes of conduct for all its contractors.

Michael Jordan, however, shrugged off similar challenges from reporters as Nike, with 37 percent of the $6.86 billion sneaker market with Jordan as its lead endorser, faced a barrage of media criticism over its decision to manufacture in Suharto's Indonesia. Jordan's hardboiled nonchalance was unavailable to Kathy Lee Gifford, whose public persona is based on a profile of emotional caring and empathizing. Nor did much dirt stick to the cartoon celebrities of Disney, target of the NLC's other summer campaign in Haiti, where Disney's fantasy world is embellished by Mickey Mouse and Pocahantas clothing sewn for starvation wages. Disney and other companies who use Haitian factories, like Sara Lee (owner of Hanes, L'Eggs, Bali, Playtex, and Champion) make donations to nonprofit causes to launder their public image, while employing workers who often toil for 50 straight hours and can still barely feed their families at the end of the week. The NLC's study of Disney operations in Haiti, and its subsequent reports on China and Bangladesh, nonetheless, helped to substantiate the argument that the doubling of workers's wages in these overseas apparel locations would have a negligible impact (2–3 percent) on the retail price of the clothing they help to produce. Three subsequent surveys of U.S. consumers showed that more than 78 percent of polled consumers declared they would be willing to pay up to 15–25 percent more for no-sweat clothing.[17]

Several other important organizations took their place alongside the NLC: Global Exchange, Sweatshop Watch, the Clean Clothes Campaign, Maquila Solidarity Network, Coalition for Justice in the Maquiladoras, People of Faith Network, the International Labor Rights Fund, Press for Change, Campaign for Labor Rights, STITCH, Committee in Solidarity with the People of El Salvadore (CISPES), and Vietnam Labor Watch. Grassroots workers' groups, formed by laid-off or threatened employees, like Fuerza Unita (San Antonio), La Mujer Obrera (El Paso), Thai and Latino Workers Organizing Committee (Los Angeles), and Chinese Staff and Workers Association (New York City) waged their own campaigns through community-based workers' centers in ways that have raised the local visibility of their issues.[18]

Two traditional institutions in this field also played their role: the U.S. Department of Labor, and the garment union, UNITE! (Union of Needletrades, Industrial, and Textile Employees—the merger union of the International Ladies' Garment Workers' Union (ILGWU) and Amalgamated Clothing and Textile Workers' Union (ACTWU)). While the Clinton administration power-steered the passage of NAFTA over and against the opposition of organized labor, its Secretary of Labor, Robert Reich, was a compensatory voice in his attempts to curtail domestic sweatshop practices, the first incumbent in fifty years to do so. After a decade of nonenforcement of most labor legislation, Reich's DOL revived the Hot Goods provision of the Fair Labor Standards Act, and began to prosecute companies in violation of this law against the interstate transport of sweated goods. With only 800 federal inspectors to cover the industry's 22,000 cutting and sewing jobs, *in addition* to the nation's other six million workplaces, enforcement in the fly-by-night sector was futile, and so the Department of Labor (DOL) resorted to the new strategy of naming names. In August 1995, a raid on the El Monte compound in Southern California uncovered 72 undocumented Thai workers behind barbed wire fences, locked up around the clock to produce garments for Montgomery Ward, Mervyn's, Miller's Outpost, and for sale at Nordstrom, Sears, Macy's, Hecht's, and Filenes. The shock produced by the raid afforded the DOL the public momentum to mount what would become its NO SWEAT campaign. After El Monte, Reich announced a "white list" of companies making a honest attempt to rid their labor of sweated processes. Those excluded would be publicly shamed. But, in the absence of any real political will to enforce regulations, Reich's strategy lacked teeth. Names on the DOL list barely grew from the initial thirty-six in December 1995, and a place on the list hardly guaranteed continued good conduct from any of the companies.[19] In the years since Reich left office, the DOL has made little headway, despite a slight increase in its staff of labor inspectors.

In response to the DOL list, the powerful National Retail Federation (NRF) established its own Retail Honor Roll for companies in compliance with labor laws, and launched a publicity war with the DOL, calling on Reich to "stop wasting millions of taxpayer dollars on counterproductive media witch hunts and devote his energies to enforcing the law."[20] By July 1996, the big retailers had been sufficiently embarrassed by the Kathy Lee Gifford—Wal-Mart scandal for many to participate in discussions about an industrywide effort at compliance and regulation, convened at Reich's fashion summit conference at Washington's Marymount University. On hand to showcase their own codes of conduct were most favored companies, like Levi Strauss (whose 1991 Global Sourcing and Operating Guidelines was a pioneer code of corporate standards), Nordstrom, Nicole Miller, Guess (the target of a homework exposé just one month later), Liz Claiborne, Patagonia, Kmart— "we are in a learning process." While the National Retail Federation president, Tracey Mullin defensively pointed a finger at immigration politics and organized crime, union representatives and journalists told harrowing tales about child and bonded labor in factories where management by terror is enforced. The few celebrity endorsers who attended—Gifford, Richard Simmons, Cheryl Tiegs—were greeted like social martyrs: "If you have a terrible outrage like El Monte or what Kathie Lee has gone through. . . ."

In April 1997, a presidential task force—the Apparel Industry Partnership (AIP)—reached an agreement on workplace codes of conduct. This group, which had first convened at the White House in August 1996, included UNITE, the National Consumers League, the Retail, Wholesale, and Department Store Union, the Interfaith Center on Corporate Responsibility, and Lawyers Committee for Human Rights, and also had industry representatives from Liz Claiborne, Nike, Reebok, Phillips-Van Heusen, Patagonia, and L.L. Bean. Agreements on health and safety, forced labor, child labor (banning employment under 15 years, except in certain countries) and antiharassment and nondiscriminatory practices had been reached early on. Accords were eventually reached on limited protections of the right to freedom of association and collective bargaining. Less satisfactory was the task force's acceptance of a 60-hour workweek as the industry norm—48 plus 12 hours overtime. Its recommendation of a 60-hour maximum, which could, however, be exceeded "in extraordinary business circumstances" (i.e., any rush order), and its commitment to a cap on "mandatory" overtime were both loose and imprecise gestures. In addition the agreements required only that workers are paid "at a rate at least equal to their regular hourly compensation" for overtime.

Predictably, the biggest split among the task-force participants had been over wages and the issue of independent monitoring. The labor and human-rights groups had pushed for a "basic-needs" standard for a "living wage," rather than the legal minimum wage, which in most offshore countries, is purposely set well below subsistence level in the hope of attracting foreign investment. In rejecting the pressure for a livable wage, the industry representatives also pushed for a system of "external monitoring" (as opposed to "independent monitoring") that would allow them to use large auditing companies like Ernst & Young, and PriceWaterhouseCooper to assess and adjudicate local and international standards that might apply to any area of compliance with the codes. Transnational corporate auditors would thus be playing the role hitherto pioneered by local NGOs familiar with the social and cultural conditions of peoples' working lives. Nor, since the agreements are voluntary, do they carry the threat of penalties. Elaine Bernard, director of Harvard's Trade Union Studies Program suggested that the agreements merely gave the "good housekeeping seal of approval to a 'kinder, gentler, sweatshop.'" The result was an impasse that led to the withdrawal of the labor and interfaith groups.

The AIP's monitoring arm, the Fair Labor Association, was set up without their participation and immediately garnered the reputation of being a corporate front. The companies on its board have a veto vote on all resolutions, they do not have to disclose their factory locations, and they are not obliged to employ independent monitors. To this day, the FLA has not made public any of its reports on any of the factory locations under investigation. Indeed, the FLA was effectively brokered by the legal aces of companies like Nike, desperate for the PR cover it provides. Nike would go further and outsource its PR to an NGO, the Global Alliance for Workers and Communities, which shills in the field of corporate responsibility. By the summer of 2000, Phil Knight was standing shamelessly by the side of Secretary General Kofi Annan at the launch of the UN's Global Compact, in the forefront of the fifty founding companies who had pledged to observe labor rights and environmental standards in their global business practices.[21] Nike's tactics illustrate the dangers involved in persuading corporations to self-regulate. Indeed, the move for companies to introduce codes of conduct and assume responsibility for ensuring the monitoring of their suppliers may be leading toward what Neil Kearney (General Secretary of the International Textile, Garment and Leather Workers' Federation) has described as "the privatization of the implementation of labor law." As more and more NGOs are involved in the process of monitoring, they may become a "permanent obstacle to trade union organization." Monitoring, in Kearney's view, will become "the new solidarismo" and the "new yellow unionism."[22]

Students and Labor

That corporations need such organizations is testimony to the heat they are feeling from grassroots activists. Arguably the most pressure in recent years has come from United Students Against Sweatshops (USAS). USAS focused on college licensing contracts, a $2.5 billion sector of the garment industry. Students at several key schools, beginning in the fall of 1998 at Duke University, petitioned their college presidents to establish codes of conduct governing the labor conditions under which licensed articles, bearing the college name, are manufactured. In the winter of 1998–99, the Collegiate Licensing Company (CLC), which brokered licensing agreements with colleges, asked college administrators to review and sign its own code of conduct, loosely based on the set of regulatory provisions drawn up by the AIP. The CLC code ran into student opposition for much the same reasons as the AIP had done with labor and interfaith groups. USAS was formed earlier that year and sparked a wave of activism. The national mobilization of students eventually resulted in campaigns, sit-ins, and occupations at almost 200 campuses, amid a blaze of media coverage. For the first time since the 1930s, students appeared to be turning in large numbers toward the cause of labor.[23]

At many of their campuses, students secured agreements about codes of conduct that were then undercut when administrators flocked to join the FLA. In response, USAS initiated a second round of campus campaigns in a bid to persuade college presidents to join the Workers Rights Consortium (WRC), a new organization, free of corporate influence, formed in April 2000. The WRC sponsors independent monitoring and verification of workers' complaints by local human-rights groups. To date, over 110 colleges have joined the WRC, and it has already successfully investigated, and partially resolved, workers' complaints in several key locations. Even when highly publicized investigations have little immediate material impact on the mass of workers' lives, they are important moves in the ongoing war of position with the major apparel companies. One day soon, they may serve as models of the kind of international action that is needed to address labor standards. Supporting workers' own local efforts to organize and remedy their grievances—the WRC model—may well be perceived as preferable to issuing companies with a sweat-free bill of health, as in the FLA model.[24]

The Challenge for Labor

Garment unions' power to bargain was forged in the early twentieth century. After the strikes of the female shirtwaist makers (the famous "Uprising of the Twenty Thousand") in 1909, and the male cloakmakers the following year, garment chieftains had met with labor leaders to sign the Protocols of Peace, the prototype of collective-bargaining agreements, mediated by Progressive jurist Louis Brandeis. The first step on the road to the suppression of the sweatshop, the Protocols established the preferential union shop, a fifty-hour week, wages going to arbitration, and rules against the permanent replacement of strikers. Organized labor learned that management would make big concessions in return for uninterrupted production, while the manufacturers found a way for labor to accept their coming creed of scientific management and industrial efficiency.

Thus were sown the seeds of labor-capital's social contract, conceived as the joint control of industrial democracy, governed by the modernist creed of productive efficiency, and committed to a more humane form of capitalism than that embodied by the sweatshop. In its Cold War heyday, organized labor's role in this contract was that of a powerful co-guarantor, blessed by a degree of government patronage unimaginable forty years before. The corporate breakup of that social contract, hastened on by the Reagan and Bush administrations' punitive war on the basic organizing rights of labor, hit the garment unions especially hard. ILGWU membership decreased from 457, 517 in 1969 (when 70 to 80 percent of New York factories were union shops) to less than 200,000 by the time of its 1995 merger with the ACTWU. UNITE!'s entire membership now stands at 250,000. With a employment peak of 1.45 million in 1973, domestic apparel jobs had fallen to 846,000 by 1995 (which saw a year's decline of 10 percent in the first big wave of NAFTA losses) and 523,000 by April 2002.

Industry and union endeavors to retain jobs have focused on a high-wage, high-tech, high-skill program, where Computer-Assisted Design, Point-of-Sale data, and Quick Response technologies maximize flexibility, minimize inventory, rationalize consumer preference and demand, and strengthen the capacity to deliver fashion goods. The emphasis is on craft, quality, and reliability unavailable offshore. But escalating competition in casual and sportwear lines has exacerbated the conditions under which domestic sweatshops proliferate. As a result, organized labor continues to be caught between a rock and hard place. Nonetheless, UNITE!'s own antisweatshop campaign, in partnership with the National Consumers League, has been an important source of consumer information (reminding us, for example, that "the care tag tells you how to treat the garment but not how the worker who made it was treated"). Union and nonunion workers' active role in the exposure of illegal conditions has often organized out of UNITE!'s Worker Centers in LA, New York, and San Francisco. A leading participant in the Southern California coalition that runs Sweatshop Watch, the union's connections in the industry has also been crucial to maintaining public pressure on converting retailers and manufacturers' public-image concerns into effective action. Just as important, UNITE! served as a crucible for the campus campaigns, supporting and participating in the work of United Students Against Sweatshops (USAS) from its roots in intern research and at the AFL-CIO Union Summers in 1996 and 1997.

For unions, the challenge of offshore organizing is even greater, especially when the local Maquiladora Manufacturers' Association, or its equivalent, can always produce a "company union" representative to mouth the regional benefits of outsourcing when U.S. reporters come calling. In developing countries under repressive rule, activism that calls for unionization is often less effective than appeals to international human-rights conventions. Countries like the U.S. can take the moral high ground in banning imports made with child labor, but they will not prefer nations that raise the level of labor protections. Without provision for its uneven impact, the 1993 Child Labor Deterrence Act pushed tens of thousands of children out of the formal workplace in countries like Bangladesh, exposing them to more hazardous and exploitative conditions in the informal economy. It is unthinkable that Congress would ever pass comparable legislation that rewards trading partners who are willing to strengthen core-labor rights.

More and more, unions have looked for leverage to citizens campaigns, often tied to consumer boycotts. Access to publicity can have a powerful effect in the streets, stores, and factories of the U.S., where 25 percent of the world's economic activity occurs. Yet the weapon of the consumer boycott is a controversial one for unionists who are more interested in improving work conditions than in chastising companies. However contentious, some boycotts have successfully taken their toll on the world of high fashion. PETA's (People for the Ethical Treatment of Animals) antifur campaigns had an immense impact for a while upon the furrier and animal-skin markets. So, too, groups whose image is distorted or ignored in fashion advertising often undertake a more diffuse form of boycott. The racially exclusive face of fashion and the preternaturally thin female body types favored in modeling have been heavily condemned for almost two decades now. African Americans, conscious of their consumer power, expect to see increased representation in advertising images from companies whose products they patronize.

Sometimes, the response can be quite complicated. For example, in 1994 Timberland ran some outrightly racist ads as part of an attempt to dissociate its name from the inner-city hip-hop youth who had adopted the trademark boots and outerwear. The ads contrasted an "out there" of white nature-lovers with the "out there" of freaky black club kids, making it quite clear which group Timberland favored. Hip-hop youth made a public point of continuing to wear Timberland in the aim of embarrassing a company that did not (officially) want their custom. A subsequent move on the part of the same consumers to patronize the preppy clothing of Tommy Hilfiger, Nautica, and Ralph Lauren proved that the game of tag which youth subcultures play with mainstream fashionwear is increasingly part of the business cycle. The vast sportswear profits generated by endorsers like Michael Jordan or Shaquille O'Neal, have helped to create high profile employment for dark-skinned African American male models who look athletic and defiant. Such images, presented as the epitome of beauty, are a notable breakthrough in a history of public aesthetics that has either denigrated or exploited the look and physique of black males. But controversy over these issues of representation are usually disconnected from the stories about garment-industry sweatshops.

Thus, many chapters of USAS found themselves in an uneasy relationship with antiracist student groups on campus, who often resented the massive publicity that the predominantly white USAS groups seemed to be able to generate on behalf of their concern for overseas workers of color. Conscious that USAS had garnered a reputation for evading domestic issues, and a capacity for dealing with race only at a distance, many activists sought to build better alliances without abandoning the focus on labor.[25] Some chapters, for example, expanded their activities to support labor struggles among campus workers—in janitorial and dining hall services—in local campaigns for a living wage, and for tomato workers in Florida exploited by Taco Bell—the sweatshops in the fields.

The Debate on Development

Critics of the sweatshop movement have seized on activists' white guilt to suggest that first-world standards are being imposed on countries that can ill afford them. Yet no one in their right mind expects to see EPZ workers achieve Northern Wage levels any time soon, and, who would dictate universal conduct throughout the global economy? Industrial elites and commentators from developing countries have also argued that the activists' cause is fundamentally protectionist. It is true that activists will often exploit anxiety about loss of domestic jobs in order to publicize their cause, and that this is a strategy which may play into the hands of domestic unions seeking to slow the decline of manufacturing jobs. Yet it is increasingly recognized, even within trade-unionist circles, that the interests of domestic workers are best served by pushing for labor-friendly growth in every country.

With somewhat more justice, anticolonial critics on the left have pointed out that the movement's portrayals of sweatshop workers as helpless victims of brutal labor conditions tends to reinforce degrading stereotypes of passive third-world women.[24] Much remains to be done in fully incorporating into the movement voices and arguments from the south, and not just those who speak on behalf of workers. Heather White, director of Verité, the human-rights monitoring group, points out that the place to begin is with basic worker literacy about the structure of wages, and then proceed to education in labor rights. Without this education, workers will "be overly dependent on outside auditors to initiate improvements.[27] So, too, activists need to emphasize provisions to educate workers, most often children, who are likely to be displaced from "improved" workplaces into the vastly inferior workplaces that far outnumber those in the export sector.[28]

Free-trade economists have gone further in their criticism of the movement by arguing that developing countries will forfeit their capacity to compete for jobs and investment if they have to prematurely accept increased labor costs.[29] Low-wage export sector jobs and the accompanying foreign investment, they argue, are needed in order to embark on the path toward development, and all countries pass through a low-wage phase on this path. In time, as civil society develops, wages will rise and labor standards will emerge in conformity with market forces. In the much-quoted words of Columbia economist Jeffrey Sachs, "My concern is not that there are too many sweatshops but that there are too few."

Most of the free-trader arguments appear to be bogus and can be rebutted succinctly. Governments have to guarantee to multinationals that wages will be kept low by suppressing workers' rights, such as free speech, the right to freedom of association, and the right to bargain collectively. Poverty does not preclude the entitlement to such rights; rights are not privileges that carry a price tag. Any increased costs incurred from observing these rights should not be borne by host nations, but by the multinational firms that reap vast profits from the sweatshop system. Even if the costs were passed on to consumers (a more practical assumption), there is a reasonable expectation that they could be absorbed without much pain. In a comparative study of garment production in Mexico and the U.S., economists Robert Pollin, Justine Burns, and James Heintz estimate that 100 percent wage increases for workers at all points of the production chain would still only translate into a retail hike ranging from 2 percent to 6 percent, well below the premium of 15 percent to 25 percent that surveyed U.S. consumers are willing to pay.[30]

Without the right to bargain for themselves, workers seldom achieve wage increases, and, with capital flowing unrestricted, higher living standards simply will not materialize. The record of free trade in countries hosting export industries with no links to the domestic economy is clear enough. Rising unemployment and falling wages are the result, in Central America and Asia alike. The NICs of East Asia are often cited as examples of how export jobs in garments and electronic assembly triggered higher levels of development and living standards. Yet, as Mark Levinson point out, the Asian tigers achieved economic growth through "trade protection, state controls on capital, and manipulated exchange rates."[31] The deregulated system that sustains today's global sweatshop in Asia and the Americas has no such controls, and is designed to ensure the free movement of capital after the model of Welch's barges. That is why wage levels have dropped not only in the South but in the North as well, where the slippage of labor standards, by comparison, has been much greater.

Until workers can self-organize and share in the wealth that they produce, Northern activists will have an important role to play, arguing not for Northern wage levels to be imposed on underdeveloped economies, but for workers to enjoy a living wage according to local standards of subsistence. If their efforts are perceived to fall short of the mark, or are considered insufficiently radical (cleaning up capitalism rather than rewriting its ground rules), as critics on the left have claimed, these charges are hardly new to the labor movement, which has long placed its faith and energy in building power incrementally by distributing it downward. At the other end of the power spectrum, the goal is to win a seat at the table of the world economic community, where elites from government and industry, unencumbered by labor representatives, make the key decisions about capital regulation.[32] Until that kind of top-level participation is achieved, labor and environmental standards will only get lip service. Even so, the elite consensus has eroded more rapidly than anyone could have imagined. Every strategy, tactic, campaign, and media exposure contributes to the pressure at all points in the chain: from world trade policy to international human rights, workplace regulation, labor organizing, consumer education and politics, and institutional activism. Whether using the powerful public vehicle of moral abhorrence or the power of reason to argue for rights and justice, the accomplishments of the second antisweatshop movement, in only seven years, have been immense. Public awareness has skyrocketed; corporations have scrambled for PR cover just as they have been forced into a concessionary stance; strategic legislation has been introduced; international coalitions have been formed; steps toward the establishment of a global monitoring structure have been taken; and a wide-ranging debate about the shape of world-trade agreements has begun. Though this is a movement with primarily economic goals, its social and political character has lent it an epochal profile with few rivals.

Notes

1. Jacob Riis, *How the Other Half Lives* (New York, Charles Scribner's Sons, 1890); Henry Mayhew, *London's Labor and the London Poor* (London, 1851); Leon Stein anthologises the best accounts at the time in *Out of the Sweatshop* (New York: Quadrangle, 1971).

2. Fredrick Abernathy, John Dunlop, Janice Hammond, David Weil, *A Stitch in Time: Lean Retailing and the Transformation of Manufacturing* (New York: Oxford University Press, 1999).

3. In "Back to the Sweatshop or Ahead to the Informal Sector?" Roger Waldinger and Michael Lapp argue that legally low wages are the real problem, and that the evidence for a sizeable underground sweatshop economy is inconclusive. The thesis of the "return of the sweatshop," they argue, was a convenient response to the enigma of large-scale immigration to postindustrial cities, but, in fact, these new Asian and Latino immigrants simply moved into entry-level apparel jobs vacated by white ethnics and other native-born workers. By contrast, participation in the "informal economy" is associated with higher status that comes with the ability to evade taxes and conduct off-the-book business.

4. Edna Bonacich and Richard Appelbaum, *Behind the Label: Inequality in the Los Angeles Apparel Industry* (Berkeley: University of California Press, 2000), 4.

5. Gus Tyler, *Look For the Union Label: A History of the International Ladies Garment Workers Union* (Armonk and London: M. E. Sharpe, 1995), pp. 18–30.

6. Peter Kwong, *Chinatown: Labor and Politics* (New York: Monthly Review Press, 1979); Edna Bonacich et al., eds. *Global Production: The Apparel Industry in the Pacific Rim* (Philadelphia: Temple University Press, 1994); and Paul Ong, Edna Bonacich and Lucie Cheng, eds. *The New Asian Immigration in Los Angeles and Global Restructuring* (Philadelphia: Temple University Press, 1994).

7. See Roger Waldinger, *Through the Eye of the Needle: Immigrants and Enterprise in New York's Garment Trades* (New York: New York University Press, 1986); and Nancy Green, *Ready-To-Wear and Ready-To-Work: A Century of Industry and Immigrants in Paris and New York* (Durham: Duke University Press, 1997).

8. For trade history, see José de la Torre, *Clothing-Industry Adjustment in Developed Countries* (New York, St. Martin's Press, 1986); Joseph Grunwald and Kenneth Flamm, *The Global Factory: Foreign Assembly in International Trade* (Washington, D.C.: Brookings Institution, 1985); Fariborz Ghadar, William Davidson and Charles Feigenoff, *U.S. Industrial Competitiveness: The Case of the Textile and Apparel Industries* (New York: D. C. Heath, 1987); Kitty Dickerson, *Textiles and Apparel in the Global Economy* (Englewood Cliffs: Prentice-Hall, 1995).

9. Annie Phizacklea, *Unpacking the Fashion Industry: Gender, Racism, and Class in Production* (London: Routledge, 1990) 9.

10. Cynthia Enloe, *The Morning After: Sexual Politics at the End of the Cold War* (Berkeley: University of California Press, 1993), 102–43.

11. In *The Power to Choose: Bangladeshi Women and Labour Market Decisions in London and Dakha* (London: Verso, 2000), Naila Kabeer studies the participation of Bangladeshi women in the garment industries of Dakha, where women went out to work in the export factories, and London, where they confine themselves to homeworking. The Dakha women were migrants from rural areas where they had endured open-ended hours in farm work, pervasive parental supervision, little autonomy in personal lives, and low self-worth in general. By comparison, their experience of urban industrial employment, for all its rigors, was preferable. The women in London were subject to the moral strictures of the Bangladeshi community, largely because of racist exclusion from the mainstream economy. As a result, these women were more dependent on their family networks, and so the gender hierarchy of skilled/unskilled labor and inside/outside work were more rigidly enforced.

12. Kathy McAfee, *Storm Signals: Structural Adjustment and Development Alternatives in the Caribean* (Boston: South End Press, 1992).

13. See Naomi Klein's analysis of the brand-building economy in *No Logo: Taking Aim at the Brand Bullies* (London: HarperCollins, 2000).

14. Bonacich and Appelbaum, *Behind the Label*, 13.

15. Jeff Ballinger, "The New Free-Trade Heel: Nike's Profits Jump on the Backs of Asia's Workers," *Harper's Magazine* (August 1992)

16. B. J. Bullert, "Strategic Public Relations, Sweatshops, and the Making of a Global Movement" (Working Paper, Joan Shorenstein Center on Press, Politics, and Public Policy, Harvard University, 2000).

17. Surveys conducted for the Center for Ethical Concerns at the Marymount University (November 1995) show that two-thirds of those polled would be willing to pay more for sweat-free clothing. A 1999 poll conducted by the Program on International Policy Attitudes at the University of Maryland showed three-quarters willing to pay up to 25 percent more. The results of an NBER survey in 1999 paralleled the previous two. See Kimberly Ann Elliot and Richard Freeman, "White Hats or Don Quixotes? Human Rights Vigilantes in the Global Economy," (NBER Conference on Emerging Labor Markets, August 2000). A counter-poll commissioned by the International Mass Retail Association showed that most consumers (46 percent) blame the government's lack of regulation for exploitative labor practices, 29 percent blame the manufacturers, while only 19 percent blame the retailers.

18. Miriam Ching Yoon Louie, *Sweatshop Warriors: Immigrant Women Workers Take on the Global Factory* (Boston: South End Press, 2001).

19. According to Robert Ross, in 1957, the Wages and Hours Division of Department of Labor had one investigator for every 46,000 workers, a ratio that held up until the mid-1970s, after which it dropped systematically. By 1996, the ratio of enforcers to workers was at a low of less than one per 150,000, with less than 800 inspectors overall. While Congress mandated a slight increase shortly thereafter to 940, inertia has prevailed since then. "Sweatshop Police," *The Nation* (September 3, 2001).

20. Press release, May 20, 1996, National Retail Federation.

21. "Still Waiting For Nike to Do It" (San Francisco: Global Exchange, 2001) In 1998, Nike's CEO and founder Phillip Knight announced in a speech at the National Press Club that his company would undertake a series of reforms. Noting that the controversy over sweatshop conditions had made his company's products "synonymous with slave wages, forced overtime and arbitrary abuse," he announced that Nike would adopt new labor policies on health and safety, child labor, independent monitoring, among other issues. Knight later described the speech as a "watershed event" that signaled a "sea change in the company culture." Yet a 2001 report by the international human-rights organization Global Exchange shows that workers making Nike products are still forced to work excessive hours, are not paid enough to meet the most basic needs of their children, and are subject to harassment, dismissal, and violent intimidation if they try to form unions or tell journalists about labor abuses in their workplace.

22. Kearney's comments are quoted in Harvard Trade Union Program's Report and Summary on a Harvard symposium in October 1998, "Global Labor Standards & the Apparel Industry: Can We Regulate Global Production?" 15.

23. See Liza Featherstone, *Students Against Sweatshops* (New York and London: Verso, 2002).

24. The Council on Economic Priorities introduced a third model code of conduct, SA 8000, which includes provisions for a living wage, and has its own accreditation agency (CPEAA).

25. See Featherstone's chapter on the politics of race within USAS *Students Against Sweatshops*, 62–68.

26. See Kabeer's critique of this tendency in *The Power to Choose*.

27. Heather White, "Educating Workers," in Archon Fung, Dara O'Rourke, and Charles Sabel, eds., *Can We Put an End to Sweatshops?* (Boston: Beacon Press, 2000), 70–72.

28. Pranab Bardhan, "Some Up, Some Down," in *Can We Put an End to Sweatshops?*, 49–53.

29. The Academic Consortium on International Trade, founded by Columbia University's Jagdish Bhagwati, is a group of prestigious free-trade economists, who formed to combat USAS influence over university administrators. Their open letter to college presidents can be found at http://www.spp.umich.edu/rsie/acit/. Their claims were combated by a counter-group, Scholars Against Sweatshop Labor, formed by Robert Pollin and James Galbraith. See http://www.umass.edu/peri/sweat.html

30. Robert Pollin, Justine Burns, and James Heintz, "Global Apparel Production and Sweatshop Labor: Can Raising Retail Prices Finance Living Wages?" Working Paper, Political Economic Research Institute (UMass, Amherst: June 2001). See http://www.umass.edu/peri/ sweat.html

31. Mark Levinson, "Economists and Sweatshops," Volume 44, Issue 4, *Dissent* (fall 1997), 11–13.

32. Richard Freeman, "What Role for Labor Standards in the Global Economy?" paper, London School of Economics (November 12, 1998).

12
Students Against Sweatshops
*A History**

LIZA FEATHERSTONE

Fourteen-year-olds, from Bangladesh to the Mexican *maquila*, working four-teen-hour days, in factories that reek of toxic fumes. Young women supporting families on some twenty cents an hour. Factory managers who forbid sick workers time off to go to the doctor. Bosses in El Monte, California, and else-where, who have, quite literally, turned factories into prisons, forcibly detain-ing workers in sweatshops surrounded by barbed wire.

More and more North Americans are familiar with such images, and the bru-tality of the garment industry has even made it to primetime TV. On a recent ER episode, sweatshop workers were killed in a fire when factory owners failed to provide adequate emergency exits. Kathie Lee Gifford slave-labor jokes are fre-quent on late-night TV. Indeed, the public is so disturbed by garment-industry abuses that in a survey conducted by Marymount University, released during the 1999 Christmas holiday season, 86 percent of consumers said they would be will-ing to pay extra to ensure that their clothing wasn't made in sweatshops.[1] In malls nationwide, it's no longer unusual to overhear shoppers in front of a Gap store debating whether to go inside. "I've heard they use sweatshop labor," one will say.

The sweatshop's new visibility is due, in large part, to the efforts of the North American antisweatshop movement, a movement now led in large part by college students. Since 1997, students on more than 200 campuses have been protesting the horrifying conditions in the collegiate apparel industry, demanding better wages and working conditions for the workers who make hats and sweatshirts bearing their school logos. Antisweatshop activists, from 1999 to 2001, were the most powerful and visible progressive presence on cam-pus since the South African divestment movement in the 1980s, and even en-joyed some concrete successes. They have also pioneered a highly pragmatic model for antiglobalization activism, one in which consumer solidarity with workers means far more than a simple refusal to buy goods tainted by ex-ploitation. It represents a sustained engagement with workers and their strug-

---

*This chapter is adapted from *Students Against Sweatshops: The Making of a Movement* (New York: Verso Books, 2002).

gles, and a commitment to build lasting institutions that can use consumers' power to help workers win victories worldwide.

This student movement emerged out of nearly a decade of activism by labor, left and religious groups. The National Labor Committee (NLC), which exposed Kathie Lee Gifford's sweatshop problem, was one of the most visible of these. But immigrant women working in the U.S. garment industry were organizing in the 1980s, through groups like the New York City's Chinese Staff and Workers Association, La Mujer Obrera in Texas and California's Asian Immigrant Women Advocates. In 1990, the same year sweatshops became the NLC's signature crusade, Fuerza Unida, a group of laid-off Levi Strauss & Co. workers in San Antonio, Texas, launched a national boycott of the company, demanding a severance package and retraining, and carrying out hunger strikes and pickets.[2]

Also in 1990, the Clean Clothes Campaign—a coalition of labor, consumer, religious, human-rights, and feminist groups which began in the Netherlands—has since spread to nine other Western European countries. In California, the Coalition to Eliminate Sweatshop Conditions attempted, unsuccessfully, throughout the early 1990s to pass antisweatshop legislation (it would eventually pass in 1999). In August 1995, a particularly horrifying garment sweatshop was discovered in El Monte, California, where seventy-two Thai immigrants were forced to labor behind razor wire, under the close watch of armed guards. The Coalition formed a single organization, Sweatshop Watch, to help the El Monte workers pressure the retailers buying from that factory. Working closely with the El Monte laborers—some of whom are now labor activists—Sweatshop Watch was able to help them collect $4 million in unpaid wages, overtime, and damages.

The United Needle and Textile Workers Union (UNITE), too, was outspoken in decrying sweatshops at home and abroad, and like the other groups mentioned here, successfully used the prominence of companies to call attention to their abuses, most notably in its mid-1990s Guess Jeans campaign. All these efforts drew press attention to the plight of sweatshop workers, and to the complicity of America's favorite brands in their immiseration.

The student movement's most important antecedents were the anti-Nike campaigns of the early 1990s, begun by Jeff Ballinger, former head of the AFL-CIO's Jakarta, Indonesia, office (who went on to found Press for Change in 1998). After spending almost four years organizing workers in Indonesia, he returned to the United States in 1992 and began raising public awareness about Nike's dollar-a-day wages in that country. Ballinger's campaign drew widespread media attention, and groups like Global Exchange, the National Labor Committee, and the People of Faith Network began anti-Nike campaigns of their own. Nike's "branding" as a sweatshop employer would later have a profound influence on students, since so many schools contract with the sneaker giant to make clothing.

In this period, many U.S. high-school students began to be horrified by the stories of faraway teenagers working in extreme heat for pennies an hour and, most saliently for many, deprived of a high-school education. Sweatshops, Abby Krasner, then a senior at Brattleboro (Vermont) High School, said in 1998, are "a student issue, because these workers are our age. If they lived here [in the U.S.], they'd be in school." Through organizations ranging from the left-liberal International Student Activism Association to chapters of the National Honor Society, these early student activists—many of whom, Krasner included, would later become leaders in the college antisweat movement—wrote letters to companies and staged protests at their local Eddie Bauer and Gap outlets. In California, hundreds of high-school and college students rallied against Guess Jeans, protests made hip by the endorsement of rock band Rage Against the Machine.

Young people were outraged on the workers' behalf, but they were also moved by a sense that their own desires were being manipulated, that the glamorous advertising aimed at youth markets was a coverup meant to distract from corporate wrongdoings. "We had been told we needed to buy these clothes to be sexy, to be popular," says Evelyn Zepeda, now a Pitzer College senior active in USAS. Realizing the work conditions behind these desperately coveted labels, she says, "We felt used." The bubble economy's excessive materialism spawned a small backlash, and a dawning consciousness of the consumer's everyday complicity in systemic evils. "The system is completely dependent," observes Liana Molina, a USAS activist from Santa Clara University, "on us going out and spending money on all this crap!"

Some companies attempted to improve their images by drafting codes of conduct, in which they deplored child labor, forced labor and other atrocities. Individual codes, however, led to little more than "self-monitoring." In 1996, the Clinton Administration, along with a coalition of apparel companies, unions, and human-rights groups, responded to activist pressure and consumer outrage by creating a unified code, and a monitoring body that would purport to enforce it. This body, called the Fair Labor Association (FLA), was so thoroughly controlled by manufacturers that it would stymie any efforts at real reform, but—vintage Clinton paternalism—it was intended to calm concerned consumers and persuade them that the problem was under control.

Meanwhile, the beginnings of a new labor consciousness were emerging on U.S. campuses, as grad students organized unions, and many undergraduates were accepting internships with the AFL-CIO's Union Summer, the program AFL president John Sweeney launched in 1996 to place college students in summer jobs with unions. In this climate, some students began to research and challenge their universities' connections to apparel companies.

They began to see that if organized, college students could play an important role in antisweatshop politics. Collegiate apparel is a $2.5 billion industry; Nike alone had multimillion-dollar contracts with University of Michigan, Duke, and the University of North Carolina (UNC), as well as smaller deals with around two hundred other schools. Students at UNC began raising questions about their school's deal with Nike, while students at University of Wisconsin-Madison, a Reebok customer, began inquiring about conditions in Reebok's factories. When Reebok fought back, citing an oddly Orwellian "No Disparagement" clause in its UW contract, which apparently meant nobody at the school could criticize the company, students and faculty were enraged at the affront to academic freedom. They began a "Disparage Reebok" campaign that embarrassed the company terribly. Reebok, easily embarrassed because it advertises itself as a paragon of social responsibility, dropped the clause.[3]

But the campus movement didn't begin in earnest until summer 1997, in UNITE!'s New York City offices. Ginny Coughlin, a newly hired UNITE! organizer, asked UNITE!'s summer interns to research the connections between collegiate apparel and sweatshops for a possible campus campaign. That campaign, UNITE! organizers reasoned, could complement the union's own antisweatshop efforts. Sensing that the FLA was helping manufacturers win the public relations battle, says Alan Howard, then-assistant to the president of UNITE!, "the union, to its credit, said, 'Here's a very important base that can help us deal with this offensive.'"

The interns researched their own schools, and found that administrators were doing next to nothing to ensure that clothing bearing their logos was made under half-decent conditions. One of those interns, Tico Almeida, then an undergraduate at Duke University, returned to school that fall. There he began a campaign to pressure the administration to pass a code of conduct requiring manufacturers of Duke apparel to maintain safe, independently monitored workplaces in which workers were free to organize. Fellow Duke students were enthusiastic and began lobbying administrators aggressively. They succeeded in getting Duke to pass the code, and the victory inspired students on other campuses to begin similar campaigns. UNITE! had been discussing a campus campaign for about six months, recalls Ginny Coughlin, but Almeida "moved it in a way that no one had been capable of moving it. I was amazed."

In the spring of 1998, students founded United Students Against Sweatshops (USAS), a network of campus antisweatshop groups (which now has an office in Washington, D.C., and several full-time staff members, and is funded by unions, foundations, and individual donors). But back on campus, most of these activists had become tortuously embroiled in meetings with administrators, negotiating the particulars of their codes of conduct. Duke students once again led the way. Occupying their president's office in spring 1999, they demanded that Duke president Nan Keohane add an even more crucial clause to her 1997 code: full disclosure of licensees' factory locations—so students and other researchers could investigate schools' sweatshop problems, and make contact with workers. After a sit-in that lasted thirty-one hours, Keohane gave in. A similar occupation won students full disclosure at Georgetown. In addition to disclosure, a sit-in at Wisconsin forced a commitment to a university-sponsored living wage study; Notre Dame and several other institutions have since followed suit with similar studies.

Is this Movement Protectionist?

The UNITE! relationship has subjected USAS to some criticism that high-school students, religious groups, and other nonunion antisweatshop activists are less likely to face. Skeptics ranging from rabid free-trade evangelist Thomas Friedman to some third-world labor unionists have denounced UNITE!'s antisweatshop campaigns as protectionist, attempting to protect American jobs while jeopardizing those of workers in the third world. The student movement, because of its relationship to UNITE!, has endured this charge as well, from its earliest beginnings.

Students are sensitive to the "protectionism" charge; they go out of their way to emphasize that their own position is not antitrade, and sometimes their image suffers from the union's lack of clarity on this point. Sue Casey, a University of Pennsylvania USAS activist, recalls an uncomfortable moment when a UNITE! official, presenting USAS with an award, thanked the student organization "'for helping us in our struggle *against imports*." Since USAS goes out of its way not to take protectionist positions, Casey says, "that really stunk."

UNITE has engaged in such anti-import rhetoric, and indeed, sometimes campaigned against lowering tariffs on imports. Defenders of this strategy argue, often persuasively, that a union is supposed to protect its own members' jobs. It has an obligation to protect the interests of its dues-paying constituents—who are, in the case of the garment workers that UNITE! represents, among the poorest workers in the U.S. labor force, and overwhelmingly black, Latina, and female. A union cannot always concern itself with the good of the entire planet, as students and religious groups are inclined to do, and at times the interests of workers in the U.S. have conflicted with those of workers in the third world. UNITE! officials also point out much of their "protectionism" has been intended to stop companies from roaming the world in search of nonunionized production-line bodies, a practice that hurts all workers. But it's become clear to many labor activists, over the past decade, that protectionism in the garment industry, one of the most mobile forms of capital, is not going to end sweatshops, not in Los Angeles, and not in Cambodia.

That's also increasingly clear to UNITE!. The union's rhetoric—and perhaps its practice—may be changing. Increasingly, because protectionism has failed—the U.S. continues to lose garment jobs to Asia despite tariffs, quotas and labor standards—UNITE's recent international efforts have emphasized solidarity with overseas organizing. The student influence here shouldn't be underestimated. "We bring a more international perspective to the labor movement," says Jackie Bray, a University of Michigan sophomore active in USAS. "Students don't have the same responsibility to membership." UNITE!'s

Ginny Coughlin agrees. "USAS has inspired us to think more globally," she said in summer of 2001, a few weeks after the union had kicked off a new anti-sweatshop initiative, the Global Justice for Garment Workers Campaign, and announced a new worldwide coalition of labor unions, religious, and human-rights groups—including USAS. Union representatives from Canada, Mexico, Thailand, Nicaragua, Hong Kong, Guatemala, Honduras and the Dominican Republic gathered in Manhattan's Judson Church, along with hundreds of UNITE! members (mostly Chinese immigrant women who work in laundries and garment factories), USAS activists from all over the country and community supporters. After labor leaders announced the beginning of the international campaign, the gathering, waving flags from around the world, assembled in the streets. Joined by several hundred more Chinese women bearing placards and parasols, the crowd marched down Broadway, despite 100-degree weather, to protest at Eddie Bauer, Banana Republic and Ann Taylor stores. The strategy, union officials explained, was to target a range of prominent retailers for the rest of the year, and see whether any of them improve workers' wages in New York City and abroad. The coalition planned to pick one particularly uncooperative company to target over the holiday season. The campaign had the strong backing of new UNITE! president Bruce Raynor, who said at Judson Church, "This isn't about protectionism. It's about improving worldwide standards." The campaign was derailed by September 11, but hopefully will endure.

Beyond "Monitoring"

Shortly after the Madison sit-in, many administrators began joining the FLA, hoping to appease students by taking some action. Students, however, scorned that organization as a corporate whitewash. They weren't alone in this assessment: Several unions and a religious group had resigned from the FLA in 1998, protesting that it was controlled by apparel companies, relied on "self-" or "voluntary" enforcement, and set no standard for a living wage. The Clinton administration tried to get USAS on board with the FLA. Gene Sperling, the president's chief economic adviser, offered to set up a monthly meeting with USAS members, but the students refused, not wanting to be used to legitimate a bogus organization. Student anger over the FLA inspired another round of sit-ins. Michigan students won full disclosure and a commitment to student input into the university's decision to join the FLA. UNC-Chapel Hill and University of Arizona students won full disclosure, and a living-wage provision in the school's code of conduct.

With these successes behind it, USAS moved on to more complicated questions. Students realized that, without a credible body to enforce them, codes of conduct were just pieces of paper. But that body had to be one that could build workers' power, rather than further erode it, as a corporate-controlled monitor might. Visiting factories and establishing relationships with workers throughout Central America and Asia, as well as working with union and living wage campaigns locally, students began to realize that unless workers have some measure of control over their own workplaces, even the nicest-sounding code of conduct is unlikely to do much good. USAS activists knew they needed to put this emerging spirit of student/labor solidarity into institutional practice. To this end, students, along with scholars, labor unions, and human-rights groups around the globe, decided to found an organization that could serve as an alternative to the FLA, one that would be free of industry influence.

The new organization, the Worker Rights Consortium (WRC) would focus on investigating worker complaints rather than certifying specific companies or factories as "sweat-free." Developing a network of workers'-rights groups in the global south, the WRC would aim to foster workers' own organizing efforts. Maria Roeper, a Haverford College student who took time off to launch the WRC, explains why it isn't much like a conventional "monitoring" agency: "The idea of 'monitoring' is in some ways disempowering to workers, like 'We're watching you.' We're not doing that. We're saying, 'What do you need?'"

In order to get the WRC off the ground, however, students would need to persuade administrators to drop out of the powerful, Nike-backed FLA, and take a gamble on their fledgling organization. At many campuses, it turned out, persuasion was not enough, and students effectively used more confrontational tactics.

"I'd Rather Go Naked . . ."

"We have the university by the balls," said Nati Passow, a University of Pennsylvania junior, in a meeting with his fellow antisweatshop protesters. "Whatever way we twist them is going to hurt." The skinny, long-haired and usually mild-mannered Passow was one of thirteen Penn students—the group later grew to forty—occupying the university president's office around the clock in early February 2000. The Penn students, along with hundreds of other members of USAS nationwide, were demanding that their university withdraw from the Fair Labor Association (FLA), and instead join the Worker Rights' Consortium (WRC).

At first the administration met the students with barely polite condescension. In one meeting, President Judith Rodin was accompanied by U-Penn professor Larry Gross, an earring-wearing fifty-something well-known on campus for his left-wing views, who urged the protesters to have more faith in the administration. Gross mocked the sit-in strategy, claiming he'd "been there, done that." President Rodin assured them that a task force would review the problem by February 29, and there was no way she could speed up its decision. She admonished them to "respect the process."

Watching the Penn students negotiate with their university's president, it was clear they weren't buying her spin. Like the other USAS activists protesting on campuses all over the nation, they had sat through many similar meetings—all ending in blithe assurances, and eventually, broken promises. They knew there was no reason to trust that the administration would meet one more arbitrary deadline after missing so many others—so they stayed in the office. After eight days of torture by folk-singing, acoustic guitar, recorders, tambourines and ringing cell phones, as well as a flurry of international news coverage, Judith Rodin met the protesters halfway by withdrawing from the FLA. (The institution joined the WRC the following school year.)

Penn's was just the first antisweatshop sit-in of that year. By mid-April, students at the universities of Michigan, Wisconsin, Oregon, Iowa and Kentucky, as well as SUNY-Albany, Tulane, Purdue and Macalester, had followed suit. And the sit-in wasn't the protesters' only tactic: Purdue students held an eleven-day hunger strike. Other students chose less somber gestures of dissent. In late February, the University of North Carolina's antisweatshop group, Students for Economic Justice, held a nude-optional party titled "I'd Rather Go Naked Than Wear Sweatshop Clothes." In late March, in an exuberant expression of the same principle, twelve Syracuse students biked across campus, 100% garment-free. The protests were a coordinated effort; members of USAS work closely with one another, a process made easier by the many listservs and Web sites that the students use to publicize actions, distribute information and help fuel turnout. Like the disclosure protests of 1999, the 2000 sit-ins were extremely focused and coordinated: While students' specific demands varied from campus to campus, all demanded that administrators join the WRC.

The WRC's code of conduct is stricter than the FLA's, including a women's rights provision, more specific language on wages and freedom of association and less wiggle room on work hours. Though WRC members are not obligated to adopt the code, many have done so, and they are obligated to, at the very least, adopt a code of their own. The WRC's participating institutions must also mandate full public disclosure of licensees' factory locations. At the time of the Penn sit-in, the FLA did not hold university members to such a requirement. Although that's changed (there's no doubt that the competition from the WRC has greatly improved the FLA), the organization still does not require disclosure from its manufacturer membership. [4]

While neither organization requires member licensees to pay a living wage, the WRC has made a commitment to define "living wage" in its code after further study. That issue has been a contentious one. Shawn MacDonald, director of accreditation for the FLA, calls the WRC's call for "study" of the issue "ironic considering so many colleges faced criticism for joining FLA and were pressured to join WRC over this very issue." But the WRC's Maria Roeper points out that the "living wage" in a particular country should be determined by the people who live there—and without some "study," it would be impossible to know what the concept means to citizens of garment-producing countries.

The FLA's structure marginalizes universities—only one university representative can serve on its board at a time—and thus is less likely than the WRC to be substantially shaped by student activist pressure. Though all such differences have been important, the most salient one—and perhaps the one least likely to change—is that the FLA's membership includes manufacturers, and the WRC's does not.

Many universities that initially rebuffed the students' entreaties to join the WRC have since backed down, a testament to the skill and energy of the student organizers. The spring 2000 wave of sit-ins was deliberately timed to precede the WRC's early April founding conference. (Before the Penn sit-in, only a handful of institutions, none of which had substantial apparel-licensing contracts, belonged to the new organization; by the end of that spring, nearly fifty had signed up.)

The WRC's founding meeting, in April 2000 at New York City's Judson Church, was attended by students or administrators from forty schools. The night before the meeting, the entire ten-school University of California system joined the organization and sent a representative to New York for the event. Some institutions joined without any building takeovers, choosing to avert bad publicity through graceful capitulation. "A lot of them joined without a sit-in because they thought there would be a sit-in the next day," says the WRC's Maria Roeper.

Indeed, student activists did manage to put administrators on the defensive. On April 7 student antisweat protesters wearing duct tape over their mouths—to protest the fact that students have no say in campus decisions—met the University of Oregon president at the airport, frightening him so badly he left the baggage claim and hid in the bathroom. The Universities of Wisconsin and Iowa sent in tear gas–wielding cops to subdue USAS activists during the WRC sit-ins, and the Madison police dragged away fifty-four students.

Recently, discussing this period, which was, at this writing in mid-2002, just over two years ago, Evelyn Zepeda said, "I remember being U-locked in the president's office. But it seems like such a long time ago. I can't believe I did that!" That sense of disconnection is understandable, because the WRC has become so effective so quickly, that it now functions more like an established NGO than the idealistic creation of a young people's protest organization. (And even most USAS chapters have had little need of confrontational protest lately, as more administrations, both out of genuine good intentions and a sense of shifting public relations imperatives, have taken the movement's demands seriously.) At this writing, 112 institutions belong, fewer than the FLA's 178,[5] but impressive for a grassroots organization with no corporate backing. It has professionalized significantly since its founding, now boasting several full-time Washington, D.C., staff, and negotiating skillfully with administrators and even apparel companies. The protest energy of students and workers lend the WRC and USAS a kind of unique power; consumers can threaten sales, while workers can threaten production. As a result, it has already managed to change work conditions, perhaps most dramatically in 2001, in a factory in the Mexican maquila.

"Sí, Se Puede!"

In January 2001, over 850 workers at Kuk-dong International Mexico, a Korean-owned garment factory in Atlixco de Puebla, went on strike when five of their co-workers were illegally fired for trying to organize an independent union. During an occupation of the factory, in which workers peacefully protested the firings, riot police violently assaulted workers. Since Kuk-dong contracts with Nike and Reebok to make sweatshirts bearing the logos of the UNC-Chapel Hill, Michigan, Oregon, and many other schools boasting active antisweatshop groups, the conflict couldn't have presented a better test case for the effectiveness of the student antisweatshop movement. The Kuk-dong struggle, said Eric Brakken in February of that year, is "the most important thing we've been a part of. If we win here, it's the beginning of a real international strategy."

Like many Mexican workers, Kuk-dong employees were at that time forced to belong to a corrupt union with close ties to management and to the local government, which pays supervisors to support it, resists dissent with brutal violence, and had never been supported by a majority of the factory's workers. The Kuk-dong workers, 90 percent of whom are young women, knew they needed a union of their own, because the union—Revolutionary Confederation of Workers and Peasants, or FCROC—had failed to respond to any of their complaints, and they were getting desperate. "From what I see, the FCROC works only for the factory," sixteen-year-old Kuk-dong worker Juana Hernandez said in an interview with USAS researchers. Alvaro Saaveda Anzures, also sixteen, agreed: "The FCROC is a union in appearance only."[6]

Wages at the factory, most workers say, are insufficient to support a single person, much less someone with children or dependents. Conditions at the factory were abominable as well; many workers accepted the job because management had promised free breakfasts and lunch, but the food Kuk-dong provided was insufficient and even worse, rancid and worm-infested. "I was sick for three days from the food I ate there," Alvaro Saavedra told USAS.[7] According to copiously sourced WRC reports–based on extensive interviews with workers and management—the Kuk-dong employees were also subjected to verbal and physical abuse, even hit with hammers and screwdrivers. The Kuk-dong factory was in clear violation, the WRC found, of the WRC's code of conduct, and those of its member universities.[8]

The workers' organizing grew out of talks with USAS activists, one of whom, David Alvarado, had been living in Puebla. The Kuk-dong workers decided to push for an independent union—an extremely bold and risky step in the *maquila*—because they knew they had powerful allies in USAS and the WRC. When the workers went on strike, students picketed Nike stores in several cities, and on campuses nationwide, urged administrators to pressure Nike and Reebok. After widely publicized WRC investigations (whose findings were largely confirmed by Verité, a monitor hired by Nike and Reebok), local media coverage and agitation from students, university administrators, and labor activists worldwide, Nike and Reebok intervened. Though the companies initially, of course, did nothing, eventually the sneaker titans forced Kukdong management to rehire a majority of the fired workers, including two of the union leaders, within two months of the dismissals.

Against all odds, the workers and students won. According to a WRC report released in late June 2001, their combined agitation had resulted in better food, wage increases for some workers, the apparent abolition of physical abuse and improved sanitary conditions. Even more surprisingly, the FCROC voluntarily left the factory that summer, management recognized that a majority of the workers support the independent union Sindicato Independiente de Trabajadoes de la Empres a Kukdong International de Mexico (SITEKIM). At USAS's instigation, U.S. Representative George Miller visited Puebla in early September 2001, and received a commitment from the governor of Puebla to grant SITEKIM official recognition. (Early USAS activist Tico Almeida was working in Miller's office and brought the situation to the congressman's attention.) SITEKIM is the first independent union in the Mexican *maquila,* and one of the few democratic unions chosen by the workers themselves. To celebrate the victory, USAS activists and Mexmode workers took a speaking tour in late November/early December of that year, which visited a dozen U.S. colleges, emphasizing the influence universities can have in improving working conditions overseas.

It is clear that Nike's interventions, though never as timely or as aggressive as workers and students would have liked, made all the difference. In response to students' exhortations not to "cut and run," both Nike and Reebok publicly committed to keeping production in Atlixco de Puebla. Of Nike's involvement, Eric Brakken of USAS said, "It's interesting, I think we've scared the fuck out of them." Like most corporate fears, however, this one needs to be constantly stoked. Throughout the fall, Nike appeared to be trying hard to extricate itself from this role, and the company placed no orders at the factory. But at the end of November, after months of student pressure, Nike sent a letter to college administrators announcing its intentions to begin contracting with the factory again in Spring 2002. Clearly workers and students will have to be willing to keep constant pressure on Nike, to ensure that the workers' don't pay for their victory with their jobs.

In March 2001, while one USAS delegation was visiting Atlixco de Puebla, another traveled to Derby—a town near Buffalo, New York—to investigate allegations of workers rights violations in the aptly-named New Era factory, which makes hats for several U.S. universities. USAS activists, interviewing some 30 workers, as well as several local officials, found that the company was responding to New Era workers' recent unionization with the Communications Workers of America (CWA) by laying off two thirds of the workforce, shifting production to its non-unionized factories and drastically cutting wages. The company, which had, during the union drive, illegally fired union leaders and threatened others with plant closings, has also failed to provide adequate compensation for its many workers who have been injured on the job. Just as Kuk-dong management justified its abuses of Mexican workers by citing the hard work and greater "efficiency" of its Indonesian workforce, New Era claimed its unionized employees in western New York weren't competitive with lower-paid workers in Alabama or Bangladesh.[9] USAS is called on universities to use their relationship with New Era to pressure the company to stop the layoffs and wage cuts, rehire workers, and honor their freedom of association. CWA, recognizing the potential of its student allies, hired a full-time campus organizer to work on the New Era campaign. In fall 2001, workers at New Era went on strike, protesting a 30 percent pay cut and continued safety and health violations; USAS held solidarity actions on campuses nationwide.

These battles represent a profound evolution in the antisweatshop movement's approach. Appropriately, while USAS's summer 2000 conference had emphasized the movement's internal dynamics, the theme of the summer 2001 conference was "solidarity," because the organization owes its success to its evolving relationships with workers and other activists. Indeed, the future of the antisweatshop movement lies in such relationships. USAS has shown that it is possible for consumers to effectively work, not on behalf of workers, but in solidarity with their struggles.

Both the New Era and Kuk-dong struggles underscore another of the group's most promising new tendencies. Like the activists worldwide who fight neighborhood gentrification and water privatization in between World Bank meetings, USAS is learning to connect the global and the local. Corporations sure do. New Era constantly—and illegally—threatens its employees with globalization: If they make trouble, production will move elsewhere and they'll lose their jobs. Telling his employees to vote against the union, the CFO told them that the company was "going global." Longtime New Era worker Terry Hilburger told USAS investigators, "I had no idea what that meant. I thought, oh, good, we're going to get lots of orders from everywhere, lots of work in the plant. But going global meant getting workers in Bangladesh to make the caps for eighty-nine cents . . . [New Era is] making millions here, but they want more millions."[10]

USAS, along with the global peace and justice movement, is seeking a better kind of globalization. In an August 14, 2001, story on USAS's triumphs at Kuk-dong, a dulcet-voiced NPR reporter praised Nike for its role in improving the situation, and said the events showed that "globalization can be a force for positive change."[11] One doesn't have to share her excessive affection for—and trust in—transnational corporations to agree with that sentiment. Like the corporations they're fighting, USAS and its allies are "going global," working toward the internationalization of their movement. In a May Day letter from SITEKIM to USAS, workers wrote:

> We know that at times our faith is lost, but as long as we are together . . . we will give each other the spirit to move forward, because we know what we do will be good for others in any part of the world. [12]

As tends to happen in politics, the old has become new again. The international solidarity that was so central to past workers' movements and rhetoric makes more sense than ever. In speeches by labor bureaucrats and even liberal politicians like Cynthia McKinney, the phrase "workers of the world unite!" has been making a decidedly nonironic comeback. So has another venerable slogan of struggle. Capturing both the optimism and the internationalism of the antisweatshop movement, the Mexmode workers ended their May Day letter with their new union's old-time motto, now frequently heard at student, labor and immigrant rights rallies this side of the "*Sí, se puede!*"

"Beyond the Horror Stories"

Initially, the movement was driven less by the sort of solidarity described above than by students' guilty sense of distance between the sweatshop and their own world, a world of calm, leafy campuses and well-stocked shopping malls. Liana Molina grew up in El Paso, not far from the *maquiladoras* and the grinding poverty of Juarez. "You see women and children begging everywhere," she says. But her experience is unusual: most USAS activists grew up nowhere near a sweatshop. In fact, they are an unusually privileged group of people. The movement began at the country's most monied universities—in a 2001 front-page story, even the *Wall Street Journal*, a close observer of the ruling class, marvelled at the extraordinary affluence of the student body at Duke, one of the schools where USAS began.[13] In a 1999 survey for a paper by economists Richard Freeman and Kimberly Ann Elliott, researcher Peter Siu found that over a third of the USAS activists reported a family income of over $100,000, more than twice the proportion of all first-year college students with that family income. Only 8 percent of USAS activists reported a family income of less than $40,000, compared to 35 percent of first-year college students.[14] That survey is dated, especially since USAS now has chapters at many public schools, from Western Michigan University to Georgia State, and is expanding its efforts to recruit students in community colleges and other state institutions. But there's no doubt that USAS still represents an unusually affluent group.

The sweatshop issue is, in a sense, a natural one for affluent students. Like many first-world antisweatshop campaigns, the student movement arose in part out of a sense of privilege. The group was born in a period of economic prosperity, when affluent students were feeling particularly fortunate, and less worried about their careers than their predecessors in the jobless early 1990s. USAS activists attend schools whose logos convey prestige, a prestige worth defending.

Partly for this reason, many activists enter the movement believing the sweatshop an aberration in a system that otherwise works well. Though USAS's public face can look quite confrontational—students occupying administration buildings and denouncing neo-liberal economics—not all students come to antisweatshop activism with a militant outlook. One Penn freshman, a USAS member who participated in a February 2000 sit-in, earnestly described himself as a "capitalist." Few would go that far in their enthusiasm for the current economic arrangements, but in interviews, countless USAS activists, usually early on in their activism, have been quick to point out that opposition to sweatshops was "not that radical."

In a sense, they are right. Sweatshops viscerally outrage mainstream America in a way that the routine exploitation of workers employed in the legal low-wage sector does not. Andrew Ross concludes his 1997 book *No Sweat: Fashion, Free Trade and the Rights of Garment Worker* by observing a "conceptual problem" with antisweatshop activism:

> . . . the growing tendency to see sweatshops, however defined, as an especially abhorrent species of labor, and therefore in a moral class of their own . . . apart from the lawful low-wage sector, which is condoned as a result . . . The fact is that virtually every low-wage job . . . fails to provide an adequate standard of living . . . Installing proper fire exits may turn a sweatshop into a legal workplace, but it remains a low-wage atrocity.

Ross underscores the importance of re-defining

> "sweatshop" as a general description of all exploitive labor conditions. . . . Given its powerful associations with inhumane and immoral treatment, and given its current visibility, the garment sweatshop may be poised . . . to serve as the crusading vector for the labor movement as a whole.[15]

No Sweat was published the same year that antisweatshop activism hit the U.S. campus. Rather than rationalizing routine exploitation, as Ross feared, the movement seems to have radicalized people in exactly the way he hoped. "People are drawn in [to antisweatshop activism] by the horror stories," says the WRC's Maria Roeper, "but then they start seeing how the whole system works."

USAS politicizes students' humanitarian impulses. There are always students with a social conscience, who are concerned about the suffering of the poor. They volunteer in soup kitchens; some even join the Peace Corps after graduation. But in the absence of any larger activist movement, they are often powerless to fight the political and economic inequalities that cause suffering. Antisweatshop activism attracts many of the students of conscience that would, in less political times, be drawn to volunteer work, and teaches them something they might not have expected to learn. Learning to think about the "whole system," to connect the sweatshop to drilling in the Arctic Circle and privatization of education, students realize that they don't just want to "help" the less fortunate. Like the authors of the Port Huron Statement, they want to live in a more egalitarian and democratic world.

USAS involvement is thus a stepping-stone, or as many students joke, a "gateway drug," to an awareness of the exploitation in all low-wage jobs, and to labor activism at home. "If I hadn't gotten involved in the sweatshop struggle I probably wouldn't have got involved in the [campus] labor issue," says James Nussbaumer, a student at the University of Southern California. Indeed, students at the University of Tennessee, Earlham in Indiana, the University of Wisconsin, Ohio State, University of Connecticut, and numerous other institutions have been fighting for better wages and work conditions for campus workers, often helping in their union drives and working closely with them. (This sort of work actually predates USAS—the first Student Labor Action Committee was established in 1994, to support locked-out workers at the A. E. Staley Company in Decatur, Illinois—but USAS has nourished it immeasurably, raising student consciousness about labor rights, and providing both networks and momentum.) At Wesleyan, Johns Hopkins, Harvard, University of Connecticut, and elsewhere, students have staged sit-ins to urge their university administrations to stop tolerating such contractors' exploitation of workers on campus, and to pressure those companies to recognize worker-organized unions. (Students objected to illegal union-busting practices, and the failure to pay workers a living wage, among other abuses.)

Part of the reason for this evolution is that the organization has moved, through its partnerships with workers, students say, from a focus on codes of conduct to an awareness that there is no substitute for workers' own organizing efforts. Though many unions are seriously flawed in practice, no code can take the place of union representation. USAS has built strong relationships with North American unions, which have, in turn, shown remarkable dedication to the new generation. The AFL-CIO contributed some $40,000 to USAS in academic year 1999–2000, and some $50,000 the following year. Many students are taking jobs as union organizers not only during the summer but also upon graduation. (Veterans of antisweatshop campaigns also go to work for groups like STITCH and the National Labor Committee.) This postgraduate labor activism has another great advantage: it keeps veterans involved in the student movement, as they are frequently hired to coordinated student/labor alliances. Turnover is one of student activism's biggest curses, and struggles entirely confined to campus usually peter out fairly quickly, precisely because there's no way to keep graduates involved. USAS's strong relationship with U.S. unions is helping the organization build domestic solidarity, and partly explains why the group hasn't dissolved after a few significant triumphs, as the 1980s antiapartheid movement did.

USAS's 2001 summer conference, at Chicago's Loyola University, passed a resolution redefining the organization's own mission, making explicit what had been a reality for some time: USAS is a broad-based student labor solidar-ity group, no longer exclusively focused on garment exploitation in the third world. Though some observers worry that the organization is spreading itself too thin, it is a welcome evolution given the urgency of economic inequality in students' backyards, and the power they have, both to bring about small but significant reforms, and to shape public consciousness.

Is student antisweatshop activism here to stay? It's difficult to say, given the volatile state of both the left and the larger world—both far more volatile since September 11—and the ever-changing nature of student activism. But Jackie Bray—as a sophomore, a relative youngster in USAS's national leadership—is hopeful. She and her fellow activists have been working hard to recruit younger members to ensure the organization's longevity; recently, a number of high schools have even established USAS chapters. After a long conversation praising her older USAS role models—especially "mentor" Laura McSpedon, a founding USAS member who now works for Jobs With Justice—she says, "I hope in four years you'll interview some first-year student, and she'll say, 'Oh yeah, Jackie Bray. She was Okay. But what we're doing works even better.' "

Coda

In early September 2001, USAS activists all over the United States received word of SITEMEX's recognition, and cheered it, knowing that their own role in this historic workers' victory had been considerable. Meanwhile, students were launching organizing campaigns to support the workers at the New Era cap company in upstate New York, who went on strike that same month. The global economic justice movement proceeded apace: Many USAS activists were preparing to go to Washington, D.C., to protest at the IMF/World Bank meetings on September 30.

On September 11, 2001, as is well known, thousands of lives were shattered, and the global political landscape was altered in ways that may take years to fully comprehend. For months, many activists feared that North America's burgeoning anticorporate movement—indeed, all emerging forms of political dissent—would become a casualty of the terrorists. The September 30 IMF/World Bank meetings—for which Washington, D.C., police had expected some 50,000 demonstrators, from the controversial hooded Anti-Capitalist Convergence (or "Black Bloc") to the AFL-CIO—were cancelled. Most protest groups cancelled their actions, too, and not only because there were no meet-ings to oppose. At a moment of sorrow and panic, demonstrators risked being ignored—or worse, reviled as unpatriotic or insensitive to the memories of the dead. In a statement explaining their withdrawal from the protests, USAS declared September in the capital "neither the time nor the place to gather in opposition." [16]

Still, a few weeks later, chastened, but still buoyed by the Kuk-dong tri-umph, USAS resumed work on the New Era campaign. New institutions continued to join the WRC, and in November, students' spirits were lifted by learning that workers had voted to unionize at BJ&B, a factory in the Dominican Republic that makes baseball caps for many USAS schools. USAS had been supporting this campaign for years—BJ&B was one of the organization's earliest efforts at cross-border solidarity—so the victory was a profound one. Students at Harvard, Stanford, Rutgers, and elsewhere continued campus living-wage campaigns.

As the response of the United States government to the September 11 attacks grew more brutal, many students threw themselves into antiwar organizing. Groups like USAS had established such strong left-student networks—and created such a ready culture of dissent—that antiwar protest was visible on many campuses before the bombs even started falling. The new antiwar—and by this writing, Palestine solidarity—organizing was much influenced by USAS, particularly in its conviction that students could force their—often reluctant—universities to become more conscientious actors in the global economy; in that vein, campus peace activists increasingly emphasize schools' military contracts.

USAS and the larger student movement face some challenges. Prolonged war—and antiwar activism—could test the warm solidarity developed in recent years between students and labor, though students and workers alike have been working hard to prevent that. There's also the problem of finite human resources: the student movement accomplishes a lot with only a handful of core activists, and sustained opposition to war—important as that is—could drain activist attention from labor issues. That's why, Jackie Bray said at the time, "There is absolute consensus in the organization that we're sticking with labor." USAS endorses peace organizing and is part of the emerging student "peace and justice movement," but feels strongly that its strength lies in its ties to the labor movement. Says Rachel Edelman, a recent University of Michigan graduate then working full-time in the USAS office, "It is more important than ever to fight in solidarity with workers, given the conservative backlash, and the fact that so many workers are losing their jobs."

There's a danger that the triple extremities of war, terror, and recession could distract the public from capitalism's everyday inequities. On the other hand, they certainly dramatize the system's problems: every post–September 11 national burden, from economic slowdown to anthrax to Enron to fighting in Afghanistan and Iraq, is disproportionately shouldered by the American working class. Many activists say that the September 11 attacks left people ever hungrier for forward-looking, optimistic social action. The global economic justice movement in particular may stand a better chance of being heard, at a time when Americans are suddenly looking at the rest of the world and wondering, "Why do 'they' hate us?" For many, September 11 underscored the need to rethink America's role in the world, and to redress global inequality. Says Jackie Bray, "People are beginning to ask questions."

Fighting sweatshops is no longer the primary focus of student activism. At this writing, struggles over the Middle East—or, at public universities like City University of New York or University of Massachusetts, draconian budget cuts—are far more visible. Yet USAS activists have been winning victories in another workers' struggle in a factory in Indonesia. The antisweatshop movement has learned to combine the antiglobalization movement's fiesty image-targeting with old-fashioned worker militance; it's a model that could work in other industries, as some activists are beginning to realize. Students and other young consumers are working closely with migrant farm workers—among the most exploited laborers in the United States—on a Taco Bell boycott, which shows great promise. The alliance between consumers and workers is a powerful and enduring one, whose potential to threaten profits may offer the best hope for justice in this particular stage of global capitalism.

Notes

1. International Communications Research (ICR). "The Consumer and Sweatshops," Marymount University Center for Ethical Concerns, 1999.
2. Miriam Ching Yoon Louie. *Sweatshop Warriors, Immigrant Women Take on the Global Factory* (Cambridge, MA: South End Press, 2001).
3. Medea, Benjamin. "Toil and Trouble: Student Activism in the Fight Against Sweatshops." In *Campus, Inc.: Corporate Power in the Ivory Tower*, Geoffrey White with Flannery C. Hauck, eds., (Amherst, NY: Prometheus, 2000).
4. The WRC and FLA codes of conduct can be found, respectively, at *www.workersrights.org* and *fairlabor.org*.
5. *www.workersrights.org; www.fairlabor.org.*
6. Collegiate Apparel Research Initiative, *La Luche Sigue: Stories from the People of the Kukdong Factory* (July 2001).
7. *Ibid.*
8. Worker Rights Consortium, *WRC Investigation Re: Complaint Against Kuk-dong (Mexico)*, June 20, 2001; *WRC Investigation Re: Complaint Against Kuk-dong (Mexico), Preliminary Findings and Recommendations*, January 24, 2001.
9. United Students Against Sweatshops. *Money Made, Workers Forgotten: The Untold Stories of the Global Race to the Bottom in Western New York*, (Spring 2001).
10. *Ibid.*
11. Burnett, John. "All Things Considered," National Public Radio, August 14, 2001.
12. Ponce, Josefina Hernandez. "Mayday Letter of Solidarity from the Kuk-dong Workers," April 30, 2001.
13. Kaufman, Jonathan. "At Elite Universities, a Culture of Money Highlights Class Divide," *Wall Street Journal*, June 8, 2001, A1.
14. Elliott, Kimberley Ann and Richard Freeman (2000). "White Hats or Don Quixotes? Human Rights Vigilantes in the Global Economy," paper for NBER Conference on Emerging Labor Market Institutions.
15. Ross, Andrew, ed. *No Sweat: Fashion, Free Trade and the Rights of Garment Workers* (New York: Verso, 1997).
16. United Students Against Sweatshops, "Statement on September 11," September 14, 2001.

13

The Ideal Sweatshop?
*Gender and Transnational Protest**

ETHEL BROOKS
Rutgers University

On a day in late June, 1995, in Miami Beach, Florida, eighteen-year-old Judith Viera stepped up to the podium at the founding convention of UNITE!, the Union of Needletrades, Industrial, and Textile Employees, to tell her story. Viera told the delegates attending the convention: "We need your help. . . . We want to have rights where we aren't abused anymore and aren't threatened with job loss for being in the union. We want to be able to work in the day so we can go to school at night. We want the bosses to stop treating pregnant women badly."[1] Viera described her co-workers' struggles to form a union at the factory where armed guards denied entry to anyone without an identification card. The men who worked as guards, Viera said, carried out full body searches of those they did allow to enter, the majority of whom were women between the ages of fifteen and thirty years old. Viera discussed the regimen of severely limited bathroom visits and forced birth control at Mandarin International, a factory producing clothing for the U.S. market, subcontracted by companies such as the Gap, J.C. Penney, and Eddie Bauer. She also told delegates about the mass firing of more than 300 Mandarin workers and a lockout of over 5,000 garment workers at the San Marcos Free Trade Zone after their most recent attempt to form a union that was recognized by the Salvadoran Ministry of Labor.[2]

Viera's testimony about unionization struggles at Mandarin was timed strategically to coincide with the founding convention of UNITE!. Her testimony, along with that of Honduran garment worker Claudia Molina, caught the attention of labor activists and U.S. consumers. The testimonies were part of a larger campaign to push the U.S.-based retailer Gap, Inc. to take responsibility for labor violations in Central American factories producing clothing

*This chapter originally appeared as part of a special issue entitled "Sweated Labor: The Politics of Representation and Reform" in *International Labor and Working-Class History*, 61 (spring, 2002). We thank ILWCH and the author for allowing us to reprint the article.

under their brand names. Viera's and Molina's testimonies about garment work, workplace abuse, and their own position as young women of color in the new international division of labor and the widespread activism that occurred as a result of their efforts jumpstarted the transnational campaign to improve working conditions at Mandarin International. The campaign ended in the agreement between the National Labor Committee and the Gap on December 15, 1995, signed at a church in Brooklyn Heights.

The Brooklyn agreement called for a reinstatement of the fired Mandarin workers, company recognition of the union and the right to organize, and an independent monitoring group made up of nongovernmental organizations and local human rights and religious groups. The independent monitoring group, which was set up and continues to monitor the Mandarin factory, now renamed Charter,[3] was to have unlimited access to the factory and inspect the factory, verify compliance with the national labor code, and guarantee union recognition by the management.

The National Labor Committee–Gap agreement and the transnational labor rights campaign with Judith Viera and Claudia Molina at the forefront were proverbial success stories replicated in subsequent labor-rights campaigns and tours of the United States by young, women garment workers from throughout the third world.[4] This article explores the role of women in transnational labor organizing. It examines the extent to which transnational protest, based in global cities like New York, Amsterdam, and San Francisco, grants agency to women employed in garment factories throughout the world. It analyzes how the cognitive and material spaces of sites of production are transformed through their connections with other sites through flows, shifts and concentrations of capital, bodies, commodities, and, in this case, political activities. Throughout, this article examines the ways in which women garment workers, garment factories and sweatshops are employed, defined and reproduced as a category in various contexts of transnational production and protest.

Transnational production and protest, concentrated in cities from Dhaka to New York to San Salvador, reproduce categories of gender, race, class and nation that are monolithic, misogynist, and difficult for workers, consumers, and activists to contest. Garment production in sites such as Mandarin/Charter in El Salvador, Seo Fashions in New York City, or Samrana Fashions in Bangladesh, deploys local practices of patriarchy and gender exploitation in producing clothing for the world's retail outlets.[5] In international protest campaigns, these categories and practices have been challenged in transnationalized, sophisticated ways by spokespeople like Judith Viera.

Transnational organizing would appear to be an example of what Lisa Lowe describes in her work on Asian-American women's activism in the garment industry:

[In] the complex encounters between transnational capital and women within patriarchal gender structures, the very processes that produce a racialized feminized proletariat both displace traditional and national patriarchies and their defining regulations of gender, space and work, and racialize the women in relation to other racialized groups.[6]

According to Lowe, these encounters have the potential to produce "new possibilities precisely because they have led to a breakdown and reformulation of the categories of nation, race, class, and gender, and in so doing have prompted a reconceptualization of the oppositional narratives of nationalism, Marxism, and feminism." The shift toward "the transnationalization of capital is not exclusively manifested in the 'denationalization' of corporate power or the nation-state," it is also expressed in the "reorganization of oppositional interventions against capital that articulate themselves in terms and relations other than the singular 'national,' 'class,' or 'female' subject."[7] While I appreciate the challenges posed by Lowe's notion of the "reorganization" of capital, corporate power, the nation-state, and oppositional interventions, as scholars and as activists we need to interrogate the ways in which these very challenges depend on the maintenance and deployment of the boundaries of the nation-state and "singular" identities. As capital has been reorganized, it has continued to depend upon the spatial and juridical boundaries of the nation-state; as protest is reconfigured as transnational, it continues to rely upon and deploy the privileges and oppressions that go along with traditional notions of identity politics. In this way, U.S.-based (white, elite) activists, protected by laws and geography, are able to mobilize U.S.-based consumers with access to "disposable income" to boycott goods from high-profile retailers in support of the labor rights of third-world and immigrant (women) garment workers.

Questions of representation are especially important in campaigns against labor abuse in garment manufacturing, whose production regimes are based on the cross-border migration of people and capital and are closely wed to consumption, style, and the fashion industry. Protest, therefore, has to rely both on crossing borders and on making counter-images. Within these border crossings and image battles, it is important to trace the workings of gender, class, and race in the tours of the United States, in the activist campaigns, and on the shop floor. Campaigns against sweatshops and sweated labor replicate globalization from above, but are framed as a new "globalization from below." Both forms of globalization use women from the south in their production regimes of clothing and images.

This article draws upon my ethnographic fieldwork, which examines three transnationally organized movements for workers' rights in the global garment industry: (1) against poor working conditions in export-processing zones in El Salvador; (2) against the use of child labor in the Bangladesh garment industry; and (3) against immigrant sweatshops in New York City.[8] In this article, I will focus on the El Salvador case study.

While the sites of transnational labor protest campaigns range from Dhaka and San Salvador to Manhattan and Brooklyn's Sunset Park, the organizers of the campaigns are more often than not located in Midtown Manhattan, Amsterdam, and San Francisco. Since the tactics of transnational negotiations and mediations depend upon access to particular resources, like Internet connections, video hookups, and telephone wires, such access plays a key role in determining how people in particular locations participate in the protest action, and how sites of production and protest are represented in the campaigns.

Because they are conceptualized as global contestations, transnational labor campaigns tend to reproduce—discursively and materially—a split between the global and the local, between sites of consumption and sites of production. In the current political moment, some sites of politics, and some agents, have been transfigured into a universal global, while others, such as sweatshops, are represented as particular, aberrant localities of globalization. It is necessary to problematize a hegemonic meta-narrative that views globalization as finance capital, advertising and consumption and to avoid relegating production relations and local forms of contestation to mere occurrences taking place in the "other" sites of globalization.

A recent analysis in the *New York Times* of working conditions at Charter pointed out that the workers there "have coffee breaks and lunch on an outdoor terrace cafeteria. Bathrooms are unlocked, the factory is breezy and clean, and employees can complain to a board of independent monitors if they feel abused." However, Charter workers such as Abigail Martínez still face long hours, "production quotas are still high, and earnings are still not enough to live on."[9] Whereas the conditions at Mandarin International before the transnational organizing campaign and the subsequent institution of independent monitoring were represented as those of a sweatshop, how do scholars and activists address the continued long hours, high quotas and low wages that remain as part of the Mandarin/Charter success story?

The organizers of transnational labor protest borrow from the signs and symbols of advertising and public relations as well as colonialist tropes and consumption practices. While symbolic politics happens at all levels, not just in advertising, research and development and consumption practices, transnational politics have tended to draw upon and redeploy particular combinations of signs and symbols in a number of localities, from the shop floor of Mandarin International to the retail outlets of Gap.

Timothy Mitchell's discussion of "the displacements opened up by the different space of the non-West and the ways in which this space is made to appear different," is helpful here.[10] The sweatshop performs a double role of being both central to capitalist production relations in certain manufacturing sectors and incompatible with the progressive rationalization of production and the humane treatment of workers. The sweatshop serves as a site of what Mitchell calls the "constitutive outside" of capitalist modernity. Timothy

Mitchell argues with reference to modernity: "Elements that appear incompatible with what is modern, Western, or capitalist are systematically subordinated and marginalized, placed in a position outside of the unfolding of history. Yet in the very processes of their subordination and exclusion, it can be shown, such elements infiltrate and compromise that history."[11] The different space of the sweatshop within the history of a progressive, rationalized capitalism is replicated both in corporations' own narrative of their production practices and in the conceptualization of the global sweatshop held by U.S.-based consumers, scholars, and activists.

The reality of sweatshops is only realized in their staging, in their performance as such for a United States consuming audience. Before the Mandarin conflict was resolved, the staging of the factory was as a sweatshop, and since the Brooklyn resolution, its reality has been transformed, and there has been no way to address, politicize or discuss the working conditions at Mandarin/ Charter. If the conditions at Mandarin/Charter or any other garment factory cannot be contained within their framing as a conflict between protectionism and free trade or workers' rights and underdevelopment, they are simply not represented. Once the egregious abuses, such as lack of bathroom breaks and physical abuse of workers, is taken care of, U.S.-based consumers, activists, and scholars accept the continuation of long hours, low pay, and high production quotas within garment production, all of which constitute the dictionary definitions of sweated labor. We accept these conditions because they *cannot* be represented as part of the resolution of the conflict. Because the definition of the "new" sweatshop has shifted to the most egregious abuses—from physical assault to forced birth control and no bathroom breaks—these other conditions which in other times would constitute sweated labor are seen as normal parts of the day-to-day running of the global garment industry. And, as the *New York Times* article points out, "the real alternative [to such conditions] is no work."[12]

The use of symbolic politics and the representation of the sweatshop has had serious implications for the ways in which gender, as it has been articulated through and alongside race, nation and class, has been utilized and reproduced within the transnational organizing campaigns. The new international division of labor in garment production, which has been the focus of a substantial body of literature, is reproduced within transnational labor organizing campaigns. Women's bodies and relations of patriarchy have been central to garment-production regimes and their maintenance and discipline on shop floors and in corporate headquarters and public-relations firms. Garment producers conceive of women garment workers as fitting into a limited range of positions within the industry. Poor women immigrants in New York City, for example, become unique targets for employment with low pay and long hours in the city's sweated garment industry. Similarly, the bodies and testimonies of women garment workers from El Salvador, Honduras, and

Nicaragua are used to appeal to conscientious consumers as part of a larger narrative that is written by U.S. and European activists to contest globalization. Gender, race, nation, class, and locality are used as markers on both sides of transnational politics: in production regimes and in protest campaigns. We can see these dynamics clearly in the protests at and around the DINDEX factory in El Salvador.

Gender and "Collective Psychosis" at DINDEX

In November 1997 at the DINDEX factory, a *recinto fiscal* in San Salvador that produced clothing for local and international markets, more than 200 women were taken to the hospital after suffering from fainting spells, dizziness, nausea, and convulsions. The women were apparently poisoned, either by the synthetic materials they worked with, by their drinking water supply, or by carbon monoxide expelled into the air by machines inside the factory.[13] At the beginning of the DINDEX workday, around 7:30 in the morning, two women fainted and were taken to the hospital. As the morning passed, more people passed out or experienced nausea, until at around 10:30 women were falling onto the factory floor "one after the other."[14] Those showing symptoms of poisoning were taken to area hospitals in ten ambulances provided by the Red Cross and the National Civil Police, while the others left the factory in fear of being poisoned.

I was in the neighborhood of DINDEX around lunchtime on that day and saw women running down the street in groups of three or four. The streets around the factory were filled with ambulances and women running in all directions away from the factory. When I asked some of those running by what was happening, they said that everyone needed to get away from the factory because they were being poisoned by contaminated water or air inside the factory. Most of the women running from the factory were quick to mention that several of those affected by the contamination were pregnant, and that some people had passed out over a period of two weeks before that day's factory-wide poisoning. All of those with whom I spoke were heading for their homes in outlying areas of the city, hoping that they, too, would not be affected by the contamination coming from the factory.[15] Unlike the factories that are inside the walls of El Salvador's various EPZs (Export Processing Zones), DINDEX is located in the center of the city in a neighborhood dotted with several *recintos fiscales*, or bonded sites of individual export-oriented factories. Therefore the women running away did not have to pass through gates or armed guards to leave the area.[16]

The DINDEX factory's windows had been bricked over during the civil war, and there was no ventilation or air circulation within the factory, where 450 people made clothing during workdays that lasted between eight and ten hours and sometimes longer.[17] The women I stopped to speak with said that during that period, they were making underwear for the Salvadoran and Central American markets, although at other times they made clothes for the U.S. and European markets. In the midst of the poisoning, employees found out that the DINDEX managers, who had been deducting social security charges from their paychecks that were supposed to cover medical visits, emergencies, and hospitalization, had never sent the money to the national social security administration.

Therefore, the women who worked at DINDEX did not have insurance coverage for their hospitalization and subsequent treatment, despite the fact that their illnesses occurred on factory grounds and that their illness was most likely caused by hazardous working conditions.[18] Those most apparently affected by the poisoning—the first to faint and have convulsions and nausea—were pregnant women who needed to remain under observation for longer periods of time. According to news reports, most of the employees had been asking about their insurance coverage for some time. The DINDEX management told its employees that they would receive their updated insurance cards as soon as the social security administration sent them. The women who worked at DINDEX then waited weeks and months to receive insurance cards that had never been paid for by the factory.[19]

Despite the lack of insurance coverage, DINDEX employees were taken by ambulance and treated at public hospitals and clinics, while El Salvador's Minister of Health, Eduardo Interiano, threatened legal action against DINDEX in order to make the factory pay for its employees' medical treatment.[20] Interiano went on to call for the intervention of the Ministry of Labor, while the head of the Salvadoran Red Cross said "the problem had been detected a week earlier, but when it arose there had been no interest on the part of the management to solve it."[21] The police cordoned off the DINDEX factory on the afternoon of the poisoning so that the Ministry of Health could determine its causes and decide whom to charge with criminal negligence.[22]

DINDEX's owner, Américo Martínez, said that there was nothing wrong with the factory and that he had always paid for the social security benefits of his employees; the problem was that the cards arrived late. Martínez said to skeptics that he regularly drank water from the cistern, adding, "Here I am now, along with everyone from the administrative area [of the factory], and until this moment nobody has had any symptoms. The way I see it, more than anything, it was panic, a shock of nerves [among the employees]."[23] According to CISPES (Committee in Solidarity with the People of El Salvador) reports, the water in the cistern appeared dirty and was contaminated with "lead, arsenic, chromium, organochlorides, and phosphorus [and also] dead insects and other debris."[24] The filter used to clean the cistern was too small to do the job and the Ministry of Health first suspected that it was the cause of the workers' illnesses. When the test results of DINDEX's water came back from the Ministry of Health and the water was declared safe enough to drink, there was intense speculation about the cause of the accident. Public health technicians inspected the site, and found both a lack of ventilation and "only ten toilets in the factory, five for [the 504] women [who work in the factory] and five for [the fifty-four] men, in disgusting, unhealthful conditions. The ideal would be one toilet for every 25 people."[25] The gender disparities in the provision of sanitary facilities among men and women were not mentioned in the inspection report.

Katia de Ramírez, an ISSS (Salvadoran Social Security Institute, the public hospital system) doctor who treated the DINDEX workers, said: "Probably the victims inhaled carbon monoxide and approximately five people were poisoned at a low level. The rest can be explained by a convulsive neurosis, that is to say, they took on the symptoms of their co-workers."[26] What Ramírez called "the rest" received more attention than both the inhalation of monoxide and the "unhealthful conditions" of the factory. Because there was no way to determine conclusively what caused the poisoning, although the health authorities think that it was most likely carbon monoxide, the public debate about DINDEX began to focus more closely on the notion of "mass psychosis" among the workers.[27] Health Minister Interiano, said that there was no doubt that some DINDEX workers had been affected by something that had poisoned them, but that many others had generated "a neurotic attitude," at the factory. Before the tests came back from the laboratories, pointing to the cause of the fainting, Interiano stated: "It is normal that, seeing their coworkers fainting, they would feel the same, but there was a bit of an exaggeration."[28] The "exaggeration," coinciding with what Interiano called the "neurotic attitude" of the women at DINDEX, echoed the factory owner Martínez's judgment that the women had suffered from a generalized panic on the shop floor.

Aihwa Ong, in *Spirits of Resistance and Capitalist Discipline*, argues that the rash of spirit possessions and "mass hysteria" that happened among garment workers in Malaysian Free Trade Zones was a way of negotiating factory disciplinary regimes and carrying out localized struggles against male domination. Ong argues:

> The eruption of spirit possession episodes in transnational companies disclosed the anguish, resistance, and cultural struggle of some neophyte female workers. Spirit attacks were indirect retaliations against coercion and demands for justice in personal terms within the industrial milieu.

In the case of the more than 200 women at DINDEX who fainted that November morning, it is impossible to categorize their symptoms as a performance of resistance either to male domination or to factory discipline. Certainly, we can examine DINDEX in light of gendered difference in the use of the feminine forms of "workers" (*trabajadoras*), "co-workers" (*compañeras*), and "employees" (*empleadas*). The feminine form was used both by the women I interviewed who were running from the factory that morning and by official sources in the press, the Ministries of Health and Labor and the factory owner to describe those who had fainted. There were certainly men working in the factory at the time, but it is unclear as to whether any of them fell ill or were poisoned at the factory on that day. From my discussions with the DINDEX workers, there was a woman manager of the factory; they were afraid that she would shut the factory down after the negative publicity and they would be left without jobs.

The citing of those most severely affected by the poisoning as pregnant women working in the factory pointed to the particular vulnerability of mothers and mothers-to-be to the rigors of factory work. As one leading news report on the DINDEX poisoning said:

> Sources at the Salvadoran Social Security Institute stated that between 10:00 in the morning and noon they saw eighty-seven employees that were in various states of illness. Three of them were pregnant and were taken to the [maternity hospital] where it was determined that despite being in serious condition, were not at risk.[29]

Other press outlets and government officials were quick to reassure the public that the pregnant workers were not in jeopardy. The women I interviewed during the evacuation of the factory were most worried about their pregnant coworkers, saying that the pregnant women were particularly undeserving of the illnesses they had experienced on the DINDEX factory floor.

The day of mass fainting and illness among the DINDEX employees also served to draw attention to the poor working conditions inside the factory. As many people pointed out, various women at the factory had been passing out over a period of several weeks, and people had complained of headaches and numbness, which accompanied a strange odor inside the factory. One DINDEX employee, Susana Sánchez, who was being treated at a local hospital, said:

> Since last November third, many of my co-workers had been experiencing fainting spells. We did not think it was too important, although a few of them went for consultations at the [hospital], but nobody gave them a medical reason for their suffering.[30]

It was not until the majority of women in the factory began to have spells of fainting and nausea on the morning of the twelfth that any attention was paid to the situation. The main coverage of DINDEX focused on the spectacle of women fainting and being carried away in ambulances, all of which was depicted in full-page color spreads in the newspapers and extensive television reports. The press coverage of DINDEX also served to draw attention to working conditions inside the factory, and put the spotlight on conditions in the industry as a whole.

The national human-rights advocate Marina de Avilés, upon being notified of the emergency at DINDEX, immediately demanded that the Ministry of Labor pay more attention to export-oriented factories, since often they do not follow Salvadoran laws. De Avilés stated: "We [the Procaduría General de

Derechos Humanos] have a study that we will soon make public that documents the number of violations suffered by these workers, which arises as a consequence of their arduous work and makes a mockery of their labor rights." The Ministry of Labor said that the DINDEX situation was "a wake-up call for the authorities, that it is their job to carry out inspections of working conditions in these places, in this case, the Ministry of Labor, in order to take advantage of the services offered them."[31]

A number of labor violations were brought to light at DINDEX during the poisoning. First, the episodes of fainting, both before and on November eleventh, exposed the possibility of conditions existing including either contaminated water or polluted air and lack of ventilation. In fact, both health and workplace violations were discovered, although the levels of water pollution were not high enough to have caused the illnesses exhibited among the workers. The air pollution and lack of ventilation, however, were cited as the most probable causes of fainting at DINDEX, clear violations of Salvadoran health and workplace safety codes. Second, once DINDEX employees needed medical attention—either a medical check-up or hospitalization—because of the on-site illnesses experienced by so many, their uninsured status was brought to public attention.[32]

The fact that hundreds of women working at DINDEX fainted in the same morning served to call attention to their working conditions, and to their daily lives, in an unprecedented fashion. It is unclear whether there was any substantive change in conditions at DINDEX or at the other factories put under the spotlight. Significantly, however, and in an echo of Ong's analysis, because so many women were taken ill that morning, they were on the front pages of the national newspapers for several days, and, for the first time, the country's highest authorities paid attention to them, their lives, and their work at DINDEX.

On the day following the fainting, only three women remained in the hospital. The rest of the women showed up to work at DINDEX the next morning, and were met with locked doors and nobody to tell them what would happen next. I went to the factory site the next day with a group of researchers and labor activists after we were told that the DINDEX management was planning to close the factory and leave the site without notice. When we arrived at the factory at 7:00 that morning there were hundreds of people in the street outside the factory gates trying to get inside. Rumors were spreading through the group gathered outside the DINDEX gates that the owners were planning to move production to another country. Some people said that the owners were, at that moment, packing up the sewing machines to ship to another site, and that nobody would get paid for the previous two weeks of work. Several people in the group claimed to have spotted various owners and managers sneaking out of the side or back of the factory to arrange its immediate closing. As one woman told a reporter in the crowd: "We have children to feed and our work is ending. We have already met the production goals for the clothing that they asked us to sew, and we want to be paid for that."[33] The woman's statement pointed to her own and her co-workers' vulnerability, and to their dependence on the biweekly paycheck. The statement also indirectly pointed to two more labor violations, namely the system of daily production quotas and payment by piece-rate rather than by hours worked, both of which are illegal under Salvadoran labor law.

The women who fainted at DINDEX, and those who camped outside the factory the next day waiting for their jobs and their paychecks, were, in essence, contesting the everyday conditions of their working lives. Despite the earlier pronouncements by the authorities calling for widespread factory inspections and respect for labor rights in El Salvador's garment industry, the day after the poisoning, most of the DINDEX employees were faced with the loss of their jobs. Many women had no idea of where to go for answers to their questions. When we talked with the women outside the DINDEX gates about the Ministry of Labor, local labor unions, or the public defender for human rights, most people did not think that they could approach any of these people for help or advice. Many women we talked with did not realize that they had any legal right to their paycheck or to their jobs, nor did they know how to contact public offices or labor unions. Some were wary of contacting unions because they were worried about being fired or blacklisted and therefore unable to find other jobs. Others continued to be suspicious of unions because of those groups' perceived linkage to the politics of the recent civil war. Even before so many people were taken ill on the shop floor and were placed under the threat of losing their livelihood, there was little alternative for women working at DINDEX to participate or contest the politics of the workplace.

It was during that November 1997 morning when half of the women in the factory passed out that they were recognized as having a particular set of needs and rights. The day after the mass illness, when everyone was waiting outside of the factory and talking among themselves about whether they would get paid and whether they would be able to keep their jobs, their moments of fear and victimization had been transformed into contestation and extended into a longer debate. At midday, dozens of women from DINDEX took buses to the Ministry of Labor to file formal complaints about factory conditions, social security deductions, and the possibility of the factory closing down without paying its employees. Others went to meet with representatives from local unions and the Mélida Anaya Montes (MAM) women's organization, El Salvador's largest grassroots feminist activist group, to discuss alternatives for organizing. For the women working at DINDEX, the poisoning and fainting were threats to both their health and livelihood, making them more vulnerable; at the same time, those threats opened up new spaces for debate and gendered agency that were not available to them before November 11.

The aftermath of the DINDEX workers' illness and the environmental conditions in the factory was covered in the news during the following week, though it received increasingly smaller newspaper coverage until it finally died down. The owner, after being threatened with legal action, agreed to pay the workers for the weeks worked and did not shut down the factory. While his employees were filing their complaints with the Ministry of Labor and meeting unions and women's groups, the owner of the factory, Américo Martínez, issued a press statement. In the statement, Martínez said: "Tomorrow afternoon, they can pick up their paychecks corresponding to the first two weeks of November." At the same time, the Salvadoran Garment Industry Association expressed its "solidarity with the affected workers."[34] The legislative branch of the FMLN (Farabundo Marti Front for National Liberation, the former guerrilla group that now is the nation's largest opposition political party) made an official statement asking that an in-depth inquiry be carried out about the massive poisoning of the DINDEX workers, and that the factory not be closed.

DINDEX Internationally

Once women from DINDEX informed MAM about their situation, MAM sent a request to the United States–based Committee in Solidarity with the People of El Salvador (CISPES) for international solidarity action on behalf of the DINDEX workers. Within a few weeks the news of DINDEX spread among United States solidarity groups. CISPES, with support from the Campaign for Labor Rights (CLR), organized a letter-writing campaign that called for a "full investigation of violations of labor, and health and safety standards at DINDEX," insisting that the Ministry of Labor "enforce the laws to ensure that this tragedy is never repeated." CISPES's "action alert" began by talking about the worker poisoning at DINDEX and pointed out that there were "several pregnant women" who were among those taken ill. Many of the workers required "artificial respiration and cardiac massage." Two weeks after the DINDEX poisoning, CISPES stated, "at least three workers remained hospitalized."

The campaign encouraged activists to send letters to the Apparel Industry Partnership (AIP) denouncing "this gross violation of garment workers' human rights."[35] The letters told the AIP: "The global anti-sweatshop code must include the right to organize and truly independent monitoring carried out by local human rights, labor, and religious groups, following the successful model in the Mandarin factory in El Salvador."[36] The U.S. letter-writing campaign in support of the DINDEX workers could potentially provide them with solidarity and international exposure in the long run, but unfortunately the campaign did not move beyond asking for independent monitoring at DINDEX. In the case of DINDEX, after the initial furor and protests died down both nationally and internationally, the poisoned workers were forgotten. While independent monitoring can be helpful, where local and international labor laws and their guarantees of the right to organize are not carried out in practice, the call for independent monitoring served only to reinforce the earlier success story of the Gap-Mandarin campaign.

The central outcome of the Mandarin-Gap agreement was the creation of the Independent Monitoring Group of El Salvador (GMIES). For the U.S.–based activists protesting in solidarity with the DINDEX workers who were poisoned, the GMIES was a key part of the model for a successful resolution to transnational labor organizing. The call for independent monitoring and the institution of corporate codes of conduct for working conditions connected Viera and the Mandarin workers with the women poisoned at DINDEX, and was seen in the United States as a way to defend the interests of the women who worked in the export-oriented garment industry.

Back to Mandarin?

Were the interests of the women garment workers, in fact, defended in the resolution of the Gap campaign or in the DINDEX campaign? The narrative of the successful labor rights campaign, seen through the prism of these shop floors in El Salvador, has required us to view the sweatshop and women who work in the world's garment factories as the outside of normal productive relations. In order to address abusive working conditions in the world's garment factories, transnational labor organizers have participated in the staging of the sweatshop as a bounded space that can be contained and eventually eliminated through the actions of well-meaning U.S. and European consumers. In the standard conception of transnational labor campaigns, consumers and activists band together to defend workers, while hierarchical relations of class, gender, race, nation, and language within production and protest can be overlooked.

My own analysis has attempted to trouble these standard conceptions of circulation within global labor protest. My work is an attempt to take into consideration the circulation of bodies, of capital, and of performance in garment production and in the transnational labor campaign. The very story of the success of the Brooklyn agreement, the institution of independent monitoring at Mandarin, and their very position as models, failed in a number of ways. What follows is an exploration of what happened at Mandarin after the success of the 1995 campaign.

Members of the all-woman union directorate of Mandarin told me in 1997 that, although thirty-five of them were rehired and working conditions have improved, their lives have been made difficult ever since their return to the factory. They also repeatedly bring up the fact that 315 of their co-unionists were *never* rehired, either because they could not be contacted, they did not respond to ads and letters used to contact them, or there were not enough jobs open at the time of the rehiring. Those 315 women were, in fact, completely left out of the negotiations, the agreement and its success story. U.S.–based activists along with representatives from the Gap—all white, North American, and mostly men—made the decisions that resulted in the Brooklyn agreement. Women are no longer forced to take birth-control pills: However, they are still not allowed to wear makeup on the factory floor because they are told it might damage the clothing they produce.

In the end, although some working conditions improved, the very women who work at Mandarin and who took the risk of forming a union on the site have been left out of the story. From the 315 workers never rehired to the thirty-five who continue to struggle as unionists at Mandarin, isolated and ridiculed, all are forgotten casualties, denied, in one way or another, the benefits of this model of transnational labor organizing.

In my discussions with Judith Viera, she told me that she was completely aware of the ways that the success of the Mandarin campaign relied at all times on her performance and her agency during the tour of the United States. According to Viera, she was the "niño símbolo," the poster child, of the Gap campaign and as such was able to garner support from the U.S. consuming audience.[37] As an account of the NLC-Gap campaign in El Salvador shows, the success stories of transnational protest have relied on gendered, racialized exclusions, and the oppositional politics they employ parallel the very relations they are attempting to contest.

The choice to employ Judith Viera on the tour of the U.S. to tell her story was determined by the same assumption behind the employment of her coworkers at Mandarin. This assumption, drawn from a long colonial, gender, and class history, is that women of color, from the third world and from immigrant areas of U.S. cities, are most useful when carrying out the work provided to them through the benevolence of foreign capital, employers, and labor activists. The work that women do, as garment workers and as symbols for protest, is not accompanied by recognition or granting of agency in the form of epistemological and discursive control over their portrayals in the campaigns and their working conditions on the shop floors.

In the 1995 tour, garment workers themselves were ostensibly addressing and redressing problems on the shop floor and in their daily lives, and contesting the ways that femininity as a category is implemented in the production process. The tour itself was nearly immune from criticism because it was framed as a means of contesting power. The tour and the campaign certainly brought international attention to working conditions in garment factories producing for the Gap, Inc. After the resolution of the campaign, however, its long-term effects on the Mandarin shop floor were ignored. As with advertising and image-making in the fashion industry, after the hype had died down, consumers did not attempt to follow what was going on in the factory. Once they ceased to be framed in terms of the sweatshop, Mandarin, DINDEX, and Salvadoran garment workers ceased to be of interest to U.S. consumers.

We need to attempt to move between the localities of the tour and the shop floor, between sites of activism and sites of production, and between the various representations of garment workers and sweatshops. It is only through close attention to the many sites of production, consumption, and capital that we are able to see the agency of women working in garment factories throughout the world. By focusing on the sweatshop as one site of modernity's constitutive outside, we can show how it is implicated in every aspect of capitalist modernity, production practices and globalization. Without an eye to all of those sites of transnational production and protest, we cannot recognize the ways in which Judith Viera, her work, and her agency, were central to the Gap campaign in 1995. Viera was no less central, in fact, than her coworkers are to Mandarin International, women who were fired, then replaced by hundreds more seeking employment in El Salvador's Free Trade Zones. The same assumptions of women, of race, and of class that determined conditions on the shop floors of Mandarin and DINDEX determined Viera's position on the tour.

The New International Division of Labor in Context

After the Gap campaign and the institution of independent monitoring, labor activists hoped that Mandarin could serve as a replicable model for future campaigns. This hope was manifested in an unspoken conviction that women working in export-oriented industries could be best defended by local human rights and religious organizations, with the support of their counterparts in the U.S. and Europe. In El Salvador, for instance, the Ministry of Labor has been lax in carrying out inspections, defending labor rights, or supporting unionization claims in the country's Free Trade Zones and bonded areas. Since local factory owners, government officials, and transnational corporations have shown that they are often unwilling to follow local and international labor laws, Salvadoran NGOs have argued that only members of civil society, i.e., the NGOs themselves, could be trusted to defend the interests of the women garment workers. In the case of Mandarin, human-rights and religious activists formed the independent monitoring group to defend the interests of those who worked inside the factory.

Can the solution to the complexity of relations, contestations, negotiations, failures, and contingencies that have marked globalized, gendered labor relations be found in the institution of independent monitoring? How are local relations and contestations understood within the dynamics of transnational campaigns, and within the institution of independent monitoring? It is important to return to a discussion of Judith Viera's tour of the United States, and her presence at the opening convention of UNITE!. What work do her presence and her story do for United States activists and consumers, and for the success and failure of organizing efforts at Mandarin?

In transnational organizing campaigns against sweatshops, from the Kathie Lee and Gap/Mandarin campaigns, to the fainting at DINDEX and others, tactics have relied upon the circulation of stories of abuses, visions of factories, and women's bodies. The founding convention of the U.S. garment workers' union, UNITE!, which merged two U.S. unions with long histories and tainted reputations, particularly in ILGWU's case, if not ACTWU's, featured Viera and

Molina.[38] For UNITE!, Judith Viera and Claudia Molina, both as individuals and as representatives of their coworkers and co-unionists, were signifiers of the union's new commitment to shop-floor organizing instead of corporate-labor pacts and to international solidarity instead of cold-war support for U.S. foreign policy. In that one moment when Judith Viera addressed the assembled unionists, her raced, national, and gendered body stood in as a solution to the fifty-year history of US nativism and national protectionism, to gender discrimination within the labor movement, and a legacy of racial exclusion in the US labor movement.[39] Viera also served to create and perform the cognitive connections between New York City–based trade unionists, San Francisco–based corporate heads and San Salvador–based garment workers.

The tours of the United States made by Viera and Molina, and by other garment workers, have their parallels in tours of former slaves in the United States and England for the cause of the abolition of slavery. In *The Black Atlantic,* Paul Gilroy argues that, before Frederick Douglass and others like him began fashioning their own slave narratives, there was an intellectual division of labor within the abolitionist movement, with sympathetic "white commentators who articulated the metaphysical core of simple, factual slave narratives." Gilroy points out that, with the work of Douglass and others, "a new discursive economy emerges with the refusal to subordinate the particularity of the slave experience to the totalising power of universal reason held exclusively by white hands, pens, or publishing houses."[40] This notion of particularity, in this case of individual garment workers in their particular factories, has been employed in the antisweatshop movement in the name of educating consumers about the means of production of each of their clothing items. The garment workers and the factories they come from serve as particular localities of globalized capital. In each instance, each worker—nonwhite, female, exploited, and living outside centers of consumption, advertising and retail decision-making—becomes yet another example of what we—often white, consuming, activist, living in centers of consumption and retail decision-making—have to fight. The shop floor is picked up as the locality of globalization, and women workers as the (gendered, raced, classed) individuals working on the global shop floor. Judith Viera and Claudia Molina, standing up on the podium at the UNITE! founding convention, are living proof of globalization and of the triumph of capital. Their presence, their words, and their experiences are circulated within the antisweatshop movement and are essential both for the success of the individual campaigns and for reminding us why the existence of UNITE! is necessary despite the weight of its troubled history.

On the other side of the circulation of images and of bodies on the tours of the United States is Kathie Lee Gifford, whose subjectivity has been utilized both as an example of the evils of globalization and, once rehabilitated, as a paragon of caring womanhood.[41] When, in 1996, Kathie Lee Gifford was confronted by unionists and labor activists with the fact that her clothing line for

Wal-Mart was being produced under sweated conditions in New York City and Honduras, she responded by crying on her television show *Live with Regis and Kathie Lee* and proclaiming her innocence in front of the audience and viewers at home. The next day, claiming that his wife was too upset to appear in public, her husband Frank Gifford handed out envelopes containing $300 each to garment workers in Manhattan who were owed tens of thousands of dollars in back pay and overtime. Both responses were orchestrated with the help of a public relations agent hired by the couple. While Kathie Lee Gifford joined New York Governor George Pataki in creating a statewide task force to improve garment-industry conditions, the nation's media outlets marked the scandal by naming its coverage in 1996 as "the summer of the sweatshop."

Kathie Lee Gifford's white, American, caring femininity, especially when taken as a foil to her husband, Frank, whose sportscaster and ex–football player image is emblematic of raced and classed notions of American masculinity, makes her particularly easily vilified and particularly salvageable. With her husband Frank supporting and defending her, Gifford was the symbol of how ties to capital can corrupt an erstwhile good person.

Kathie Lee Gifford's race, nationality, and gender position also serve to make her stand in for well-meaning consumers caught buying clothes from sweatshops despite their best intentions. Both Gifford and U.S. consumers are guilty, it would seem, because they did not know how the clothing was made, and it is this very innocence that makes it possible for them to be saved by the simple act of changing their purchasing or subcontracting habits. Because agency, in the case of Viera and Molina, in the case of Gifford, and in the case of consumers and activists, is subsumed in the totality of the global, a victim-model dichotomy and salvation story is possible. Gifford and U.S. consumers are just as much victims of corporate greed as Judith Viera or the DINDEX workers; this victimization is the capital circulated by campaigns and women labor, spokespeople for the whole movement. Once women are cast in the role of victim, or, for that matter, model, in relation to capitalist production and consumption regimes, one wonders about the possibility of their ever reclaiming agency.

In the case of DINDEX, many of the women affected by the poisoning and by the threat of losing their jobs were doing a number of things to contest their situation. The women working at DINDEX before and after the poisoning were working long hours for their pay, and after the poisoning were organizing themselves to protect their jobs and their livelihoods. They were attempting to organize themselves in the face of possible layoffs and continued illness. At the same time, in the global (United States, global-urban) arena, a system of independent monitoring at the factory was being demanded in their name. Because independent monitoring was seen as a successful resolution to an earlier, similar, problem, it was then resuscitated as the solution to another example of abuse. The examples of sweatshop conditions at Mandarin International and

DINDEX have become particular localities within the universalistic idiom of globalization. While being seen as particular localities, they are at the same time shown to be repetitions of one another, as identical but particular sites with identical, but specific, sweatshop conditions that can be solved through identical tactics and outcomes.

Representing the Sweatshop

Many stories of successful transnational campaigns against sweatshops and the global system of subcontracting in fact reinforce the totality of globalization. Most of the DINDEX workers have long since left MAM, hundreds of workers are still killed every year because of fires and locked doors in Bangladeshi factories, and, two years after she spoke at the UNITE! convention, Judith Viera was working at a gasoline station outside of San Salvador. Long after the end of the campaigns the images of the women garment workers at their center continue to circulate in the antisweatshop movement as victims of globalization and superexploitation and as models of successful resistance against corporate domination. As models for the antisweatshop movement, however, women garment workers have not been granted the status of protesters. Within the politics of the sweatshop, the hierarchies that are a part of production regimes are both shifted and deployed for the use of protesters in North America and Europe. Garment workers and sweatshops have become part of a circulation of signs and symbols, of virtual factories and perpetual victimhood.

These transnational campaigns have been held up as models for global, woman- and worker-centered activism, while they actually have reinforced the categories of nation, race, class and gender, often reproducing the new international division of labor within the movements themselves. While women (of color, white, third world, first world, working, immigrant, Latina, Asian, African) are included, they are presented as part of spectacle, image-making, and marketing. Consumer-directed transnational protest campaigns against sweatshops would not succeed without relying on the testimony, the body and the performance, of Judith Viera, Claudia Molina, or Kathie Lee Gifford. Gender, race, nation, class, and the garment workers themselves, do the work that holds the process of transnational protest together while fields of local agency are channeled into a politics of performance.

Transnational organizing, as it has been carried out in these model campaigns that would seem to place women first, actually continues to rely on gendered and racialized hierarchies. This image-making is parallel to advertising images and to images from earlier anthropological and developmentalist discourse, cleaned up and made attractive and consumable. Even when women's participation seems open and obvious, analyses of gender and how it works with race and nation remain submerged. Certain women's bodies are used to market jeans, while others are used for protesting. Still others are used to produce the jeans and to produce the narrative of victim/model for the benefit of U.S.-based leftists.

What of the possibilities invoked by Lowe? In fact, the successes of transnational labor organizing over the past few years have not led to a breakdown and reformulation of categories of nation, race, class and gender. Their very success has relied on the maintenance and reproduction of these categories both in the campaigns and on the shop floor. My examination of transnational campaigns for labor rights, and the coalitions that they engender, raises further questions about the possibilities of "global" civil society, the centers of which are located, more often than not, in a select few of the world's global cities. It also raises questions about the possibility of creating transnational social movements able to negotiate gendered, raced, classed, and nation-based differences within and among participants in transnational efforts to widen citizenship in all sites of transnationality.

What possibilities are opened up by a focus on the sweatshop in transnational organizing? If we take as an example the summer of 1996, called the "Summer of the Sweatshop" in print and television media, we can see that the use of child labor, the setting of impossible production quotas, the underpayment of wages, body searches, women's work, forced birth control, and pregnancy testing were all part of public discourse for the first time in nearly a century. Furthermore, production practices were firmly linked to consumption practices and privileged consumers were linked to women workers struggling to survive on low wages. Gender, race, nationality, and work were united under the antisweatshop banner, and United States–based activists and consumers pushed for elimination of the worst abuses and the labor movement in the United States began to revitalize. Through the rise of what Manuel Castells calls the network society, labor activism was carried out in spaces where, through the Internet and other media, communication lines are open with the international community.[42]

What is foreclosed by the politics of the sweatshop? For one thing, sweatshop politics has not been able to address effectively activism around complicated stories that have no straightforward remedy, nor does it address the high production quotas and low earnings faced by women workers at places like Mandarin/Charter. Everyday forms of violence in garment producing sites and communities, along with everyday battles to organize women working in garment factories throughout the world, are marginalized when they cannot be represented or sold to a consuming Northern audience. Because the sweatshop in its newer and older forms is both the excess of and integral to capitalist manufacturing, it is only representable as an *other* space, and its workers as victims of excessive abuses or static models of resistance who can only be saved through the agency of those on the outside.

The transnational relies upon, reproduces, and troubles politics within the boundaries of modernity. Just as the new sweatshop is the always-outside, the elsewhere of globalization, within garment production and protest, garment workers are central both to contest and to reproduce globalization-as-empire. Sweatshops, garment workers, Export Processing Zones, and the clothes that they produce are the material of the cross-border imaginaries of global politics. The production, maintenance, and replication of globalization relies upon, uses, extracts from its others in San Salvador, Dhaka, Brooklyn, and Manhattan's Chinatown both materially and symbolically, from clothing to extracted surplus value to political mobilization to contestations of citizenship and corporate control.

Certainly, images of the sweatshop have been used to improve working conditions in the factories that are the focus of contention. While transnational activists and the antisweatshop movement are working to contest corporate hegemony, the very disruptions they engender rely upon discursive splits between globalization and particular localities, between global and other cities, between malls and Export Processing Zones, and between the stock market and the sweatshop. They rely on third-world and immigrant women's bodies, on gender, class, race, and nationalist notions of citizenship, while at the same time contesting the very deployment of those categories. This poses a dilemma for activists and scholars alike: How can women's work and spaces of production, protest, and everyday life, global and elsewhere, be reimagined? Such a reimagining would recognize the ways in which protest, production, and politics both rely upon *and* contest these cross-border imaginaries, creating openings and providing spaces for the others of global cities, while working within the borders of globalization and empire. In the current period, however, our notions of fair-labor practices have more often than not arisen out of the staging of capitalism's excess, of its others, in the form of the new, global sweatshop.

Notes

1. Muriel Cooper, "Latina Teens Air Human Cost of Greed," *AFL-CIO News,* July 31, 1995, 16.
2. See Ethel Brooks, "The Consumer's New Clothes: Global Protest, The New International Division of Labor and Women's Work in the Garment Industry" (Ph.D. Dissertation: New York University, 2000), Chapter 1, for a detailed discussion of 1995's Mandarin-Gap Campaign.
3. In order to avoid the confusion involved with having two names for the same site I will call the factory Mandarin when referring to the period before the campaign and Charter for the current period. If I am talking about the factory through both periods of time, I will refer to it as Mandarin/Charter.
4. The speaking tours of the United States by garment workers had roots in the abolitionist movement, when former slaves would provide testimony about their experiences in slavery in order to educate the (white, nonslaveholding) public. See Paul Gilroy, *The Black Atlantic* (Boston: Harvard University Press, 1993), 68–70.
5. For discussions of such gendered, raced, classed and local practices, see Aihwa Ong, *Spirits of Resistance and Capitalist Discipline* (Albany: SUNY Press, 1987); Maria Mies, *Patriarchy and Accumulation on a World Scale* (London: Zed, 1986); María-Patricia Fernandez-Kelly, *For We are Sold, I and My People: Women and Industry in Mexico's Frontier* (Albany, 1983: SUNY Press); and Sheila Rowbotham and Swasti Mitter, eds., *Dignity and Daily Bread: New Forms of Economic Organizing among Poor Women in the Third World and the First* (New York: Routledge, 1994).

6. Lisa Lowe, "Work, Immigration, Gender: The New Subjects of Cultural Politics," in Lisa Lowe and David Lloyd, *The Politics of Culture in the Shadow of Capital* (Durham: Duke University Press, 1997), 360.
7. Lowe, "Work, Immigration, Gender," 360.
8. Brooks, "The Consumer's New Clothes."
9. Leslie Kaufman and David González, "Labor Standards Clash with Global Reality," *New York Times*, April 24, 2001, A1.
10. Timothy Mitchell, "The Stage of Modernity," in Timothy Mitchell, ed., *Questions of Modernity* (Minneapolis: University of Minnesota Press, 2000), 27.
11. Timothy Mitchell, "Introduction," in Mitchell, ed., *Questions of Modernity*, xiii.
12. Kaufman and González, "Labor Standards Clash with Global Reality."
13. Author's interviews with DINDEX workers, San Salvador, November 1997. "Intoxicación Masiva," *La Prensa gráfica* (San Salvador, November 12, 1997: 4); "Intoxicación Masiva," *El Diario de Hoy* (San Salvador, November 12, 1997: 1–3); "Update: Salvadoran Workers Poisoned by Carbon Monoxide," CISPES Alert, December 8, 1997.
14. "Intoxicación masiva en maquila," *La Prensa gráfica*.
15. Interviews with DINDEX workers, San Salvador, November 1997.
16. Although the women running by were not wearing distinctive clothing or other signs that they worked in a *maquila*, they were identifiable as garment workers to my colleagues and me from the UCA. Guessing that they were garment workers, we stopped them to ask what was happening and which factory they worked for.
17. CISPES Action Alert, December 7, 1997.
18. "Trabajadoras no tenían certificados del ISSS," *La Prensa Gráfica* (San Salvador, November 12, 1997), 4.
19. "Víctimas dadas de alta," *El Diario de Hoy* (San Salvador, November 13, 1997), 6.
20. "Salud procederá legalmente contra maquiladora DINDEX," *El Diario de Hoy* (San Salvador, November 13, 1997), 6.
21. "Víctimas dadas de alta," *El Diario de Hoy*, 6.
22. "Desmayos y pánico en la factoría," *El Diario de Hoy* (San Salvador, November 12, 1997), 3.
23. "Sin conocerse causa de intoxicación," *La Prensa Gráfica* (San Salvador, November 13, 1997), 6.
24. "Salvadoran Workers Poisoned by Carbon Monoxide," CISPES Action Alert, December 8, 1997.
25. "Sin conocerse causa de intoxicación," *La Prensa Gráfica*, 6.
26. "Intoxicación masiva en maquila," *La Prensa Gráfica*, 4.
27. "Salud procederá legalmente contra maquiladora DINDEX," 6.
28. "Interiano asegura que 'hubo exageración,'" *La Prensa Gráfica* (San Salvador, November 13, 1997), 6.
29. "Trabajadores no tenían certificados del ISSS," *La Prensa Gráfica* (San Salvador, November 12, 1997), 4.
30. "Hay un olor extraño," *El Diario de Hoy* (San Salvador, November 12, 1997), 3.
31. "Salud procederá legalmente contra maquiladora DINDEX," 6.
32. Article 30, Item 10 of the Labor Code of El Salvador states: "It is prohibited that management reduce, directly or indirectly, the salaries that they pay, by either supplementing or reducing social welfare benefits that administered to their workers, except when there is legal cause." (Ricardo Mendoza Orantes, ed., *Codigo de Trabajo con Reformas Incorporadas*, República de El Salvador, 1997), 17.
33. "Víctimas dadas de alta," *El Diario de Hoy*, 6.
34. ASIC, the Spanish acronym for *Asociación Salvadoreña de la Industria de la Confección*, is the factory owners and employers association. "Piden investigar intoxicación," *El Diario de Hoy* (San Salvador, November 14, 1997), 2.
35. For a discussion of the founding of the AIP, see Brooks, "The Consumer's New Clothes," Chapter 3.
36. CISPES Action Alert, "Salvadoran Workers Poisoned by Carbon Monoxide," December 8, 1997.
37. Brooks, "The Consumer's New Clothes," 65.
38. UNITE! was founded in 1995 through the merger of the Amalgamated Clothing and Textile Workers Union (ACTWU) and the International Ladies Garment Workers' Union (ILGWU), when they faced severely dwindling membership and criticism for their brand of "business unionism" and lack of shop floor organizing.

39. It should be noted that STET instituted outreach programs in immigrant communities and backed immigration reform.

40. Gilroy, *The Black Atlantic*, 68–69. For an in-depth discussion of the antislavery debate, and its relationship to capitalism, see Thomas Bender, ed., *The Anti-Slavery Debate* (Berkeley: University of California Press, 1992).

41. See Brooks, "The Consumer's New Clothes," Chapter 3, for a discussion of Kathie Lee Gifford and the antisweatshop movement.

42. Manuel Castells, *The Rise of Network Society* (Cambridge, MA: Blackwell, 1996).

Contributor Biographies

Richard P. Appelbaum is professor of sociology and global and international studies at the University of California at Santa Barbara. He is the co-editor of *Behind the Label: Inequality in the Los Angeles Garment Industry* (2000) and has authored and edited several major works in social theory, political economy and global economics.

Xiaolan Bao is professor of history at California State University, Long Beach. Her recent publications include: *Holding Up More Than Half the Sky: Chinese Women Garment Workers in New York City, 1948–1992* (2001); and "Politicizing Motherhood: Chinese Garment Workers' Campaign for Daycare Centers in New York City, 1977–1982," in *Asian/Pacific Islander American Women: A Historical Anthology* (2003). Her research has focused on Chinese American women workers, diasporic feminism, and women's movements in China.

Daniel E. Bender is an assistant professor of history at the University of Waterloo in Ontario, Canada. His articles have appeared in *Radical History Review, International Labor and Working-Class History*, and the *Journal of Women's History*. He is the author of *Sweated Work, Weak Bodies: Anti-Sweatshop Campaigns and Languages of Labor* (2003) and is currently writing about the use of evolutionary theory to understand the effects of American industrialization, urbanization, and immigration.

Edna Bonacich is professor of sociology and ethnic studies at University of California at Riverside. She is the editor of *Global Production: The Apparel Industry in the Pacific Rim* (1994); *Behind the Label: Inequality in the Los Angeles Garment Industry* (2000) and the author of *Immigrant Entrepreneurs* (1991) among other works.

Eileen Boris, the Hull Professor of Women's Studies at the University of California, Santa Barbara, specializes in gender, race, and the welfare state. She is the author of *Home to Work: Motherhood and the Politics of Industrial Homework*, which won the 1995 Philip Taft Prize in Labor History, and co-editor of *Complicating Categories: Gender, Class, Race, and Ethnicity* (1999), *Homework: Historical and Contemporary Perspectives on Paid Labor at Home* (1989). She also has edited the Winter 2004 special issue of *The Journal of Women's History* on "Women's Labors" and is finishing a book tentatively titled *Bodies on the Job, Citizens at Work*. In her spare time, she is active in the Santa Barbara Coalition for a Living Wage and the Women's Economic Justice Project of CAUSE (Central Alliance United for a Sustainable Economy) and works for welfare rights as part of the Women's Committee of 100.

Ethel Brooks is an assistant professor of women's and gender studies and sociology at Rutgers University. Her research explores areas of critical political economy, globalization, social movements, feminist theory, comparative sociology, nationalism, urban geographies and postcolonialism, with close attention to epistemology.

Liza Featherstone writes for *The Nation, The Washington Post* and many other publications. With United Students Against Sweatshops, she is co-author of *Students Against Sweatshops*, published by Verso in 2002. Her next book, *Woman's Work*, will be about sex discrimination against Wal-Mart workers.

Nancy L. Green is Directrice d'études (Professor) at the Ecole des Hautes Etudes en Sciences sociales (Paris), where she teaches comparative immigration history. Her study of sweatshops in the garment industry appeared as *Ready-to-Wear and Ready-to-Work: A Century of Industry and Immigrants in Paris and New York* (Duke University Press, 1997) and she has published widely on French and American migration history.

Richard A. Greenwald, assistant professor of history at the United States Merchant Marine Academy, is the author of *Law and Order in Industry: The Protocols of Peace, the Triangle Fire and Industrial Democracy in the Making of Modern Labor Relations in Progressive Era New York* (2004). He is currently researching the history of American maritime labor.

Jennifer Guglielmo is assistant professor of history at Smith College. She is currently writing a book on Italian women and working-class politics in New York City, 1880–1945, and beginning research on working-class women, race, and the politics of coalition in New York City's postwar grassroots movements. She is also co-editor of *Are Italians White? How Race Is Made in America* (2003).

Peter Liebhold shares curatorial responsibilities for the manufacturing, management, iron and steel, mining, and petroleum collections of the Division of Technology, National Museum of American History, Smithsonian Institution. He has published articles on business practice, invention, management and industrial photography. He has curated several exhibitions that include *Who's in Charge: Workers and Managers in the United States, Images of Steel: 1860–1994*, and *Between a Rock and a Hard Place: A History of American Sweatshops, 1820-Present.*

Immanuel Ness is associate professor of political science at Brooklyn College, City University of New York. His research focuses on the labor movement, low-wage workers, and organizing. He is currently working on a book on organizing among new immigrant workers.

Andrew Ross is professor and director of the Program in American Studies at New York University. He is the author of several books including *No-Collar: The Humane Workplace and Its Hidden Costs*, and *The Celebration Chronicles: Life, Liberty and the Pursuit of Property Value in Disney's New Town.* He has also edited several books, including *No Sweat: Fashion, Free Trade, and the Rights of Garment Workers.*

Harry R. Rubenstein shares curatorial responsibilities for the political history, reform movements, and labor history collections of the Division of Social History, National Museum of American History, Smithsonian Institution. He is the co-author of *Design for Victory: World War II Posters on the American Home Front* and *The American Presidency: A Glorious Burden.* He has curated several exhibitions that include *Badges of Pride: Symbols and Images of American Labor, Who's in Charge: Workers and Managers in the United States*, and *Between a Rock and a Hard Place: A History of American Sweatshops, 1820–Present.*

Daniel J. Walkowitz is professor of history at New York University, where he also directs the Metropolitan Studies Program. Presently engaged in book and video projects on English country dance and the culture of liberalism in the twentieth-century United States (the video with the Smithsonian Center for Folklife), he is the author of *Working With Class: Social Workers and Politics of Middle-Class Identity* (1999).

Kenneth C. Wolensky is a historian with the Pennsylvania Historical and Museum Commission, Harrisburg. His research focuses on labor, industrial, social, and public policy history. He is co-author (with Robert and Nicole Wolensky) of *Fighting for the Union Label: The Women's Garment Industry and the ILGWU in Pennsylvania,* the first comprehensive study of the women's garment industry and its major labor union in the Keystone State. He is also a faculty member in American Studies at Penn State, Harrisburg, and co-authored *The Knox Mine Disaster.*

Index

AAMA. *See* American Apparel
    Manufacturer Association (AAMA)
Activist unions, 97–98
ACTWU. *See* Amalgamated Clothing and
    Textile Workers Union (ACTWU)
ACWA, 189
ACWU. *See* Amalgamated Clothing and
    Workers Union (ACWU)
Addams, Jane, 80
Adler, Yacob, 28
A.E. Stanley Company, 260–261
A & H Sportswear, 67
AIP. *See* Apparel Industry Partnership
    (AIP)
Alabama, 258
Almeida, Tico, 216
Amalgamated Clothing and Textile
    Workers Union (ACTWU), 107,
    169, 237, 240
Amalgamated Clothing and Workers Union
    (ACWU), 78, 84, 86, 208
Amalgamated Clothing Workers of America
    (ACWA), 189
American Apparel Manufacturer
    Association (AAMA), 63, 65, 66, 69
American College of the Applied Arts, 162
American Federal of Labor, 80
American industrial evolution
    history, 23
American sweatshop
    global and historical perspective, 1–15
Angretina, Susanna, 191
Annual Academy Awards, 158
Antisweatshop movement, 225–246
    tactics and strategies, 233–239
Anzures, Alvaro Saaveda, 256
Apparel Industry Partnership (AIP), 215,
    238, 239, 276
Apparel Industry Task Force, 135
Apparel trade
    light industrial structure, 38
Appelbaum, Richard, 153, 218, 229
Asia, 145, 148, 244
Asian Pacific American Legal Center, 69
Assembly line, 38
Atlantic Crossings, 6

Badami, Minnie, 196
Baker, Newton D., 208
Bali, 236
Ballinger, Jeff, 234, 248
Balmara, 60
Bambace, Angela, 195
Bambace, Giuseppina, 191
Bangladesh, 145, 147, 236, 247, 258
Bao Zhi Ni, 123, 124
Beniko, 60
Benjamin, Medea, 215
Benstrom, Bill, 64
Bepop Clothing, 156
Bernard, Elaine, 238
Between a Rock and a Hard Place: A History of
    Sweatshops, 1820–Present, 13, 57–73
Beverly Hills, 57
Beyer, Clara, 211
Biological competition, 24
Bisno, Abraham, 27, 30
Blair, Toni, 154
Blanck, Max, 80, 154
Blue eagles, 208–212
Bonacich, Edna, 229
Boris, Eileen, 14, 48
Brakken, Eric, 257
Brody, David, 82
Bugle Boy, 145–146, 153
Bullert, B.J., 234
B.U.M. Equipment, 146
Bum International, 60
Bunch, Lonnie, 61
Burma, 142
Burns, Justine, 243
Burton, Dan, 69
Bush administration, 240
Business services, 161
Buttoners, 120
    wages and hours, 122

Cacici, Tina, 189
Calapso, Jole, 187
California, 141
California Apparel News, 152, 158
California Department of Industrial
    Relations, 59

California Design College, 162
California Fashion Association (CFA), 63, 64, 155
California Fashion Industries, 148–149
CaliforniaMart, 159–160
Calvin Klein, 67, 216
Campaign for Labor Rights, 236
Campaigns, 203–224
Canada, 252
Cantonese
  v. Fujianese, 130–134
Capital, 38, 143
Caribbean, 144
Caribbean Basin Initiative (CBI), 232
Carole Little, 148–149
Carpenter, Jesse, 45
Cash, 123
Castells, Manuel, 39
CBI, 232
Central America, 144, 146, 151, 244
Certified public accountants, 161
CFA. *See* California Fashion Association (CFA)
Chaikin, Sol "Chick," 109
Champion, 236
Chauvin International Ltd., 146
Cheap labor, 142
Checks, 123
Cherkes, William, 94
Cherokee, 153
"Chickens in soy sauce," 127
Chile, 152
China, 24, 142, 151, 163, 234, 236
Chinatown, 170, 171
Chinatown Garment Industry Study, 119
Chinese festivals, 126
Chinese shops
  Sunset Park. *See* Sunset Park Chinese shops
Chinese Staff and Workers' Association (CSWA), 14, 139, 170, 175–176, 177
Chinese workers, 126
Ching Yoon Louie, 219
Choo, Marcia, 70
Chorus Line, Inc., 147–148
Cigar Makers' International Union, 205
CISPES. *See* Committee in Solidarity with the People of El Salvadore (CISPES)
City Girl, Inc., 156
Class, 20, 26–28, 122
  barriers, 27
CLC, 239–240
Clean Clothes Campaign, 236, 248

Cleaners
  wages and hours, 122
Clinton administration, 11, 144–145, 249, 252
Cloakmakers, 81
Cloakmakers Strike of 1910, 82
Clothing imports, 142
Clothing trade
  foreign-born labor, 20
Cloth particles, 51
Coalition for Justice in the Maquiladoras, 236
Cocoran, Tom, 84
Coffin, Judith, 48
Cohen, Ben, 84
Collegiate Licensing Company (CLC), 239–240
Committee in Solidarity with the People of El Salvadore (CISPES), 236, 276
Committee on Resolutions, 42
Commons, John R., 3, 4
Compensation
  timely payment, 129
Competition, 51, 132, 138
Conforti, Rosalie, 191
Consumers' League (New York), 30, 211
Contracting, 44–45, 174
Contractors, 45
Controversy, 62
Coocha, Anna, 191
Costa Rica, 148, 155
Cost compression, 45
Coughlin, Ginny, 250, 252
Cowie, Jefferson, 77
Crew, Spencer, 61, 66
Criminals, 95
CSWA. *See* Chinese Staff and Workers' Association (CSWA)
Cultural practices, 126
Cultural products, 157–158

Daily News (New York), 10
Darwinian evolution, 25
Davril, Paul, 155
Dayton Hudson, 213
De Avilés, Marina, 273
De Cara, Rose, 191
Degradation, 21, 25
Delfino, Albina, 197
Deng Ying Yi, 124, 128
Denning, Michael, 193
Depression, 49
De Ramírez, Katia, 272

Detection
  avoidance, 59
Development
  debate, 242–245
Diaz, Wendy, 214
Di Guglielmo, Laura, 191
Di Maggio, Margaret, 195, 196
DINDEX, 270–276
  internationally, 276–277
Dirt, 48, 51
Discriminatory treatments, 128
Disease, 48, 98
Disney, 203, 214, 226, 236
Domestic apparel industry
  imports, 107
Dominican Republic, 145, 148, 252
Douglas, Paul, 103
Drago, Dorothy, 196
Dubai, 147
Dubinsky, David, 92, 94, 96, 97, 107
Dublin, Mary, 209, 211
Duke University, 216, 239–240, 249, 250
Dust, 48, 51

East Asia, 244
Eastern-European Jews, 3, 19, 20, 23, 25,
  28, 29
Eastern Out-of-Town Department, 92
Echaveste, Maria, 63, 69
Economic competition, 23
Economic conditions, 40
Economic Development Administration
  (EDA), 104
Economics, 3–6
Ecuador, 155, 178
EDA, 104
Eisner, Michael, 226
Elliott, Kimberly Ann, 259
El Monte, California, 1, 11, 51, 57–73, 214,
  248
El Salvador, 232, 233
Ely, Richard, 23
Emancipation of women, 189
Emotions, 48
Employee health insurance, 99
Employers Mutual Protective Association,
  80
English Factory Act, 7
English tailors, 23
Enloe, Cynthia, 232
Enola Gay, 69
EPZ, 270
Ernst & Young, 238

Ethical consumption, 204–208
Ethnicity, 20
European countries, 144
Excessive hours, 51
Exertion, 48
"Exodus of children," 188
Exploiting workers, 128
Export Processing Zones (EPZ), 270

Facism, 193–197
Factory, 43–44
Fair Labor Association (FLA), 215, 226, 239,
  253, 254
Fair Labor Standards Act of 1938 (FLSA),
  10, 78, 83, 84, 203, 210
Family ties, 125
Family wages, 121
Farruggia, Angelina, 196
Fashion, 37–55, 41
Fashion Center, 177
Fashion designers, 158
Fashion Institute of Design and
  Merchandising, 162
F-40 California, 60
Featherstone, Liza, 1
Federal Industrial Commission on
  Immigration, 19
Federated Department Stores, 174
Feinstone, Morris, 27, 28
Female homeworkers, 31
Female inspectors, 30
Ferrara, Rosalina, 191
Fetter, Frank, 24
Fire hazards, 51
FLA. *See* Fair Labor Association (FLA)
Flexibility, 51
Flexible specialization, 37–55
Flood, Daniel J., 103, 105
Flood-Douglas Area Redevelopment Bill,
  104
Floor workers, 120
  wages and hours, 122
FLSA. *See* Fair Labor Standards Act of 1938
  (FLSA)
Ford, Henry, 38
Foreign, 19–37
Foreign-born labor
  clothing trade, 20
Foreperson, 120
  wages and hours, 122
Francine Browner, Inc., 155
Fraser, Steven, 84
Freeman, Richard, 259

Free trade, 2, 110
Free Trade Zone, 228
French Canadians, 23
Friedman, Thomas, 251
Fujianese
    v. Cantonese, 130–134
Furio, Colomba, 192
Fuzhou, 130–134

Gabaccia, Donna, 187
Gaeta, Tina, 186, 191
Gap, 174, 203, 214, 234, 278
Gap-Mandarin campaign, 276
Garment contract shops, 19
Garment production, 143
Garments
    mixed legacy, 227–230
Garment unions, 77
Garment work, 2
Garment workers
    classes, 102
Garment Workers' Justice Center, 177, 178
GATT. *See* General Agreement on Tariffs
    and Trade (GATT)
Geft, Liebe, 70
Gender, 28–32, 122
Gender hierarchy, 120
General Agreement on Tariffs and Trade
    (GATT), 143, 144, 212, 231
General Electric, 225
Gibson, Ted, 151
Gifford, Frank, 281
Gifford, Kathy Lee, 63, 69, 214, 235, 237,
    247, 279, 280, 281, 282
Gilroy, Paul, 280
Gingold, David, 96, 97
Giuliani, Rudolph, 218
Glass, Mitch, 149
Glenn, Susan, 122
Global American sweatshop, 6–12, 11
Global consumption
    inequalities, 8
Global Exchange, 203, 236
Globalization, 2
Globalization and worker organization
    New York City garment industry,
    169–182
Global Justice for Garment Workers
    Campaign, 252
Global production
    growth, 142–145
GMIES, 277
Godkin, E.L., 7

Gompers, Samuel, 82
Governor's Commission (New York State),
    44
Gray, Hanna, 66
Great Depression, 77, 78, 83, 91
Green, Nancy, 122
Gross, Larry, 253
Guangdong, 130–134
Guatemala, 92, 142, 145, 148, 155, 171, 232,
    252
Guerrero, Mario, 235
Guess, Inc., 141, 151–153
Guglielmo, Jennifer, 14
Guglielmo, Thomas A., 199
Gutstein, Leo, 95

Haas, Robert, 69
Haiti, 171, 232, 233, 236
Hall, Floyd, 67
Handling fee, 123
Hanes, 236
Harris, Isaac, 80
Harris, Randall, 64
Hazardous environment, 123
Heat, 138
Heintz, James, 243
Heinze, Andrew, 30
Hemmers
    wages and hours, 122
Herman, Alexis M., 11, 66, 67
Hernandez, Juana, 256
Herrick, Elinore, 211
Heyman, I. Michael, 65
Hilburger, Terry, 258
Hillman, Sidney, 78, 84, 85, 208, 210
Hine, Lewis, 207
Hobson, John, 25
Homework, 46–48
    recrudescence after World War II, 47
Honduras, 145, 148, 155, 214, 233, 252
Hong Kong, 109, 142, 143, 144, 145, 252
Hot Goods Bill, 129
Hours, 123
House of Representatives committee, 19
Hubbell, Web, 69
Hull House, 80
Hyperinnovation, 157–158

Ideal sweatshop, 265–285
ILGUW. *See* International Ladies' Garment
    Workers' Union (ILGUW)
Illness, 98
ILO, 40, 41

Immigrant Jews, 25
Immigrants, 3, 4
  poor, 21
  sick, 28–32
  undocumented, 181
Immigrant sweatshop, 26–28
Immigrant workers, 173
  Jewish, 25, 27
Immigration and Naturalization Service
  (INS), 59
Immigration quotas, 9
Immigration restrictions, 9
Imports
  domestic apparel industry, 107
Incomes, 121
  underreporting, 123
Independent Monitoring Group of El
  Salvador (GMIES), 277
India, 24, 142
Indonesia, 142, 145, 147, 171, 234
INS, 59
Inspectors, 25, 29
  vs. workers, 27
Internal Revenue Service (IRS), 129
International Labor Rights Fund, 236
International Labour Office (ILO), 40, 41
International Ladies' Garment Workers'
  Union (ILGUW), 13, 49, 80, 83, 84,
  86, 91, 94, 96–97, 104, 107, 169, 185,
  194, 212–213, 237, 240
  biennial membership, 108
  Pennsylvania, 113
  post-industrial era, 107–113
  restoration, 10
  strike of 1913, 188
  Wyoming Valley, 105
International migration, 172
Invisibility blues, 85–86
IRS, 129
Israel, 147
Italian-American women
  New York City needle trades, 185–202
Italian-American women's radicalism,
  193–197
Italians, 3, 23, 24
Italy, 187

J. Michelle, 154
Japan, 24, 142, 144
Jasukaitis, Michele, 67
J.C. Penney, 150, 228
Jewish immigrant workers, 25, 27
Jewish LA Westsiders, 57

Jews, 23
Jews' low racial status, 24
Johns, Rebecca, 213
Johnson, Hugh S., 209
Johnson, Sam, 65
Jordan, Michael, 226, 236, 242
Journalists, 1, 29
Just-in-time ordering, 41

Kane, Karen, 64, 162
Kane, Lonnie, 64, 156
Kanter, Larry, 155
Karen Kane Co., 156
Karp, Roberta, 215
Karp, Robi, 66
Kearney, Neil, 239
Kelley, Florence, 203, 205, 206, 208, 210
Kenny, Mary, 80
Keohane, Nan, 250
Kessler, Judi, 149
Klopp, Bent, 145
Kmart, 67, 69, 156, 174, 213, 228
Knight, Phil, 216, 234, 246
Knox Coal Company, 94
Konheim, Bud, 66
Korea, 109, 142, 145
Kotkin, Joel, 156
Krasner, Abby, 249
Kuk-dong International Mexico, 256
Kurtzman, Ben, 142
Kyser, Jack, 153

LA basin, 228
Labor
  challenge, 240–241
Labor conditions, 48–49
Labor costs, 163, 172
Labor laws, 37, 118, 134–136
Labor organization, 38
Labor pool, 95
Labor unions, 41
Labor violations, 274
  reporting, 129
Lamarckian evolution, 25
Lapp, Michael, 50
Latin America, 172
Laundry by Shelli Segal, 155
Laura Hyun Yi Kang, 220
Law enforcement
  Sunset Park Chinese shops, 134–136
Lawrence Strike of 1912, 188
Lax, Bernard, 154
Leader, George M., 103, 104, 105, 106

League of Women Shoppers (LWS), 211
League of Women Voters, 208
Lee, Joseph, 31, 153
Lee, Sara, 236
L'Eggs, 236
Leichter, Franz S., 49
Leisure
  emblems, 30
Leonard, Gus, 155
Leslie Faye, Inc., 92, 110
  bankruptcy, 115
  insolvency, 111
  strike, 111
Levine, Louis, 82
Levinson, Mark, 244
Levi Strauss, 67, 69, 153
Levitan, Mark, 123, 137
L.F. Sportswear, 60
Liberals, 77–90
Liberti, Frank, 196
Liebhold, Peter, 1, 13
Light, Gene, 147
Liguori, Yolanda, 196
Lii, Jane H., 117
Little, Carole, 162
Little Laura, 154
Living-room workshop, 30
Liz Claiborne, 66, 215
Logan, Karl, 162
Lombardi, Giordana, 191
Loosening regulation, 51
Los Angeles, 146, 147, 150, 151, 153
  attractions, 157
Los Angeles Times, 64, 154, 156
Los Angeles Trade-Technical College, 162
Lowe, Josephine Shaw, 205, 267
Lower East Side, 24
Low-margin operations, 45
Low pay, 51
Loyola University, 261–262
LWS, 211
Lyons, Clementine, 100

Macalester, 254
MacDonald, Shawn, 254
Machine operators, 120, 121
  wages and hours, 122
Malaysia, 8, 130–134, 142, 145
Manasurangkun, Suni, 58, 59–60
Mandarin International, 265, 266, 277–279
Manetta, Lina, 191
Manhattan's Chinatown, 118
Manufacturers, 41

Maquila Solidarity Network, 236
Maria Fose Fashion, 67
Martin, Kenneth, 148
Martin, Larry, 63, 66
Martínez, Américo, 271, 276
Mason, Lucy Randolph, 211, 212
Matheson, Bill, 97, 100, 104, 106
Matheson, Min Lurye, 97, 98, 105, 106
Mauldin Mills, 67
Mazur, Jay, 63, 66, 69, 107
McKay, George, 24, 26, 29
McSpedon, Laura, 262
Mervyn's, 60
Metchek, Ilse, 70, 155, 156
Mettler, Suzanne, 210
Mexico, 109, 141, 144, 145, 146, 147, 148,
  149, 150, 151–153, 152, 153, 154,
  155, 156, 163, 178, 247, 252
MFA, 9, 144, 231
Miami, 265
Migrations, 85–86
Migratory pattern, 109
Millan, Jose, 61, 63
Miller, Frieda, 211
Miller, George, 65
Miller, Nicole, 66
Millers Outpost, 60
60 Minutes, 235
Mirenda, Josephine, 195
Mitchell, Timothy, 268–269
Molina, Claudia, 265, 280, 282
Molina, Liana, 249, 259
Mongolia, 142
Montgomery Ward, 60
Monthly Labor Review, 85
Morality, 3–6
Moral repulsion, 2
Moral weight, 8
Morse, Barney, 159, 160
Morse, David, 160
Morse, Harvey, 160
Morse, Sidney, 159
Morse-Lebow, Susan, 160
Moss Adams, 161
Mowdy, Jeff, 155
Moynihan, Patrick, 66
Ms. Tops, 60
Mullin, Tracy, 63, 67
Multi Fiber Arrangement (MFA), 9, 144,
  231
Museum, 57–73
Museum of Tolerance, 57–73
Myers, Melanie, 150

NAFTA. *See* North American Free Trade Agreement (NAFTA)
Nation, 7
National borders, 9
National Child Labor Committee, 208
National Consumers' League (NCL), 83, 205
National Council of Jewish Women, 208
National Labor Committee, 203, 248
National Labor Committee (NLC), 235, 236
National Labor Committee-Gap agreement, 266
National Labor Relations Act of 1933 (NLRA), 84
National market
consolidate, 10
National Mobilization Against Sweatshops, 219
National Museum of American History, 61
National Organization for Public Health Nursing, 208
National Recovery Act, 47
codes, 42
National Retail Federation (NRF), 63, 65
Nautica, 242
NCL, 83, 205
Needlepoint, 98, 99, 101, 102, 104
Newcomers
opportunities, 44
New Deal, 78, 83–84, 209
codes, 49
labor laws, 203
New England textile mills, 23
New Italy, 195
New York City, 25, 92
garment industry
9/11 and aftermath, 170–171
decline, 171–172
failure explained, 176–178
globalization and worker organization, 169–182
organizing strategies, 174–176
spontaneous strike, 178–179
worker power and organizational failures, 173
Lower East Side, 19
needle trades
Italian-American women, 185–202
New York State Factory Investigating Commission, 47
New York State licensing laws, 46
New York Times, 65, 117, 185, 269

New York Women's Trade Union League (WTUL), 79–80
NGO, 214
Nicaragua, 252
Nightline, 235
Nike, 7, 203, 216, 226, 234, 236, 239, 250, 257
9/11
New York City garment industry, 170–171
NLC, 235, 236
NLRA, 84
Nongovernmental organizations (NGO), 214
Nordstrom, 66
North American Free Trade Agreement (NAFTA), 110, 141, 148, 150, 152, 155, 163, 212, 232
consequences, 149–153
Northeastern Pennsylvania Stakeholders Alliance, 111
North Korea, 142
Novak, Pearl, 112
NRF, 63, 65

Odencrantz, Louise, 188
OECD, 50
OEM, 143
Offshore production, 141–167, 142, 143
O'Neal, Shaquille, 242
"One country, two systems," 128
Ong, Aihwa, 272
On-site training, 126
Operators
wages and hours, 122
Organization for Economic Cooperation and Development (OECD), 50
Organized labor, 137
Original Equipment Manufacturing (OEM), 143
Orleck, Annelise, 190
Orsi, Robert, 198
Otis College of Art and Design, 162
Our Manager's Column, 98
Outside subcontractors, 38

Pacific Rim, 109, 147
Pakistan, 145
Passow, Nati, 253
Pataki, George, 281
Paychecks, 127
Pennsylvania anthracite region, 94–96
economic recovery efforts, 114

Pennsylvania garment factories
migration, 91–115
Pennsylvania Industrial Development
Authority (PIDA), 105, 106
Pennsylvania Power & Light, 95
Pennsylvania State University Extension
Campus
Wilkes-Barre, 102
People of Faith Network, 236
PEP, 101
Perkins, Frances, 78–79, 84, 93, 211
Perot, Ross, 153
Perspectives, 39
Peru, 152
Petras, Elizabeth McLean, 79
Philadelphia Shirtwaist Union, 80
Philippines, 145, 147, 171
Pianos, 30
Piccone, Robin, 162
PIDA, 105, 106
Piece-rate system, 121, 174
Piecework, 23
Pig market, 45
Pinchot, Gifford, 93
Piore, Michael, 51, 78
Pittston, 95
Pitzer College, 220, 249
Platinum Clothing, 162
Playtex, 236
Pocono Mountain vacation retreat, 101
Podell, Tony, 155, 156
Poles, 23
Political Education Program (PEP), 101
Pollin, Robert, 243
Polo, 153
Pomerantz, Fred, 110
Pomerantz, John, 110
Poor immigrants, 21
Pope, Jesse, 23
Portes, Alejandro, 39
Poverty, 123
Precut cloth, 19
Pressers, 121
wages and hours, 122
Press for Change, 236
Prestianni, Maria, 191
Price Club, 160
PriceWaterhouseCooper, 238
Privileges, 128
Protective tariffs, 9
Protocol of Peace, 10
Public concern, 1
Purdue, 254

Race suicide, 21, 24
Racial barriers, 27
Racial degeneration, 20, 21, 28–32
Radonphon, Maliwan, 60
Raitano, Lillie, 195
Ralph Lauren, 242
Raynor, Bruce, 6
Reagan administration, 51, 213, 235, 240
Recruitment, 127
Red scare, 193–197
Reebok, 250, 257
Reich, Robert, 66, 214, 236, 237
Reinis, Richard, 154
Reisberg, Elias, 96, 97
Retailers, 109
Richards, Jeff, 146
Rigby, David, 157
River Slope Mine, 94
Rodgers, Daniel, 6
Rodin, Judith, 253, 254
Rodriguez, Joe, 64, 151, 157
Roeper, Maria, 255, 260
Romualdi, Lucia, 195
Roosevelt, Eleanor, 209
Rosenberg, Abraham, 28
Rosenfeld, Morris, 27
Ross, Andrew, 14, 260
Rubenstein, Harry, 1, 13
Rubinstein, Howard, 236
Runaway factories, 109
Runaway shop, 85–86, 93
Russian Jews, 23

Sabel, Charles F., 37
Sachs, Jeffrey, 243
Salerno, Salvatore, 194
Samson, David, 67
Sanitation, 24
San Salvador, 268, 270
San Souci Amusement Park, 103
Satthaprasit, Rampha, 58
Schedule, 58
Schoelen, Dorothy, 162
Schools, 161–164
Scott, Allen, 157
Scottish tailors, 23
Sears, 213, 228
Seasonal fluctuation, 42
Seasonal manufacture, 41
Second industrial revolution, 38
Sentences, 59
Sicily, 187
Sick immigrants, 28–32

Sindicato Independiente de Trabajadoes de la Empres a Kukdong International de Mexico (SITEKIM), 257
Singapore, 109, 145
Sing Tao Daily, 128
SITEKIM, 257
Siu, Peter, 259
60 Minutes, 235
Sklar, Kathryn Kish, 206
Slow season, 40–43
Smith, Carol, 40
Smithsonian curators, 1, 13
Smithsonian's traveling exhibition, 57–73
Social Investment Forum, 66
Social reformers, 30
Solidarity, 218–220
Sorters, 120
Southeast Asia, 130–134
South Korea, 234
Space, 39–40, 43
Spagnoletti, Ginevre, 188, 191
Specialization, 41
Speed, 51
Sperling, Gene, 252
Sphatt, Marcus, 156
Spirits of Resistance and Capitalist Discipline, 272
Spontaneous strike
    New York City garment industry, 178–179
Sportsclothes Ltd., 142
Sportswear, 147
Squalid conditions, 49
Squillante, Anna, 191
Sri Lanka, 142, 145, 147, 171
Stench, 24
STITCH, 219, 236
Stollberg, Benjamin, 82
Storrs, Landon, 84, 211
Strike
    Leslie Faye, Inc., 111
    spontaneous
        New York City garment industry, 178–179
Students, 239–240, 247–264
Students Against Sweatshops, 216
Su, Julie, 57, 63, 69
Subcontracting, 44–45
Sunset Park Chinese shops, 117–139, 228, 268
    Cantonese v. Fujianese, 130–134
    co-ethnic conspiracy, 125–130
    division of labor, 120–122

law enforcement, 134–136
wages and hours, 122–125
working environment, 119–120
Support Team International for Textileras (STITCH), 219, 236
Surveillance, 187
Sweatshop
    defining, 21, 48, 229
    home, 31
    progressive era, 79–83
    return, 48–52
    use of word, 33
Sweatshop feminism, 185–202
Sweatshop USA, 12–15
Sweatshop Watch, 203, 236
Sweeney, John, 249
Syrians, 23

Taiwan, 109, 142, 145, 234
Target, 174, 203
Tenement apartments, 19
Tension
    local and transnational, 2
Textile Workers Union, 107
Thailand, 142, 234, 252
Thai workers, 1, 51, 58
Timberland, 242
Time, 39–40, 40–43
Tirreno, Millie, 191
Toiling, 48
Tomato, 60
Tommy Hilfiger, 242
Toni Blair, 154
Topson Downs, 60
Torres, Esteben, 66
Trade
    politics, 230–233
Trade unions, 173, 214
    leaders, 4
Transnationalizing American history, 8
Transnational migrant workforce, 172
Triangle Shirtwaist Factory fire, 191
Trimmers, 120
    wages and hours, 122
Tulane, 254
Turkey, 145
Tyler, Gus, 82

Undocumented immigrants, 181
Union Bank, 161
Unionization, 135–136
    strategies, 9
    victory, 81

Union of Needle, Industrial, and Technical
    Employees (UNITE!), 1, 6, 14, 49,
    63, 66, 69, 107, 108, 124, 128, 137,
    152, 170, 171, 174, 176, 177, 203,
    213, 216, 237, 241, 248, 250, 251, 265
  detractors, 175–176
Unions, 51
  activist, 97–98
  culture, 137
  garment, 77
  labor, 41
  parochialism, 137
  pressures, 49
  trade, 173, 214
UNITE!. *See* Union of Needle, Industrial,
    and Technical Employees (UNITE!)
United Nations Organization for
    Migration, 172–173
United Students Against Sweatshops
    (USAS), 1, 216, 239–240, 241, 242,
    250, 260–261, 263
University of Iowa, 254
University of Kentucky, 254
University of Michigan, 254
University of North Carolina, 249, 254
University of Pennsylvania, 253
University of Wisconsin, 254
University of Wisconsin-Madison, 250
Urban garment shops, 37
U.S. Industrial Commission, 4, 23, 26
  sweating system defined, 3
USAS. *See* United Students Against
    Sweatshops (USAS)

Valesh, Eva McDonald, 24
Versatility, 41
Viera, Judith, 265, 266, 279, 280, 282
Vietnam, 142, 171
Vietnam Labor Watch, 236
Vural, Leyla, 213

Wages, 58–59, 171, 174
  withholding, 129
Waldinger, Roger, 50
Walling, William English, 80
Wall Street Journal, 259
Wal-Mart, 150, 156, 160, 174, 213, 214, 228,
    235, 236, 237, 281
Wanamaker, John, 206, 207
War Labor Board, 78

Warnaco, 216
Welch, Jack, 225
Wenzhou, 130–134
White, Heather, 243
White House Apparel Industry
    Partnership, 11
White House Apparel Partnership, 66
White Label campaign, 206
Wiesenthal, Simon, 57
Wilkes-Barre, 94, 99
  Pennsylvania State University Extension
    Campus, 102
Wing Lam, 175–176
Wolensky, Ken, 77
Wolff, Goetz, 154
Women, 28, 29
Women fainting, 274–276
Women's garment industry, 38
  history, 113
Women's propaganda group, 189
Women's Trade Union League (WTUL), 186
Women's Wear Daily, 158
Women's wear sector, 40
Wong, Sue, 162
Woodbury University, 162
Work conditions, 187
Worker power and organizational failures
  New York City garment industry, 173
Worker Rights Consortium (WRC), 216,
    226, 253, 254, 255, 260–261
Workers
  empathy with employers, 126–127
  vs. inspectors, 27
  tension, 132
Work ethic, 95
Working conditions, 134–136, 136
Workplace agitation, 189
World Trade Organization, 145
WRC. *See* Worker Rights Consortium
    (WRC)
WTUL, 79–80, 186
Wyoming Valley, 95
Wyoming Valley garment factory, 94
Wyoming Valley International Ladies'
    Garment Workers' Union (ILGUW),
    105, 108

Yin li, 121

Zepeda, Evelyn, 220, 249, 255